BESTSELLING BOOK SERIES

Seattle & the Olympic Peninsula For Dummies®, 2nd Edition

Downtown Seattle

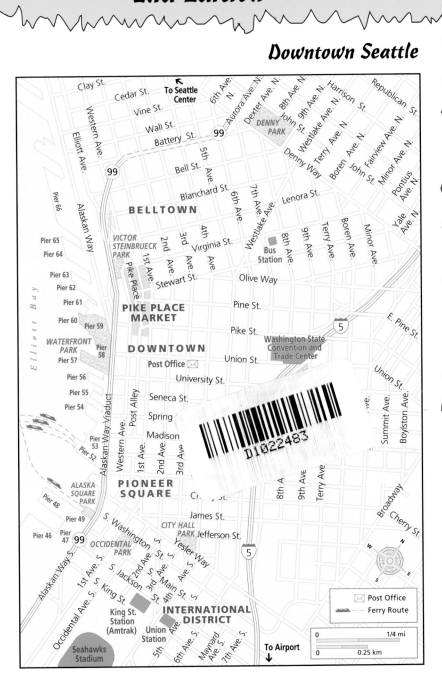

Clay St. · Cedar St. · To Seattle Center · Vine St. · Wall St. · Battery St. · 6th Ave. N. · Aurora Ave. N. · Dexter Ave. N. · 8th Ave. N. · 9th Ave. N. · Harrison St. · Republican St.

DENNY PARK

Western Ave. · Elliott Ave. · 99 · Bell St. · 5th Ave. · Blanchard St. · 6th Ave. · John St. · Denny Way · Westlake Ave. N. · Terry Ave. N. · Boren Ave. N. · John St. · Fairview Ave. N. · Minor Ave. N. · Pontius Ave. N. · Yale Ave. N.

Pier 66 · Alaskan Way · BELLTOWN · 7th Ave. · Westlake Ave. · Lenora St.

Pier 65 · Pier 64 · VICTOR STEINBRUECK PARK · 2nd Ave. · 3rd Ave. · 4th Ave. · Virginia St. · Bus Station · 8th Ave. · 9th Ave. · Terry Ave. · Boren Ave. · Minor Ave.

Pier 63 · Pier 62 · Pike Place · 1st Ave. · Stewart St. · Olive Way

Pier 61 · Pier 60 · Pier 59 · **PIKE PLACE MARKET** · Pine St.

Elliott Bay · WATERFRONT PARK · Pier 58 · Pier 57 · **DOWNTOWN** · Pike St. · Washington State Convention and Trade Center · E. Pine St. · 5

Pier 56 · Post Office ☒ · Union St. · Union St.

Pier 55 · Pier 54 · University St. · Summit Ave. · Boylston Ave.

Post Alley · Seneca St.

Alaskan Way Viaduct · Western Ave. · Spring · Madison · 1st Ave. · 2nd Ave. · 3rd Ave.

Pier 53 · Pier 52

Pier 48 · ALASKA SQUARE PARK · **PIONEER SQUARE** · Cherry St. · 8th Ave. · 9th Ave. · Terry Ave. · Broadway

Pier 49 · Pier 46 · Pier 47 · 99 · S. Washington St. · James St. · CITY HALL PARK · Jefferson St. · Cherry St.

OCCIDENTAL PARK · Yesler Way · 5

Alaskan Way S. · Occidental Ave. S. · 1st Ave. S. · S. Jackson St. · 2nd Ave. S. · 3rd Ave. S. · S. King St. · S. Main St. · 4th Ave. S.

King St. Station (Amtrak) · Union Station · **INTERNATIONAL DISTRICT** · 5th Ave. S. · 6th Ave. S. · Maynard Ave. S. · 7th Ave. S. · To Airport ↓

Seahawks Stadium

D102483

Legend:
☒ Post Office
⛴ Ferry Route

0 ——— 1/4 mi
0 ——— 0.25 km

N · S · E · W

Seattle & the Olympic Peninsula For Dummies, 2nd Edition

Cheat Sheet

The Olympic Peninsula

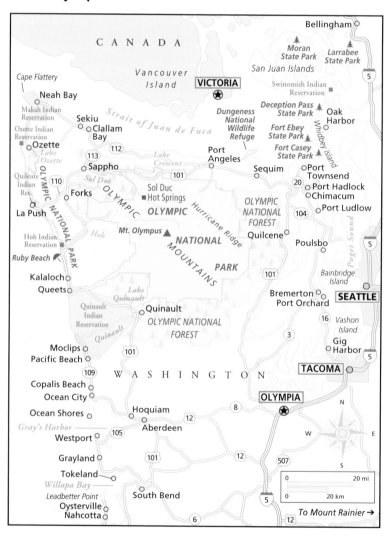

Copyright © 2004 Wiley Publishing, Inc.
All rights reserved.

Item 3921-3.

For more information about Wiley Publishing,
call 1-800-762-2974.

For Dummies: Bestselling Book Series for Beginners

Seattle & the Olympic Peninsula

FOR

DUMMIES®

2ND EDITION

by Jim Gullo

WILEY

Wiley Publishing, Inc.

Seattle & the Olympic Peninsula For Dummies,® 2nd Edition

Published by
Wiley Publishing, Inc.
111 River St.
Hoboken, NJ 07030
www.wiley.com

About the Author

When not downing numerous cups of coffee or mowing his way through the Pike Place Market's food stalls, Seattle-based writer **Jim Gullo** travels the world on assignment for magazines that include *Islands, Sunset,* and the *Alaska Airlines Magazine.* He is also the author of *Just Let Me Play,* the autobiography of golfer Charlie Sifford, and *The Importance of Hillary Rodham Clinton,* a supplemental textbook for middle-school readers. You can find him on various playgrounds around the city hoisting jump shots or challenging all comers to games of two-on-two with his 14-year-old son, Michael, or swinging with his three-year-old son, Joe.

Dedication

To Christopher, with an uncle's fondest regards.

Author's Acknowledgments

Many thanks to all of the restaurateurs, hoteliers, tour operators, and public relations mavens who so generously provided information and access for this book. A special thanks to Lorne and Louis Richmond of Richmond Public Relations in Seattle, along with their dynamic staffers Hamilton McCulloh and Erica Klump; Norma Rosenthal and Tamara Wilson; Scott Wellsandt and Cynthia Nims for telling me every single good thing they eat; and Alexis Lipsitz Flippin, Elizabeth Albertson, and Stephen Bassman of Wiley for their editorial help and support. Enormous gratitude to my wife Kris for all of her loving support and encouragement, not to mention slogging through endless discussions about the best places in Seattle.

Publisher's Acknowledgments

We're proud of this book; please send us your comments through our Dummies online registration form located at www.dummies.com/register/.

Some of the people who helped bring this book to market include the following:

Editorial

Editors: Elizabeth Albertson, Development Editor; Kelly Ewing, Project Editor

Cartographer: Elizabeth Puhl

Editorial Manager: Michelle Hacker

Senior Photo Editor: Richard Fox

Cover Photos: *Front Cover:* © Dave Bartruff/Corbis; *Back cover:* © Kevin Schafer/Corbis

Cartoons: Rich Tennant, www.the5thwave.com

Production

Project Coordinator: Kristie Rees

Layout and Graphics: Amanda Carter, Stephanie D. Jumper, Jacque Schneider

Proofreaders: TECHBOOKS Production Services, Brian H. Walls

Indexer: TECHBOOKS Production Services

Publishing and Editorial for Consumer Dummies

  Diane Graves Steele, Vice President and Publisher, Consumer Dummies

  Joyce Pepple, Acquisitions Director, Consumer Dummies

  Kristin A. Cocks, Product Development Director, Consumer Dummies

  Michael Spring, Vice President and Publisher, Travel

  Brice Gosnell, Associate Publisher, Travel

  Kelly Regan, Editorial Director, Travel

Publishing for Technology Dummies

  Andy Cummings, Vice President and Publisher, Dummies Technology/General User

Composition Services

  Gerry Fahey, Vice President of Production Services

  Debbie Stailey, Director of Composition Services

Contents at a Glance

Introduction *1*

Part 1: Getting Started *9*

Chapter 1: Discovering the Best of Seattle and
    the Olympic Peninsula 11
Chapter 2: Deciding When to Go 15
Chapter 3: Planning Your Budget 23
Chapter 4: Planning Ahead for Special Travel Needs 33

Part 11: 1roning Out the Details *41*

Chapter 5: Getting to Seattle and the Olympic Peninsula 43
Chapter 6: Deciding Where to Stay 57
Chapter 7: Booking Your Room 63
Chapter 8: Taking Care of the Remaining Details 69

Part 111: Settling in to Seattle *77*

Chapter 9: Location, Location, Location: Seattle 79
Chapter 10: The Best Hotels in Seattle 87
Chapter 11: Orienting Yourself in Seattle and Getting Around 109
Chapter 12: Money Matters 121
Chapter 13: The Lowdown on the Seattle Dining Scene 123
Chapter 14: Seattle's Best Restaurants 129

Part 1V: Exploring Seattle *159*

Chapter 15: Seattle's Top Sights and Cool Things to Do 161
Chapter 16: A Shopper's Guide to Seattle 189
Chapter 17: Five Great Seattle Itineraries and
    Three Dandy Day Trips 199
Chapter 18: Living It Up after the Sun Goes Down:
    Seattle Nightlife 215

Part V: Discovering Olympic National Park *221*

Chapter 19: Getting to Know Olympic National Park 223
Chapter 20: Planning Your Visit to the Park 229
Chapter 21: Enjoying the Park 237
Chapter 22: Deciding Where to Stay and Eat in the Park 249

Part V1: Exploring the Olympic Peninsula *255*

Chapter 23: The Olympic Peninsula 257
Chapter 24: Port Ludlow to Port Hadlock 261
Chapter 25: Port Townsend 265
Chapter 26: Sequim and Port Angeles 273

Part VII: The Part of Tens 279
    Chapter 27: Ten Northwest Taste Treats You Simply Can't Miss 281
    Chapter 28: Ten Quintessentially "Northwest" Things to Do 285

Appendix A: Quick Concierge: Seattle 289

Appendix B: Quick Concierge: The Olympic Peninsula and Olympic National Park 293

Worksheets 295

Index 301

Maps at a Glance

Greater Seattle...81
Downtown Seattle...82
Downtown Seattle Accommodations 88
Seattle Accommodations — North & Northeast.......................92
Downtown Seattle Dining...130
Seattle Dining — North & Northeast...136
Downtown Seattle Attractions 163
Seattle Attractions—North & Northeast...................................164
Seattle Center...171
Seattle Excursions 200
Olympic National Park 224
The Olympic Peninsula 259

Table of Contents

Introduction *1*
    About This Book 2
    Foolish Assumptions 3
    How This Book Is Organized 4
        Part I: Getting Started 4
        Part II: Ironing Out the Details 4
        Part III: Settling in to Seattle 5
        Part IV: Exploring Seattle 5
        Part V: Discovering Olympic National Park 5
        Part VI: Exploring the Olympic Peninsula 5
        Part VII: The Part of Tens 6
    Conventions and Icons Used in This Book 6
    Where to Go from Here 7

Part 1: Getting Started *9*
Chapter 1: Discovering the Best of Seattle and the Olympic Peninsula 11
    Of Mountains and Water 12
    A Palette of Northwest Flavors 12
    A-Hiking We Will Go 12
    Because Bill Gates Lives Here 13
    Provisioning for the Gold Rush 13
    The Show Must Go On 13
    No Island Is a Man 14
    Exploring Towns and Scenic Byways 14

Chapter 2: Deciding When to Go 15
    The Secret of the Seasons 15
    Seattle Calendar of Events 19
        January 19
        May 19
        July 19
        September 20
        December 20
    The Olympic Peninsula's Calendar of Events 20
        January 20
        February 20
        March 21
        April 21
        May 21
        July 21
        August 21
        September 21

October 22
November 22

Chapter 3: Planning Your Budget 23

Adding Up the Elements 24
Lodging 24
Transportation 25
Dining 25
Attractions 26
Shopping and entertainment 26
Watch Out for Hidden Expenses! 27
Choosing Traveler's Checks, Credit Cards, or ATMs 27
ATMs 27
Traveler's checks 28
Credit cards 29
Hot Tips for Cutting Costs 30

Chapter 4: Planning Ahead for Special Travel Needs 33

Making Family Travel Fun 33
Journeying Senior Style 35
Accommodating Travelers with Disabilities 36
Traveling Tips for Gays and Lesbians 37
Discovering Traveling Tips for Black Travelers 38
Flying Solo 39
Walking the Dog Away from Home 40

Part II: Ironing Out the Details 41

Chapter 5: Getting to Seattle and the Olympic Peninsula ...43

Travel Agent: Friend or Foe? 43
Travel Insurance: Do You Need It? 44
Trip-cancellation insurance 44
Medical insurance 45
Lost-luggage insurance 45
Escorted General-Interest Tours: Sit Back and Enjoy the Ride ...45
Packages for the Independent Traveler: Going It Alone 47
Getting to Seattle 48
By plane 48
Getting through the airport 51
By car, train, and bus 54
Getting to the Olympic Peninsula 55
By car 55
By plane 55
By bus 56

Chapter 6: Deciding Where to Stay 57

The Chains: Tried and True 57
Motels and Motor Inns: No Frills 58
Hostels and B&Bs: Close Encounters 58
Inns and Converted Apartment Houses: The Personal Touch 59
The Big Corporate Hotels: Grand and Glitzy 59

Boutique Hotels: Quiet Luxury 60
The Upper-Crust Hotels: Top of the Line 60
What You Get for the Money 60

Chapter 7: Booking Your Room 63

Uncovering the Truth about Rack Rates 63
Getting the Best Room at the Best Rate 64
Navigating Reservations Services and Hotlines 64
Seattle 64
The Olympic Peninsula 65
Surfing for Hotels 65
Figuring Out What to Do If You Arrive Without
a Reservation 66

Chapter 8: Taking Care of the Remaining Details 69

A Car-Rental Checklist 69
Getting the Best Deal on a Car Rental 70
Looking Out for Your Health 71
Staying Safe 72
Making Reservations and Getting Tickets in Advance
for Restaurants, Events, and Sightseeing 73
Seattle and the Olympic Peninsula on the Web 73
Packing for the Flannel Curtain 74
Dress for comfort 74
Prepare for a drizzle — or two 74
Pack lightly 75

Part III: Settling in to Seattle 77

Chapter 9: Location, Location, Location: Seattle 79

The Downtown Experience 80
Queen Anne's Lace 84
Bunking Down in the Neighborhoods 84

Chapter 10: The Best Hotels in Seattle 87

Seattle Hotels from A to Z 90
Hostelling: No Room at the Inn? 104
Index of Accommodations by Price 106
Index of Accommodations by Neighborhood 107

Chapter 11: Orienting Yourself in Seattle
and Getting Around 109

Getting from the Airport to Your Hotel 110
Arriving by Car 111
Arriving by Train 112
Getting Around Once You're Here 112
Getting around by car 112
Getting around by bus 115
Getting around by taxi 116
Getting around by Waterfront Streetcar and monorail ...117
Getting around by ferry 117

Getting around by bike 118
Getting around on foot 118

Chapter 12: Money Matters 121

Where to Get Cash in Seattle 121
What to Do If Your Wallet Is Stolen 122
Taxing Matters 122

Chapter 13: The Lowdown on the Seattle Dining Scene ...123

Discovering the Latest Trends, the Hot Seats,
  and the Star Chefs 123
Eating Like a Local 125
  Seafood is king 125
  Seattle's coffee fix 126
  Fresh from the farm to your table 126
Dressing to Dine, Seattle Style 126
Making Reservations 126
Cost-Cutting Tips for Dining Out 127

Chapter 14: Seattle's Best Restaurants 129

Seattle Restaurants from A to Z 132
On the Lighter Side: Top Picks for Breakfast, Snacks,
  and Meals on the Go 150
  Breakfast on the half-shell 150
  Living the high life in caffeine city 150
  Exploring the food stalls at Pike Place 152
  Asian snacks in the International District 152
  Quick eats on the street 153
Index of Accommodations by Price 155
Index of Accommodations by Neighborhood 156
Index of Accommodations by Cuisine 157

Part IV: Exploring Seattle 159

Chapter 15: Seattle's Top Sights and Cool Things to Do 161

The Top Attractions from A to Z 161
More Cool Things to Do and See 173
  Seattle just for kids 174
  Seattle just for teens 177
  Seattle for romantics 179
  Seattle for nature and outdoors lovers 180
And on Your Left, the Space Needle: Seeing Seattle
  by Guided Tour 183
  Touring Seattle on land 183
  Touring Seattle by air 185
  Touring Seattle by water 185
  Touring Seattle by Duck 187

Chapter 16: A Shopper's Guide to Seattle 189

Making the Shopping Scene 189
The Big Boys (and Girls) of Retailing 190

Prowling the Market(s) 191
Seattle's Great Shopping Neighborhoods 192
Belltown 192
Capitol Hill 193
The Shopping District 193
Pioneer Square 193
The Waterfront 194
Queen Anne 194
Neighborhoods north of downtown 194
Seattle Stores by Merchandise 196
Antiques and retro wares 196
Books and music 196
Fashion 197
Home decor 197
Outdoor clothing and gear 197
Salmon and specialty food items 198
Souvenirs and collectibles 198
Toys 198

**Chapter 17: Five Great Seattle Itineraries and
Three Dandy Day Trips** **199**
Great Itineraries 199
Seattle in Three Days 201
Day one 201
Day two 201
Day three 202
Seattle for Nature Lovers 202
Seattle for Coffee and Snack Lovers 203
Seattle for the Tragically Hip 203
Seattle with Kids 204
The Best Day Trips 205
Day trip #1: The Mountain Loop — The North
Cascades Highway 205
Day trip #2: The San Juan Islands 206
Day trip #3: Mount Rainier National Park 212

**Chapter 18: Living It Up after the Sun Goes Down:
Seattle Nightlife** **215**
What's Happening: Getting the News 215
Where to Get Tickets 215
The Play's the Thing: The Local Theater Scene 216
Music, Dance, and More: The Performing Arts 217
The Seattle Symphony 217
The Seattle Opera 218
The Pacific Northwest Ballet 218
Hitting the Bars and Clubs 218
Live! Music and dancing 218
Party time: Bars with attitude 219
Social magnets: Restaurant and hotel bars 219

Part V: Discovering Olympic National Park 221

Chapter 19: Getting to Know Olympic National Park 223

Olympic National Park: Beaches, Glaciers, Mountains,
Lakes, and Rainforest 223
Must-See Attractions 227

Chapter 20: Planning Your Visit to the Park 229

Getting There 229
Driving in 229
Flying in 230
Busing in 231
Planning Ahead 231
Reserving a room or a campsite 231
Packing for the park 232
Figuring Out the Lay of the Land 232
Arriving in the Park 234
Finding information 234
Paying fees 235
Getting around 235
Remembering Safety 235

Chapter 21: Enjoying the Park 237

Enjoying the Park 237
Exploring the top attractions 237
Taking a hike 241
One-day wonder 243
If you have more time 245
Ranger programs 245
Keeping active 247
Escaping the rain 248

Chapter 22: Deciding Where to Stay and Eat
in the Park 249

Where to Stay in Olympic National Park 249
Lodging in the park 250
Campgrounds 251
Where to Eat 253

Part VI: Exploring the Olympic Peninsula 255

Chapter 23: The Olympic Peninsula 257

Orienting Yourself on the Olympic Peninsula 258
Obtaining Visitor Information on the Olympic Peninsula 260

Chapter 24: Port Ludlow to Port Hadlock 261

Port Ludlow 261
Getting there 261
Visitor information 262
Exploring the area 262

Staying in style 262
Dining out 262
Chimacum and Port Hadlock 263

Chapter 25: Port Townsend 265

Getting There 266
Finding Information 266
Exploring the Area 267
Exploring the town 267
Exploring Fort Worden State Park 269
Exploring Port Townsend from the water and air 270
Staying in Style 270
Dining Out 271

Chapter 26: Sequim and Port Angeles 273

Getting There 274
Finding Information 274
Exploring the Area 274
Enjoying Outdoor Adventures 275
Bicycling 275
Camping 276
Llama trekking 276
Sea kayaking and canoeing 276
Whale-watching 276
Staying in Style 277
Choosing Where to Dine 277

Part VII: The Part of Tens 279

Chapter 27: Ten Northwest Taste Treats You Simply Can't Miss 281

Crab Cocktails 281
Piroshky!, Piroshky! 281
Copper River Salmon 282
Pie at the Dahlia Lounge 282
Kerry Sears' Oysters 282
A Darn Fine Cuppa Joe 283
Apple Pancakes in Sequim 283
Jumbo Lump Crab Cakes 283
Halibut and Chips 283
Larsen's Danish 284

Chapter 28: Ten Quintessentially "Northwest" Things to Do 285

Ride a Ferry across Puget Sound 285
Go to the Top of the Space Needle 285
Watch the Salmon, Eat the Salmon 286
Have a Latte at the Pike Place Market 286

Paddle a Kayak 286
Soak in the Panorama at Hurricane Ridge 287
Take a Peek at Bill Gates's House 287
Ride a Floatplane to the San Juan Islands 287
Snap Pictures of Mount Rainier 288
Attend Bumbershoot and the Lavender Festival 288

Appendix A: Quick Concierge: Seattle *289*
Fast Facts 289

Appendix B: Quick Concierge: The Olympic
Peninsula and Olympic National Park *293*
Fast Facts 293

Worksheets *295*

Index *301*
General Index 301
Accommodations Index 313
Restaurant Index 314

Introduction

What do you think you know about Seattle and Washington's Olympic Peninsula — that great, dense chunk of urban and mountainous real estate that occupies the upper left-hand portion of your map of the United States? I ask, because more than most places, Seattle seems to be the object of very subjective thinking by many people, including the national media. Choose your stereotype: Seattle's the coffee capital of America and the place that (good or bad) brought you Starbucks; it's inhabited by a bunch of yuppies whining over their collapsed stock options; it's full of web-footed creatures who enjoy nothing more than a good downpour; it's a thriving, enviably clean, and safe city with a European cafe ambiance; it's made up of *poseurs* who flirted with big-city culture and importance in the '90s but have since retreated into their crabby, Northwest shells. It's almost as if Seattle exists as a state-of-mind (or even worse, a TV show) in the collective American consciousness.

I'll leave it up to you to find your own version of Seattle. Maybe the perfect characterization of the place will come to you as you study the grounds in your latte cup; maybe it will hit you as you ponder the city from atop a glorious hiking trail in Olympic National Park. However, here's Seattle in a nutshell from my point of view: For a long time, we made all of those "Best Places to Live" lists, and media stories extolled the beautiful views, the clean air, the low crime statistics and the forward-thinking urban planning of Seattle. That caused about a million Californians to move here — only to leave a year or two later because it rained too much in the winter. Then, for some reason, the winter rains detoured south, and for several years the Pacific Northwest enjoyed near-perfect weather while Los Angeles flooded.

Seattle went on to make more news: downtown demonstrations, riots in the streets, and *boom!*, a major earthquake, the biggest in these parts in more than 50 years. The high-tech and Internet industries created another kind of boom here and then almost as quickly collapsed, leaving the state of Washington with one of the highest unemployment rates in the country. Boeing, which started in a little red barn that you can still visit, picked up its airplanes and left, moving its corporate headquarters to Chicago. The media, ever happy to pop the very balloons they inflated, bashed Seattle with stories about its precipitous decline and how (gasp!) Portland and Vancouver had become much hipper than Seattle. So what, you may ask, is really going on in the Pacific Northwest?

The short answer is that everything is just fine. The streets are safe, the earthquake damage has been swept away, and the weather continues to be just lovely, if you call a 70°F summer day with eggshell-blue skies perfect, as I do. I have to laugh at the Northwest weather naysayers when it is 50° degrees in February, the entire East Coast is blanketed in snow, and I'm mulling over the options of playing golf or going for a long bike ride. Those who have chosen to make the Northwest their home are very, very fond of the place and eager to show it off at a moment's (or a relative's) notice. Hence, I've written this guidebook, which attempts to steer you toward the places I know and what I love about Seattle and the spectacular Olympic Peninsula, which provides daily doses of Olympian inspiration every time you look upon its craggy peaks from across Puget Sound.

You're coming at a good time, whether it's your first visit or you're returning for another slice of the Northwest pie. If you haven't been to Seattle since the early 1990s, you won't recognize the place — the city has undergone major renovations and renewal in the last five years. The high-tech boom was very generously shared by all those Microsoft millionaires who invested in the community. They helped fund, among other things, a new symphony hall, a sparkling new ballpark and football stadium, new museums, and a downtown library, and they helped transform whole neighborhoods like Belltown into little urban oases of culture. At the same time, Olympic National Park continues to be one of America's outdoor wonderlands, a fabulous place to get away from city congestion and absorb some raw natural beauty. And the Olympic Peninsula continues to be a great getaway full of beautiful lakes and beaches and charming towns. With the exception of traffic, which continues to be lousy, these places have managed to hang on to a high quality of life that is cherished by the locals. This book is the first step toward helping you discover the best of the Pacific Northwest in general, and Seattle and the Olympic Peninsula in particular.

About This Book

This book is designed to get you quickly acclimated to Seattle and the Olympic Peninsula and to provide you with the best, most essential ingredients for a great vacation. As a travel writer who's been in the business for several years, I find that traditional guidebooks often drown the reader in too much information — leaving the reader high and dry, trying to make sense of it all. Here, I've done the legwork for you, offering my expertise and not-so-humble opinions to help you make savvy, informed decisions in planning your trip. What you *won't* find here is a numbing phone-book-style directory of every single place to eat, sleep, and do your laundry in Seattle, or statistics of people who have registered satisfaction with a particular restaurant or attraction. Frankly, those kinds of guidebooks make my eyes glaze over.

In *Seattle & the Olympic Peninsula For Dummies,* 2nd Edition, I cut to the chase. I've chosen my favorites in many categories and put them into a form you can easily access to make your own decisions, whether it's from your living room couch while you're watching *Frasier* (which is set in Seattle), or wandering the Pike Place Market looking for Frasier (he doesn't actually live here, I'm sorry to tell you). I also want to give you a good idea of where to go to find things on your own, because I feel that an important part of travel is the discovery of your own favorite places and experiences along the way.

This book is designed for you to flip to the exact information you want at any given moment. Dog-ear the pages, make notes in the margins, attack it with a highlight pen, spill mustard on the parts you don't need, or tear them out and throw them to the winds (but if you want to act like a Northwesterner, you'll recycle them). You can even find pages in the back to use for notes, along with worksheets to help you plan your budget and other facets of your trip.

The publisher's esteemed legal team (the highly annoying Fractious, Soomee, and Torte) wishes to add that the travel industry changes rapidly, especially in terms of prices. In other words, if things cost a tad more (or less) by the time you use this book, don't blame me. Rates are always subject to change, and you should call, surf the Web, or fax ahead of time to make sure that places are still open, restaurants are still seating, ballgames are still being played, and kids are still welcome before you embark on your trip to the great Northwest. And if you find that a certain coconut-cream pie I've highly recommend is less than scrumptious, I'm sorry about that, too. (But I'm betting you'll love it.) Finally, if you're nose-deep in my brilliant analysis of Belltown and you trip over a Dungeness crab on the sidewalk, it's not my fault. In that event, the author of this book is Joe Shmoe, not me, and your own legal team should contact him directly. Fractious, Soomee, and Torte have spoken.

Foolish Assumptions

In writing this book, I made some of the following assumptions about you, the reader:

- ✔ You may be an inexperienced traveler who is interested in Seattle and the Olympic Peninsula and wants to know when to go and how to arrange your trip. Maybe you're a little nervous about traveling to such a distant corner of the country, and you want to know exactly what to expect.

- ✔ You may be an experienced traveler who has visited the region before, but you want an informed opinion to help you plan your latest vacation; you want to know what's new, and you want to quickly access information.

✔ If you live practically anywhere in the United States, Seattle and the Olympic Peninsuala are a heck of a long way away, and making the trek to the Northwest may involve a significant portion of your vacation time and budget — so you want to be sure you do it right and plan the best vacation possible.

✔ You're not alone, and you realize that hundreds of thousands of visitors come to the Northwest every year. I want to give you the tools to make your own, unique choices in Seattle and along the Olympic Peninsula so that you aren't simply following the crowds from place to place.

If any of these assumptions ring a bell with you, then *Seattle & the Olympic Peninsula For Dummies,* 2nd Edition, is your guidebook of choice.

How This Book Is Organized

This book is divided into seven parts, which cover all of the major aspects of your planning and your trip. Because I cover two major destinations here, I combine some of the up-front information (such as how to plan your budget), but then break Seattle and the Olympic Peninsula down separately into their own bite-size parts. Within each of the seven major parts, you find a number of chapters that help you quickly locate the specific information you want and need. The Table of Contents at a Glance and the complete Table of Contents that preceded this introduction are perfect tools for finding general and specific information. At the back of the book, you find worksheets and quick listings of helpful service information and phone numbers.

Part 1: Getting Started

Here's where that old proverbial ball gets rolling with some information on when to plan a trip to the Northwest, some events to keep in mind, and a framework for establishing your budget, as well as a preliminary list of good reasons why the area is so much fun to visit.

Part 11: Ironing Out the Details

Details, details. Should you look into a package tour? What kind of lodging is right for you? How can you get the best bang for your buck? Should you buy travel insurance? Do you need traveler's checks? After you read this part, the suitcase is pretty much on the bed and ready to be packed!

Part III: Settling in to Seattle

Arriving in a new city and getting acclimated are two of the great joys of travel, and this part makes it easy. Here's where you really get to know the Emerald City and address those two very basic human needs: food and shelter. You find out where things are located in the city, get reviews of hotels, figure out how to get around town, and (after you've worked up a good appetite) read about the best places to eat.

Part IV: Exploring Seattle

The Space Needle beckons, the Experience Music Project invites you inside, and the Pike Place Market reserves a flying fish in your name in this part, which offers information on the best things to do and see in and around Seattle, with special sections on exploring the city with kids and teens. You also find invaluable tips on organizing your time in order to explore the city more efficiently.

Part V: Discovering Olympic National Park

Some of the joys of the Olympic Peninsula include hiking Hurricane Ridge, paddling lovely Lake Crescent, walking a rugged Pacific beach that's studded with driftwood, or simply sitting in a rented cabin with a fire roaring in the hearth and a good book at your side. This chapter brings you the wonders of Olympic National Park, with tips and details on everything you need to know to maximize your time exploring one of the country's great natural wonders.

Part VI: Exploring the Olympic Peninsula

From feasting on fresh crab at Dungeness to enjoying the wild and wacky festivals of Port Townsend, this section brings you the Olympic Peninsula in all its splendor. You may come for the wilderness and scenery of the National Park, but you may well find that some of your favorite moments take place in the charming small towns of the region. With info on Port Angeles, Port Townsend, and Port Ludlow, among other places, I provide plenty of tips on maximizing your experience in this unique little corner of the continent.

Part VII: The Part of Tens

I offer some tips on some not-to-miss food sensations to be found in the area. I also give you the lowdown on some quintessential Northwest experiences.

Conventions and Icons Used in This Book

I list the hotels, restaurants, and attractions in this book alphabetically. I use the following series of abbreviations for credit cards in the hotel and restaurant reviews:

> **AE:** American Express
>
> **DC:** Diners Club
>
> **DISC:** Discover Card
>
> **MC:** MasterCard
>
> **V:** Visa

For most of you, cost is a factor in choosing hotels and restaurants. To cut out the hassle of closely reading to find out the exact prices of places, I denote the relative cost of things with dollar signs. My scale ranges from one dollar sign ($) to four ($$$$) for restaurants and accommodations. To see the breakdown for each price scale, go to the Seattle hotel and dining chapters.

I also include several icons scattered around the book to alert you to special cases or particularly useful information.

The Tip icon delivers some inside information and advice on things to do or ways to best handle a specific situation that can save you time or money.

The Heads Up icon tells you when you should be especially aware of a situation that may be potentially dangerous, a tourist trap, or, more likely, a rip-off. In other words, Heads Up!, and be especially alert.

Families with kids in tow may appreciate the Kid Friendly icon, which identifies places and attractions that are welcoming or particularly suited to kids.

Bargain! Bargain! The Bargain Alert icon tells you when you're about to save a bundle, or suggests ways that you can cut costs.

Especially created for this book is the Northwest icon, which points to attractions or events that you shouldn't miss that are unique to Seattle, Olympic National Park, the Olympic Peninsula, or the Pacific Northwest.

Where to Go from Here

Huh? I thought that was obvious. Get on a bus, plane, train, or car and head to Seattle as fast as you can and have a blast. You may find, as so many other people have, that this is your favorite place in the whole country to visit, and you'll be reaching for this book again soon to plot your return.

Part I
Getting Started

The 5th Wave   By Rich Tennant

"Don't worry, son. By the looks of it, I imagine that cloud's headed straight for Seattle."

In this part . . .

The Pacific Northwest is primed for visitors, boasting stellar sights and attractions in a majestic setting. Here in Part I, I help you plan your trip soup to nuts, with loads of helpful insider information and advice. I've done all the planning legwork for you, taking you through every aspect of trip preparation — from budgeting your vacation to finding the best value in airfares to working with travel agents. Want to know the best season to come? Are discounts available for seniors or children? Can tacked-on taxes tip a tight budget? Look no further; the answers are here. You get a calendar of events, money-saving tips, and special advice for seniors, gay and lesbian travelers, and travelers with disabilities. All the major planning bases are covered here so that once you get to Seattle and the Olympic Peninsula, all you have to do is sit back and enjoy.

Chapter 1

Discovering the Best of Seattle and the Olympic Peninsula

In This Chapter

▶ Taking in views you only see in the Northwest

▶ Exploring a palette of new flavors

▶ Enjoying gorgeous gardens and fine wines

▶ Living it up in Mr. Gates's neighborhood

▶ Finding the outerwear that makes the Northwesterner

*O*utside my window, as I write this chapter, a floatplane is flying across the city on its way home from the San Juan Islands. It's superimposed against a section of the tall, craggy, snow-blanketed Olympic mountain range in the distance, and below it are glimpses of a blue waterway. Spread out before me are hills blanketed with trees and houses. It's no exaggeration to say that my favorite view of Seattle is the one from my office window.

I'm not alone. Plenty of people who call Seattle their home enjoy sensational vistas from their own front doors. You, too, will come away from the Emerald City with your own favorite moments and scenes. Maybe it will be the view at sunrise of **Mount Rainier** or **Mount Olympus,** or the sight of a solitary ferry crossing **Puget Sound** from your hotel window. Maybe it will be a tour of a gorgeous garden, a breathtaking hike, a paddle on a pristine lake, or the fun your family has together on a perfect summer day. In the following pages, I offer up a few images for you to savor as you contemplate your trip, a kind of appetizer to the fully laden buffet that follows. With all of the attention to details that a big trip or vacation requires — from budgeting, to buying tickets, to packing, to making sure that the cat's fed while you're gone — it's good to remember the payoff you receive when you finally arrive. Come back to this chapter whenever you need to remember *why* you're taking a visit to the Northwest, and the planning and plotting will only get easier.

Of Mountains and Water

The landscapes of the Pacific Northwest, surrounding Seattle and Olympic National Park, are truly unlike anything you've ever seen. Seattle is flanked by high mountain ranges on two sides: the **Cascades** to the east and the **Olympics** to the west. Both ranges are dusted with snow almost all year long and make for great scenery from nearly every corner of the city. To the south of the city lies magnificent **Mount Rainier,** one of the tallest peaks in the continental United States, which looms overhead like a giant sentinel. **Olympic National Park** on the Olympic Peninsula is a geologic wonderland that encompasses tall mountains, alpine lakes, a rainforest, and incredibly rugged Pacific beaches that have been pounded by wind and water into fantastic landscapes. And the varieties of water views in both areas are incredible. Seattle has **Puget Sound** and its many bays, which lap up against the city's western edge, and two big urban lakes (Union and Washington) that are connected to the sound by a placid canal that's ideal for paddling. Strolling and biking along canal-side paths is another favorite activity. Mountains, water, and trees are the defining physical features of this area, and you'll not want for splendid photo opportunities.

A Palette of Northwest Flavors

Oysters and clams are raised in the bays and estuaries of Puget Sound and the Pacific Ocean. Dungeness crabs are piled high on fishmongers' tables. Salmon and halibut are flown in fresh from Alaska. Washington grows more apples than any other state, as well as peaches and cherries. Oregon's hazelnuts, Pinot Noir wines, and wild mushrooms make it to the table. It all adds up to an embarrassment of local culinary riches and a distinctive cuisine that Northwest restaurants cook up with vigor and finesse.

Many restaurants also take advantage of the myriad Asian influences that have permeated Pacific Northwest cooking. In addition to traditional and fusion Northwest restaurants, the region offers a broad selection of excellent French, Italian, and Continental-style restaurants. Many people are happy to graze their way through the **Pike Place Market,** with its lunch-counter-style restaurants and food sellers, to gain an instant appreciation for the diversity of foods that the region offers. Finish off your Pike Place visit with a slice of huckleberry pie and, of course, a cup or three of cafe latte for the full Northwest experience.

A-Hiking We Will Go

Be sure to pack your hiking boots (the waterproof ones, of course) and day pack, because this area has tons of trails to explore. In **Olympic**

National Park, you can enjoy miles and miles of alpine trails at **Hurricane Ridge** (which you can traverse on cross-country skis in the winter), as well as 63 miles worth of undisturbed (and undeveloped) beaches. Seattle is home to some of the largest urban parks in the country, and the area boasts national and state forests that have beautifully maintained trails thanks to the vigilance of local outdoor clubs.

Because Bill Gates Lives Here

Seattle is in the midst of a renaissance, a fine symbol of which is the presence of Bill Gates, the world's richest man, who continues to live and work here. Although you may not see Bill or his equally affluent sidekick Paul Allen, their influence is spread across the region. Seattle has become known for its philanthropies: The Gates Foundation is the largest charitable organization in the world and donates millions to health, education, and computer-literacy programs. Allen is very active in preserving forests and funding medical research. You can see the benefits of local philanthropy when you visit the new symphony hall, football and baseball stadiums, and museums like Allen's **Experience Music Project.** You can also drive out to the suburb of Redmond to see the campus of Microsoft or take a boat tour that passes by the waterfront estate that Gates built a few years ago.

Provisioning for the Gold Rush

Seattle has been a center of commerce since the days when gold-rushers (including my personal favorite rusher, Jack London) stopped here to buy provisions for their expeditions north. Eddie Bauer grew up here, as did a whole outdoor culture embodied in the REI cooperative. The city is known for producing fine activewear and has a casual, comfortable, active-living approach to fashion. You probably won't need your suit or tux here, and plenty of local stores can outfit your own personal expedition into the Northwest-casual lifestyle of jeans, flannels, comfortable shoes, and outerwear.

The Show Must Go On

Grunge may be dead (although you can always find bands playing very loud, very unmelodic music somewhere in the city), but despite dwindling budgets, the arts scene is still very strong in Seattle. Theater companies like the **Seattle Rep** and **Intiman** have national reputations and continue to attract the best playwrights, directors and actors; the **Seattle Opera** is about to move into a completely renovated space as of this writing; and the **Seattle Symphony** and **Pacific Northwest Ballet** are thriving. The city also has one of the liveliest cinema and book-reading scenes in the country, with lots of places to see new movies or hear authors reading their work. You won't find a lack of things to do at night (all the more reason to drink lots of coffee).

No Island Is a Man

Islophiles (and anyone else who just likes to be surrounded by water), take note: Seattle is a great place to use as a base while you explore a number of utterly charming islands. Located in Puget Sound and easily reached by ferries from downtown Seattle, **Vashon** and **Bainbridge Islands** are delightful little rural enclaves with parks and beaches and pleasant villages to explore. You have to drive through Bainbridge Island on the way to Olympic National Park, and it's well worth a stop. The beautiful **San Juan Islands** to the north are accessible by ferry and catamaran service. And although technically not an island, the **Olympic Peninsula** certainly feels like one. The peninsula is bordered on three sides by bodies of water — the Hood Canal, the Pacific Ocean, and the entrance to Puget Sound — with far-off Vancouver Island and the city of Victoria in the distance.

Exploring Towns and Scenic Byways

If you're a country person, you'll find that the Olympic Peninsula is exactly the opposite of Seattle. The towns are small and quaint, the forests are thick, and there are plenty of lovely, pastoral views to go around. I direct you to places like **Port Townsend,** a lively Victorian town with its own counterculture sensibility; tiny **Chimacum,** with its outstanding cafe; and the peaceful enclaves of **Port Angeles** and **Port Ludlow.** I also point out some great drives that offer up tons of scenery — including a drive on one of the newest National Scenic Byways in the country.

Chapter 2

Deciding When to Go

In This Chapter

▶ Choosing the best time to go

▶ Checking out the calendars of events for Seattle and the Olympic Peninsula

Rain or shine, Seattle and the Olympic Peninsula are year-round destinations, pulsing with events and activities spring, summer, fall, and winter. So no matter when you come, you're guaranteed to experience the best that the Pacific Northwest has to offer.

The Secret of the Seasons

It's a myth! It's a fantasy! It's a vicious lie perpetuated by disgruntled Californians! No, it doesn't rain *all* the time in the Pacific Northwest; it only rains when you come to visit (just kidding). Yes, Seattle is known the world over for its soggy climate, but if you come expecting constant, steady deluges of rain, you may be in for a surprise.

As the tourism board is quick to point out, in terms of annual rainfall, Seattle receives less rain than New York and Boston. It usually rains more than 200 days a year here, with periods of steady drizzle interspersed with sun breaks. On the plus side, however, it rarely freezes or snows in this neck of the woods — in Seattle, one snowfall per year is about the norm, and it rarely sticks around for more than a day. Winter high temperatures generally hover around a mild 50 degrees. Locals will take that and a little rain over blizzards and bone-chilling lows anytime.

The Olympic Peninsula has a variety of climate zones. The low-lying areas near the water are as mild as Seattle. However, the exposed north and west sides of the peninsula see more rainfall and harsher weather. Olympic National Park is dominated by central mountains that are covered in snow for much of the fall and winter. During the other months of the year, expect rain — lots and lots of rain — in the Park, and be pleasantly surprised if you catch a few sunny days in a row. Keep this rainy weather in mind if you're planning an extended hike or camping trip in the Park.

Table 2-1 lists, by month, average high and low temperatures recorded in Seattle.

Table 2-1	**Average High & Low Temperatures in Seattle (Fahrenheit/Celsius)**											
	Jan	*Feb*	*Mar*	*Apr*	*May*	*June*	*July*	*Aug*	*Sept*	*Oct*	*Nov*	*Dec*
High °F	44.6	49.0	52.2	57.5	64.1	69.4	75.0	74.7	69.4	59.4	50.4	45.4
High °C	7	9.4	11.2	14.2	17.8	20.8	23.9	23.7	20.8	15.2	10.2	7.4
Low °F	34.7	36.7	38.0	41.2	46.4	51.3	54.5	54.8	51.3	45.3	39.5	35.8
Low °C	1.5	2.6	3.3	5.1	8.0	10.7	12.5	12.7	10.7	7.4	4.2	2.1

Source: Official readings of the Western Regional Climate Center taken at Seattle-Tacoma International Airport from 1931–2000.

Table 2-2 lists, by month, the average rainfall in Seattle.

Table 2-2		**Seattle Average Monthly Rainfall (inches)**									
Jan	*Feb*	*Mar*	*Apr*	*May*	*June*	*July*	*Aug*	*Sept*	*Oct*	*Nov*	*Dec*
5.35	4.03	3.77	2.51	1.84	1.59	0.85	1.22	1.94	3.25	5.65	6.00

Source: University of Utah Department of Meteorology.

Spring

Spring is great in Seattle and the Olympic Peninsula for the following reasons:

- ✔ The crocuses and daffodils begin to bloom as early as late February, and the trees of the Pacific Northwest begin to bud and flower.

- ✔ Safeco Field opens up again for a new season with the Seattle Mariners baseball club, a perennial playoff contender in the American League West. Tickets are generally available in the early months of the season, but get tougher to find when summer rolls around.

- ✔ The rivers flow fast from winter runoff, and salmon begin to reappear in local streams and Puget Sound. At the same time, seasonal delicacies like Copper River Salmon from Alaska swim onto the menus of local restaurants.

But keep in mind that:

- ✔ The weather can be maddeningly cool and damp this time of year, with the same gray, 50 degree days in February continuing right up until the first of July.

- ✔ If you plan to spend the day outdoors, you may need to wear layers — a turtleneck under a fleece jacket under an overcoat, for example — that you can peel away as the day warms up . . . or keep on if it doesn't.

Summer

Summer is superb in Seattle and the Olympic Peninsula. Many people think that the area has the finest summer weather in the country for the following reasons:

- ✔ From July 5 to the end of September, the weather is typically gorgeous and sunny, averaging 75 to 80 degrees nearly every day.

- ✔ Thanks to daylight savings time and northern latitudes, summer sunlight can extend well past 8:30 p.m.

- ✔ Opportunities to participate in the Northwest's range of outdoor activities — hiking, boating, paddling, bicycling, and beach-combing — are unlimited. Summer is the time to plan that long hike or extended camping trip in the Olympics, or to set up camp on the shores of a gorgeous lake and spend time swimming, fishing, and paddling. It's also the perfect time for hanging out on the beach, but don't expect much swimming in the rough waters of the Pacific or the frigid waters of Puget Sound, which rarely exceed 53 degrees. Prepare your kids (who may automatically equate a trip to the beach with swimming) for the disappointment and bring towels and extra clothes, because they're going to get wet anyway.

- ✔ Seattle puts on its biggest and best annual festivals, drawing hundreds of thousands of residents and visitors alike for food, music, and entertainment.

But keep the following things in mind if you visit during this time:

- ✔ Summer is the peak season for visitors. The hotels are all packed and charge top dollar, and you may have plenty of competition for space in restaurants, seats on ferries, and downtown parking spaces.

- ✔ June is typically the most disappointing month, weather-wise — you keep expecting summer to unfold, and the gray dampness lingers; July and August are the best times to visit.

Fall

Fall is great in Seattle and the Olympic Peninsula for the following reasons:

- ✔ Most tourists clear out after Labor Day, but the September weather is clear and gorgeous, leaving you to enjoy summer-style activities with far fewer crowds.

- ✔ Northwest produce is at its peak, and along with berries, apples, and mushrooms, you have access to the freshest crabs, oysters, and salmon from Northwest waters.

- ✔ The leaves begin to turn color in October, with beautiful, New England-like landscapes to explore in many parts of the Northwest.

- ✔ You can practically have the whole Olympic Peninsula to yourself, as the locals return to school and work, and the tourists head home. Those gorgeous hiking trails and lakes are still in prime condition during the fall. Autumnal festivals in towns like Port Townsend and Port Angeles begin to crank up, and you can celebrate with the locals.

But keep in mind that:

- ✔ The end of daylight savings time means that darkness descends on the Northwest before 6 p.m.

- ✔ Gray, cloudy weather begins to move in for days at a time by mid-October.

Winter

Winter is great for the following reasons:

- ✔ Seattle hotels compete like crazy to offer discounted rates, with a price-reduction program that's available through and sponsored by the local tourist boards. On the Olympic Peninsula, cabins are easy to come by and offer a cozy, dry retreat from big storms that whip in from the Pacific.

- ✔ The cultural seasons of the city are in full swing, with new exhibitions opening at art museums, plays premiering, and opera, ballet, and symphony available nearly every night.

- ✔ The downtown areas are spruced up and alive with holiday shoppers, and stores offer the best sales of the year.

But keep in mind that:

- ✔ The parks will be mushy and wet, colors are muted, and days can be gray and dark from dawn to early dusk.

- ✔ You need your raincoat, waterproof shoes, and a hat (but not an umbrella, which marks you as a tourist).

Seattle Calendar of Events

In this section, I list a select few of Seattle's nonstop annual festivals and events. Please check the Web sites or call the numbers I give to confirm dates and times before you plan your vacation; events are subject to change.

January

Seattle kicks the year off with the **Seattle International Boat Show,** a huge exhibition of sailboats, yachts, kayaks, and canoes for the boating-crazy Northwest at the Stadium Exhibition Center. Call ☎ **206-634-0911;** Internet: www.seattleboatshow.com. Late January.

May

The Seattle Center is the site for the **Northwest Folklife Festival,** a weekend of international folk entertainment that draws thousands of people to Seattle Center for dance, music, crafts, and food. Call ☎ **206-684-7300;** Internet: www.nwfolklife.org. Memorial Day weekend.

Also in May, the **Seattle International Film Festival** holds premieres and international screenings at theaters around the city. Call ☎ **206-464-5830;** Internet: www.seattlefilm.com. Late May to mid-June.

July

During the **Bite of Seattle,** the city's top restaurants set up booths for zillions of visitors who stroll around Seattle Center, forks in hand, sampling small dishes from several of their favorite eateries. Go early and bring an appetite. Call ☎ **206-684-7200;** Internet: www.seattlecenter.com. Third weekend in July.

Seafair is Seattle's biggest festival of the year, with parades downtown, foot races, hydroplane boat races on Lake Washington, and appearances by the Blue Angels aerobatic team. Call ☎ **206-728-0123;** Internet: www.seafair.com. From early July through early August.

The **4th of July** is huge in Seattle, with two competing fireworks shows every year that attract thousands of spectators. At **Gas Works Park,** on Lake Union, people begin to arrive in the early morning to jockey for the best viewing positions for the evening fireworks extravaganza. Fireworks are shot from barges in the middle of the lake, and huge speakers play a musical soundtrack. The whole lake and surrounding hillsides of Queen Anne, Capitol Hill and Wallingford become a natural amphitheater for the show. At **Myrtle Edwards Park,** on the downtown waterfront, a local restaurant chain hosts a day-long festival of food and music, culminating in a spirited fireworks show that is shot from the water. Call ☎ **206-461-5840**; Internet: www.seeseattle.org. July 4.

September

Bumbershoot, the Seattle Arts Festival, is a delirious weekend of entertainment, with every venue at Seattle Center open and jammed with patrons taking in popular music, dance, literary readings — the works. Save yourself a long wait in line by buying advance tickets at a participating retailer (usually Starbucks). Call ☎ **206-281-1111**; Internet: www.bumbershoot.com. Labor Day weekend.

December

Don't miss **New Year's Eve at the Space Needle,** when crowds at Seattle's favorite landmark usher in the New Year under a grand fireworks show at midnight. Call ☎ **206-443-2111**; Internet: www.seattlecenter.com. New Year's Eve.

The Olympic Peninsula's Calendar of Events

In this section, I list a select few of the Olympic Peninsula's annual festivals and events. Please check the Web sites or call the numbers I give to confirm dates and times before you plan your vacation; events are subject to change.

January

Centrum's Winter Chamber Musical Festival brings renowned musicians to Port Townsend's Fort Worden for outstanding chamber music. Call ☎ **360-385-3102**; Internet: www.centrum.org. Generally held the last weekend in January.

February

The **Sekiu Winter Salmon Derby** is a three-day fishing event where anglers vie for the largest salmon and rockfish. Even if you're not fishing, it's fun to see the catches weighed and proudly displayed on the docks. Call ☎ **360-963-2311;** Internet: www.olympicpeninsula.org. Generally held the nearest weekend to February 15.

March

Spring Carnival at Hurricane Ridge is a fun weekend festival held on the snow at the base of a ski hill in Port Angeles, with ski races, a barbeque, and games for kids. Call ☎ **360-457-4519;** Internet: www.portangeles.org. Third weekend in March.

April

The community of Forks celebrates **RainFest,** a weekend festival of crafts, art, theater and more. Call ☎ **360-374-2531;** Internet: www.forkswa.com. Second weekend in April.

May

The town of Sequim has been holding an **Irrigation Festival** for 108 years and isn't likely to stop soon. Arts and crafts, games, music, food, and a parade are featured. Downtown Sequim. Call ☎ **360-683-6197;** Internet: www.irrigationfestival.com. May Day weekend.

In Port Angeles, the **Juan de Fuca Festival** is an annual celebration defined by music, dance, and arts. Call ☎ **360-457-5411;** Internet: www.juandefucafestival.com. Memorial Day weekend.

July

Sequim's **Celebrate Lavender Festival** celebrates this sweet-scented flower with entertainment, a street fair, crafts, pick-your-own lavender, and lavender farm and garden tours. Call ☎ **800-500-8401;** Internet: www.lavenderfestival.com. One weekend in mid-to-late July.

August

Makah Days, in Neah Bay, is a celebration of the Makah tribe's culture, with a parade, a street fair, canoe races, traditional games, food, and more. Call ☎ **360-374-2531;** Internet: www.makah.com/days. Last weekend in August.

September

Port Townsend's **Wooden Boat Festival** is the premier event of its kind in the country, with exhibits, demonstrations, and races of classic wooden boats. Call ☎ **360-344-3436;** Internet: www.woodenboat.org. First weekend after Labor Day.

October

Taste Dungeness crab, a local delicacy, as well as local produce, at the **Dungeness Crab & Seafood Festival**. Held at the John Wayne Marina in Sequim. Call ☎ **360-457-6110;** Internet: www.crabfestival.org. Second weekend in October.

November

Port Townsend's excellent artists and craftsmen display their wares in the annual **Port Townsend Arts Guild Holiday Crafts Fair**, a juried show open only to local artists. The event is located in the Port Townsend Community Center. Call ☎ **360-379-3813;** Internet: www.ptguide.com. Last weekend in November.

Chapter 3

Planning Your Budget

· ·

In This Chapter

▶ Building a budget for your trip to Seattle and the Olympic Peninsula

▶ Uncovering hidden expenses

▶ Planning what to bring: Traveler's checks, cash, and credit cards

▶ Discovering cost-cutting tips for the savvy traveler

· ·

Anybody remember John D. Hackensacker III? He was a wealthy rube played by Rudy Vallee in Preston Sturges's great comedy *The Palm Beach Story*. John D. was rich beyond compare, but he had a niggling little habit: He loved to whip out a notebook and record every single expense he incurred, to the last nickel, all the while wooing Claudette Colbert on a journey to Palm Beach. Claudette was not amused by this Uncle Scrooge-like behavior, and in the end, it was someone other than poor John D. who got the girl.

I'm not saying that budgeting your trip isn't important. It is. You can get a good idea of the expenses you can expect to pay on your visit to Seattle and/or the Olympic Peninsula by utilizing the "Making Dollars and Sense of It" worksheet in the back of this book. This worksheet breaks down the approximate hotel, transportation, food, and entertainment expenses from the minute you leave home until the moment you return. But don't let a budget rule your life: Think of it as a framework that gives you an approximate idea of your financial limitations. Passing up a great Northwest meal of Dungeness crab or fresh salmon, missing an opportunity to see a Mariners or Seahawks game, or forgoing a production of the Seattle Opera's vaunted *Ring* trilogy (if you're lucky enough to get tickets) would truly be a pity.

Build a good 20 percent cushion into your budget so that you won't feel deprived when opportunities present themselves during your trip. And they will. But don't worry: Seattle and the Olympic Peninsula are very reasonably priced places to visit, with few or none of the stratospherically priced temptations that are regularly available in New York or San Francisco. You can find plenty of ways to cut corners and get back on budget, and I offer suggestions on how to do so in this chapter. Just promise me that you won't have your nose stuck in an accounting notebook when a pod of killer whales swims by the ferryboat in Puget Sound. Take heed from the sorry tale of John D. Hackensacker.

Finally, keep in mind that the travel and tourism industries have taken a significant hit due to the economic woes occurring in the first years of the 21st century. In Seattle in particular, many new hotels and lodgings were built with all the money that was just lying around during the final years of the late '90s stock market boom, only to find a reduced market for travelers once they opened. In short, the visitor industry in Washington will welcome you with proverbial open arms and practically get down on its knees to thank you for coming. Deals are everywhere to lure your buying dollar in order to recoup some of the ongoing losses that the visitor industry has sustained. It's definitely a buyer's market, and you'll be thrilled with the deals you can find.

Adding Up the Elements

Your vacation budget consists of the following main elements. Depending on your preferences (and your appetite), where you lay your head at night should run about equal with food as your major expenses in Seattle, but beware of those pesky hidden expenses. In the Olympic Peninsula, your accommodation costs will likely exceed your dining costs. Here, I list what you should expect to pay, on average, for lodging, transportation, dining, attractions, and shopping and entertainment in Seattle and on the Olympic Peninsula.

Lodging

Seattle has a wide range of lodging opportunities, and you don't have to head to the outskirts of town in order to save money on hotels. Aside from the big, downtown luxury hotels, where rooms set you back $250 per night and up, you have several options for centrally located cheaper accommodations. Midsize hotels and the plethora of boutique hotels in Seattle offer rooms for around $150, and budget accommodations can be had for $100 or less a night. Hostelers who don't mind sharing bathrooms can find beds for under $20 in a great downtown location. Each city also has several B&B options for rooms in the $75 to $90 range, and many inexpensive new hotels built out of restored apartment houses offer rooms with furnished kitchenettes. One of the newest trends on the Seattle hotel scene is the opening of several all-suite hotels in the neighborhoods just north of downtown that give you extra space for the same (or better) price that you would pay for a single, downtown room.

On the Olympic Peninsula, you'll find a more modest selection of lodging options, ranging from collections of log-cabin-style cottages and standard, side-of-the-road motels to elegant, Victorian-era hotels with rooms that are all decorated in lace. A few high-end hotels offer rooms

with the kind of services and amenities that most Seattle hotels offer.
You would be hard-pressed to spend more than $150 a night on a whole
cabin, with many single rooms coming in at under $50. Families or
groups of friends traveling together will find terrific options for sharing
cabins and saving even more bucks.

Many inns include breakfast in the tariff, which can save you a few
more bucks every day. See Chapters 6 and 7 for a more thorough breakdown of money-saving lodging opportunities.

Transportation

Use of public transportation and cabs can cut your transportation
costs down dramatically in Seattle, particularly if you're staying in the
downtown area and don't need a rental car for most of your visit (see
Chapter 11). You can rent a car from a downtown agency for any day
trips you want to take. You definitely need a car to explore the wide-
open spaces of the Olympic Peninsula and Olympic National Park.

In the downtown area, parking is extremely limited, difficult to find, and
very expensive. (Most Seattle hotels charge $18 per day for parking.)
Instead of driving downtown, take advantage of the inexpensive, comprehensive public transportation system. If you do have a car in the
city, park it on a street in an outlying neighborhood for free and then
take a handy bus ride to and from your parking place.

If you're spending the bulk of your trip in the Olympic Peninsula and
will be visiting Seattle only briefly, you can save a great deal of driving
and parking hassle by leaving your car at a parking lot of the ferry terminals at either Bremerton or Winslow (Bainbridge Island) and walking
onto the ferry, which deposits you in the middle of downtown Seattle,
an easy walk from many hotels and attractions. Traveling on the ferries
without a car is also a great deal cheaper.

Dining

Food is such a huge part of the Northwest experience that budgeting
yourself out of the chance to eat well in Seattle and the Olympic
Peninsula would be a shame. Sure, the city has fast-food joints and the
same family-style chain restaurants that you can find in every burg
from Missoula, Montana, to West Orange, New Jersey. But where else
can you get fresh king salmon and Northwest oysters; hazelnuts, blackberries, and Rainier cherries; clams, mussels, and Dungeness crabs;
fresh apples and asparagus; and those ubiquitous cups of caffe latte?
And while you're in the neighborhood, shouldn't you try an award-
winning bottle of Oregon pinot noir, Washington merlot or chardonnay,
or one of the dozens of excellent microbrew beers so renowned in the
Pacific Northwest? Of course you should!

You can eat very well indeed at the many upscale restaurants springing up in Seattle's **downtown core** for $40 to $80 per person, not including wine. I say make room in your budget for at least one of these splurges and then cut costs by eating inexpensively, but well, at places like the **Pike Place Market** in Seattle, diners, or local family restaurants. Food doesn't cost nearly as much on the Olympic Peninsula; save your splurges for Seattle. This is one corner of the country where you can easily avoid fast-food chain places altogether without compromising your budget.

Attractions

The sightseeing attractions in Seattle and the Olympic Peninsula may end up being the biggest bargains on your trip. Plenty of attractions and activities are free, and the area museums, tours, and other attractions (with the exception of the wildly overpriced **Experience Music Project** in Seattle, at $20 per adult and $15 per child) are very reasonable. It costs very little to hike at **Mount Rainier** or **Hurricane Ridge,** watch the waves crash onto **Ruby Beach,** or let your kids play in the big, computerized fountain at **Seattle Center.** Even if you don't want to spring for the price of a ballgame at **Safeco Field,** you can tour the ballpark on most off days for a modest fee.

You can easily balance your activities budget by mixing expensive outings or big events with cheap fun like going to **parks,** watching the salmon and boats run through the **Ballard Locks,** visiting the excellent **zoo** in Seattle, or just taking a **ferryboat ride.** Lingering at a **sidewalk cafe** with a glass of microbrew beer or caffe latte and watching the parade of Northwesterners pass by is an awfully inexpensive way to enjoy a nice morning or afternoon. If you're splitting your time between Seattle and the Olympic Peninsula, plan to spend about three-quarters of your going-out budget in the city and enjoying the quieter and cheaper pleasures of nature in the country.

Shopping and entertainment

With half of the people in Seattle (and practically everybody on the Olympic Peninsula) dressed casually in jeans and light sweaters, you probably won't feel a huge, overwhelming urge to blow a fortune shopping for new clothes while you're here. You certainly can do so if you like, and then you can break the rest of the bank on cool housewares and gifts. But fashion isn't an overwhelming part of the local scene, and the only time you will feel underdressed is when your shoes aren't waterproofed. To that end, if you feel like your activewear wardrobe needs a boost, this area is a great place to pick up a whole new set of duds for exploring the great outdoors.

As far as activities go, it's up to you and your lifestyle when it comes to the importance of going out every night and spending money on music, beer, and entertainment. Grunge may be dead, but Seattle still has plenty of bars and clubs with live music where microbrews run $3 and $4, and cover charges are usually a modest $5 or so. Even fairly pricey activities have bargain opportunities. You can purchase cheap theater, music, and symphony tickets, for example, at half-price ticket windows at two locations in Seattle.

If you're interested in seeing the **Seattle SuperSonics** basketball team, family tickets are offered every month for just $10 a ticket (including a hot dog and soft drink). You can only buy these tickets from the Key Arena box office with all family members in tow.

Watch Out for Hidden Expenses!

Oh, those hidden charges — they can blow up a budget faster than you can say, "Have you seen my wallet, honey?"

Washington has no state income tax, so the state makes up for it with a hefty 8.8 percent sales tax, plus an additional tax on hotel rooms. Rental-car taxes are nearly through the roof, with surcharges added when you pick up your car at the airport. (That's why you should make a point of enjoying **Safeco Field** when you visit Seattle; you and a zillion other tourists paid for it through special taxes.)

If your budget is tight, inquire about all the added taxes when you make your hotel or car reservation, because the added tax can really make a difference in how many days you decide to rent or stay. Keep in mind that when you buy tickets to concerts, ballgames, or special events from Ticketmaster, you pay a surcharge. Try to buy tickets directly from each event's box office to get the best price.

Choosing Traveler's Checks, Credit Cards, or ATMs

When it comes to carrying money in the Northwest, should you bring traveler's checks or use ATMs? What about paying with credit cards? In this section, I tell you what you need to know about each option.

ATMs

The easiest and best way to get cash away from home is from an ATM (automated teller machine). The **Cirrus** (☎ **800-424-7787;** Internet: www.mastercard.com) and **PLUS** (☎ **800-843-7587;** Internet: www.visa.com) networks span the globe; look at the back of your bank card to see which network you're on and then call or check online for ATM locations at your destination. Make sure that you know your personal identification number (PIN) before you leave home and be sure to find out your daily withdrawal limit before you depart. Also keep in mind that many banks impose a fee every time a card is used at a different bank's ATM. On top of this charge, the bank from which you withdraw cash may charge its own fee. To compare banks' ATM fees within the U.S., visit www.bankrate.com.

You can also get cash advances on your credit card at an ATM. Keep in mind that credit-card companies generally charge a higher interest rate for cash advances.

Seattle has a zillion ATMs, not only at banks throughout the downtown areas and the neighborhoods, but in convenience stores, grocery stores, and public places like **Seattle Center, Safeco Field,** and the **Pike Place Market.** (See Chapter 12 for specifics on getting to your money in Seattle.)

The pickings for easy access to your cash get slimmer when you cross Puget Sound and head off to the Olympic Peninsula. To find an ATM there, you'll have to head to the main population centers at **Poulsbo, Port Angeles,** and **Port Townsend.**

Tribal casinos are all the rage in many of the areas surrounding Olympic National Park, and inside, you'll find cash machines a-plenty. You can't miss the casinos' huge signs and Vegas-style flashing lights as you drive down major roads like Hwy 101. In addition to ATMs, the casinos also offer inexpensive food and cheap drinks and entertainment. Just make sure that you leave with more cash than you arrived with, which is easier said than done in a casino.

Traveler's checks

Traveler's checks are something of an anachronism from the days before the ATM made cash accessible at any time. Traveler's checks used to be the only sound alternative to traveling with dangerously large amounts of cash. They were as reliable as currency, but, unlike cash, could be replaced if lost or stolen.

Small change

When you change money, ask for some small bills or loose change. Petty cash can come in handy for tipping and public transportation. Consider keeping the change separate from your larger bills, so that it's readily accessible and you won't look like a tourist when you step onto a bus and pull out a wad of $20s in search of a $1 bill.

These days, however, traveler's checks are less necessary because most cities have 24-hour ATMs that allow you to withdraw small amounts of cash as needed. However, keep in mind that you'll likely be charged an ATM withdrawal fee if the bank is not your own, so if you're withdrawing money every day, you may be better off with traveler's checks — provided that you don't mind showing identification every time you want to cash one.

You can get traveler's checks at almost any bank. **American Express** offers denominations of $20, $50, $100, $500, and (for cardholders only) $1,000. You'll pay a service charge ranging from 1% to 4%. You can get American Express traveler's checks over the phone by calling ☎ **800-221-7282**; Amex gold and platinum cardholders who use this number are exempt from the 1% fee. AAA members can obtain checks without a fee at most AAA offices.

Visa offers traveler's checks at Citibank locations nationwide, as well as at several other banks. The service charge ranges between 1.5% and 2%; checks come in denominations of $20, $50, $100, $500, and $1,000. Call ☎ **800-732-1322** for information. **MasterCard** also offers traveler's checks. Call ☎ **800-223-9920** for a location near you.

If you choose to carry traveler's checks, be sure to keep a record of their serial numbers separate from your checks in the event that they're stolen or lost. You'll get a refund faster if you know the numbers.

I don't want to suggest that you forgo bringing traveler's checks — they're still the safest way of carrying money — but you may not need them here in the Northwest as much as you would in other parts of the country or abroad. Seattle is a very safe city, and incidences of street crimes, like mugging or pickpocketing, are few and far between. On top of that, many small businesses and restaurants are reluctant to cash traveler's checks, especially in amounts over $20. You just may find that traveler's checks are more trouble than they're worth.

Credit cards

Credit cards are a safe way to carry money, and they provide a convenient record of all your expenses. You can also withdraw cash advances from your credit cards at banks or ATMs, provided you know your PIN number. If you've forgotten yours, or didn't even know you had one, call the number on the back of your credit card and ask the bank to send it to you. It usually takes five to seven business days, though some banks will provide the number over the phone if you tell them your mother's maiden name or some other personal information.

See Chapter 12 for information on what to do if your credit card or traveler's checks are lost or stolen.

Hot Tips for Cutting Costs

Even people with the biggest pockets don't like to throw money away for no good reason. There's a little cost-cutter in everyone, I say. Here are some savvy money-saving tips for chipping away at your vacation budget:

- ✔ **Take advantage of seasonal rates.** Hotel rates are generally lower in the slower seasons. The time of year you decide to visit may affect your bargaining power more than anything else. During the peak season — basically summer — when a hotel is booked up, management is less likely to extend discount rates or value-added package deals. In the slower season — winter — when capacity is down, they're often willing to negotiate.

  Seattle's Super Saver promotion lists some three dozen hotels, most of which are in the downtown core, that cut prices dramatically between November and March. (Call the reservations line directly at ☎ 800-535-7071 or book online at www.seattle supersaver.com.) Almost all the lodgings on the Olympic Peninsula lower their rates after the summer season.

- ✔ **Make use of membership discounts.** Membership in AAA, AARP, or frequent-flier/traveler programs often qualifies you for discounted rates. You may also qualify for corporate, student, or senior discounts even if you're not an AARP member, although I highly recommend joining (see Chapter 4 for details). Members of the military or those with government jobs may also qualify for price breaks.

- ✔ **Ask about package deals.** Even if you're not traveling on an all-inclusive package, you may be able to take advantage of packages offered by hotels and condos directly. See Chapter 5 for more details on package tours.

- ✔ **Call the hotel direct in addition to going through central reservations.** See which one gives you the better deal. Sometimes the local reservationist knows about packages or special rates, but the hotel may neglect to tell the central booking line.

- ✔ **Surf the Web to save.** A surprising number of hotels advertise great value packages via their Web sites, and some even offer Internet-only special rates. (See Chapter 7 for more on Internet booking services.)

- ✔ **Consult a reliable travel agent.** A travel agent can sometimes negotiate a better price with certain hotels and assemble a better value complete travel package than you can get on your own. Even if you book your own airfare, you may want to contact a travel agent to price out your hotel. On the other hand, hotels, condos, and even B&Bs sometimes discount your rate as much as 30 percent — the amount they'd otherwise pay an agent in commissions — if you book direct. For more advice on the pros and cons of using a professional go-between, see Chapter 5.

✔ **Book your rental car at weekly rates when possible.** If you simply must have a car, keep in mind that weekly rates are generally considerably lower than daily rates. See Chapter 11 for details.

✔ **Reserve a hotel room with a kitchenette or a condo with a full kitchen and do your own cooking.** You may miss the pampering that room service provides, but you can save lots of money. Even if you only prepare breakfast and an occasional picnic lunch in the kitchen, you still save significantly in the long run.

✔ **Ask whether the kids can stay in your room.** A room with two double beds usually doesn't cost any more than one with a king-size bed, and most hotels don't charge an extra-person rate when the additional person is your kid.

✔ **Enjoy a takeout lunch in a picnic setting.** Get something to go from **Pike Place Market** in Seattle, for example, and take it to **Myrtle Edwards Park** or **Discovery Park.** Or take your feast on the ferry and enjoy a picnic in any number of quiet, outdoor places on the Olympic Peninsula. See Chapter 13 for more tips on cutting food costs.

Chapter 4

Planning Ahead for Special Travel Needs

● ●

In This Chapter

▶ Planning a no-fuss family vacation

▶ Discovering special deals for seniors

▶ Enabling the disabled

▶ Using resources for African-American travelers

▶ Finding gay-friendly communities and resources

● ●

*T*ravelers of all sizes, stripes, and ages flock to Seattle and the Olympic Peninsula, and the area responds in kind, happy to put out the welcome mat for any and all. (Okay, so sometimes it's a wet, drippy welcome mat, but Seattleites can't help that.) Here are some travel tips and invaluable resource information for travelers with special needs or preferences.

Making Family Travel Fun

If you have enough trouble getting your kids out of the house in the morning, dragging them thousands of miles away may seem like an insurmountable challenge. But family travel can be immensely rewarding, giving you new ways of seeing the world through smaller pairs of eyes. I keep a special eye out for readers who are traveling with the whole crew by mentioning kid-friendly attractions, restaurants, and hotels throughout the book. Look for the "Kid Friendly" icon to guide your way. You'll find that Seattle is a very kid-friendly city, with plenty of activities to keep the little ones amused and loads of outdoor spaces to let them blow off excess energy. Keep in mind that not all hotels have swimming pools, and the few that have outdoor pools keep them open for only a few months of the year. If your kids think that it just isn't a proper vacation if the lodging doesn't have a pool, then make sure that your hotel choice has one — preferably indoors. By the same token, don't expect to catch much swimming time on a Puget Sound or Pacific Ocean beach: The water is freezing, even during the hottest part of the summer. I point out in my hotel recommendations which places have pools and which have in-room Nintendo.

On the Olympic Peninsula, kids will enjoy plenty of parks, beaches and wide-open spaces. You'll have to do a bit more searching and spend some extra dollars to find lodging with a pool, but they're available. The same goes for in-room Nintendo: Not widespread, but definitely available. Make sure that you always carry a towel in the car or backpack and a change of clothes or two, because kids won't have to work too hard to get wet on a surging Pacific beach ("I just wanted to look at the waves, Mom!"), a gurgling creek ("I was just throwing rocks into the water!"), or a trail through a rainforest ("What made you lay down in that bed of dripping-wet ferns?"). A spare pair of shoes also can come in handy when the first one gets soaked.

You'll do a fair amount of walking in the city, and a good stroller is an absolute necessity if you're traveling with toddlers. Seattle is a very hilly city that rivals San Francisco for grueling, uphill walks in some areas. Younger children may climb your leg and beg you to carry them after three steps up one of these monster inclines. A sturdy child-carrying backpack goes a long way toward keeping the peace, both in Seattle and on scenic hikes in Olympic National Park. When museums and sightseeing get to be too much for the young ones, head to the wonderful neighborhood parks, many of which have swings and slides. Ask your hotel's front desk for the nearest one, or look in the City of Seattle Government pages in the phone book under "Parks and Recreation" for a list. Kids also love the amusement park rides in **Seattle Center,** the winter carousel at **Westlake Center,** and the indoor carousel on the **Waterfront.**

When it comes to food, you needn't forgo a great Northwest meal if your child's idea of eating seafood is fish sticks. Most restaurants either have kids' menus or offer kid-friendly burgers or pastas. You can let kids pick and choose their own meals from the familiar options at the food court at **Westlake Center** or the stalls at **Pike Place Market,** which sell everything from noodles to fresh doughnuts.

For those moms and dads who crave a night on the town without children in tow, many hotels offer baby-sitting services. If your hotel doesn't have such a service, try **Best Sitters (☎ 206-682-2556)** in Seattle.

If you get to the point where you're all sick and tired of sightseeing or it's pouring buckets outside, keep in mind that Seattle is a film lover's dream, and you're likely to find a movie theater within a few blocks of your accommodations. By the same token, the city has several large, inviting bookstores, and most of them have areas for children to sit and read, as well as cafes where you can enjoy a cup of coffee and a magazine.

Following are some great resources for planning your trip with children:

✔ **Familyhostel** (☎ **800-733-9753;** Internet: www.learn.unh.edu/
  familyhostel) takes the whole family, including kids ages 8 to 15,
  on moderately priced domestic and international learning vacations. A team of academics leads the lectures, fields trips, and
  sightseeing.

✔ You can find good family-oriented vacation advice on the Internet
  from sites like the **Family Travel Network** (Internet: www.
  familytravelnetwork.com), an extensive site offering a free
  newsletter, listings of hot travel deals for families, tips for traveling with kids, and much more; **Traveling Internationally with
  Your Kids** (Internet: www.travelwithyourkids.com), a comprehensive site offering sound advice for long-distance and international travel with children; and **Family Travel Files** (Internet: www.
  thefamilytravelfiles.com), which offers an online magazine
  and a directory of off-the-beaten-path tours and tour operators
  for families.

For more information on traveling with children to Olympic National
Park, check out our sister publication, *Frommer's Family Vacations
in the National Parks* (Wiley Publishing). Another great reference
to have is *How to Take Great Trips with Your Kids* (The Harvard
Common Press), which is full of good general advice that can apply
to travel anywhere.

Journeying Senior Style

People over the age of 60 are traveling more than ever before. And why
not? Being a senior citizen entitles you to some terrific travel bargains,
and Seattle and the Olympic Peninsula are no exceptions. Senior discounts are available at many hotels, restaurants, and attractions; even
a ride on a Washington State Ferry is discounted by nearly 50% for passengers over the age of 65. Just remember to always mention the fact
that you're a senior citizen when you make your travel reservations.

Members of **AARP** (formerly known as the American Association of
Retired Persons), 601 E St. NW, Washington, DC 20049 (☎ **800-424-3410**
or 202-434-2277; Internet: www.aarp.org), get discounts on hotels, airfares, and car rentals. AARP offers members a wide range of benefits,
including *AARP: The Magazine* and a monthly newsletter. Anyone over
50 can join.

The **U.S. National Park Service** offers a **Golden Age Passport** that
gives seniors 62 years or older lifetime entrance to all properties
administered by the National Park Service — national parks (including
Olympic National Park), monuments, historic sites, recreation areas,
and national wildlife refuges — for a one-time processing fee of $10.

You must purchase the pass in person at any NPS facility that charges an entrance fee. Besides free entry, a Golden Age Passport also offers a 50% discount on federal-use fees charged for such facilities as camping, swimming, parking, boat launching, and tours. For more information, go to the Web site www.nps.gov/fees_passes.htm or call ☎ **888-467-2757.**

Many reliable agencies and organizations target the 50-plus market. **Elderhostel** (☎ **877-426-8056;** Internet: www.elderhostel.org) arranges study programs for those aged 55 and over (and a spouse or companion of any age) in the U.S. and in more than 80 countries around the world. Most courses last five to seven days in the U.S. (two to four weeks abroad), and many include airfare, accommodations in university dormitories or modest inns, meals, and tuition.

Recommended publications offering travel resources and discounts for seniors include the quarterly magazine *Travel 50 & Beyond* (Internet: www.travel50andbeyond.com); *Travel Unlimited: Uncommon Adventures for the Mature Traveler* (Avalon); *101 Tips for Mature Travelers,* available from Grand Circle Travel (☎ **800-221-2610** or 617-350-7500; Internet: www.gct.com); *The 50+ Traveler's Guidebook* (St. Martin's Press); and *Unbelievably Good Deals and Great Adventures That You Absolutely Can't Get Unless You're Over 50* (McGraw Hill).

Accommodating Travelers with Disabilities

Most disabilities shouldn't stop anyone from traveling. Travelers with disabilities have more options and resources available than ever before. For the most part, Seattle is well-equipped for disabled travelers. Most of Seattle's city buses have wheelchair lifts, and drivers will help a wheelchair-bound traveler get to a secure space on the bus. The city's hills can be awfully difficult to negotiate, but planning excursions carefully can help flatten the journey. With its packed sidewalks and cobblestone streets, the **Pike Place Market** in Seattle can be tough to negotiate by wheelchair, but the Market has elevators that can lift you to or from Western Avenue and the waterfront. **Experience Music Project** has an elevator on Fifth Avenue that can lift you to the level of its main entrance.

The major towns on the Olympic Peninsula, including Port Angeles and Port Townsend, have handicapped-accessible lodgings and restaurants, as well as streets and boardwalks that are easily negotiable by wheelchair. The Olympic National Park Visitors Center in Port Angeles (see Chapter 21 for information) can provide information on wheelchair travel in the park. The U.S. National Park Service offers a **Golden Access Passport** (☎ **888-467-2757;** Internet: www.nps.gov/fees_passes.htm) that gives free lifetime entrance to all properties

administered by the National Park Service — national parks, monuments, historic sites, recreation areas, and national wildlife refuges —
for persons who are blind or permanently disabled, regardless of age.
You may pick up a Golden Access Passport at any NPS entrance fee area
by showing proof of medically determined disability and eligibility for
receiving benefits under federal law. Besides free entry, the Golden
Access Passport also offers a 50% discount on federal-use fees charged
for such facilities as camping, swimming, parking, boat launching,
and tours.

Many travel agencies offer customized tours and itineraries for travelers with disabilities. **Flying Wheels Travel** (☎ **507-451-5005;** Internet:
www.flyingwheelstravel.com) offers escorted tours and cruises
that emphasize sports and private tours in minivans with lifts.
Accessible Journeys (☎ **800-846-4537** or 610-521-0339; Internet: www.
disabilitytravel.com) caters specifically to slow walkers and
wheelchair travelers and their families and friends.

Organizations that offer assistance to disabled travelers include the
Moss Rehab Hospital (Internet: www.mossresourcenet.org), which
provides a library of accessible-travel resources online; the **Society for
Accessible Travel and Hospitality** (☎ **212-447-7284**; Internet: www.
sath.org; annual membership fees: $45 adults, $30 seniors and students), which offers a wealth of travel resources for all types of disabilities and informed recommendations on destinations, access guides,
travel agents, tour operators, vehicle rentals, and companion services;
and the **American Foundation for the Blind** (☎ **800-232-5463;**
Internet: www.afb.org), which provides information on traveling with
Seeing Eye dogs.

For more information specifically targeted to travelers with disabilities,
the community Web site **iCan** (Internet: www.icanonline.net/
channels/travel/index.cfm) has destination guides and several
regular columns on accessible travel. Also check out the quarterly
magazine **Emerging Horizons** ($14.95 per year, $19.95 outside the
United States; Internet: www.emerginghorizons.com); **Twin Peaks
Press** (☎ **360-694-2462**; Internet: http://disabilitybookshop.
virtualave.net/blist84.htm), offering travel-related books for
travelers with special needs; and *Open World Magazine,* published
by the Society for Accessible Travel and Hospitality (☎ **212-447-7284**;
Internet: www.sath.org; subscription: $18/yr., $35 outside the U.S.).

Traveling Tips for Gays and Lesbians

Seattle is welcoming and tolerant of gay lifestyles, but keep in mind
that when you leave the city and venture out into parts of rural
Washington, the acceptance levels can go south in a hurry. Seattle's
most gay-friendly neighborhood is **Capitol Hill,** where a popular
Gay Pride March is conducted down Broadway every year in June.

The *Seattle Gay News* (☎ 206-324-4297) is a free community newspaper that you can find in most Capitol Hill bars and restaurants, as well as most of the city's public libraries. The *Pink Pages* (☎ 206-238-5850) is a directory of gay-friendly businesses. You can find both of these publications at the **Beyond the Closet Bookstore,** 518 East Pike St. (☎ 206-322-4609; Internet: www.beyondthecloset.com), which has a great deal of gay and lesbian resources information, plus a bulletin board listing gay and lesbian events. A **Lesbian Resource Center** at 2214 South Jackson St. (☎ 206-322-3953; Internet: www.lrc.net) also offers many resources and can refer you to other lesbian organizations.

The International Gay & Lesbian Travel Association (IGLTA) (☎ 800-448-8550 or 954-776-2626; Internet: www.iglta.org) is the trade association for the gay and lesbian travel industry and offers an online directory of gay and lesbian-friendly travel businesses; go to its Web site and click Members.

Many agencies offer tours and travel itineraries specifically for gay and lesbian travelers. **Above and Beyond Tours** (☎ 800-397-2681; Internet: www.abovebeyondtours.com) is the exclusive gay and lesbian tour operator for United Airlines. **Now, Voyager** (☎ 800-255-6951; Internet: www.nowvoyager.com) is a well-known San Francisco–based gay-owned and operated travel service. **Olivia Cruises & Resorts** (☎ 800-631-6277 or 510-655-0364; Internet: www.olivia.com) charters entire resorts and ships for exclusive lesbian vacations and offers smaller group experiences for both gay and lesbian travelers.

The following travel guides are available at most travel bookstores and gay and lesbian bookstores, or you can order them from **Giovanni's Room** bookstore, 1145 Pine St., Philadelphia, PA 19107 (☎ 215-923-2960; Internet: www.giovannisroom.com): *Out and About* (☎ 800-929-2268 or 415-644-8044; Internet: www.outandabout.com), which offers guidebooks and a newsletter ten times a year packed with solid information on the global gay and lesbian scene; *Spartacus International Gay Guide* and *Odysseus,* both good, annual English-language guidebooks focused on gay men; the *Damron* guides, with separate, annual books for gay men and lesbians; and *Gay Travel A to Z: The World of Gay & Lesbian Travel Options at Your Fingertips,* by Marianne Ferrari (Ferrari Publications; Box 35575, Phoenix, AZ 85069), a very good gay and lesbian guidebook series.

Discovering Traveling Tips for Black Travelers

Seattle has long been known as a place of tolerance and peaceful coexistence among all races. The kind of racial tension that can be a part of daily life in many eastern cities simply has never existed here. That image has been shaken in recent years because the black community, which is centered in the Central District east of downtown, has protested unfair treatment, mostly at the hands of the police department. For information and news about local issues, *The Seattle Medium* (Internet: www.seattlemedium.com) is a black-owned newspaper that has been serving the African-American community since 1970.

Keep in mind that Seattle is an overwhelmingly white city, with blacks making up only 8.4% of the local population. That number drops to 3.2% in the state of Washington. In other words, you probably won't see many people of color, but we're not aware of any incidents of racial intolerance that have taken place on the Olympic Peninsula in the last decade.

The Internet offers a number of helpful travel sites for the black traveler. **Black Travel Online** (Internet: www.blacktravelonline.com) posts news on upcoming events, and includes links to articles and travel-booking sites. **Soul of America** (Internet: www.soulofamerica.com) is a more comprehensive black travel Web site, with travel tips, event information, family reunion postings, and sections on historically black beach resorts and active vacations.

For more information, check out the following collections and guides: *Go Girl: The Black Woman's Guide to Travel & Adventure* (Eighth Mountain Press), a compilation of travel essays by writers including Jill Nelson and Audre Lorde, with some practical information and trip-planning advice; *The African American Travel Guide* by Wayne Robinson (Hunter Publishing; must be bought direct at Internet: www.hunterpublishing.com), with details on 19 North American cities; *Steppin' Out* by Carla Labat (Avalon), with details on 20 cities; *Travel and Enjoy Magazine* (☎ 866-266-6211; Internet: www.travelandenjoy.com; subscription: $24/yr), which focuses on discounts and destination reviews; and the more narrative *Pathfinders Magazine* (☎ 877-977-PATH; Internet: www.pathfinderstravel.com; subscription: $15/yr.), which includes articles on everything from Rio de Janeiro to Ghana.

Flying Solo

Many people prefer traveling alone. For independent travelers, solo journeys offer infinite opportunities to make friends and meet locals. Unfortunately, if you like resorts, tours, or cruises, you're likely to get hit with a "single supplement" to the base price. Single travelers can avoid these supplements, of course, by agreeing to room with other single travelers. An even better idea is to find a compatible roommate from one of the many roommate locator agencies before you leave for your trip. In Seattle, you can contact **Events and Adventures**

(☎ 425-882-0838; Internet: www.localsingles.org) to meet local singles and join scheduled activities. In addition, check out the following resources:

- ✔ **Travel Companion Exchange (TCE)** (☎ 631-454-0880; Internet: www.travelcompanions.com) is one of the nation's oldest room-mate finders for single travelers. Register with them and find a travel mate who will split the cost of the room with you.

- ✔ **TravelChums** (☎ 212-787-2621; Internet: www.travelchums.com) is an Internet-only travel-companion matching service with elements of an online personals-type site, hosted by the respected New York–based Shaw Guides travel service.

- ✔ **Backroads** (☎ 800-462-2848; Internet: www.backroads.com) offers more than 160 active trips to 30 destinations worldwide, including Bali, Morocco, and Costa Rica.

For more information, check out Eleanor Berman's *Traveling Solo: Advice and Ideas for More Than 250 Great Vacations* (Globe Pequot), a guide with advice on traveling alone, whether on your own or on a group tour. (It was updated for 2003.) Or turn to the **Travel Alone and Love It** Web site (Internet: www.travelaloneandloveit.com), designed by former flight attendant Sharon Wingler, the author of the book *Travel Alone and Love It*. Her site is full of tips for single travelers.

Walking the Dog Away from Home

By all means, don't leave Precious at home (or Fluffy, Spike, Rex or Bowser), particularly if you're an outdoor person who will be spending lots of time hiking and exploring. Seattle is very pet-friendly, and many hotels make a special fuss about catering to their guests' dogs. Parks and walkways are nearby for that all-important daily walk (bring your own bags and use them, please), and the city even has a half-dozen leash-free areas in city parks where dogs can run free in a large, fenced space and get to know their Northwest brethren. The best dog runs are at **Magnuson Park** alongside Lake Washington in the Northeast district of the city, near the University of Washington, and **Marymoor Park** in the eastside suburb of Redmond. Ask your hotel for information or look up "Parks & Recreation" in the City of Seattle Government pages of the phone book.

Dogs are allowed on the ferries, but they must either be on a leash on the car decks (not upstairs among other passengers) or in the car. Remember to never leave your pet in the car for an extended period of time on a hot day. On the Olympic Peninsula, you'll find plenty of wide-open spaces to run your dog, but keep in mind that most public parks require dogs to be leashed at all times.

Part II
Ironing Out the Details

The 5th Wave By Rich Tennant

THE HARRISONS PREPARE FOR THEIR MOUNTAIN BIKING VACATION IN OLYMPIC NATIONAL PARK.

Awesome move, Mom.

In this part . . .

In Part I, I lay out the groundwork for your trip to Seattle and the Olympic Peninsula. In this part, I get down to the nitty-gritty, offering hard-working advice on the best ways to get around once you're there, how to avoid driving in rush-hour traffic, how to book tickets and reservations online, and the pros and cons of package tours. I provide invaluable tips on packing and what kind of clothes to bring, what to do if you get sick away from home, and advice on when to make reservations for events or special meals — all the last-minute details you need to help make your trip a smooth and safe one!

Chapter 5

Getting to Seattle and the Olympic Peninsula

● ●

In This Chapter

▶ Using a travel agent

▶ Buying travel insurance

▶ Comparing escorted tours and package tours

▶ Making your own travel arrangements

▶ Finding the best airfare

▶ Getting to Seattle and the Olympic Peninsula by car, train, or bus

● ●

*Y*ou know about all the great attractions that Seattle and the Olympic Peninsula have to offer. You're sold on the notion that either would make a great vacation destination, and you're rarin' to go. Now it's simply a matter of figuring out the best way to get there.

Travel Agent: Friend or Foe?

A good travel agent is like a good mechanic or a good plumber: hard to find, but invaluable once you've got the right person. And the best way to find a good travel agent is the same way you found that good plumber or mechanic — by word of mouth. Any travel agent can help you find a bargain airfare, hotel, or rental car. But a good travel agent stops you from ruining your vacation by simply trying to save a few dollars. The best travel agents can tell you how much time you should budget for each destination, find a cheap flight that doesn't require that you change planes three times, get you a hotel room with a view for the same price as a lesser room, arrange for a competitively priced rental car, and even give recommendations on restaurants.

Travel agents work on commission. The good news is that *you* don't pay the commission — the airlines, accommodations, and tour companies do. The bad news is that unscrupulous travel agents often try to persuade you to book the vacations that land them the most money in commissions.

In the past few years, some airlines and resorts have begun limiting or eliminating travel agent commissions altogether. The immediate result has been that travel agents don't bother booking these services unless the customer specifically requests them. But some travel industry analysts predict that if other airlines and accommodations follow suit, travel agents may have to start charging customers for their services.

Travel Insurance: Do You Need It?

Although it's not like embarking on a trip to Australia or South Africa, Seattle and the Northwest still is a long way from home for a vast majority of people in the United States, and if you have to cancel or curtail your trip due to unforeseen circumstances, you may find yourself eating the expenses of fairly hefty plane tickets. In this section, I discuss the pros and cons of travel insurance in order to help you make an informed decision. Check your existing insurance policies and credit-card coverage before you buy travel insurance. You may already be covered for lost luggage, cancelled tickets, or medical expenses. The cost of travel insurance varies widely, depending on the cost and length of your trip, your age, health, and the type of trip you're taking.

Trip-cancellation insurance

Trip-cancellation insurance helps you get your money back if you have to back out of a trip, if you have to go home early, or if your travel supplier goes bankrupt. Allowed reasons for cancellation can range from sickness to natural disasters to the State Department declaring your destination unsafe for travel. (Insurers usually won't cover vague fears, though, as many travelers discovered when they tried to cancel their trips in October 2001 because they were wary of flying.) In this unstable world, trip-cancellation insurance is a good buy if you're getting tickets well in advance — who knows what the state of the world, or of your airline, will be in nine months? Insurance policy details vary, so read the fine print. Especially make sure that your airline or cruise line is on the list of carriers covered in case of bankruptcy. For information, contact one of the following insurers: **Access America** (☎ **800-284-8300;** Internet: www.accessamerica.com); **Travel Guard International** (☎ **800-826-1300;** Internet: www.travelguard.com); **Travel Insured International** (☎ **800-243-3174;** Internet: www.travelinsured.com); and **Travelex Insurance Services** (☎ **800-228-9792;** Internet: www.travelex-insurance.com).

Medical insurance

Most health insurance policies cover you if you get sick away from home, but check, particularly if you're insured by an HMO. If you require additional medical insurance, try **MEDEX International** (☎ **800-527-0218** or 410-453-6300; Internet: www.medexassist.com) or **Travel Assistance International** (☎ **800-821-2828;** Internet: www.travelassistance.com; for general information on services, call the company's Worldwide Assistance Services, Inc. ☎ **800-777-8710**).

Lost-luggage insurance

On domestic flights, checked baggage is covered up to $2,500 per ticketed passenger. If you plan to check items more valuable than the standard liability, check whether they're covered by your homeowner's policy, get baggage insurance as part of your comprehensive travel-insurance package, or buy Travel Guard's "BagTrak" product. Don't buy insurance at the airport, as it's usually overpriced. Be sure to take any valuables or irreplaceable items with you in your carry-on luggage, as many valuables (including books, money, and electronics) aren't covered by airline policies. If your luggage is lost, immediately file a lost-luggage claim at the airport, detailing the luggage contents. For most airlines, you must report delayed, damaged, or lost baggage within four hours of arrival. The airlines are required to deliver luggage, once found, directly to your house or destination free of charge. Delivery is usually quick and easy if you're staying in downtown Seattle, which is just a half-hour from the airport, but it can get trickier if you're planning on camping or moving around in the Olympic Peninsula.

Escorted General-Interest Tours: Sit Back and Enjoy the Ride

Escorted tours are structured group tours, with a group leader. The price usually includes everything from airfare to hotels, meals, tours, admission costs, and local transportation. Many people derive a certain ease and security from escorted trips. Escorted tours — whether by bus, motor coach, train, or boat — let travelers sit back and enjoy their trip without having to spend lots of time behind the wheel. Tour organizers take care of all the little details; you know your costs up front and have few surprises. Escorted tours can take you to the maximum number of sights in the minimum amount of time with the least amount of hassle, so you don't have to sweat over the plotting and planning of a vacation schedule. Escorted tours are particularly convenient for people with limited mobility.

On the downside, an escorted tour often requires a big deposit up front, and lodging and dining choices are predetermined. As part of a cloud of tourists, you'll get little opportunity for serendipitous interactions with locals. The tours can be jam-packed with activities, leaving little room for individual sightseeing, whim, or adventure — plus, they often focus only on the heavily touristed sites, so you miss out on the lesser known gems.

If you want to undertake a long tour of the Pacific Northwest, ending up in Seattle, several tour companies will be happy to put you on the bus for one of those "If this is Thursday, that must be the Space Needle" tours. **Globus Tours** (☎ **303-797-2800;** Internet: www.globusandcosmos. com) is a huge international tour operator that moves more than 500,000 tourists a year and can take you to Seattle or Antarctica with equal ease. The company offers a 12-day trip from San Francisco to Seattle that stops in Olympic National Park (and all points in between).

Another good option is **Gray Line of Seattle** (☎ **800-426-7505;** Internet: www.graylineofseattle.com), a motorcoach tour company that offers a number of package options throughout the Northwest. Besides offering city tours of Seattle (see Chapter 15 for specifics), the company concentrates on moving visitors between Seattle and the Canadian cities of Victoria and Vancouver. The Northwest Triangle tour is a seven-day, six-night journey from Seattle, with a city tour and visits to Mount Rainier, to Victoria, British Columbia, and to Vancouver, Canada. Another weeklong option goes from Seattle to the San Juan Islands, then to Vancouver, and then to the ski resort town of Whistler, British Columbia, before returning to Seattle via Victoria. Gray Line of Seattle offers three different hotel pricing options (moderate, first-class, and deluxe), utilizing the Holiday Inn Express (moderate), Paramount Hotel and Warwick Hotel (first-class), and Renaissance Madison Hotel (deluxe).

Before you invest in an escorted tour, ask about the **cancellation policy.** Is a deposit required? Can the company cancel the trip if it doesn't get enough people? Do you get a refund if the company cancels? If *you* cancel? How late can you cancel if you're unable to go? When do you pay in full? If you choose an escorted tour, think strongly about purchasing trip-cancellation insurance, especially if the tour operator asks you to pay up front. See the section on "Travel Insurance," earlier in this chapter.

You'll also want to get a complete **schedule** of the trip to find out how much sightseeing is planned each day and whether enough time has been allotted for relaxing or wandering solo.

The **size** of the group is also important to know up front. Generally, the smaller the group, the more flexible the itinerary, and the less time you'll spend waiting for people to get on and off the bus. Find out the

demographics of the group as well. What is the age range? What is the gender breakdown? Is this mostly a trip for couples or singles?

Discuss what is included in the **price.** You may have to pay for transportation to and from the airport. A box lunch may be included in an excursion, but drinks can cost extra. Tips may not be included. Find out whether you'll be charged if you decide to opt out of certain activities or meals.

If you plan to travel alone, you'll need to know whether a **single supplement** will be charged or whether the company can match you up with a roommate.

Packages for the Independent Traveler: Going It Alone

Going it on your own without a travel agent or group tour? No problem, you have all the tools that you need at your disposal to book your trip just the way that you want it. Before you start your search for the lowest airfare, you may want to consider booking your flight as part of a travel package. *Package tours* aren't the same thing as escorted tours. Package tours are simply a way to buy the airfare, accommodations, and other elements of your trip (such as car rentals, airport transfers, and sometimes even activities) at the same time and often at discounted prices — kind of like one-stop shopping. Packages are sold in bulk to tour operators, who resell them to the public at a cost that usually undercuts standard rates.

One good source of package deals is the airlines themselves. Most major airlines offer air/land packages, including **American Airlines Vacations** (☎ 800-321-2121; Internet: www.aavacations.com), **Delta Vacations** (☎ 800-221-6666; Internet: www.deltavacations.com), **Continental Airlines Vacations** (☎ 800-301-3800; Internet: www.coolvacations.com), and **United Vacations** (☎ 888-854-3899; Internet: www.unitedvacations.com). Several big **online travel agencies** — Expedia, Travelocity, Orbitz, Site59, and Lastminute.com — also do a brisk business in packages. If you're unsure about the pedigree of a smaller packager, check with the Better Business Bureau in the city where the company is based, or go online at www.bbb.org. If a packager won't tell you where it's based, don't fly with them.

For Seattle-specific tours, look to the airlines, which package vacations by combining airfare and hotel rooms with an option for a rental car. **Alaska Airlines** (☎ 800-547-9308; Internet: www.alaskaair.com), and its sister airline, **Horizon Airlines** (same phone and Web), can set you up in Seattle with rooms at the Roosevelt, W Seattle, or Paramount

hotels. **American Airlines Vacations** (☎ 800-433-7300; Internet: www.
aavacations.com) offers hotel packages in Seattle, with rooms at the
Madison Renaissance or Edgewater hotels.

If you book a package tour that winds up in Seattle, ask whether the
tour operator offers an extension on your hotel room rate that allows
you to stay put for a few days after the official tour ends. You may be
able to get a better rate this way, but check on other offers to be sure
that you get the best deal possible.

Travel packages are also listed in the travel section of your local
Sunday newspaper. Or check ads in the national travel magazines such
as *Arthur Frommer's Budget Travel Magazine, Travel & Leisure, National
Geographic Traveler,* and *Condé Nast Traveler.*

Package tours can vary by leaps and bounds. Some offer a better class
of hotels than others. Some offer the same hotels for lower prices.
Some offer flights on scheduled airlines, while others book charters.
Some limit your choice of accommodations and travel days. You're
often required to make a large payment up front. On the plus side,
packages can save you money, offering group prices but allowing for
independent travel. Some even let you add on a few guided excursions
or escorted day trips (also at prices lower than if you booked them
yourself) without booking an entirely escorted tour.

Before you invest in a package tour, get some answers. Ask about the
accommodation choices and prices for each. Then look up the hotels'
reviews in this guide and check their rates for your specific dates of
travel online. If you need a certain type of room, ask for it; don't take
whatever is thrown your way. Request a nonsmoking room, a quiet
room, a room with a view, or whatever you fancy.

Finally, look for **hidden expenses.** Ask whether the total cost includes
airport departure fees and taxes, for example.

Getting to Seattle

The following sections cover the various modes of transportation that
you can use to get to Seattle.

By plane

The advantage of flying to Seattle is that it's the quickest way to get to
the city from many places. The following sections cover the ins and
outs of choosing an airline, getting an inexpensive fare and making
your way through the airport.

The airline players in the Northwest

Seattle's Sea-Tac Airport is served by most of the big hitters in the airline biz. Major regional carriers, with the most arrivals and departures from and to West Coast cities, are **Alaska Airlines** (☎ 800-426-0333; Internet: www.alaskaair.com) and its regional carrier, **Horizon Airlines** (☎ 800-547-9308; Internet: www.horizonair.com), which serves smaller airports in Washington, Oregon, Montana, Idaho, and northern California; **Southwest** (☎ 800-435-9792; Internet: www.southwest.com); and **United** and **Shuttle by United** (☎ 800-241-6522; Internet: www.ual.com). The big boys who come into the region are **American Airlines** (☎ 800-433-7300; Internet: www.aa.com), **America West** (☎ 800-235-9292; Internet: www.americawest.com), **Continental** (☎ 800-525-0280; Internet: www.flycontinental.com), **Delta** (☎ 800-221-1212; Internet: www.delta.com), **Northwest** (☎ 800-225-2525; Internet: www.nwa.com), and **US Airways** (☎ 800-428-4322; Internet: www.usairways.com).

International carriers who fly directly into Seattle are **Air Canada** (☎ 800-776-3000; Internet: www.aircanada.ca), **British Airways** (☎ 800-247-9297; Internet: www.british-airways.com), **Asiana Airlines** (☎ 800-227-4262; Internet: www.air.asiana.co), and **Scandinavian Air** (☎ 800-221-2350; Internet: www.flysas.com). For a complete list of all carriers who use Sea-Tac, check out the airport's Web site at www.portseattle.org/seatac.

Don't forget that airlines are consolidating and cross-promoting each other's frequent-flier programs like crazy these days. Alaska Airlines, for example, has co-benefits with American, Northwest, and several international carriers, and if you fly an Alaska Airlines flight, you can charge the miles to your frequent-flier account on those airlines, or vice-versa. Be sure to check with your frequent-flier program to see which regional carriers are included, and make sure that they enter the appropriate frequent-flier account when you buy the ticket or check in for your flight.

Surfing for airfares

The "big three" online travel agencies, Expedia.com, Travelocity.com, and Orbitz.com sell most of the air tickets bought on the Internet. (Canadian travelers should try expedia.ca and Travelocity.ca; U.K. residents can try expedia.co.uk and opodo.co.uk.) Each site has different business deals with the airlines and may offer different fares on the same flights, so shopping around is wise. Expedia and Travelocity will also send you **e-mail notification** when a cheap fare becomes available to your favorite destination. Of the smaller travel agency Web sites, **SideStep** (Internet: www.sidestep.com) has gotten the best reviews from *For Dummies* authors. It's a browser add-on that purports to "search 140 sites at once," but in reality only beats competitors' fares as often as other sites do.

Travel in the age of bankruptcy

At press time, two major U.S. airlines were struggling in bankruptcy court, and most of the rest weren't doing very well either. To protect yourself, **buy your tickets with a credit card,** as the Fair Credit Billing Act guarantees that you can get your money back from the credit-card company if a travel supplier goes under (and if you request the refund within 60 days of the bankruptcy). **Travel insurance** can also help, but make sure that it covers against "carrier default" for your specific travel provider. And be aware that if a U.S. airline goes bust mid-trip, a 2001 federal law requires other carriers to take you to your destination (albeit on a space-available basis) for a fee of no more than $25, provided you rebook within 60 days of the cancellation.

Also remember to check **airline Web sites,** especially those for low-fare carriers such as Southwest, JetBlue, AirTran, WestJet, or Ryanair, whose fares are often misreported or simply missing from travel agency Web sites. Even with major airlines, you can often shave a few bucks from a fare by booking directly through the airline and avoiding a travel agency's transaction fee. Most airlines now offer online-only fares that even their phone agents know nothing about.

Great **last-minute deals** are available through free weekly e-mail services provided directly by the airlines. Most announcements come on Tuesday or Wednesday and must be purchased online. Most are only valid for travel that weekend, but some (such as Southwest's) can be booked weeks or months in advance. Sign up for weekly e-mail alerts at airline Web sites or check mega-sites that compile comprehensive lists of last-minute specials, such as **Smarter Living** (Internet: smarterliving. com). For last-minute trips, site59.com in the U.S. and lastminute.com in Europe often have better deals than the major-label sites.

If you're willing to give up some control over your flight details, use an **opaque fare service** like **Priceline** (Internet: www.priceline.com; Internet: www.priceline.co.uk for Europeans) or **Hotwire** (Internet: www.hotwire.com). Both offer rock-bottom prices in exchange for travel on a "mystery airline" at a mysterious time of day, often with a mysterious change of planes en route. The mystery airlines are all major, well-known carriers. The possibility of being sent from Philadelphia to Chicago via Tampa is remote; the airlines' routing computers have gotten a lot better than they used to be. But your chances of getting a 6 a.m. or 11 p.m. flight are pretty high. Hotwire tells you flight prices before you buy; Priceline usually has better deals than Hotwire, but you have to play their "name our price" game. If you're new at this scenario, the helpful folks at **BiddingForTravel** (Internet: www.biddingfortravel.com) do a good job of demystifying Priceline's prices. Priceline and Hotwire are great for flights within

North America and between the United States and Europe. But for flights to other parts of the world, consolidators will almost always beat their fares.

For much more about airfares and savvy air-travel tips and advice, pick up a copy of *Frommer's Fly Safe, Fly Smart* (Wiley Publishing, Inc.).

Flying for less: Tips for getting the best airfare

Passengers sharing the same airplane cabin rarely pay the same fare. Travelers who need to purchase tickets at the last minute, change their itinerary at a moment's notice, or fly one-way often get stuck paying the premium rate. Here are some ways to keep your airfare costs down.

- Passengers who can book their ticket **long in advance,** who can **stay over Saturday night,** or who **fly midweek** or **at less trafficked hours** will pay a fraction of the full fare. If your schedule is flexible, say so, and ask whether you can secure a cheaper fare by changing your flight plans.

- You can save on airfares by keeping an eye out in local newspapers for **promotional specials** or **fare wars,** when airlines lower prices on their most popular routes. You rarely see fare wars offered for peak travel times, but if you can travel in the off-months, you may snag a bargain.

- Search the **Internet** for cheap fares. See the section "Surfing for Airfares," earlier in this chapter.

- **Consolidators,** also known as *bucket shops,* are great sources for international tickets, although they usually can't beat the Internet on fares within North America. Start by looking in Sunday newspaper travel sections; U.S, travelers should focus on *The New York Times, Los Angeles Times,* and *The Miami Herald.* Beware: Bucket-shop tickets are usually nonrefundable or rigged with stiff cancellation penalties, often as high as 50 to 75% of the ticket price, and some put you on charter airlines with questionable safety records.

- Join **frequent-flier clubs.** Accrue enough miles, and you'll be rewarded with free flights and elite status. You don't need to fly to build frequent-flier miles — **frequent-flier credit cards** can provide thousands of miles for doing your everyday shopping.

For many more tips about air travel, including a rundown of the major frequent-flier credit cards, pick up a copy of *Frommer's Fly Safe, Fly Smart* (Wiley Publishing, Inc.).

Getting through the airport

With the federalization of airport security, security procedures at U.S. airports are more stable and consistent than ever. Generally, you'll be fine if you arrive at the airport **1 hour** before a domestic flight and **2 hours** before an international flight; if you show up late, tell an airline employee, and she'll probably whisk you to the front of the line.

Bring a **current, government-issued photo ID** such as a driver's license or passport. If you've got an e-ticket, also print the **official confirmation page;** you'll need to show your confirmation at the security checkpoint, and your ID at the ticket counter or the gate. (Children under 18 don't need photo IDs for domestic flights, but the adults checking in with them need them.)

Security lines are getting shorter than they were during 2001 and 2002, but some doozies remain. If you have trouble standing for long periods of time, tell an airline employee, and the airline will provide a wheelchair. Speed up security by **not wearing metal objects** such as big belt buckles or clanky earrings. And what about those clever workboots that you fancy: Do they have steel toes? If so, I hope you're wearing socks, because those steel toes will trigger the metal detector. If you've got metallic body parts, a note from your doctor can prevent a long chat with the security screeners. Keep in mind that only **ticketed passengers** are allowed past security, except for folks escorting disabled passengers or children. If that's the case, you'll need to get a pass from your airline's ticket agent before security lets you through the gate.

Federalization has stabilized **what you can carry on** and **what you can't.** The general rule is that sharp things are out, nail clippers are okay, and food and beverages must be passed through the X-ray machine — but security screeners can't make you drink from your coffee cup. Bring food in your carry-on rather than checking it, as explosive-detection machines used on checked luggage have been known to mistake food (especially chocolate, for some reason) for bombs. Travelers in the United States are allowed one carry-on bag, plus a personal item such as a purse, briefcase, or laptop bag. Carry-on hoarders can stuff all sorts of things into a laptop bag; as long as it has a laptop in it, it's still considered a personal item. The Transportation Security Administration (TSA) has issued a list of restricted items; check its Web site at `www.tsa.gov/public/index.jsp` for details.

Special advice for knitters: Long, metal knitting needles are one of those gray areas; they may get flagged as sharp objects, and then you're stuck at security without your knitting. I've heard from screeners that you should try to switch to plastic or bamboo needles, preferably circular, and make sure that you have some rows started, because nobody wants you to tear up the socks that you've begun to make for Grandma.

In 2003, the TSA is phasing out **gate check-in** at all U.S. airports. Passengers with e-tickets and without checked bags can still beat the

ticket-counter lines by using **electronic kiosks** or even **online check-in.**
Ask your airline which alternatives are available; if you're using a kiosk,
bring the credit card you used to book the ticket. If you're checking
bags, you'll still be able to use most airlines' kiosks; again call your airline for up-to-date information. **Curbside check-in** is also a good way to
avoid lines, although a few airlines still ban curbside check-in entirely;
call before you go.

At press time, the TSA is also recommending that you **not lock your
checked luggage** so that screeners can search it by hand, if necessary.
The agency says to use plastic "zip ties" instead, which can be bought
at hardware stores and can be easily cut off.

Scary scenarios to avoid

The following three airport horror stories can happen to even the most
savvy travelers. Try to ensure that they don't occur on your trip.

- ✔ **The late-check-in scenario:** If you want to experience true horror,
  arrive less than an hour before your flight leaves at the busy, over-
  worked Sea-Tac airport — with bags to check in. In peak tourist
  seasons, lines spill out of the concourses onto the sidewalk, with
  more enormous lines waiting to get through the security checks.
  Do yourself a favor and get to the airport at least an hour and a
  half before your flight leaves during the busy seasons. If you're
  late, try to check your bags with a skycap (tip him a dollar per
  bag) and then race to the gate for your boarding pass.

- ✔ **The late-to-the-gate scenario:** Want to experience more true
  horror? You've raced to your gate after arriving late to the airport
  and made it with minutes to spare. The doors are still open, and
  they're boarding the last of the passengers, but guess what?
  They've given away your seat. If you don't check in ten minutes
  before a domestic flight (more for international flights), the airlines begin to release seats to stand-by passengers, and no
  amount of screaming or sobbing can get your seat back. If you're
  cutting it close, try to get to a ticket agent fast — any ticket agent
  for your airline — to secure your seat.

- ✔ **The missed-flight scenario:** Even more horror: You miss your
  flight. If so, then whine, plead, and beg the gate agent to try to
  confirm you on the next flight out. If that one is full, get on the
  waiting list for standbys right away. The closer you get to the top
  of that list, the better your chances for averting total travel disas-
  ter. If all else fails, check with other airlines to see whether they'll
  honor your ticket and put you on their own flight to the same
  destination; most of them will say that they can't, but they can,
  and will, if seats are available and you look pitiful enough while
  explaining your predicament.

By car, train, and bus

Flying may be the quickest way to get to Seattle, but you can make a real adventure out of your travel time by driving, riding the rails, or hopping a bus. Here are your nonflying alternatives.

By car

Have some time on your hands and want to get a sense of how vast the American West really is? Get into your car, fill it up, and head to the Pacific Northwest. Seattle is a good, hard, two-day drive from San Francisco and a three-day excursion from Los Angeles or Las Vegas. Chicago is a long, lonely, four- to five-day trek across the Dakotas and Montana, and the Eastern seaboard is farther than you even want to think about unless you happen to have a *lot* of time on your hands. It takes five hours to cross the state of Washington from Seattle to Spokane, three hours from Seattle to Portland, and a little more than two hours from Seattle to Vancouver, British Columbia.

Seattle is located on the I-5 corridor that stretches all the way down to Southern California. Seattle is reached from the east by I-90. If you're coming from the west, either cross Puget Sound by the fine **Washington State Ferries (☎ 800-84-FERRY** or **206-464-6400)**, with connections for passengers and cars to the Olympic peninsula towns of Bremerton and Southworth, or use Hwy 101 or 16, which cross the Tacoma Narrows Bridge and then connect to I-5.

For information, maps, and roadside assistance, a membership in the **American Automobile Association (AAA)** can be invaluable. Call ☎ **800-222-4357.**

By train

Amtrak (☎ 800-872-7245; Internet: www.amtrak.com) services downtown Seattle, as well as Tacoma and Everett, with several trains a day. The Amtrak Cascades route connects Vancouver, British Columbia, Seattle, Portland, and Eugene, Oregon, on a route that roughly parallels I-5 but also hugs the Puget Sound coastline, with some great views along the way. The Coast Starlight route goes all the way south to Los Angeles on a long, scenic run. Heading east, Amtrak's Empire Builder connects Seattle to Spokane and points east. Check train schedules carefully if you're not going to or coming from a major city, because many Amtrak routes to the Northwest include bus service through some sections of the routes.

By bus

Greyhound (☎ 800-231-2222) serves Seattle, with connections to other cities throughout the country. The bus terminal is located in the heart of downtown, within walking distance of hotels and hostels.

Getting to the Olympic Peninsula

Reaching Olympic National Park and the Olympic Peninsula towns of Port Ludlow, Port Townsend, and Port Angeles is easy, thanks to the international airport near Seattle, which is a relatively short car ride — or shuttle flight — from the park. Heck, you can even reach the park from the sea, thanks to the docks at Port Angeles and the ferries that arrive there from Victoria, British Columbia.

By car

Seattle is the closest major gateway to Olympic National Park, which anchors Washington State's peninsula in the Pacific. From the city, you can reach the east side of the park either by taking a ferry across Puget Sound or by heading south on Interstate 5 to Tacoma, then taking Washington 16 north to Bremerton, and finally, heading north on Washington 3 to HWY 101. To reach the park's western side, drive west from Olympia on Washington 8 to Aberdeen and then north on HWY 101.

If you take the ferry across the sound from Seattle, you find park entrances along HWY 101 at Port Angeles, Hurricane Ridge, Elwha, Lake Crescent, and Sol Duc.

Traveling up HWY 101 from Aberdeen, you have the choice of entering the park in the Quinault or Queets valleys, or at Kalaloch Beach, the Hoh Rain Forest, or Mora. You reach Ozette in the northwestern corner via a road off Washington 112. From spur roads off HWY 101 on the east side of the park, you can reach Staircase and the park's entrance at Dosewallips. You find an entrance to Hurricane Ridge on the southern border of Port Angeles, and you can reach Deer Park via a road that heads south off HWY 101 just east of Port Angeles.

Some entrances may close in the winter, so check with the park visitor center at ☎ 360-565-3130 before setting out for Olympic.

For Puget Sound ferry schedules, contact **Washington State Ferries** (☎ 206-464-6400). For ferries arriving in Port Angeles from Victoria, British Columbia, contact **Black Ball Transportation** (☎ 360-457-4491) in Port Angeles. **Victoria Express** (☎ 800-633-1589 or 360-452-8088), offers seasonal, walk-on ferry service from Victoria, British Columbia to Port Angeles.

By plane

If you want to fly to the park, **Horizon Air** provides service to **Fairchild International Airport** (☎ 360-457- 8527) in Port Angeles from Seattle

Tacoma International Airport. **Budget Rent-A-Car** has an outlet at Fairchild. (See the Appendix A for toll-free numbers for Horizon and Budget.)

The closest major airport is the **Seattle Tacoma International Airport** (☎ **800-544-1965** or 206-431-4444), known as Sea-Tac, located 15 miles south of Seattle on Interstate 5. Most major airlines and car-rental agencies are here; see Appendix A for toll-free numbers. For bus service from the airport, see the next section, "By bus."

By bus

Olympic Bus Lines (☎ **360-417-0700**) offers twice daily service to and from Seattle and Seattle Tacoma International Airport to Port Angeles, Sequim, and Port Townsend. Fares are $29 one-way to or from downtown Seattle; $49 round-trip between Seattle and Port Angeles; and $43 one-way to or from the airport. **Pennco Transportation** (☎ **360-582-3736**), which is more expensive, makes nine trips daily between the airport and Port Angeles; it also provides transportation between Port Angeles and Port Townsend, Port Ludlow and Silverdale. Other bus companies on the peninsula include **Clallam Transit** (☎ **800-858-3747** or 360-452-4511), which operates Monday through Saturday within Port Angeles with commuter services to Sequim, Joyce, Lake Crescent, Forks, Neah Bay, and La Push; **Jefferson Transit** (☎ **360-385-4777**), which is based in Port Angeles and serves Brinnon and connects with Clallam Transit in Sequim; **Grays Harbor Transit** (☎ **800-562-9730** or 360-532-2770), which operates from Olympia and Aberdeen with service to Lake Quinault; and **Mason County Transit** (☎ **800-374-3747** or 360-427-5033), which runs between Shelton, Olympia, Bremerton, and Brinnon.

On the peninsula, **Olympic Tours** (☎ **360-457-3545**) offers park tours for groups as large as 30 people and can shuttle you to or from trailheads for backpacking treks.

Chapter 6

Deciding Where to Stay

. . . .

In This Chapter

▶ Sorting out lodging alternatives

▶ Choosing the place that's best for you

▶ Getting your money's worth

. . . .

*H*otels, motels, inns, guesthouses, and hostels: All are places where you can lay your head and feel at home during your visit to the Pacific Northwest, but the differences between these accommodations can be enormous. Lodgings in Seattle and the Olympic Peninsula range from a simple bed in a stark, spare room with an adjoining or shared bathroom, to a luxurious, top-of-the-line hotel with dazzling furnishings, 24-hour room service, a full array of amenities, and staff to meet your every need. The kind of place that works best for you depends on your desires and budget. An understanding of the different types of accommodations can help you make your choice. Remember that, in general, *you get what you pay for.*

In this chapter, I give you a general discussion of the different lodging options in Seattle and the Olympic Peninsula For specific details on individual lodgings in each area, see Chapter 10 for Seattle lodgings and Chapters 22 through 26 for Olympic National Park and Olympic Peninsula lodgings. A breakdown of prices and amenities follows at the end of this chapter to give you an idea of the types of places you can expect to find in your price range.

The Chains: Tried and True

Chain hotels and motels are the accommodations that you can find in virtually every city and state in the country. You recognize the names: Holiday Inn, Marriott, Comfort Inn, and Embassy Suites. They make a lot of money by offering hotel rooms that are pretty much the same regardless of what part of the country you visit, with standard rooms and rates. The room decor and furnishings are simple and basic, with a minimum of color or style; the services are the same in each hotel; and the rates are similar from one end of the country to the other. You can find these kinds of properties in the Northwest, but I haven't listed many of them in my breakdowns of the top hotels in Seattle and the Olympic Peninsula simply because both places offer so many better, more stylish, and more quintessentially Northwest options. If you dislike surprises in your choice of lodging, a chain place may be right for you, but it's a little like going all the way across the country to eat at a fast-food burger joint: You could have had the same experience at home. I prefer to try out new and unusual places in big cities and stick to the chains in more rural areas, such as when I leave Seattle and set off across the states of Washington and Oregon.

Motels and Motor Inns: No Frills

Motels are budget havens that consist of strips of rooms, usually with an outside entrance to each one, or long corridors of rooms that are stacked atop each other, and a sign out front that indicates VACANCY or NO VACANCY. These lodgings are generally the least expensive in a city, and they're frequently located on the outskirts of town or in close proximity to the major highways — largely because their biggest distinction from hotels is that they offer parking and cater to people who are driving. They generally don't have elevators or staff available to help you carry bags, and in-room amenities are limited to phones and cable TV, with (if you're lucky) a bar of soap in the bathroom and a coffeemaker (bring your own coffee). In the Northwest, it's rare to find a motel with a pool, but most motels offer nonsmoking rooms. Give the furniture a good sniff before you settle in to see whether the previous guests stuck to the rules, and if it smells smoky, ask to be moved into another room. Motels in the Northwest range from chain brands to independent lodgings that aren't affiliated with a larger company. Don't be shy about asking to see a room and testing the bed before you put your money down. If you're driving, you can save as much as $18 a day in parking charges by staying at a motel rather than a downtown hotel.

Hostels and B&Bs: Close Encounters

Hostels, frequently known as "youth hostels," are usually the sparest of accommodations, meant for travelers on extremely low budgets. They're called youth hostels because they're often occupied by teenagers and college kids, who don't mind sleeping in a same-sex dormitory room with 20 or more beds lined up in rows, with shared group bathrooms. Many hostels have a few private rooms, which cost a few dollars more than the shared dormitories and provide a modicum of privacy. Seattle has a highly rated hostel in a good location at the Pike Place Market that attracts young people, backpackers, and couples on a tight budget. Families may not feel safe because of the large numbers of people who come and go. Hostels are popular with international travelers and are a good place to meet people. Most hostels have shared kitchen facilities that you can use.

Bed-and-breakfasts, or B&Bs, are generally private homes or converted mansions with rooms that are rented out, with breakfast included in the price. There may be a shared living room that you can use to sit and read or to meet other guests. Guest rooms frequently don't have television sets or private phones. Breakfast may be served at a communal dining table and can range from a meal of cereal and toast to a full spread of bacon, eggs, and freshly baked bread or coffeecake. B&Bs are a good choice in neighborhoods with few or no hotels or motels, and they're a good place to meet locals who can give you the lowdown on places to go in the city. Prices are generally lower for B&B rooms than hotel rooms, and equal to or slightly more than motel rates. The downside is that you may have to sacrifice some privacy.

Inns and Converted Apartment Houses: The Personal Touch

Inns used to be very basic lodgings, often located in a converted home, where you could get a meal and a comfortable bed, usually with a shared bathroom. Now an inn can refer to anything from a bed-and-breakfast lodging to a luxurious suite hotel. For the most part, an inn is a lodging with fewer than 50 rooms and no on-premises food service (with the exception of a cold breakfast buffet) with accommodations that range from the downright rustic (shared baths and no TVs or phones in the rooms) to plush and luxurious (rooms with private baths and adjoining living rooms). In Seattle in particular, several converted apartment houses are now called hotels or inns (I list the better ones in the guide to the city's hotels in Chapter 10). These accommodations have small sitting areas and kitchenette units where you can cook your own meals, thus saving a bundle on restaurant prices. Most inns include a continental breakfast of coffee, juice, and rolls or cereal (at the least) in the price of the room.

The Big Corporate Hotels: Grand and Glitzy

Every big city has its grand, expansive hotels that cater to the convention trade and business travelers, and Seattle is no exception. Hotel chains like Sheraton and Westin operate large hotels with hundreds of rooms, two or more restaurants, and amenities that range from doormen to valet parking, 24-hour room service, and on-site health clubs and pools. Convention hotels are often bustling places with above-average rooms and services, but the sheer volume of people who come and go contributes to the feeling of being an anonymous minnow in a particularly large school of fish. Club-level rooms are generally offered at higher prices; these have a private sitting area where you can partake of the complimentary continental breakfast, afternoon cocktail, and wine service. These hotels are typically located right in the thick of things in the most vibrant parts of the city, and they convey that big-city feeling from the moment you enter their lobbies.

Boutique Hotels: Quiet Luxury

In recent years, European-style boutique hotels have become a popular alternative for travelers, particularly business travelers, who prefer a quieter, more serene lodging to the usual large corporate or convention hotels. A boutique hotel is, by definition, a smaller, intimate lodging, usually with fewer than 100 rooms. The rooms are tastefully decorated and often quite comfortable, with thick comforters on the beds and full bathrooms that may include hot tubs. Most boutiques also offer a warm, cheery, living-room-style lobby with a fireplace or library for guests to use. These hotels are generally adjoined to a good restaurant, and a crack staff is on hand to greet guests and attend to their needs. Boutique hotels beautifully fit the laid-back, comfortable lifestyle of the Pacific Northwest and are some of the best bets for accommodations in Seattle.

The Upper-Crust Hotels: Top of the Line

These no-expense-spared, high-end hotels — the kinds of places where you'd want to have your wedding if you or your family had cash to burn — are the most elegant and expensive accommodations in a city. Rooms are superbly appointed, and staff is on hand to attend to your every need, from providing around-the-clock dining, to procuring theater or restaurant reservations, to ironing your shirts. Rooms are generally large, with nice views, classy furnishings, and huge bathrooms. The hotels usually have at least one very formal, very plush dining room that serves exquisite food created by a talented chef. You may find yourself rubbing elbows with a visiting celebrity or star athlete over afternoon tea in the beautifully decorated lobby.

What You Get for the Money

So, how far do your lodging dollars go in Seattle and the Olympic Peninsula? In my lists of hotels, I break down the various options with $ signs, and, as you can well guess, the more $ signs, the merrier, in terms of service, views, and space.

Keep in mind that I base prices on the hotels' listed rack rates — the standard rates posted for a lodging's rooms. Most accommodations offer discounts on the rack rates at different times throughout the year, and tour operators and special-interest group members (such as AAA club members) may also receive discounts off the rack rate. Hotel prices also rise and fall with the seasons and can be influenced by whether a big convention is coming to town, so don't be surprised if my quoted prices are slightly different when you call to make a reservation. Also, see Chapter 7 for tips on getting the best lodging rates. Here's an idea of what the dollar signs represent, and what it buys for you.

$

($50–$80)

This low-end category covers most motels, hostels, and B&Bs in Seattle, as well as bare-bones chain hotels, and most of the accommodations that you'll find on the Olympic Peninsula. You get a room with one or two queen-size beds (or a dormitory bed in a hostel), usually away from the center of the city or town's action, with either a shared bathroom or a small, private bath that may only have a shower and not a bathtub. Check the beds at the lower end of this scale to make sure that they're not lumpy or damaged. Cable television and a phone are usually included at the upper end of this scale, and breakfasts (if they're offered) often consist of a light continental spread. Few other amenities or services are offered.

$$

($80–$125)

This price category includes rooms at newer, more centrally located chain hotels, and rooms in older and slightly run-down deluxe hotels. On the Olympic Peninsula, this price will get you a cabin that can sleep as many as ten people, or a nice room in a Victorian hotel. B&Bs and inns at this level are nicer and better decorated, and the breakfasts are often heartier. Rooms in the older deluxe hotels are on the small side, but they have views from the upper floors; the newer chain hotels in this price category may have a pool or fitness room. All have private bathrooms and some bath amenities, like shampoos and body lotions. Most lodgings have either a restaurant or coffee shop on the premises or are closely located to a number of eateries.

$$$

($125–$175)

Travelers who are willing to spend in this price range have the maximum number of pickings in downtown Seattle. You get quite a nice room in the top inns and boutique hotels, or one of the cheaper rooms in a big, deluxe convention and/or luxury hotel. Amenities like wine tastings, fitness rooms, or access to local health clubs are offered, as well as in-room movies and games, room service, and a restaurant. Rooms are spacious and nicely decorated with art and fine furnishings, and they frequently have a separate sitting area or sofa. Most rooms feature king-size beds. Each room has two or more phones with multiple lines, as well as Internet service on a fast connection. Services may include concierges to help with reservations and procuring tickets to events, bell staffs to assist with luggage, and attendants to valet park your car. On the Olympic Peninsula, this price category will get you a comfortable room or cabin in a lodging with amenities such as a pool, great views or an on-site restaurant.

$$$$
($175–$250)

The top-of-the-line price category gets you a standard room at the most deluxe hotels in town, or a suite (which consists of a bedroom and a separate sitting room) at a boutique hotel. Location is right in the thick of things, near shopping, restaurants, attractions, and businesses. The large rooms have views of either water or the downtown area, and the bathrooms have two sinks and a separate tub and shower and are often trimmed in marble. Amenities may include plush bathrobes; high-quality shampoos and lotions in the bathrooms; minibars stocked with sodas, beer, wine, and liquors; 24-hour room service from a high-end menu; and staff to assist with most needs. The lobby is grand and spacious, with lots of meeting rooms and ballrooms available for private functions. Two or more high-quality restaurants usually serve food throughout the day. On the Olympic Peninsula, this price category includes the best, most comfortable lodgings at full-service resort hotels. It also includes superior oceanfront cabins, many of which have full kitchens and large soaking tubs in the bathrooms.

Chapter 7

Booking Your Room

. . . .

In This Chapter

▶ Avoiding rack rates

▶ Getting your dream room at the best rate

▶ Discovering the Northwest's premier reservations services

▶ Using the Web as a bargain-hunter's resource

▶ Finding last-minute lodging

. . . .

Seattle offers a wide range of accommodations, from top-of-the-line to no-frills motel basic. You can shoot for the stars in a luxury suite or save by staying in a perfectly reliable (and perfectly priced) chain, small inn, or B&B. The Olympic Peninsula also has a number of lodging choices, from inexpensive motels to fancy rooms in Victorian hotels, but without the upper end of full-service hotels that the city offers. This chapter offers tips and insider advice on finding your dream accommodations when you visit the Pacific Northwest.

Uncovering the Truth about Rack Rates

The *rack rate* is the maximum rate that a hotel charges for a room. It's the rate you get if you walk in off the street and ask for a room for the night. You sometimes see this rate printed on the fire/emergency exit diagrams posted on the back of your hotel room door.

Hotels are more than happy to charge you the rack rate, but listen up: You don't have to pay it! Hardly anybody does. You can avoid paying the rack rate by simply asking for a cheaper or discounted rate. Try it — you may be pleasantly surprised at the result.

Getting the Best Room at the Best Rate

Summer is the high season in both Seattle and the Olympic Peninsula (see Chapter 2 for more information), and any special offers that hotels make to lure customers are lean during these months. The city has plenty of new hotel rooms to go around, and it's very unlikely that you'll be shut out altogether, but you may not get your first choice of lodging if you don't book well in advance for a summer visit.

In the winter, it's a different story altogether. You can get substantial savings on accommodations. Hotels and other lodgings offer programs with discounts of up to 50 percent in the slower winter months. Seattle calls its promotion "Super Saver" and lists some three dozen hotels, most of which are in the downtown core, that cut prices dramatically between November and March. The Hotel Edgewater, for example, has rooms for $129 (down from $265). To get the special rates, you have to call the reservations line directly (☎ 800-535-7071) or book online at the Internet site www.seattlesupersaver.com.

If you deal with hotels directly during the winter season, ask whether they can deepen the discount with a room rate cut, an upgrade, or an amenity such as free parking. Go on — it never hurts to ask.

Package tours can also be a way to get good hotel prices. Tour operators designate rooms for package tours ahead of time and can offer substantial savings when they combine the rooms with airfare, tours, and/or car rentals. See Chapter 5 for information on tour operators.

Navigating Reservations Services and Hotlines

Whether you do your travel planning over the phone, by mail, by fax, or by computer, you want access to the best resources to get the information you need. Here are some of the top local reservations services and hotlines for finding the right accommodations in the Seattle area and on the Olympic Peninsula.

Seattle

For help in securing a room reservation, turn to the **Seattle Hotel Hotline** (☎ 800-535-7071), a service of the Convention & Visitors Bureau. This service is the only source for booking reduced-rate hotel rooms under the off-season "Seattle Super Saver" package. **Pacific Northwest Journeys** (☎ 800-935-9730) is a booking service that plans whole itineraries to the Northwest area (including the Olympic Peninsula); it charges a fee for booking you a hotel room, but it frequently knows about and takes advantage of unadvertised specials or discounted rates.

To find a room in a private home or bed-and-breakfast, contact the **Seattle Bed and Breakfast Association** (☎ **800-348-5630** or 206-547-1020; Internet: www.seattlebandbs.com). **A Pacific Reservation Service** (☎ **800-684-2932** or 206-439-7666; Internet: www.seattle bedandbreakfast.com) offers a wide variety of lodging options, from inns and yachts to cabins and condos. In greater Seattle, contact the **Northwest Bed and Breakfast Reservation Service** (☎ **503-243-7616**) for rooms in outlying towns. The latter two companies also represent some lodgings on the Olympic Peninsula.

The Olympic Peninsula

The Olympic Peninsula has no centralized reservations bureau, but the **North Olympic Peninsula Visitor & Convention Bureau** (☎ **800-942-4042** or 360-452-8552; Internet: www.olympicpeninsula.org) can direct you to dozens of accommodations. The Web site also has links to member lodgings and to Web special deals offered by individual properties.

Surfing for Hotels

Of the "big three" sites, **Expedia.com** may be the best choice, thanks to its long list of special deals. **Travelocity.com** runs a close second. Hotel specialist sites **hotels.com** and **hoteldiscounts.com** are also reliable. An excellent free program, **TravelAxe** (Internet: www.travelaxe.net), can help you search multiple hotel sites at once, even ones you may never have heard of.

Priceline and **Hotwire** are even better for hotels than for airfares; with both, you're allowed to pick the neighborhood and quality level of your hotel before offering up your money. Priceline's hotel product even covers Europe and Asia, though it's much better at getting five-star lodging for three-star prices than at finding anything at the bottom of the scale. *Note:* Hotwire overrates its hotels by one star — what Hotwire calls a four-star is a three-star anywhere else.

While the major travel booking sites (such as Travelocity, Expedia, Yahoo! Travel, and Cheap Tickets) offer hotel bookings, you're better off using a site devoted primarily to lodging because you may find properties that aren't listed on more general online travel agencies. Some lodging sites specialize in a particular type of accommodations, such as bed-and-breakfasts, which you won't find on the more mainstream booking sites. Others, such as TravelWeb (see the upcoming bulleted list in this section for contact information), offer weekend deals on major chain properties, which cater to business travelers during the week and have more empty rooms on weekends.

Here is a sampling of lodging sites on the Internet:

✔ Although the name **All Hotels on the Web** (Internet: www.all-hotels.com) is something of an exaggeration, the site *does* have tens of thousands of listings for hotels throughout the world. Bear in mind that each hotel has paid a small fee (of $25 and up) to be listed, so it's less an objective list than a book of online brochures.

✔ **InnSite** (Internet: www.innsite.com) has B&B listings in all 50 U.S. states and more than 50 countries around the globe. Find an inn at your destination, see pictures of the rooms, and check prices and availability. This extensive directory of bed-and-breakfasts includes listings only if the proprietor submits one (it's free to get an inn listed). The innkeepers write the descriptions, and many listings link to the inn's own Web sites. Try also the **Bed and Breakfast Channel** (Internet: www.bedandbreakfast.com).

✔ **Places to Stay** (Internet: www.placestostay.com) lists one-of-a-kind lodgings in the U.S. and abroad that you may not find in other directories, with a focus on resort accommodations. Again, the listing is selective — this list isn't a comprehensive directory, but it can give you a sense of what's available at different destinations.

✔ **TravelWeb** (Internet: www.travelweb.com) lists more than 26,000 hotels in 170 countries, focusing on chains such as Hyatt and Hilton, and you can book almost 90 percent of these online. TravelWeb's "Click-It Weekends," updated each Monday, offers weekend deals at many leading hotel chains.

Figuring Out What to Do If You Arrive Without a Reservation

You're not necessarily out of luck if you come to the Northwest on the spur of the moment and without reservations, even in the height of the summer. You just have significantly reduced options. In Seattle, try calling the local **Hotel Hotline** (☎ 800-535-7071 or 206-461-5840) to see whether any member hotels have rooms available. If all else fails, cruise the strip of motels on **Aurora Avenue North,** just north of downtown Seattle, where vacancy signs alert you to the availability of rooms. If nothing else, you can get a bed for the night (if not by the hour) and a telephone to help you find something more desirable.

The Olympic Peninsula doesn't have a similar service, but a call to the **North Olympic Peninsula Visitor & Convention Bureau** (☎ **800-942-4042**, 360-452-8552) may provide you with some leads. Towns are far apart on the Olympic Peninsula, and you don't want to begin a wild goose chase of driving from one to another in search of rooms. A telephone is your best tool; get on the horn and see whether you can find any vacancies. Your best bet will be the town of **Port Angeles**, which has a string of motels that are likely to turn up a vacant room.

Chapter 8

Taking Care of the Remaining Details

. . . .

In This Chapter

▶ Getting the lowdown on rental-car companies and insurance

▶ Securing the best tables and tickets to the hottest attractions before you leave home

▶ Exploring Seattle and the Olympic Peninsula on the Internet

▶ Packing for your trip (bring lots of flannels!)

▶ Using computers and cell phones on vacation

. . . .

*Y*ou bought your plane tickets, reserved your accommodations, and plotted out where and how you want to tour the city. Now is the time to take care of the last-minute details of your vacation.

A Car-Rental Checklist

Not sure whether you should rent a car in Seattle? Table 8-1 gives you a checklist to help you decide. Put a mark by the statements that are the most important to you and see whether the pros outweigh the cons.

Table 8-1	The Pros and Cons of Renting a Car
Pros	**Cons**
Want ultimate freedom of movement	Don't want to pay for expensive downtown parking
Want to explore distant parts of the city	Don't want to look for street parking, which can be tough to find
Need to carry and store lots of gear, such as strollers, camera stuff, and bags	Don't have much excess gear

(continued)

Table 8-1 (continued)

Pros	Cons
Know that walking more than three or four blocks makes you tired and grumpy	Know that driving in urban traffic makes you tired and grumpy
Have to get back to the airport from a place that isn't readily cab-accessible	Can easily take a cab or hotel van to the airport
Don't want to wait for cabs or buses	Don't want to pay the whopping 28.3% tax in Seattle if car rented
Know that you look good in a leather bucket seat	Know that you look good in running shoes

Getting the Best Deal on a Car Rental

Car-rental rates vary even more than airline fares. The price depends on the size of the car, the length of time you keep it, where and when you pick it up and drop it off, where you take it, and a host of other factors.

Asking a few key questions can save you hundreds of dollars. For example, weekend rates may be lower than weekday rates. Ask whether the rate is the same for pickup Friday morning as it is for pickup Thursday night. If you're keeping the car five or more days, a weekly rate is often cheaper than the daily rate. Some companies may assess a drop-off charge if you don't return the car to the same renting location; others, notably National, do not. Ask whether the rate is cheaper if you pick up the car at the airport or at a location in town. (Rates are often lower in downtown Seattle than at the airports.) If you see an advertised price in your local newspaper, be sure to ask for that specific rate; otherwise, you may be charged the standard (higher) rate. Don't forget to mention membership in AAA, AARP, frequent-flier programs, and trade unions. These affiliations usually entitle you to discounts ranging from 5 to 30%. Ask your travel agent to check any and all of these rates.

And don't forget: Most car rentals are worth at least 500 miles on your frequent-flier account!

On top of the standard rental prices, other optional charges apply to most car rentals. The Collision Damage Waiver (CDW), which requires you to pay for damage to the car in a collision, is covered by many credit-card companies. Check with your credit-card company before you go so that you can avoid paying this hefty fee, which can be as much as $15 per day.

The car-rental companies also offer additional liability insurance (if you harm others in an accident), personal accident insurance (if you harm yourself or your passengers), and personal effects insurance (if your luggage is stolen from your car). If you have insurance on your car at home, you're probably covered for most of these scenarios. If your own insurance doesn't cover you for rentals, or if you don't have auto insurance, you should consider the additional coverage. (The car-rental companies are liable for certain base amounts.) But weigh the likelihood of getting into an accident or losing your luggage against the cost of these coverages (as much as $20 per day combined), which can significantly add to the price of your rental. Some companies also offer refueling packages, in which you pay for an entire tank of gas up front. The price is usually fairly competitive with local gas prices, but you don't get credit for any gas remaining in the tank. If you reject this option, you pay only for the gas you use, but you have to return it with a full tank or face charges of $3 to $4 a gallon for any shortfall. If a stop at a gas station on the way to the airport may make you miss your plane, then by all means take advantage of the fuel purchase option. Otherwise, skip it.

If you're booking rental cars online, you can usually find the best deals at rental-car company Web sites, although all the major online travel agencies also offer rental-car reservations services. Priceline and Hotwire work well for rental cars; the only "mystery" is which major rental company you get, and for most travelers, the difference between Hertz, Avis, and Budget is negligible.

Looking Out for Your Health

Seattle has a wide range of health-care facilities, the water is fine to drink straight from the tap, and the lakes and Puget Sound (with the exception of Green Lake, which suffers from algae blooms) are clean and safe for swimming, if rather cold. One thing is for sure: You have to try pretty hard to get a sunburn in Seattle and the Olympic Peninsula. If you had an acute trauma or life-threatening injury or illness, you would likely be taken to Seattle's Harborview Medical Center, which is the major trauma center in the Northwest. People with health concerns can rest assured that Seattle is the home of world-class health-care facilities, not to mention research centers like the Fred Hutchinson Cancer Research Center and the University of Washington Medical Center. Harborview Medical Center, located on First Hill (which is fondly called Pill Hill because of all the hospitals and health-care centers are there), is the No. 1 acute trauma facility in the Northwest. Ask your hotel about the all-night pharmacies throughout the city if you're in need of a prescription drug late at night.

In most cases, your existing health plan will provide the coverage you need. But double-check; you may want to buy **travel medical insurance** instead. Bring your insurance ID card with you when you travel.

If you suffer from a chronic illness, consult your doctor before your departure. For conditions like epilepsy, diabetes, or heart problems, wear a **Medic Alert Identification Tag** (☎ 800/825-3785; Internet: www.medicalert.org), which will immediately alert doctors to your condition and give them access to your records through Medic Alert's 24-hour hotline.

Pack **prescription medications** in your carry-on luggage and carry prescription medications in their original containers, with pharmacy labels — otherwise, they won't make it through airport security. Also bring along copies of your prescriptions in case you lose your pills or run out. Don't forget an extra pair of contact lenses or prescription glasses.

Staying Safe

Seattle is generally a very safe city. Incidents of violent street crime, such as muggings or assaults, are rare, and there are very few places where we'd advise you not to walk alone at night. The exceptions to this rule are Pioneer Square after midnight, when alcohol from the many bars and vagrancy can create a combustible mix, and the seedy area of downtown centered around Third Avenue and Cherry Street (which, coincidentally or not, is where the county courthouse sits).

Keep in mind that Seattle is a city, and you need to protect your personal belongings by keeping cars locked and valuables, such as cameras and purses, hidden out of sight. Your hotel room is a far safer place to keep valuables than a car. If you must put your belongings in a car, keep them in the trunk. In tourist areas like the Pike Place Market and Seattle Center, try to not display wads of cash, particularly at night. You're better off keeping your small bills handy in a separate purse or pocket instead of pulling out your entire stash of money in order to pay for a $3 hamburger.

For tips on safety when exploring Olympic National Park, refer to Chapter 20.

Making Reservations and Getting Tickets in Advance for Restaurants, Events, and Sightseeing

At certain times of the year — when the sports teams are in town, when the big arenas are rocking with name acts, and when theaters and symphony halls light up — Seattle has an awful lot of entertainment going on. Big events always sell out quickly, so make sure that you don't forget to book your Pearl Jam tickets, Mariners seats, or a table at that hot new restaurant by making reservations.

Seattle Center's huge arts festivals, such as **Bumbershoot** and **Northwest Folklife,** offer tickets at the gates, but you have to wait in mammoth lines to score them. You can save lots of time by buying advance tickets at a sponsoring retailer (usually Starbucks; see the events' Web sites in Chapter 2 for specific info), even on the day you want to attend.

As far as restaurants are concerned, the most popular places in town can book up fast, particularly on Friday and Saturday nights. Really special events, such as **Rover's** over-the-top Halloween feast (13 courses, and everyone in costume) sell out months in advance. In Seattle, call well ahead for a table at **Cascadia, Brasa, El Gaucho, Canlis, Rover's,** or the **Dahlia Lounge.**

Your hotel concierge is always a good source for obtaining tickets or hard-to-come-by restaurant reservations. If you can, contact the concierge before you come to town to get advice on good seats to a hot show or restaurant reservations. To buy directly in Seattle, call **TicketMaster (☎ 206-622-HITS;** Internet: www.ticketmaster.com) or **Pacific Northwest Ticket Service (☎ 206-232-0150).**

Seattle and the Olympic Peninsula on the Web

For listings of what's happening in sports, entertainment, and the arts, check out www.seattleinsider.com (which also offers cool cam views from atop the Space Needle and Queen Anne Hill), or the sites for the **Seattle Weekly** (Internet: www.seattleweekly.com) or **Seattle Post-Intelligencer** (Internet: www.seattle-pi.com) newspapers. **City Search** also gets into the act with a Web site for Seattle (Internet: www.seattle.citysearch.com), with listings and feature articles on the local dining, club, and entertainment scene. You can access **The Seattle-King County Convention & Visitors Bureau** (☎ 206-461-5840) through www.seattleinsider.com, which has links and calendars for all of the arts organizations and sports teams in town. For the Olympic Peninsula, go straight to the **North Olympic Peninsula Visitor & Convention Bureau** (☎ 800-942-4042; Internet: www.northwestsecret places.com) for information on activities and events. The Visitor & Convention Bureau Web site has links to all of the communities on the Olympic Peninsula and their individual Web sites.

Packing for the Flannel Curtain

Call it the Northwest Flannel Curtain. When you enter the state of Washington, leave your fine suits and designer clothes behind and slip into some comfortable blue jeans and loose flannel shirts. I can't emphasize it enough: Seattle, despite its veneer of sophistication and software wealth, is utterly, completely, resolutely casual. You'll feel as out of place walking the streets of **Belltown** or **Ballard** in a fine suit (Armani or Chanel) and overcoat as you would walking into a ritzy Manhattan restaurant in a sweatsuit. People simply don't dress up at night; you can find the proof in the dress codes of restaurants, where only one place in Seattle — *one place!* — even suggests that gentlemen wear a jacket to dinner (**Canlis,** and even there, they won't give you much attitude if you show up without one). Wearing stylish black designer clothes, Los Angeles or New York style, immediately brands you as a conspicuous outsider in most neighborhoods in Seattle.

Dress for comfort

Dress for comfort and you can go just about anywhere. Call it a gift or a curse, depending on your fashion sensibilities, but it's not unusual at any event — the opera, the symphony, or a fine restaurant — to see attorneys and executives who come straight from work in suits mingling freely with people in jeans and Topsiders. At least folks don't wear sweatsuits in public here, as some people do in Los Angeles and Phoenix (not to point fingers or anything).

Prepare for a drizzle — or two

Bring a raincoat, but leave the umbrella at home. Most people don't bother with umbrellas here; the rain clouds come and go too quickly. If you want to look like a local, wear a hat or a baseball-style cap when it starts to drizzle, or leave your head bare to enjoy the fine moisturizing. Also, keep in mind that just because it's June, it's not necessarily summer. It can still be chilly and damp right up to the 4th of July, so bring along a light sweater and jacket.

Pack lightly

As airplanes get more stuffed with passengers, airlines have gotten tighter with restrictions on carry-on baggage. You're generally limited to one carry-on bag per person in addition to a purse or small brief-case, and that bag had better be small enough to fit under the seat in front of you if you don't want it eye-balled and gate-checked by an agent.

Part III
Settling in to Seattle

The 5th Wave By Rich Tennant

"It's a little known fact that the same people who designed the Seattle Space Needle also designed pilot uniforms."

In this part . . .

*I*n this part, I provide the lowdown on visiting the Emerald City, giving you all the information you need to familiarize yourself with the city's different neighborhoods, find the lodging that's just right for you, and choose among Seattle's fine assortment of restaurants. I tell you the best ways to get around the city, whether by car, train, monorail, or ferry, and where you can find delicious eats.

Chapter 9

Location, Location, Location: Seattle

In This Chapter

▶ Lodging in Downtown: Where the beds are

▶ Staying in a neighborhood that's fit for a queen (Queen Anne, to be precise)

▶ Finding out where to go to live like a local

*I*n your fondest hotel dreams (and come on, I know you have them), are you staying in the thick of things in a vibrant city, with the best restaurants, shopping, and nightlife just steps from your door? Or do you prefer to spend your nights in a neighborhood where the locals live, in order to experience how the natives work, shop, and play? Or would you like to be near parks or beaches in order to soak up as much nature as possible during your visit? If budget is your sole consideration, are you willing (and logistically able) to bed down in the part of town that's largely known for its cheap motels?

In this chapter, I discuss the location choices for lodging in Seattle. In the case of the Emerald City (a nickname for Seattle derived from the city's lush, green setting), this overwhelmingly means staying downtown in the heart of Seattle. But even within that rather wide chunk of the city, you find plenty of choices to help you select the downtown location that best suits your style, budget, and mood.

The pickings get slimmer if you're determined to go out among the people and live in a neighborhood populated by dyed-in-the-flannel Seattleites, but it's still possible. The street life and activity of near-north neighborhoods like Ballard, Fremont, Green Lake, and Wallingford (see Chapter 11 for more information on these neighborhoods) are definitely worth experiencing, but you have to settle for far fewer lodging options. The neighborhood of Queen Anne has the best of both worlds, providing a variety of lodgings in a near-downtown setting that is also home to some lovely residences with astonishing views.

And, finally, if budget is your primary consideration, I can send you to a part of town with more cheap, gritty motels than you've ever seen outside of a Quentin Tarantino movie. But keep in mind that you need a car for exploring — and the ambience is just this side of dreadful.

The Downtown Experience

Downtown, meaning roughly the large area of central Seattle between Pioneer Square and Lake Union, is where all but a few hardy travelers wind up laying their heads during their visit to Seattle. Why? To paraphrase a certain well-known bank robber, you stay in downtown Seattle because that's where the beds are. It's the home of the city's biggest and finest hotels, including the only waterfront lodgings in town. It's also the location for most of the best new restaurants, much of the best shopping, and many of Seattle's top attractions and festivals. It's safe, too, and relatively easy to get around on foot. (See Chapter 8 for a discussion of whether you need to rent a car.)

It may seem that your only choice is to reside alongside skyscrapers and shopping malls, but look closer: Downtown Seattle is separated into a number of manageable divisions, each with its own singular charm and character. **The Market** refers to the blocks on First Avenue adjacent to the lovely Pike Place Market, where open stalls sell flowers, produce, fresh fish, and delicatessen foods. Staying in the middle of the Market, with close proximity to the Seattle Art Museum, sidewalk cafes, and several fine restaurants, reminds many people of visiting Europe.

Just a few blocks north on First Avenue is **Belltown,** a neighborhood centered on Bell Street that has become the hippest part of downtown Seattle. Here, you can barely walk down the street without bumping nose-first into a chef who has just hung out his shingle on a fabulous new restaurant, or young high-tech types who have snapped up the million-dollar condos that overlook Elliott Bay. Belltown has Seattle's hottest new restaurants, bars, and nightclubs.

The **Waterfront,** on the edge of Belltown that meets Elliott Bay, is popular with visitors who enjoy its souvenir shops, tour boats and ferries, and seafood restaurants. Two nice hotels, including a brand-new Marriott that just opened in spring 2003, give you that living-on-the-waterfront feeling.

In the middle of the downtown area, centered roughly around 5th Avenue and Pine Street, is the **Shopping District.** The city's largest retailers (see Chapter 16 for shopping tips) and the city's biggest and finest hotels are located within a block or two of the Shopping District. Chapter 10 discusses the many options in this area, the heart of downtown, which features both big, convention hotels and intimate boutique hostelries, all within a block or two of lots of shops and restaurants. On the fringes of the Shopping District and at the very edges of downtown are even more lodging choices. Keep in mind that this entire area, from the Market to the Shopping District, is easily walkable and convenient to just about every downtown lodging.

Greater Seattle

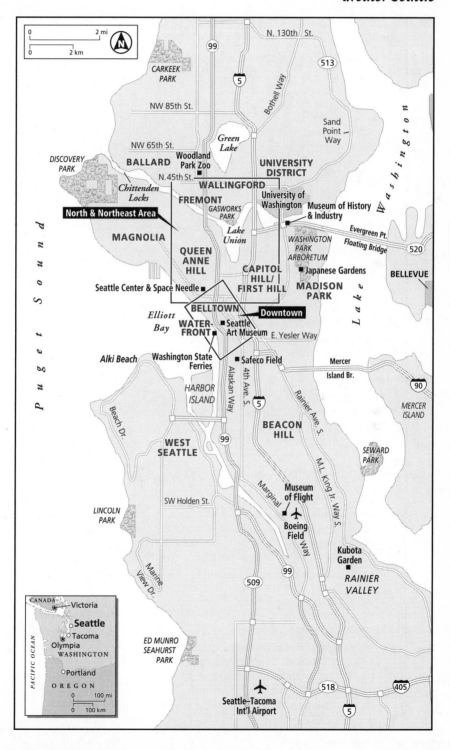

Downtown Seattle

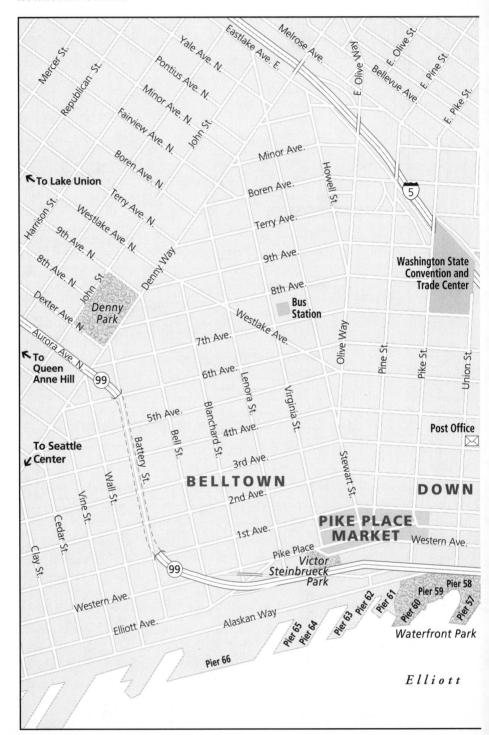

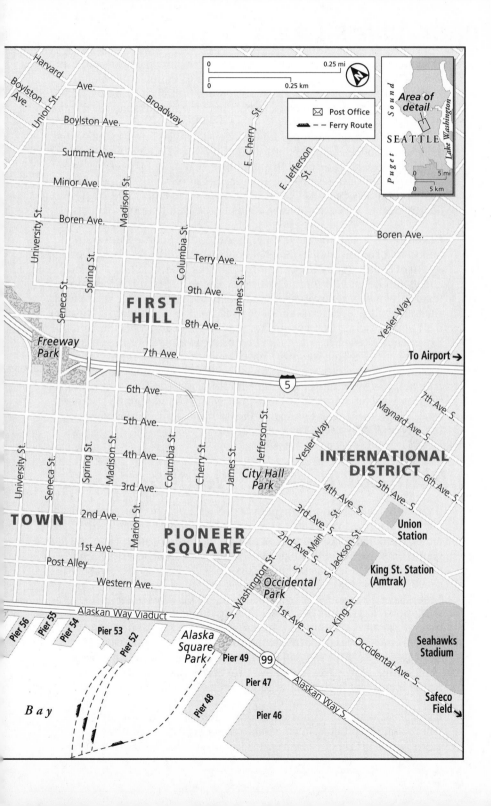

0   0.25 mi

0   0.25 km

⊠ Post Office
━━ ╌ ╌ Ferry Route

Area of
detail

SEATTLE

Puget Sound

Lake Washington

0   5 mi

0   5 km

Harvard Ave.

Boylston Ave.

Union St.

Broadway

Boylston Ave.

Summit Ave.

Minor Ave.

Boren Ave.

E. Cherry St.

E. Jefferson St.

University St.

Madison St.

Columbia St.

Terry Ave.

Boren Ave.

Spring St.

9th Ave.

James St.

**FIRST
HILL**

8th Ave.

Yesler Way

Seneca St.

Freeway
Park

7th Ave.

To Airport →

5

6th Ave.

5th Ave.

Jefferson St.

7th Ave. S.

University St.

Spring St.

Madison St.

4th Ave.

Columbia St.

Cherry St.

James St.

Maynard Ave. S.

Seneca St.

3rd Ave.

City Hall
Park

Yesler Way

**INTERNATIONAL
DISTRICT**

5th Ave. S.

6th Ave. S.

2nd Ave.

4th Ave. S.

TOWN

Marion St.

1st Ave.

3rd Ave. S.

2nd Ave. S.

Main St.

S. Jackson St.

**Union
Station**

Post Alley

**PIONEER
SQUARE**

Western Ave.

S. Washington St.

Occidental
Park

1st Ave. S.

King St.

**King St. Station
(Amtrak)**

Alaskan Way Viaduct

Pier 56

Pier 55

Pier 54

Pier 53

Pier 52

Alaska
Square
Park

Pier 49

99

Occidental Ave. S.

**Seahawks
Stadium**

Pier 47

Pier 48

Alaskan Way S.

**Safeco
Field ↘**

Bay

Pier 46

Queen Anne's Lace

Creating a kind of transition zone between downtown Seattle and the near-north neighborhoods is the **Queen Anne** section of town. It begins just north of Denny Way in a cluster of retail shops and apartment houses, climbs a steep hill (with Queen Anne Avenue N., the main thoroughfare), and winds up in a quiet, residential neighborhood alongside the Ship Canal. Here you find residential-style hotels in converted apartment houses near the bottom of the hill and budget accommodations on the eastern edge of the neighborhood, near 5th Avenue and Roy Street. Several new all-suite properties have opened up in recent years on the west side of Queen Anne, near busy Elliott Avenue; I profile the best of these accommodations in the next chapter.

Queen Anne is also the closest neighborhood to **Seattle Center,** the multiblock complex where Seattle's big festivals, like Bumbershoot and A Bite of Seattle (see Chapter 2 for a calendar of events), are staged and which houses KeyArena (the home of the SuperSonics basketball team), the newly renovated Opera House, the Pacific Northwest Ballet, several legit theaters for plays (including the Seattle Children's Theater), the Pacific Science Center, and the Seattle Children's Museum, and the Experience Music Project. And, of course, towering over the entire complex is the **Space Needle,** Seattle's most beloved landmark. Lower Queen Anne provides a good base for walking to Seattle Center events and facilities, hopping a cab or bus into downtown Seattle, or exploring the city's neighborhoods by car. Upper Queen Anne Avenue also has a retail district with great shops and restaurants and sterling views of the city and Mount Rainier on a clear day.

Bunking Down in the Neighborhoods

If you want to live among the people of Seattle (a cheerful, web-footed lot, I assure you), you have to cross the Ship Canal, heading north, on either the Ballard, Fremont, Montlake, I-5 or Aurora bridge. Here you find gentle hills packed with single-family houses — Seattle's bedrooms — interspersed among parks, retail corridors, and lovely views. No full-service hotels yet exist in the urban neighborhoods of Fremont, Ballard, Green Lake, or Wallingford, but you can find bed-and-breakfast accommodations and motels. A string of cheap, budget motels line Aurora Avenue North beginning on the northern end of Fremont. To stay close to the **University of Washington** (known locally as "U-Dub"; "Go Huskies" is your rallying cry), you find several hotel and motel choices just off the freeway in the **University District,** or U-District, as the locals call it, that make good bases of operations.

If budget is your main consideration — meaning that you don't care where you sleep because you plan to be on the go most of the day anyway — a string of cheap motels lies on Aurora Avenue North beginning right after the Ship Canal in Fremont and stretching roughly up to 175th Street and the outer limits of Seattle proper. The lodgings that I list in Chapter 10 (see the section "Hosteling: No Room at the Inn?") are all clean and safe, but this part of town is admittedly less than desirable — if not outright seamy — for walking or sightseeing. You definitely need a car to get around, and you get virtually none of the ambience, street life, or views that make Seattle such a great place to visit. You are, however, just minutes away from many of the city's best neighborhoods for exploring, within easy reach of movie theaters at the Oak Tree shopping center, and just a 10-minute drive straight into downtown on Aurora Avenue North (also called Route 99). Several budget-priced motels are also scattered around the area where Denny Way and Aurora Avenue meet on the northern end of downtown. Again, the ambience isn't terrific, and you won't soak up much local atmosphere until you leave that part of town.

Chapter 10

The Best Hotels in Seattle

· ·

In This Chapter

▶ Analyzing a complete breakdown of Seattle's best lodgings

▶ Sorting accommodations by price and location

▶ Figuring out where to go and what to do if the best hotels are booked solid

· ·

*I*n this chapter, I bounce on the mattresses and snoop through the closets of my favorite hotels in Seattle in order to give you all the information you need to make the right choice. The following lodging recommendations are the places I'd book if I were visiting the Emerald City. Remember that summer is high season, and if you find that your favorite hotel choices are booked solid, look to the list at the end of this chapter for some runners-up that I can also recommend.

In Chapter 9, I give you a breakdown on the neighborhoods and sub-neighborhoods of the city. Here, I discuss the lodgings in those parts of town and let you know which are closest to shopping, nightlife, and museums, and which have the best views. Most of Seattle's hotels are located in the downtown corridor, but even within that area several subneighborhoods offer different flavors of the city.

Throughout the chapter, look for the Kid-Friendly icons, which point out lodgings that are especially good for families.

Feel free to use the margins of the book to check or note the hotels that seem just right for your needs and then go to the "Sweet Dreams: Choosing Your Hotel" worksheet at the back of the book to help narrow down your choices. Happy hunting!

Downtown Seattle Accommodations

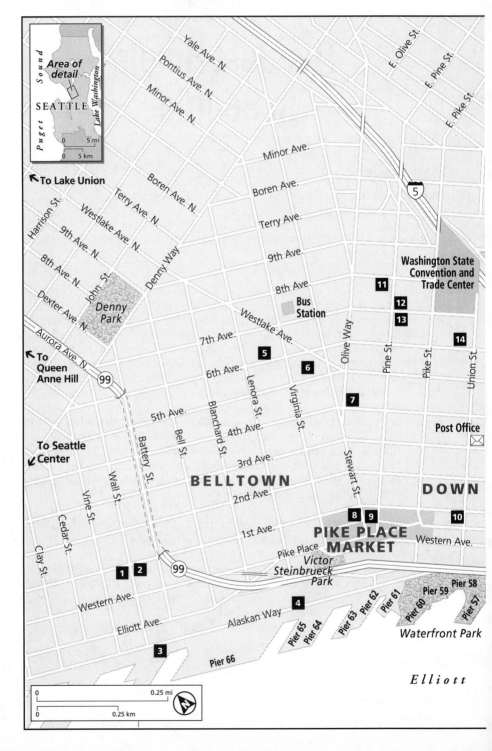

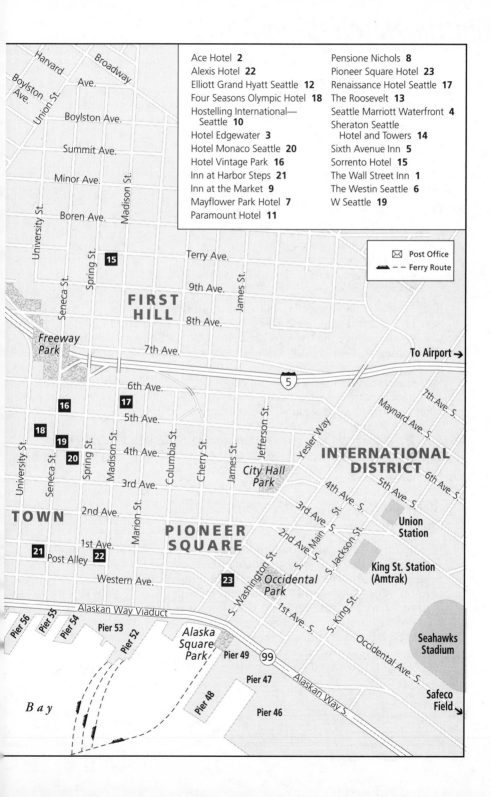

Ace Hotel 2
Alexis Hotel 22
Elliott Grand Hyatt Seattle 12
Four Seasons Olympic Hotel 18
Hostelling International—
Seattle 10
Hotel Edgewater 3
Hotel Monaco Seattle 20
Hotel Vintage Park 16
Inn at Harbor Steps 21
Inn at the Market 9
Mayflower Park Hotel 7
Paramount Hotel 11
Pensione Nichols 8
Pioneer Square Hotel 23
Renaissance Hotel Seattle 17
The Roosevelt 13
Seattle Marriott Waterfront 4
Sheraton Seattle
Hotel and Towers 14
Sixth Avenue Inn 5
Sorrento Hotel 15
The Wall Street Inn 1
The Westin Seattle 6
W Seattle 19

Post Office
Ferry Route

Seattle Hotels from A to Z

The breakdown on hotel prices is as follows. The dollar signs accompanying every listing are based on the hotel's posted rack rates for a standard room. Suites are much more expensive. Keep in mind that rates fluctuate, and rack rates are generally at the top of a hotel's pricing range. You should be able to find considerable discounts during the winter and off-season months.

$	$50–$80
$$	$80–$125
$$$	$125–$175
$$$$	$175–$275

Ace Hotel

$ Belltown

New York and San Francisco have tons of places like this one, but in Seattle, the trendy, minimalist Ace is a curiosity that caters to the truly hip. Located above the Cyclops bar in the heart of Belltown's restaurant-and-nightclub scene, it's all spare: The rooms, which have cinder-block walls, feature white-washed walls and floors, low beds on simple platforms, and stainless-steel sinks and counters. Most of the 34 rooms share a bathroom with the other rooms on the floor — perhaps a visiting rock band or performance artist will be sharing yours.

2423 First Ave. at Wall Street; entry is unassuming, but look for big Cyclops sign. ☎ *206-448-4721. Internet:* www.theacehotel.com. *Rack rates: $75–$95. AE, DISC, MC, V.*

Alexis Hotel

$$$$ Pike Place Market

One of the city's premier boutique hotels, the Alexis is artfully decorated and hip, featuring everything from an art gallery on the main floor that rotates shows by local artists to suites named for the likes of John Lennon, Miles Davis, and Jerry Garcia, each containing drawings and memorabilia of its distinguished namesake. The hotel occupies a handsome older building on First Avenue near the Seattle Art Museum. The rooms are spacious and well-appointed. The most luxurious rooms are the fireplace suites, which have whirlpool baths, wet bars, king-size beds, and black bathrooms trimmed in marble and stocked with bath amenities from the in-house Aveda spa. Light a fire and call for a massage in your room for the ultimate sybaritic experience and then head to the lobby for an evening wine tasting, followed by dinner at the stylish Library Bistro restaurant. Pets are more than welcome here; they're treated like royalty, with special amenities and packages offered. A perfume shop at street level is one of the best places in the city to pick up delicious scents.

1007 First Ave. on Madison Street, halfway between Pioneer Square and the Market. ☎ *800-426-7033 or 206-624-4844. Fax: 206-621-9009. Internet:* www. alexishotel.com. *Rack rates: $230–$250 (fireplace suites are $440). AE, DC, DISC, MC, V.*

Chambered Nautilus Bed & Breakfast Inn
$$ University District

This six-room B&B, in a 1915 Georgian Colonial home, is located in a quiet residential neighborhood a few blocks from the noise and bustle of the University of Washington. Great for visiting parents but perhaps too sedate for students, the rooms feature queen-size beds and private baths and are decorated with antiques and floral motifs. Hardy souls who don't mind the hike may enjoy the third-floor Crow's Nest Chamber, with a fireplace and nautical window that offers mountain views.

5005 22nd Ave. NE. Take I-5 to NE 50th Street, head west, turn left on 20th Ave. NE, right on NE 54th St., and right on 22nd Ave. NE. ☎ *800-545-8459 or 206-522-2536. Fax: 206-528-0898. Internet:* www.chamberednautilus.com. *Rack rates: $99–$124; full breakfast included. AE, MC, V.*

Courtyard by Marriott
$$ Lake Union

If I had to choose one of the Marriotts in the Seattle area, I'd pick this one over the Residence Inn (which is situated just a few blocks away on the other side of Lake Union and is reviewed later in this section) because it's newer, has a pool and whirlpool, and is better situated for quick drives into downtown, Seattle Center, Queen Anne, and Fremont. The cookie-cutter approach to decorating gives you a tried-and-true, if utterly bland, room with a bed, bathroom, and coffee machine. Ask for a room with a view of the lake, where you can often spot sailboats and floatplanes. The pool makes this hotel especially kid-friendly.

925 Westlake Ave. N. Take I-5 to Mercer St., go right off ramp, left onto Valley St., and right onto Westlake Ave. N. ☎ *800-321-2211 or 206-213-0100. Fax: 206-213-0101. Internet:* www.marriott.com. *Rack rates: $99–$269. AE, DC, DISC, MC, V.*

Seattle Accommodations — North & Northeast

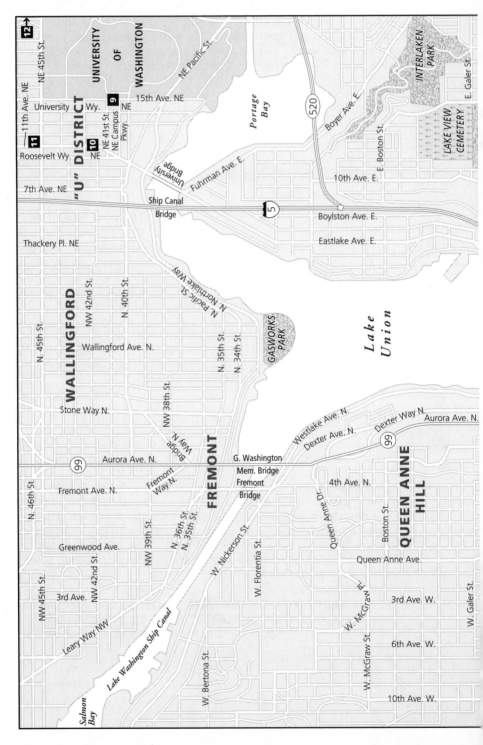

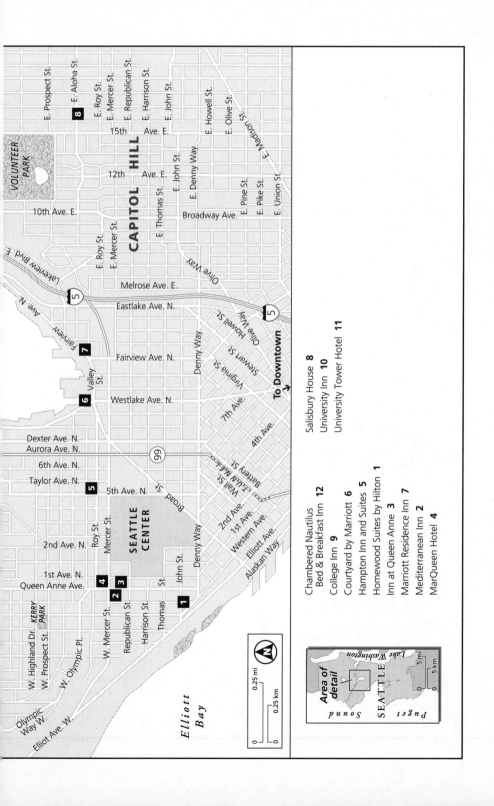

Salisbury House **8**
University Inn **10**
University Tower Hotel **11**

Chambered Nautilus
Bed & Breakfast Inn **12**
College Inn **9**
Courtyard by Marriott **6**
Hampton Inn and Suites **5**
Homewood Suites by Hilton **1**
Inn at Queen Anne **3**
Marriott Residence Inn **7**
Mediterranean Inn **2**
MarQueen Hotel **4**

Four Seasons Olympic Hotel
$$$$ **Shopping District**

An Italian Renaissance beauty in the heart of downtown, the Four Seasons is Seattle's most elegant lodging. The plush lobby is decorated with chandeliers and enormous vases brimming with flowers, and the ballrooms are what brides-to-be dream of. The rooms aren't especially large given the steep tariff you pay for them, but they contain all kinds of amenities, from ironing boards to terrycloth bathrobes, that you expect from a Four Seasons. The beds are large enough to easily accommodate the NBA players who bunk here. The Garden Court restaurant/lounge is a wonderful place to bring your mother for afternoon tea, and chef Gavin Stephenson turns out classic continental fare in the Georgian Room. Younger children swoon over the Teddy Bear Suite, a public room that's decorated every holiday season with adorable bears and a Christmas tableau, with free cookies for all visitors.

411 University St., between 4th and 5th avenues. University Street is one-way heading north. ☎ *800-223-8772 or 206-621-1700. Fax: 206-682-9633. Internet:* www.fourseasons.com. *Rack rates: $325–$355. AE, DC, DISC, MC, V.*

Grand Hyatt Seattle
$$$$ **Shopping District**

The latest and grandest megahotel in Seattle was built for big convention business, but it makes a great lodging for individual travelers as well, with a perfectly situated spot in the center of downtown. The rooms are posh, with leather desks, glassed-in showers, and enormous TV sets. Services are considerable, from good concierges to valets. The hotel is wired to the max with high-speed Internet access in every room and bed-side buttons to close the drapes or put out the Do Not Disturb sign. Best of all is the location: Right across the street from the upscale Pacific Place shopping center, movie theaters, Gameworks, and all of downtown's shopping and attractions.

721 Pine St., on the corner of 7th Avenue. ☎ *800-233-1234 or 206-774-1234. Fax: 206-774-6120. Internet:* http://grandseattle.hyatt.com. *Rack rates: $235–$259. AE, DC, DISC, MC, V.*

Hampton Inn and Suites
$$$ **Queen Anne**

A couple of years ago, two hotels were combined to form this big, all-suite property. It's in a quiet area of lower Queen Anne, just behind Tower Records and a ten-minute hoof from Seattle Center and the main Queen Anne retail corridor. The commom areas aren't incredibly welcoming — most of the guests are too busy dashing off to business meeting or tourist attraction to linger. The two-room suites are rather bland, although large TVs and cheerful fireplaces (in some rooms) perk things up a bit.

Kitchenette suites are available for extended stays. Continental breakfast is included.

700 Fifth Ave. N., on the corner of Roy Street in lower Queen Anne. ☎ ***800-426-7866*** *or 206-282-7700. Fax: 206-282-0899. Internet:* www.hampton-inn.com. *Rack rates: $139–$179. AE, DC, DISC, MC, V.*

Homewood Suites by Hilton
$$$ Queen Anne

If you like to cook, you'll appreciate the full kitchens — with rangetops, microwaves, and large fridges — that are part of these roomy suites. The hotel's location on a busy corner of lower Queen Anne gives you quick access to the waterfront and the main thoroughfare to Ballard and points north, but it's too close to the traffic noise on busy Western Avenue to feel homey. A breakfast buffet is included, as is a beer-and-wine reception in the afternoon (and sodas for the kids), and a light meal is served at night if you need a quick bite. Views of Elliott Bay are fair from some rooms, but I'd save the premium you'll pay for the view and spend it on pizza and a movie on Queen Anne Avenue.

206 Western Ave. W. Go west on Denny Avenue, and it curves onto Western Avenue W.; the hotel is two blocks away on the right. ☎ ***800-CALL-HOME*** *or 206-281-9393. Fax: 206-283-5022. Internet:* www.homewood-suites.com. *Rack rates: $149–$189. AE, DC, DISC, MC, V.*

Hostelling International–Seattle
$ Pike Place Market

Popular with the international backpacking set, this hostel is superbly situated in the lower reaches of the Pike Place Market, a short walk from Pioneer Square and the waterfront. Clean and comfortable, the 1915 building is broken down into dorm rooms that sleep six to ten and share a bath; semiprivate dorm rooms that sleep four and share a bath; and private rooms for families or couples that have a private bath and a kitchenette. A lounge, library, and self-service kitchen and laundry provide public space for guests to stretch out in, linens are available, and unlike most hostels, it has no curfew.

84 Union St. (between Western Avenue and Post Alley on the bottom of the Pike Place Market). ☎ ***888-622-5443*** *or 206-622-5443. Internet:* www.hiseattle.org. *Rack rates: $20–$23 for dorm rooms. AE, MC, V.*

Hotel Edgewater
$$$ Waterfront

How can it be that in a city that is famous for its aquatic environment, the Edgewater is the only full-service lodging that's directly on the water? That's one of the reasons this hotel is packed throughout the year. It can't hurt that it's in a marvelous setting on pilings over Elliott Bay with non-stop views of Bainbridge Island, the Olympic Mountains, and ferries criss-crossing Puget Sound. The lodge-style rooms are decorated in plain, peeled pine furniture; fireplaces were added to all the rooms in 2000 to up the charm quotient a notch. Be sure to ask for a water view and plan to spend some time on your smallish balcony overlooking the bay. Don't miss Myrtle Edwards Park to the north for strolling and biking, and the marvelous Seattle Aquarium to the south. And yes, the Beatles slept here back in 1964, and you can buy a poster of the Fab Four in the hotel's gift shop.

2411 Alaskan Way, north end of the waterfront at the foot of Wall Street. ☎ *800-624-0670 or 206-728-7000. Fax: 206-441-4119. Internet:* www.noblehousehotels. com. *Rack rates: $149–$239. AE, DC, DISC, MC, V.*

Hotel Monaco Seattle
$$$$ **Shopping District**

A San Francisco-style export from the Kimpton Group, which has opened Monacos in Denver, Chicago, and San Francisco, the Monaco Seattle is anything but a chain hotel. Decorated extravagantly and beautifully, it has a gorgeous lobby filled with murals and sculptures. The boudoir-like guestrooms, exuding comfortable elegance, are decorated with striped walls, draped fabrics, and bold colors. Rooms are equipped with fax machines and stereos with CD players, and suites boast VCRs in addition to whirlpool tubs in the spacious bathrooms. Billed as a "boutique" hotel, it has a big-hotel feel, with a fitness center, 24-hour room service, evening wine tastings, and a crackerjack concierge and service staff. Next door, the Sazerac restaurant is a Cajun place with terrific food and a crackling urban atmosphere (see Chapter 14).

1101 Fourth Ave., corner of Spring Street. ☎ *800-945-2240 or 206-621-1770. Fax: 206-624-0060. Internet:* www.monaco-seattle.com. *Rack rates: $225–$235. AE, DC, DISC, MC, V.*

Hotel Vintage Park
$$$$ **Shopping District**

A sister property to the Hotel Monaco, the Vintage Park is a slightly older and more understated version of a boutique hotel, with the Kimpton Group's same commitment to providing business travelers with an alternative to big, impersonal convention hotels. The lobby is a cozy, living-room-style space with a fireplace, books, and evening wine tastings. Access to an off-premises health club is offered, as well as valet parking and 24-hour room service. Guestrooms are all named after local wineries, with a purple-and-green grapevine motif on the bedspreads, and maroon and hunter green walls. For business travelers, the hotel is wired to the max, with fax machines and high-speed Internet access. Deluxe rooms are a good way to go, featuring half-canopy beds and granite-trimmed baths.

The adjoining Tulio Restaurant is one of the better Italian eateries in town. Businesspersons appreciate the quick access to I-5, but shoppers find that it's a long walk to the best department stores and downtown malls.

1100 Fifth Ave., corner of Seneca Street. ☎ *800-624-4433 or 206-624-8000. Internet:* www.hotelvintagepark.com. *Rack rates: $200–$230. AE, DC, DISC, MC, V.*

Inn at Harbor Steps

$$$ **Pike Place Market**

Four Sisters Inns, which operates distinctive B&Bs on the West Coast, took a chance on this unique property on the bottom floors of a high-rise apartment/condo building at the Pike Place Market. The spacious rooms are tastefully appointed with modern art and designer linens. All rooms have sitting areas and fireplaces. Although rooms have no worthwhile views, they open onto a peaceful courtyard garden. Guests can use the building's excellent fitness center, lap pool, and basketball court, and continental breakfast is served. A wood-trimmed library is a great place to read the morning newspaper from the comfort of deep leather chairs. Kids may appreciate the pool and gym here.

1221 First Ave. at Seneca Street, just south of Harbor Steps public stairway. ☎ *888-728-8910 or 206-748-0973. Fax: 206-748-0533. Internet:* www.foursisters.com. *Rack rates: $160–$225. AE, DC, MC, V.*

Inn at the Market

$$$$ **Pike Place Market**

Located in the heart of the Market, this French-inspired inn has long been the boutique getaway of choice for those who want a small, intimate hotel experience in Seattle. It's still pretty tough to beat, with its views of Elliott Bay, expansive rooms trimmed in silk and chenille, bay windows overlooking the waterfront, oversize bathrooms, rooftop patio above the Market, and room service coming from the exquisite Campagne restaurant (see Chapter 14). For a fee, you can use the Seattle Club, one of the better health clubs in town, a few blocks away at the north end of the Market.

86 Pine St. in the Market between Pike Place and First Avenue. ☎ *800-446-4484 or 206-443-3600. Fax: 206-443-0631. Internet:* www.innatthemarket.com. *Rack rates: $190–$265. AE, DC, DISC, MC, V.*

MarQueen Hotel

$$$ **Queen Anne**

A uniformed doorman with an Eastern-European accent greets you at this converted apartment building in a great location on lower Queen Anne, a short walk from Seattle Center. The hardwood-floor rooms are quirky and old, with small sitting areas and full kitchenettes, which makes this hotel a great bargain for families who don't mind cooking in for some meals. With its refurbished lobby, featuring dark mahogany and new carpets, you get the feeling that you've stepped into an elegant, old-city residence. You won't get room service or a restaurant, but a dozen eateries lie within two blocks; some offer the option for hotel guests to charge meals to their bill at the hotel.

600 Queen Anne Ave. N. at the corner of Mercer Street. ☎ ***888-445-3076*** *or 206-282-7407. Fax: 206-283-1499. Internet:* www.marqueen.com. *Rack rates: $139–$179. AE, DC, DISC, MC, V.*

Marriott Residence Inn
$$$ Lake Union

Because of its location on busy Fairview Avenue N., this all-suite hotel has a decided "motel-ish" feeling, but the two-room suites are roomy and comfortable, a hot breakfast is included, kids will enjoy the indoor pool, and several of the better Lake Union restaurants are right across the street (if you decide to brave the traffic). This hotel isn't my top pick for an all-suite lodging because of the location, but you could do worse.

800 Fairview Ave. N. Take I-5 to Mercer St., turn right off ramp and go right on Fairview Avenue N. ☎ ***800-321-2211*** *or 206-624-6000. Fax: 206-223-8160. Internet:* www.marriott.com. *Rack rates: $129–$159. AE, DC, DISC, MC, V.*

Mayflower Park Hotel
$$$ Shopping District

This grand old property in a 1927 building harks back to the days when wealthy businessmen enjoyed grand lodgings in the heart of a big city. The location is superb: In the heart of the downtown shopping district, with an attached walkway to Westlake Center shopping and the monorail to Seattle Center. The lobby is elegant and expansive, and the floor-to-ceiling windows in Oliver's — the on-site bar that makes the best martinis in town — provide great views of the passing scene on Fourth Avenue. Where the Mayflower Park always comes up a bit short is in its smallish rooms, which are blandly decorated. This place is the kind of stodgy, faded businessman's lodging that makes you understand why they started building Embassy Suites and Marriotts. Ask for a corner room or suite if you don't want to feel cramped and be sure to eat at Andaluca, the fine Mediterranean restaurant in the basement (see Chapter 14).

405 Olive Way at Fourth Avenue. ☎ ***800-426-5100*** *or 206-623-8700. Fax: 206-382-6997. Internet:* www.mayflowerpark.com. *Rack rates: $150–$195. AE, DC, DISC, MC, V.*

Mediterranean Inn
$ Queen Anne

This hotel is a great find for single travelers or couples who want to be in the thick of the action but don't need lots of space. The inexpensive rooms in this new hotel come with a queen bed or a full-size hide-a-bed, a little counter with a microwave (which the hotel owners optimistically call a kitchenette), and a TV with VCR. The bonus is that you're right on Queen Anne Avenue, across the street from the movie theater, a block away from Seattle Center, and within a ten-minute walk of tons of restaurants and coffeeshops. The already-low rates get even lower for extended stays of a week or more.

425 Queen Anne Ave. N. Heading west on Denny Way, turn right on 1st Avenue N. and left on Republican St.; hotel is on corner of Republican and Queen Anne Avenue N. ☎ **866-525-4700** *or 206-428-4700. Fax: 206-428-4699. Internet:* www.mediterranean-inn.com. *Rack rates: From $79. AE, DC, DISC, MC, V.*

Paramount Hotel
$$$$ Shopping District

The Paramount has a reputation as an upscale rock-and-roll hotel that houses the big acts that play at the nearby Paramount Theater. The lobby certainly doesn't dispel that image, with its polished marble fireplace and plump sofas. But I find the rooms to be surprisingly mundane, with beige decor and old prints. An Executive King on an upper floor is much more exciting, with a jetted bathtub and view of downtown. Pacific Place's shopping and restaurants are right across the street.

724 Pine St. across from Pacific Place. ☎ **800-426-0670** *or 206-292-9500. Fax: 206-292-8610. Internet:* www.westcoasthotels.com/paramount/. *Rack rates: $220–$240. AE, DISC, MC, V.*

Renaissance Hotel Seattle
$$$ Shopping District

A big convention hotel affiliated with Marriott, the Madison suffers from a less-than-ideal location at the far end of the shopping district, a steep hill climb from the waterfront and Pike Place Market. However, fitness buffs and families with kids love the rooftop health club and its indoor swimming pool, whirlpool, and fitness room. For a few extra dollars, the Club Floor offers extra amenities, such as a continental breakfast and afternoon cocktails in a private lounge.

515 Madison St. between 5th and 6th avenues. ☎ **800-278-4159** *or 206-583-0300. Fax: 206-624-8125. Internet:* www.renaissancehotels.com. *Rack rates: $140–$240. AE, DC, DISC, MC, V.*

The Roosevelt
$$$ **Shopping District**

Built in 1929, the centrally located Roosevelt has benefited from a recent renovation. The old dowager still has some pretty tiny rooms at the lower price levels, but the dark-wood-paneled lobby is cheerful, and the new fitness center is top-notch. Upgrade to a hot tub room with a big whirlpool tub if you want a bathroom that doesn't feel tiny and cramped.

1531 Seventh Ave. and Pine Street, across from Pacific Place. ☎ *800-426-0670 or 206-621-1200. Fax: 206-233-0335. Internet:* www.westcoasthotels.com. *Rack rates: $135–$190. AE, DC, DISC, MC, V.*

Salisbury House
$$ **Capitol Hill**

If you want to bed down in one of Seattle's most elegant older neighborhoods, this B&B in a lovely section of Capitol Hill is a good choice. The turn-of-the-(19th)-century mansion is outfitted with five cozy rooms (only one of which has a TV) and a guest library with maple floors and beamed ceiling. You're a short walk from Volunteer Park and the Seattle Asian Art Museum, as well as the urban bustle of Broadway. It's fun to walk the back streets of the neighborhood and see the stately homes of Seattle's former gentry, most of which are now divided into apartments.

750 16th Ave. E., Capitol Hill, on the corner of Aloha Street. ☎ *206-328-8682. Fax: 206-720-1019. Internet:* www.salisburyhouse.com. *Rack rates: $95–$155. MC, V.*

Salish Lodge & Spa
$$$$ **North Bend**

While fans of David Lynch's *Twin Peaks* recognize this place as "The Great Northern," today's comfort seekers simply know the woodsy Salish as a prime getaway destination from the city. The lodge is located in the town of North Bend, where the television series was filmed, an hour's drive east of Seattle. The 91 rooms and suites have wood-burning fireplaces and big, soaking tubs. The spa is the best in the area. Snoqualmie Falls roars outside (ask the front desk how to hike to the base of it), and you can enjoy the nearby Snoqualmie Pass ski area and lots of gorgeous North Cascades hiking trails — but only if you can tear yourself away from the cozy comforts of your plush (and expensive) room.

6501 Railroad Ave., Snoqualmie, WA. ☎ *800-2-SALISH or 425-888-2556; . Fax: 425-888-2533. Internet:* www.salishlodge.com. *Rack rates: $229–$419. AE, DC, DISC, MC, V.*

Seattle Marriott Waterfront

$$$ Waterfront

Seattle's newest hotel opened in April 2003 as the city's second lodging on the waterfront. (The Hotel Edgewater, which is reviewed earlier in this section, is the other one.) The trouble is that the Seattle Marriott Waterfront isn't exactly smack up against Elliott Bay, but across busy Alaskan Way, with the Seattle Streetcar track in the way. Still, nearly all the rooms have water views, you're a quick walk from the aquarium and a streetcar ride from Safeco Field or the Pike Place Market, and you can't beat that brand-new hotel feeling, not to mention the indoor-outdoor pool (always popular with kids). Book early, because this hotel is sure to become popular quickly, especially when all those cruise-ship passengers get wind of it.

2100 Alaskan Way, at Bell Street. ☎ ***800-228-9290*** *or 206-239-0144. Fax: 206-254-1229. Internet:* www.gowest.marriott.com/seattlewaterfront. *Rack rates: $159–$199. AE, DC, DISC, MC, V.*

Sheraton Seattle Hotel and Towers

$$$$ Shopping District

Seattle's biggest, most bustling convention hotel has a little of something for everyone. The lobby resembles Grand Central Station at rush hour, with groups of conventioneers and diners coming and going. You may fondly remember exquisite dinners at Fullers, but don't bother to drop by for a meal now: The restaurant, once the best in Seattle, is open only to groups now. Happily, the Pike Street Café still offers a calorie-laden (but oh-so-soothing) dessert bar. Standard rooms are modestly appointed and blandly decorated, but big enough to not feel cramped. Concierge-level floors at the top have their own reception and lounge. The health club on the 35th floor is among the best in town, with a large indoor pool that kids seem to love, a whirlpool, and a fitness center. Snag a north-facing room for the best views of Lake Union and the Space Needle; a west-facing room looks out on an enormous, view-blocking skyscraper.

1400 Sixth Ave. at Union Street. ☎ ***800-325-3535*** *or 206-621-9000. Fax: 206-621-8441. Internet:* www.sheraton.com. *Rack rates: $240–$280. AE, DC, DISC, MC, V.*

Sorrento Hotel

$$$$ First Hill

This Italianate mansion, with a lovely courtyard and fountain at the entrance, would be one of the finest lodgings in town — if it *were* in town. Instead, the Sorrento is perched on a hillside on busy Madison Street, near First Hill's (nicknamed Pill Hill) hospitals — a steep walk from downtown. A complimentary limousine service into the downtown core eases the pain somewhat. The hotel itself is utterly stylish, with beautifully decorated rooms and public areas. A suite upgrade costs as little as $20 more a night and provides an extra sitting area. Views from the west-facing rooms take in all of downtown Seattle. I hear that the penthouse is awfully elegant, too, for those nights when only a $1,000 room will do.

900 Madison St. at Terry Avenue, north of downtown core. ☎ *800-426-1265 or 206-622-6400. Fax: 206-343-6155. Internet:* www.hotelsorrento.com. *Rack rates: $230–$250. AE, DC, DISC, MC, V.*

University Tower Hotel

$$ University District

Art Deco styling is the main attraction of this high-rise hotel, formerly called the Edmond Meany Hotel until new ownership took over and changed it to a Best Western property. The rooms are large, thanks to their corner locations, with smallish baths. Get a room on an upper floor to escape the traffic noise from busy 45th Street and enjoy the best views of the Cascade and Olympic mountains. Proximity to the UW campus and I-5 are big draws, along with the Deco styling and furnishings. Services include a restaurant in the basement and an espresso bar and bakery off the lobby, in-room coffeemakers and ironing boards, and a continental breakfast. Parking is free, too, making this hotel a very good bargain.

4507 Brooklyn Ave. NE at NE 45th Street. ☎ *800-899-0251 or 206-634-2000. Fax: 206-547-6029. Internet:* www.meany.com. *Rack rates: $99–$179. AE, DC, DISC, MC, V.*

The Wall Street Inn

$$ Belltown

It may sound businesslike and corporate, but this cheerful inn is a great find in Belltown, with large rooms overlooking Elliott Bay and four-poster beds. A comfy living room with leather furniture and a fireplace doubles as a breakfast room for big, homemade breakfasts, and fresh flowers brighten the sun-filled space nicely. If you'd like to cook in, a patio deck has a barbecue grill, but don't bother: Downstairs is El Gaucho, one of Seattle's best steakhouses.

2507 First Ave. at Wall Street. ☎ *800-624-1117 or 206-448-0125. Fax: 206-448-2406. Internet:* www.wallstreetinn.com. *Rack rates: $85–$145. AE, DC, DISC, MC, V.*

W Seattle

$$$$ Shopping District

Yes, Virginia, there is some style in Seattle. Dressed in dark chocolates and ecrus, with chrome, glass, and leather accents, the W Hotel gives stubbornly unfashionable Seattle a rare infusion of New York/L.A. style. This stylishness of the W Seattle is not surprising, because this local branch is affiliated with the other trendy W hotels in New York, L.A., Atlanta, and Sydney. Seattle's version gives you more of the same: a reception desk that's backed by a wall of modernist oils, a lobby that resembles a living room filled with plush, velvety furniture and silver knick-knacks, and rooms wired with great electronics, including a VCR, a CD/cassette player, Internet access, and cordless phones. Need some substance to go with the style? The feathery beds are simply the best in town.

1112 Fourth Ave. at Seneca Street, across from Hotel Monaco and Four Seasons Olympic. ☎ *206-264-6000 or 877-W-HOTELS. Fax: 206-264-6100. Internet:* www. w-hotels.com. *Rack rates: $390–$450. AE, DC, DISC, MC, V.*

The Westin Seattle

$$$$ **Shopping District**

With nearly 900 rooms occupying two cylindrical towers, the Westin, now owned by megaconglomerate Starwood Resorts, is one of Seattle's top business and convention hotels. Bill Clinton stayed here during the APEC conference and is probably the only head of state to order McDonald's delivered to his room from across the street. Equipped with everything you need in a convention hotel, from an indoor pool and spa to business-equipped rooms with fax machines and Internet access, the Westin bustles with big-city vibrancy, but it's also curiously cold and impersonal. The hotel's Kid's Club program offers special amenities and services (such as cribs, high chairs, and souvenir items) for the younger set.

1900 Fifth Ave. at convergence of Stewart Street and Westlake Avenue. ☎ *800-WESTIN-1 or 206-728-1000. Fax: 206-728-2259. Internet:* www.westin.com. *Rack rates: $225–$330. AE, DC, DISC, MC, V.*

Willows Lodge

$$$$ **Eastside**

If you'd like to experience a luxurious Northwest-style lodge — the kind of place where Microsofties stay after cashing in a few dozen stock options — head out to this spectacular boutique hotel in the eastside suburb of Woodinville. The lodge is beautifully situated near wineries and the Red Hook brewpub facility, and you can waddle home across the parking lot after a nine-course dinner at the fabulous Herbfarm restaurant (see Chapter 14). Inside, you'll find a lobby of Douglas fir beams and an enormous stone fireplace, plus cozy rooms with thick duvets, fireplaces, and jetted bathtubs. This place is well worth an out-of-town splurge and is probably the single most romantic lodging in the area.

14580 NE 145th St., Woodinville, across Lake Washington on I-90 and north on I-405; Web site has complete directions. ☎ *877-424-3930 or 425-424-3900. Fax: 425-424-2585. Internet:* www.willowslodge.com. *Rack rates: $260–$320. AE, DC, DISC, MC, V.*

Woodmark Hotel
$$$$ **Eastside**

If you're looking for a luxurious hotel at the edge of one of Seattle's pretty lakes, travel across Lake Washington to the tony eastside suburb of Kirkland to find this fancy lodging. Boutique-sized and elegant, the service is terrific, and the rooms are plush and spacious. The nightly midnight buffet of cold cuts and bread (effectively allowing guests to "raid the pantry") is just one of the many classy touches that this expensive property offers. Kirkland's main drag has several high-end shops and restaurants, but you're looking at a 45-minute-plus drive into Seattle over the busy Hwy. 520 bridge.

1200 Carillon Point, Kirkland, on the eastern shore of Lake Washington, just north of the 520 bridge. ☎ *800-822-3700 or 425-822-3700. Fax: 425-822-3699. Internet:* www.thewoodmark.com. *Rack rates: $205–$275. AE, DC, DISC, MC, V.*

Hostelling: No Room at the Inn?

In high season, Seattle's accommodations choices can be limited. If my favorites (listed earlier in this chapter) are booked solid, the following selections are perfectly fine options.

College Inn
$ **University District**

4000 University Way NE. ☎ **206-633-4441**. *Fax: 206-547-1335. Internet:* www.speakeasy.org/collegeinn/. *Rack rates: $65–$80. MC, V.*

Inn at Queen Anne
$$ **Queen Anne**

505 First Ave. N. ☎ **800-952-5043** *or 206-282-7357. Fax: 206-217-9719. Rack rates: $99–$109. AE, DC, DISC, MC, V.*

Pensione Nichols
$$ **Pike Place Market**

1923 First Ave. ☎ **800-440-7125** *or 206-441-7125. Fax: 206-448-8906. Rack rates: $100. AE, MC, V.*

Pioneer Square Hotel
$$–$$$ **Downtown**

77 Yesler Way. ☎ **800-800-5514** *or 206-340-1234. Fax: 206-467-0707. Rack rates: $99–$199. AE, MC, V.*

Sixth Avenue Inn

$–$$$ **Shopping District**

2000 Sixth Ave. ☎ **800-648-6440** *or 206-441-8300. Fax: 206-441-9903. Rack rates: $79–$131. AE, DC, DISC, MC, V.*

University Inn

$$ **University District**

4140 Roosevelt Way NE. ☎ **800-733-3855** *or 206-632-5055. Fax: 206-547-4937. Rack rates: $92–$119. AE, DC, DISC, MC, V.*

So where do I stay?

Are you confused at this point? Head swimming in a soup of hotel details? Let me make it easy for you. Here are my choices given the following criteria, in order of preference:

If budget is my main concern:

Mediterranean Inn	Wall Street Inn
Marriott Residence Inn	Salisbury House
Homewood Suites by Hilton	Hampton Inn and Suites
Hostelling International–Seattle	Courtyard by Marriott

If being cool and in the thick of city life are important:

Inn at the Market	Alexis Hotel
Ace Hotel	Wall Street Inn
Inn at Harbor Steps	Grand Hyatt Seattle
MarQueen Hotel	Mediterranean Inn
Four Seasons Olympic Hotel	Mayflower Park Hotel
Paramount Hotel	Sheraton Seattle Hotel and Towers

For great views:

Hotel Edgewater	Seattle Marriott Waterfront
Inn at the Market	Woodmark Hotel
Sorrento Hotel	Courtyard by Marriott
Marriott Residence Inn	

(continued)

(continued)

For romance:

Willows Lodge

Hotel Monaco Seattle

Woodmark Hotel

Inn at Harbor Steps

Hotel Vintage Park

Salish Lodge & Spa

Sorrento Hotel

Inn at the Market

W Seattle

For kids:

Seattle Marriott Waterfront

Westin Seattle

Marriott Residence Inn

Renaissance Hotel Seattle

Sheraton Seattle Hotel and Towers

When money is no object:

Four Seasons Olympic Hotel

Willows Lodge

Grand Hyatt Seattle

Sorrento Hotel

Woodmark Hotel

Index of Accommodations by Price

$

Ace Hotel
College Inn
Hostelling International–Seattle
Mediterranean Inn
Sixth Avenue Inn

$$

Chambered Nautilus Bed & Breakfast
    Inn
Courtyard by Marriott
Inn at Queen Anne
Pensione Nichols
Salisbury House
University Inn
University Tower Hotel
The Wall Street Inn

$$$

Hampton Inn and Suites
Homewood Suites by Hilton
Hotel Edgewater
Inn at Harbor Steps
MarQueen Hotel
Marriott Residence Inn
Mayflower Park Hotel
Pioneer Square Hotel
Renaissance Hotel Seattle
The Roosevelt
Seattle Marriott Waterfront

$$$$

Alexis Hotel
Grand Hyatt Seattle
Four Seasons Olympic Hotel

Hotel Monaco Seattle
Hotel Vintage Park
Inn at the Market
Paramount Hotel
Salish Lodge & Spa
Sheraton Seattle Hotel and Towers

Sorrento Hotel
W Seattle
The Westin Seattle
Willows Lodge
Woodmark Hotel

Index of Accommodations by Neighborhood

Belltown
Ace Hotel
The Wall Street Inn

Eastside
Salish Lodge & Spa (located in
    Snoqualmie, the far Eastside)
Willows Lodge
Woodmark Hotel

First Hill/Capitol Hill
Salisbury House
Sorrento Hotel

Lake Union
Courtyard by Marriott
Marriott Residence Inn

Pike Place Market
Alexis Hotel
Hostelling International–Seattle
Inn at Harbor Steps
Inn at the Market
Pensione Nichols

Queen Anne
Hampton Inn and Suites
Homewood Suites by Hilton

Inn at Queen Anne
MarQueen Hotel
Mediterranean Inn

Shopping District
Grand Hyatt Seattle
Four Seasons Olympic Hotel
Hotel Monaco Seattle
Hotel Vintage Park
Mayflower Park Hotel
Paramount Hotel
Pioneer Square Hotel
Renaissance Hotel Seattle
The Roosevelt
Sheraton Seattle Hotel and Towers
Sixth Avenue Inn
W Hotel
The Westin Seattle

University District
College Inn
Chambered Nautilus Bed &
    Breakfast Inn
University Tower Hotel

Waterfront
Hotel Edgewater
Seattle Marriott Waterfront

Chapter 11

Orienting Yourself in Seattle and Getting Around

- -

In This Chapter

▶ Arriving by air, car, or train

▶ Driving in Seattle

▶ Experiencing the Seattle bus adventure

▶ Taking monorails, streetcars, and ferries

▶ Hitting the town on two wheels — or two feet

- -

*H*ere's a little-known civic skeleton-in-the-closet that you can use to goad your new Seattle friends: Seattleites are profoundly envious of Portland's light-rail transportation system. It's a source of local shame that Seattle never got its act together to build a decent public-transportation system, as Portland did, and now you can see the results in the form of daily traffic jams and downtown parking woes. Sure, Seattle has buses, a trolley car, ferries, and even an old monorail that has but two stops, but the bottom line is that Seattle drives to where it's going. (A light-rail system finally broke ground in 2003, but it won't be built and ready to use for years. Similarly, residents have been bickering for years about building a new monorail that will connect downtown to neighborhoods like Ballard and Fremont, and if they're lucky, their grandkids will one day ride it.)

For travelers whose main objective is to stick to the attractions clustered around the city's downtown core, the lack of public transit matters little. But for those who want to see much more of Seattle and its surrounding environs, it's a good idea to know a bit about your transportation options before you arrive.

Getting from the Airport to Your Hotel

Located 15 miles from downtown Seattle and about the same distance from downtown Tacoma (hence the name, **Sea-Tac International Airport**), Seattle's airport, originally built in the mid-1940s, is surprisingly small for such a large metropolitan area, which is both good and bad news for travelers. The good news is that it's relatively easy to find your way around the airport, get your bags quickly, and head over to ground transportation. The bad news is that the airport is congested and perennially under construction — in 2002, it moved 26.7 million people through a facility that was designed to handle about half that number — with projected expansions into the first decade of the 21st century, including plans for a much-debated third runway that will add even more air traffic and subsequent congestion.

You arrive at one of five concourses (a sixth is being renovated and won't reopen until 2004). From most of these concourses, it's a quick, easy five-minute walk to the main terminal and lower-level baggage claims, but from the north and south terminals, you need to take a subway train to the baggage claim. The train goes in only one direction, and it's virtually impossible to get lost on it. At the baggage claim, the 15 baggage carousels are clearly marked for each airline, and baggage retrieval is generally fast. If you need cash, you can find ATMs in the main concourse between the ticket counters and the gates, as well as on the baggage claim level. Of course, several espresso vendors who would love to pour you your first cup of hot Seattle coffee also line the baggage claim level and the main concourse. An information desk at the baggage-claim level is supposed to assist travelers with ground transportation information, but don't count on people actually being there to help out, particularly late at night.

You then have a few options for getting into town. All shuttles and taxis have been moved into the parking garage, which is reached by covered walkways from the terminal. From baggage claim, take the escalators (or elevators, if you have bulky items or carts) to the mezzanine level and then walk 50 yards or so on the skybridge to the parking garage. Head to the third floor (more elevators and escalators are available) and look for signs directing you to the taxi stand or shuttle services. Taxis can drive you the 20 minutes into downtown Seattle (for about $30). Also in the parking garage is Shuttle Express, a shared-van service that can take you to any address — *except major hotels* — in the metropolitan area for about $21 for the first passenger and $7 for accompanying passengers. If you'd like a town car, Lincoln Continental transfers are offered for $50 to downtown points. The cheapest option is to wait (up to a half-hour) for Gray Line buses that meet in front of the baggage claim (with stops outside of doors 6 and 26) and stop at all the major downtown hotels. These cost $8.50 per person one-way or $14 round trip. City buses also stop at the airport (outside of the baggage claim's door 6) and head downtown for $1.50, but it's a long, circuitous trip, and I don't recommend taking them.

Rental-car companies are located on the baggage claim level. They can sign you up and put you into a courtesy van for a quick ride to their parking areas.

Courtesy vans for services that use the airport have also all been shunted into the adjoining parking garage. If you're looking for a hotel van, rental-car van, or shuttle to an airport parking lot, you need to continue from the baggage claim up an escalator to a covered bridge that connects the terminal to the parking garage; go downstairs one level once you get there and wait at one of several courtesy-van stopping points, where phones are available to call your hotel or rental-car company for a pick-up.

If, ten minutes after you leave the airport, you feel as if you're going around in circles because another airport is visible from the highway, don't fret or yell at the driver. You're simply passing Boeing Field, a manufacturing and testing facility for Seattle's favorite aerospace conglomerate as well as a small airstrip for charters and private jets.

Arriving by Car

Driving into Seattle? Lucky you! You get to see right away how hideous traffic can be on Seattle's major transportation arteries. Because the city is surrounded by water to the east and west, you either arrive from the north or south on **Interstate 5,** which can experience major congestion at any time of the day or night, or from the east on **Interstate 90,** which crosses Lake Washington by bridge and grinds to a standstill during rush hours or on the many nights when major sporting events are scheduled at the downtown arenas. From I-5, enter downtown from the Seneca Street or Mercer Street exits (both left-lane exits if you're coming from the south). Continuing north on I-5 past Mercer Street puts you onto a bridge over the Ship Canal, with the first exit being NE 45th and 50th streets for the University District, Green Lake, and the near-north neighborhoods. Heading west past Mercer Island and Lake Washington, I-90 dead-ends shortly after you pass the I-5 interchange, putting you into downtown Seattle on 4th Avenue South.

The million-dollar question: Should you rent a car?

The answer is no and yes, but mostly no. If you're staying in the downtown area and are intent on exploring Seattle's best attractions, you can get by quite well with a judicious use of shoe leather, public transportation, and the odd cab ride. You rarely find that you even need a car. And don't forget that the cost of parking (and the time spent searching for parking) can be prohibitive. If after a few days of scouring Seattle's core you want to venture farther afield — an excursion or day trip to the city's far-flung neighborhoods or islands, say or to Mount Rainier National Park or Olympic National Park — you can easily rent a car downtown, take your trip, and then return the car to the agency and let them deal with parking. All the big rental-car agencies have downtown locations, and you can save a considerable amount on taxes if you rent from downtown locations rather than picking up your car at the airport.

Arriving by Train

Showing up in Seattle on Amtrak's **Coast Starlight** train, which originates in San Diego and runs through Portland, is a fine way to arrive in the Emerald City. The rather dingy and little-used train station is located in the Pioneer Square section of downtown Seattle. The first thing that you'll see upon leaving the station is the handsome new Seahawks football stadium. A cab ride from the station to a downtown hotel takes just five to ten minutes and costs a few bucks. If you're traveling light, you can walk to many downtown hotels. But don't do so late at night: That part of Pioneer Square can get rowdy and ominous after the sun goes down.

Getting Around Once You're Here

Transportation, particularly the attendant hassles of keeping and parking a car, can make or break your trip to the Emerald City. Fortunately, most of Seattle is very easily strolled, and buses in the Ride Free Zone can whisk you from one end of downtown to the other. Heed the following advice carefully, and you can spend far more time sightseeing and far less time dealing with transportation hassles as you explore the metro area.

Getting around by car

You can get along just fine in Seattle without a car, particularly if you're only interested in seeing the main attractions in the core of the city.

But lots of visitors to Seattle wouldn't think of missing out on the myriad spectacular sights in close range of the city. Whether you're using a car for the full duration of your vacation or simply to take a day trip outside the city, here are some tips on navigating the highways and byways of Seattle.

Although they look fat, desirable, and accessible on the map, the main highways of Seattle are frequently the worst places to drive. **Interstate 5,** the major north-south artery, is choked with traffic throughout the day, particularly where it passes under the Convention Center downtown in a bewildering tangle of exits and ramps. For some reason, the worst traffic on Interstate 5 seems to be on weekends. **I-90** and **SR520,** the two highway bridges that carry workers and residents into the city from the eastern suburbs, have some of the worst traffic snarls in the country. These tangles exist not only at rush hours but on sports nights when Sonics fans are coming to Seattle Center to watch a basketball game or when Mariners fans are headed to Safeco Field to catch a ballgame. The bottom line: Try to avoid I-5 at all costs during your visit to save yourself lots of time and aggravation or schedule your drives during off-peak hours.

If you're heading east, it's usually better to use **I-90** across Mercer Island, but absolutely don't do it during either rush-hour period of the day. On the east side, **I-405,** the bypass route that stretches from just north of the airport to the northern suburb of Lynnwood, can be viciously plugged throughout the day and is worth avoiding if you can help it.

Make Route 99 your best friend in Seattle. Also known as Aurora Avenue, this north-south road is the best way to get from downtown to the near-north neighborhoods, or south to the airport. It's much less traveled than I-5 and easier to access. It's also a great way to get to the neighborhood of West Seattle and to the ferries to Vashon Island and Southworth.

Most downtown streets are one-way and relatively well-marked. Seattle drivers are, for the most part, very courteous, and they generally give way if you signal your desire to change lanes.

Street smarts: Where to pick up information

For more information and local maps, head to the **Washington State Convention and Trade Center** at 8th Avenue and Pike Street downtown, where the Seattle-King County Convention and Visitors Bureau (☎ **206-461-5840**) can provide you with brochures and information. If you just need a map, any self-respecting gas station or convenience store should have several maps of the local area.

Right on red is the law in Washington and is restricted only at the few intersections posted with "No Right on Red" signs. Many intersections are unmarked on the side streets of most Seattle neighborhoods, so stay alert; don't barrel through intersections and remember that the car on the right has the right-of-way.

Seattle's hilly topography and narrow streets can quickly confuse you and get you lost. Don't ever assume that, say, N. 49th Street will lead to NW 49th Street; take my word that it doesn't. Instead, always use the major "arterial" routes to get as close to your destination as possible. Don't try to save time by using the side streets: They're usually blocked by both-sides-of-the-street parking, and the going is slow. When two cars are trying to occupy a street that only one car can fit onto, local etiquette says that the car closest to a driveway or shoulder should yield.

Parking downtown can be a real hassle, not to mention costly if your hotel charges a daily parking fee, but it's doable if you're willing to park a few blocks away from the busiest parts of the city and walk the rest of the way. Here are some tips on where and when to park, how to find free parking, and how to keep your parking costs from becoming prohibitively high:

- ✔ On-street parking runs $2 per hour in Seattle and is enforced every day except Sunday and holidays until 6 p.m. The meters accept quarters and dimes only, and most go up to just two hours.

- ✔ Unless you get up at 5 a.m. before the city starts to fill up with workers, you won't find street parking in the downtown core. You may have better luck finding parking in the northern part of downtown, on the streets north of Bell Street as you head toward Denny Way. You can also use the lots at Seattle Center near the Space Needle, which charge about $6 per day, and then take the monorail or a bus into downtown for sightseeing.

- ✔ Downtown parking lots charge between $10 and $15 a day, with early-bird rates of $6 to $8 offered before 9 a.m. Most lots are unattended and require you to stuff your payments into little slots in a central payment box, so make sure that you have lots of dollar bills handy. The lots are zealously monitored, and they charge a stiff fine (traceable to you through your rental-car contract) for nonpayment of parking fees.

- ✔ In the main Shopping District, merchants give you an Easy Streets token for every $20 purchase you make in their stores, which knocks a dollar off the price of parking at most nearby lots.

- ✔ Neighborhoods like Ballard, Queen Anne, and Capitol Hill have plenty of free street parking off the main commercial streets. Just drive a block or two away from Market Street, Queen Anne Avenue North, or Broadway, respectively, to find neighborhood parking. Keep an eye out for restricted parking signs in some neighborhoods that only allow street parking by permit (for residents).

✔ If you park your car on one of Seattle's many hills, always point your front tires to the curb, or you may be liable for a fine.

✔ The Pike Place Market's parking garage, located on Western Avenue just opposite the Market, offers free parking for the first hour of shopping. After an hour, you pay $5 for the second hour, and $2.50 an hour for each hour after that. An hour gives you plenty of time to run into the Market and grab enough fruit, cheese, and baked goods to make a picnic without having to pay for parking.

✔ Most downtown restaurants offer valet parking. It isn't free (prices are usually around $5 with validation from the restaurant), but it's generally cheaper than parking lots and much more convenient.

Getting around by bus

Chalk it up to Seattle's hilly topography and network of twisting, "arterial" streets (the main routes around town), but the city's **Metro bus system** (☎ **800-542-7876** or 206-553-3000) can get a trifle confusing if you're trying to reach distant points in the city. To reach the Ballard Locks (see Chapter 15), for example, you need to choose one of eight different routes between First and Fourth avenues downtown, wait for a bus heading north, bump your way around and through parts of Queen Anne, cross the Ballard Bridge, get off on Market Street with a transfer (you get it from the bus driver when you pay), and wait for another bus heading west — a process that can take over an hour for a 15-minute trip. It's not a bad way to see the city, if you have the time and the inclination to sort out bus schedules and wait for transfers, but if you're in a hurry, it's hard to justify. Buses generally run until about midnight, and fares cost $1 to $1.75, depending on the distance you travel and when you travel (riding during commuter hours means higher fares). A big sign on the cash box tells you the fare. You need exact change (dollar bills are accepted), or you can purchase a book of tickets that are valid on all Metro routes and the Waterfront Streetcar (see the section "Getting around by Waterfront Streetcar and monorail") by calling ☎ **206-624-PASS.** Don't forget to ask for a transfer if you need to board a connecting bus.

Riding the bus for free

The best thing about the bus system is that most of downtown Seattle has been established as a Ride Free Zone between 6 a.m. and 7 p.m. This is where you can really use the bus to your advantage, as you hop from Belltown (the Ride Free Zone begins at Battery Street) to the Pike Place Market or Pioneer Square (the Zone ends at South Jackson Street, just a few blocks from Safeco Field), or up the steep hills from the waterfront to Sixth Avenue and the Shopping District without paying a dime. In the Ride Free Zone, you can board and exit the bus from either of the two doors; the driver announces when you're nearing the edge of the Zone. If you continue past the Zone, you exit from the front door and pay on your way out.

Not sure whether you're in the Ride Free Zone or if you're past the hours of free rides? You can tell by looking to see whether people are boarding the bus from the front and the rear at the same time, or if the driver holds his hand over the cash box when you board, signaling that you don't have to pay.

The great thing about the Ride Free Zone is that you can board nearly any bus heading in your direction, and you don't have to deal with schedules or routes. Just stay on the bus until it approaches your destination, or if it veers off in another direction, get off at the next exit and grab the next bus going your way. Because it's free, you won't need transfers or tickets.

The electric Kool-Aid bus system

Seattle's one big concession to easing downtown traffic was to build a 1.3-mile-long tunnel underneath the downtown area that is used solely by electric buses. Five stations are located between the Convention Center (entrance at 8th Avenue and Pine Street) and the International District, with a central stop near Pioneer Square at 3rd Avenue and James Street. Because it's in the Ride Free Zone, trips through the tunnel are all free during the Ride Free hours of 6 a.m. to 7 p.m. It's a quick way to get from the Shopping District to Pioneer Square, and the underground stations are all decorated with interesting public art.

Getting around by taxi

Seattle is not a city where you can hail taxis on the street, but it has a number of competing cab companies that can come and pick you up at a hotel or attraction. And you can always find cabs lined up and ready to be boarded at major downtown hotels like the Sheraton, the Four Seasons Olympic, and the Westin. Taking cabs is a good way to get around when walking or taking the bus is not feasible, but if you find that you're taking cabs more than two or three times a day, it can quickly get cost-prohibitive (versus renting a car). The fare is $1.80 for the flag drop and $1.80 for every mile. Try **Yellow Cab** (☎ 206-622-6500), **Farwest Taxi** (☎ 206-622-1717), or **Graytop Cab** (☎ 206-782-TAXI).

Taxis in Seattle have been chided in recent years for their less-than-stellar customer service, and it can take forever to dispatch a car to an out-of-downtown location. Don't expect to just call and get a quick pick-up from any spot in the city; it may take an hour or more for the cab company to pry a driver away from the downtown area. If you take a cab to a far-flung corner of the city (like the Arboretum or the Museum of Flight), make sure that the driver knows when to pick you up again for the return trip. You might even ask the driver to wait for you for an hour. (Try to get him or her to do it off the meter.)

If you want to make sure that you always have a ride, and you don't mind paying a premium for the service, call a limousine company to have a town car and driver at your disposal. **Express Car,** a division of Shuttle Express (☎ 425-981-7077), provides Lincoln Continental town-cars for one-way trips or hourly charters ($55 per hour).

Getting around by Waterfront Streetcar and monorail

Downtown Seattle has two quaint transportation alternatives that aren't much for moving the masses but that work well for tourists who want to see the city. **Metro** (☎ 800-542-7876 or 206-553-3000) operates an old-fashioned streetcar along the Alaskan Way waterfront from Pier 70 (near the Edgewater Hotel) to Pioneer Square. The fare is $1 ($1.25 during peak hours) in exact change. The streetcar runs about every 20 minutes until 10:45p.m.

If you have a car to park, you have a much better chance of finding a spot for it under the Alaskan Way viaduct near Pioneer Square or all the way north on Alaskan Way near Myrtle Edwards Park. Then you can take the Waterfront Streetcar to waterfront attractions like the Aquarium and the Omnidome Film Experience and to elevators or steps leading up to the Pike Place Market.

Similarly, the **Seattle Monorail** (☎ 206-441-6038) can shoot you directly from its station at Seattle Center near the Space Needle and Experience Music Project to the heart of the downtown shopping district at Westlake Center in just 90 seconds. Alas, these are its only two stops (lots of locals want it to be extended), and the ride is more of a tourist attraction than serious public transportation. It's a great way to get around between those two central points, however, and costs only $1.25 each way, with attendants on hand to make change. It runs until 11 p.m. most nights.

Getting around by ferry

Although it's long past the heyday of the Mosquito Fleet days, when all manner of ships dotted Puget Sound, delivering people and goods to far-flung communities on the water, the **Washington State Ferry system** (☎ 206-464-6400 or 800-84-FERRY) is a quintessential Northwest experience that you shouldn't miss. Ferryboats can't get you around Seattle proper, but they can transport you to Bainbridge and Vashon islands or the Kitsap Peninsula towns of Bremerton and Southworth (see Chapter 15). You can go by car or on foot to Bainbridge Island, with fares set at $5.40 for passengers and $9 for cars ($12 during peak tourist months in the summer). Ferries leave from Pier 52 on the downtown waterfront and from the Fauntleroy Terminal in West Seattle.

Getting around by bike

Keeping in mind that Seattle is a big, active city, getting around by bicycle can be an alternative if you're an experienced rider. Many Metro buses (see "Getting around by bus," earlier in this chapter) are equipped with bike racks, and the city has several dedicated bike paths. You can easily negotiate Alaskan Way and the lovely waterfront path at Myrtle Edwards Park by bike, but I wouldn't recommend riding through the busy shopping district unless you're very experienced. North of the Ship Canal, the Burke-Gilman Trail, along with a few side streets, connects all the neighborhoods from Ballard to the University District with a dedicated bike-and-jogging trail that easily allows you to explore Ballard and its Locks, Fremont, Gasworks Park, Wallingford, and U-District by bike. For a lovely ride, the Burke-Gilman Trail meets Lake Washington at Matthews Beach (at NE 93rd Street) and continues along the lake several miles to Kenmore.

To get to the near-north neighborhoods and the Burke-Gilman Trail from downtown by bike, take Westlake Avenue, a wide, safe thoroughfare that runs down the west side of Lake Union, turn right onto the Fremont Bridge (you can use the sidewalk to safely cross it), and then look for the bike path going in either direction on the north side of the ship canal. Going right leads to Wallingford and the U-District; left heads to Ballard.

Getting around on foot

Downtown Seattle is surprisingly compact and, except for a few nasty, San Francisco-style hills, easy to walk. The Pike Place Market and Belltown, for example, are just a few blocks apart from one another on flat First Avenue, and the center of the Shopping District, at 5th and Pine, is just four long blocks from the Market. An ambitious walker could scour the entire downtown area in one long day (with several stops for rejuvenating lattes). You face some nasty hills from the waterfront heading east toward the Shopping District — if you head in that direction, you might consider taking a bus instead. Otherwise, when faced with a steep hill to climb from one avenue to the next, simply head a block or two north or south, and you may find that the inclines recede. In some places, like Queen Anne Hill, you won't have any option but to suck it up and climb the steep hill, but your effort is rewarded at the top with some marvelous vistas of the city, the mountains, and the water below.

You can see many of Seattle's neighborhoods on foot. Simply take the bus or park your car on one edge of Fremont, Capitol Hill, or Wallingford and then spend a few hours strolling among the old houses and retail corridors. The Burke-Gilman Trail (see the preceding section) is also a great way to get from one near-north neighborhood to another without encountering any traffic.

Jaywalking is taken seriously in Seattle. It may seem comical or out-right crazy to you to be standing at a clear intersection with no cars in sight, particularly if you're from New York, but Seattleites won't cross that street until the light changes. And if one of Seattle's Finest catches you jaywalking, you have some 'splainin' to do and a hefty fine to pay.

Chapter 12

Money Matters

In This Chapter

▶ Accessing your cash on the road

▶ Salvaging your vacation if your wallet is stolen

▶ Taxing tourists, the Seattle way

*Y*ou've plotted your budget in advance, figuring what it will cost you (and your family) on average to stay, dine, and enjoy the sights in Seattle during your vacation. Now you need to know exactly where in the city you can access cash, where to get more if your wallet is stolen, and just how deep a bite the local taxman plans to take out of your finances.

Where to Get Cash in Seattle

You won't have any problem accessing cash in Seattle. The city is loaded with ATMs, and there seems to be a bank on every corner in most neighborhoods. With the exception of Washington Mutual (keep reading for more information), most banks charge a service fee ($1 to $1.50) when noncustomers use their ATMs. So minimizing the number of cash withdrawals you make is a smart move. The major banks in town are **Bank of America** (☎ 206-461-0800), with dozens of locations; **Washington Mutual** (☎ 800-756-8000), which at the time of this writing was not charging noncustomers a service fee to use its ATMs; **KeyBank** (☎ 800-KEY-2YOU); **Wells Fargo Bank** (☎ 800-869-3557); and **U.S. Bank** (☎ 800-US-BANKS).

Prominent tourist areas that have ATMs are **Safeco Field,** the **Pike Place Market** (one is located right behind the ticket booth near Rachel, the Pig; another is inside near the chili parlor), **Pacific Place,** and **Seattle Center,** which has Bank of America kiosks on many of the walkways leading into the Center, as well as inside the **Seattle Center House.** Many convenience stores also have ATMs, but they charge the highest service fees ($1.50 to $2). Debit cards with a Visa logo are widely accepted at shops and restaurants.

A smart way to use your debit card to access cash without having to pay a service charge is to buy something at a grocery store like **Safeway** (☎425-455-6444) or **QFC** (☎425-455-3761), pay for it with your debit card, and get cash back.

What to Do If Your Wallet Is Stolen

Almost every credit-card company has an emergency 800-number that you can call if your wallet or purse is stolen. Your credit-card company may be able to wire you a cash advance off your credit card immediately; in many places, it can get you an emergency credit card within a day or two. The issuing bank's 800-number is usually on the back of the credit card, but that won't help you much if the card was stolen. Copy the number on the back of your card onto another piece of paper before you leave and keep the copy in a safe place just in case. **Citicorp Visa's** U.S. emergency number is ☎ **800-847-2911. American Express** cardholders and traveler's checks holders should call ☎ **800-221-7282** for all money emergencies. **MasterCard** holders should call ☎ **800-307-7309.**

If you opt to carry traveler's checks, be sure to keep a record of their serial numbers so that you can let police know how many checks (and which ones) were stolen or lost. You should always keep the list of numbers in a safe and separate place so that you're ensured a refund if the checks are lost or stolen. If you need quick cash, you can always have someone wire you money in Seattle. **Western Union** has several offices in Seattle, with locations at 539 Queen Anne Ave. N. (☎ **206-285-1400**) and 201 Broadway E. (☎ **206-324-8740**).

Odds are that if your wallet is gone, you've seen the last of it, and the police aren't likely to recover it for you. However, after you realize that it's gone and you cancel your credit cards, you should call to inform the police. You may need the police report number for credit card or insurance purposes later.

Taxing Matters

Washington's sales tax is a hefty 8.8 percent, which partially makes up for the zero state income tax that residents (don't) pay. Visitors get hit with additional taxes. There's a total tax of 15.6 percent (after a "convention and trade tax" of 7 percent is tacked on to the existing sales tax) on hotel rooms within the Seattle city limits. Car rentals get hit the hardest, with an 18.3 percent rental surcharge (which includes taxes levied to pay for the lovely new baseball stadium — remember *that* when you're stuck in ballgame traffic), and yet another 10 percent if you pick up the car at the airport. Holy Toledo, that's 28.3 percent! You can save some of that cost by renting from a downtown agency.

Chapter 13

The Lowdown on the Seattle Dining Scene

- -

In This Chapter

▶ Asking dress code? What dress code?

▶ Dining out among the locals

▶ Discovering the hottest trends and happenings in Seattle's restaurants

▶ Keeping food costs down

▶ Knowing where and when to make reservations

- -

Call it Seattle's Golden Age of good eating. The Internet and high-tech money that fueled the city's economic growth in the late '90s also brought a whole lot of wild Alaskan salmon, foie gras, thick steaks, and crème brûlée to town. The taste for fine food stuck around even after the economy went south, and Seattleites continue to support the best restaurants in town.

The competition among restaurateurs is nothing but good news for visitors, who can enjoy delicious Pacific Northwest cuisine at any number of venues in a variety of price categories. If, by some chance, you tire of salmon and chowder, Seattle offers plenty of places to sample excellent Italian, pan-Asian, American heartland, and French dishes.

Discovering the Latest Trends, the Hot Seats, and the Star Chefs

Steak has arrived in town with a vengeance, thanks in large part to the success of **El Gaucho,** which serves up huge portions of tender cow. In the last two years, Seattle has found room for several upscale steakhouse chains, such as **Fleming's, Morton's,** and **Ruth's Chris Steak House.** If you add local favorites like the **Metropolitan Grill, Daniel's Broiler,** and the **Union Square Grill** to the picture, you find that a whole lotta good meat is being consumed in these parts. (I include descriptions of my favorite steak spots in Chapter 14.) Of course, that doesn't mean that the city has forgotten about seafood, for which Seattle continues to be famous. In recent years, the seafood-consuming experience has been raised a notch due to the addition of classy seafood restaurants like the **Oceanaire Seafood Room** and **Waterfront,** which compete with tried-and-true favorites like **Flying Fish, Etta's, Palisade,** and **The Brooklyn Seafood, Steak & Oyster House** to get the freshest fish to the table. Today's breed of seafood restaurant is reaching beyond local seafood to bring fresh fish from international waters to the table, which means on any given day you may be choosing between Australian lobster tails, Hawaiian mahi-mahi, Columbia River sturgeon, Dungeness crab, and three different kinds of Alaskan and Atlantic salmon.

After tucking away your two pounds of prime beef and one pound of fish, you may be thinking about a luscious dessert, of course. The best restaurants in town go out of their way to provide unique dessert menus with the name of the pastry chef prominently featured. Wrap yourself around a warm pumpkin brioche, a molten chocolate cake, or a perfect *tarte tatin* (upside-down apple tart), and you may never go back to colored gelatin again. Local star chef Tom Douglas has gone so far as to open a retail bakery alongside the newly relocated **Dahlia Lounge** to meet the demand for his insanely delicious coconut-cream pie, which is tall and creamy and covered in shavings of white chocolate.

The hottest restaurant neighborhood of late has been **Belltown,** where you can hardly walk down the street without bumping into a chef who has just opened his own fine-dining establishment. But the sheer saturation of restaurants in the neighborhood, as well as the dearth of available rental space, is good news for other up-and-coming sections of town, such as **Ballard** and **Capitol Hill.** The city's general mania for good food extends also to the new delis and takeout kitchens that are popping up in communities and cooking whole meals for families to take home and reheat.

Seattle's top chefs have solidified their standing with second-generation projects that have matured and become local favorites. Standout cooks like Kerry Sears, Tamara Murphy, and Christine Keff continue to dazzle at, respectively, **Cascadia, Brasa,** and **Fandango.** Tom Black moved out to the **Barking Frog** restaurant at Willows Lodge, and Johnathan Sundstrom opened **Earth & Ocean** at the W Hotel. These chefs continue to grow in confidence and experience, as they apply their skills to new variations on Northwest, Mediterranean, and Latin foods. Restaurants are on the move literally as well: Tom Douglas picked up and moved his first restaurant (out of the three he now runs), the **Dahlia Lounge,** a few blocks down Fourth Avenue into a bigger, better space, and **Wild Ginger,** the city's favorite Asian restaurant, left its nook under the Pike Place Market for more expansive digs on Third Avenue.

Eating Like a Local

Yes, Seattle has its fair share of hot-shot chefs and big-city dining experiences, but the culinary landscape would be much diminished if the regional bounty were not as rich and varied as it is. Here are the staples of land and sea that drive the local diet.

Seafood is king

Seafood is king in Seattle, and I don't just mean king salmon. I'm talking chinook salmon, silver salmon, farm-raised salmon, hook-and-line-caught salmon, and salmon that comes with a pedigree from a specific fishery in Alaska. People around here know the difference between a Yukon River salmon and a Copper River salmon. (They hail from different parts of Alaska and have slightly different textures and flavors.) Locals can tell the difference between a Judd Cove oyster from Orcas Island and a Quilcene oyster from the Olympic Peninsula.

Go to any supermarket in town or visit the fishmongers who hawk (and throw) fresh fish at the Pike Place Market, and you begin to discover the myriad varieties of coldwater fish that Northwesterners love. Besides salmon, there's black cod, a buttery, rich fish that is a wonder in either fresh or smoked form; halibut steaks from Alaska; chewy, lobsterlike halibut cheeks that resemble large scallops; monkfish (which has been called "the poor man's lobster"); and trout, sturgeon, and steelhead from local rivers.

Puget Sound is also a huge producer of shellfish, much of which winds up on local tables. Oysters, clams, mussels, and crab are all available throughout the year (less so during the summer months, when harvests are leaner), and the harvesting of rare, wild razor clams is allowed by the state — people race to their fish markets to get some of the sweet, chewy razor clam meat. (See Chapter 14 for some of my favorite restaurants for seafood.)

To many people, the word "seafood" equals "expensive." That's not necessarily so in Seattle. You can get a fine plate of fish and chips made from lingcod or halibut for under $6 at many places around the city (see Chapter 14 for more on quick and cheap eats), and the local clam chowder — a thick, creamy white soup laden with clams and potatoes — is a steal at under $3 a bowl. Even Dungeness crab can be had during the spring at ridiculously cheap prices: As low as $3.99 per pound at fishmarkets and supermarkets, both of which will clean your crab and sell you a cup of excellent cocktail sauce for a buck — the perfect Northwest picnic. (Look for more tips on saving money while still eating well, later in this chapter.)

Seattle's coffee fix

Seattleites love their coffee and develop strong loyalties to the local coffee shops and brands, whether it's Seattle's Best Coffee, Tully's Coffee, or Starbucks (otherwise known as McCoffee, thanks to their global expansion). Besides those Big Three, you'll find local chains like Uptown Espresso and Caffe Ladro dotted around town, as well as dozens of independent shops. In Seattle, expect to find a coffee bar or three on most major intersections of the city and drive-through espresso shacks serving up quick fixes of the local elixir. I list some of my favorites in Chapter 14.

Fresh from the farm to your table

Finally, I can't overemphasize the value of the **Pike Place Market** to the local culinary scene. It's so much more than just a tourist experience; it's the best place to find Washington fruits, fish, and vegetables in season. The success of the market has spawned satellite markets in neighborhoods around the city where farmers come to sell their produce. You can find them on weekends, during the summer and fall months, in the University District, Fremont, and South Seattle.

Dressing to Dine, Seattle Style

Seattle is utterly casual and informal in its attitudes toward dressing up to eat. I know of only one restaurant, **Canlis,** that even *suggests* that men wear a jacket to dinner. Ties are about as prevalent as spats. Even in upscale places like **El Gaucho,** which attracts a suit-and-tie crowd of attorneys and downtown professionals, it's not unusual to find a casual blue-jean and sweater crowd chowing down at the table next to the suits.

Indeed, you're more likely to feel out of place in most Seattle restaurants if you're overdressed, not underdressed. Dress casually and comfortably, and you should fit in fine nearly everywhere. If you're not sure what to wear, call the restaurant ahead of time.

Making Reservations

Seattle's best restaurants do fill up, especially on weekends, but you won't be shut out if your schedule is flexible. Lunch rarely calls for a reservation, and if you don't mind eating dinner before 7 p.m., you have a better chance of getting into a hot spot. You definitely need a reservation if you're trying to arrange seating for more than four diners at a time. Be sure to call ahead in any event, because sometimes a private party may take over a whole restaurant. If you have one or two eateries on your list that you absolutely don't want to miss, call ahead at least a week in advance to be sure to secure a table.

For a unique dining opportunity, check to see whether your restaurant offers a Chef's Table in the kitchen, where you can watch the staff prepare your dinner. You'll feel as if you have the whole place to yourself. Restaurants like **Buca di Beppo** and the **Georgian Room** have very popular Chef's Tables that sell out well in advance, and more restaurants are following suit.

Cost-Cutting Tips for Dining Out

It would be a pity to miss out on trying some Northwest food favorites like salmon, crab, and oysters because you're trying to keep food costs down. Spend your vacation eating at fast-food joints or national chains, and you miss a big part of what makes the Northwest unique. You can minimize your food costs by remembering some of the following suggestions and then use your savings to splurge for a fine meal:

- ✔ Coffee bars and espresso stands are cheap spots to go for breakfast, with muffins, rolls, and bagels available alongside the brew. Many stands also carry ready-made sandwiches and salads for lunch.

- ✔ Don't forget to take advantage of the continental breakfast if your hotel offers one.

- ✔ Kids are often perfectly happy with a big bowl of inexpensive cereal in the morning, with milk from any corner grocery store in the city.

- ✔ You can make one of your daily meals an inexpensive one by ordering takeout food, pizza, or sandwiches, or by grazing the inexpensive food stands at **Seattle Center,** the **Pike Place Market,** or **Westlake Center.**

- ✔ Seattle's supermarkets, such as **Safeway, QFC,** and **Thriftway,** have all expanded their ready-made-foods departments, with extensive offerings of inexpensive sandwiches, sushi, fresh soups and chili, and Chinese food. Buying a whole roasted chicken, fresh bread, tossed or prepared salads, and a pie for dessert is a delicious and cheap way to feed the family at a picnic in the park.

- ✔ Dungeness crabs are always cooked directly at sea when they're caught. You can save a bundle on restaurant prices by buying your crabs in season (September through May) from fish markets or supermarkets and making them the featured attraction of a picnic or in-room meal. Ask the store to clean your crab by removing its hard cap and washing out the insides; they should do it at no additional charge. Then crack the shells with your hands or a fork, and pick the meat out. It's delicious cold, especially with a zesty cocktail sauce.

Just as Seattle's hotels try to lure visitors with cost-cutting moves in the slower winter season, Seattle's restaurants offer seasonal promotions to diners. In March, some of the best restaurants in the city team up for the "25 for $25 Dine Around Seattle" promotion, when 25 restaurants offer a three-course prix fixe meal for $25 (not including beverages or tip) from Sunday to Thursday. You get to choose from a couple of appetizers, three or four entrees and a couple of desserts. It's an absolute steal of a deal when you consider that an entrée alone at some of these places costs more than $20 bucks. The promotion is often repeated in November. Check the Web sites of the **Seattle Post-Intelligencer** (www.seattle-pi.com) newspaper or the **Seattle-King County Convention & Visitors Bureau** (www.seattleinsider.com) to see whether restaurants are offering deals when you're coming to town.

Chapter 14

Seattle's Best Restaurants

. . . .

In This Chapter

▶ Discovering top restaurants in the city

▶ Listing restaurants by location, price, and the type of food served

▶ Finding snacks and quick bites

▶ Chowing down on oysters and eggs: The Northwest breakfast

▶ Getting your caffeine fix: A coffee bar on every corner

▶ Market-grazing and food for picnicking

. . . .

1 wish that you had a month in Seattle to try out all the restaurants that I recommend, though even a month isn't enough time to sample all the wonderful places the city has to offer. The dining scene here is varied, thriving, and very exciting — great chefs compete in this world-class culinary arena. Food is an important part of the local culture, and many places on this list represent the best in Northwest cuisine.

Each listing in this chapter includes typical prices for standard entrees, along with a quick-reference dollar sign guide to prices that follows these guidelines for a three-course meal of appetizer, entree, dessert, a beverage, and a tip (from 15 to 20 percent of the total check), per person:

$	Under $20 (cheap eats in a place with little or no decor)
$$	$20 to $30 (moderate prices for an ethnic dinner or a fancy lunch at a nice restaurant)
$$$	$30 to $40 (nicer decor and service and finer dining opportunities)
$$$$	$40 to $50 (top-of-the-line at most of the finer places)
$$$$$	More than $50 (most exclusive places in town, with multiple courses and great decor)

Downtown Seattle Dining

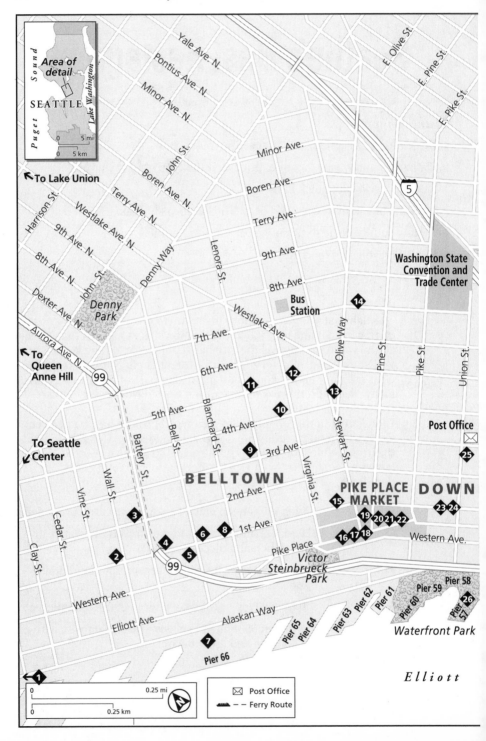

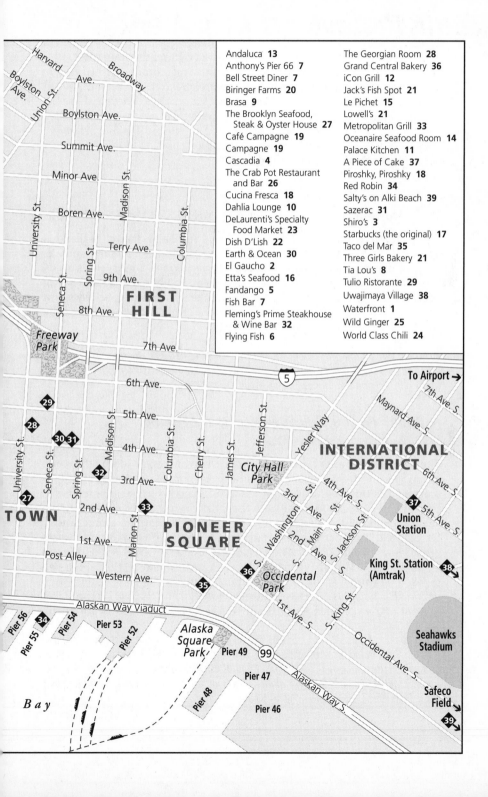

Andaluca **13**
Anthony's Pier 66 **7**
Bell Street Diner **7**
Biringer Farms **20**
Brasa **9**
The Brooklyn Seafood,
   Steak & Oyster House **27**
Café Campagne **19**
Campagne **19**
Cascadia **4**
The Crab Pot Restaurant
   and Bar **26**
Cucina Fresca **18**
Dahlia Lounge **10**
DeLaurenti's Specialty
   Food Market **23**
Dish D'Lish **22**
Earth & Ocean **30**
El Gaucho **2**
Etta's Seafood **16**
Fandango **5**
Fish Bar **7**
Fleming's Prime Steakhouse
   & Wine Bar **32**
Flying Fish **6**

The Georgian Room **28**
Grand Central Bakery **36**
iCon Grill **12**
Jack's Fish Spot **21**
Le Pichet **15**
Lowell's **21**
Metropolitan Grill **33**
Oceanaire Seafood Room **14**
Palace Kitchen **11**
A Piece of Cake **37**
Piroshky, Piroshky **18**
Red Robin **34**
Salty's on Alki Beach **39**
Sazerac **31**
Shiro's **3**
Starbucks (the original) **17**
Taco del Mar **35**
Three Girls Bakery **21**
Tia Lou's **8**
Tulio Ristorante **29**
Uwajimaya Village **38**
Waterfront **1**
Wild Ginger **25**
World Class Chili **24**

Seattle Restaurants from A to Z

In this section, I give you a good selection of different restaurants with varied cuisines and price ranges. None of the restaurants described here were thrown in just because they were cheap or offered an unusual type of food. Big chain restaurants aren't listed here either, because almost without exception they don't measure up to the quality and service that you get from an independent eatery. If money is a big consideration, see Chapter 13 for some tips on cutting food costs in order to maximize your food budget.

Andaluca

$$$$ **Downtown/Shopping District** **MEDITERRANEAN**

Dark and atmospheric, with carved booths and hand-painted walls, this restaurant is one of Seattle's finest for pan-Mediterranean fare, such as Spanish paellas, Italian risottos and bruschettas, and a marvelous appetizer of artfully prepared vegetables. You can easily make a meal out of several of the small plates from the "shareables" menu of appetizers. But then you'd miss out on the Spanish beef tenderloin entree with its exquisite Marsala glaze and side of grilled pears.

407 Olive Way at the Mayflower Park Hotel. ☎ *206-382-6999. Reservations recommended. Main courses: $18.50–$27.95. AE, DC, DISC, MC, V. Open: Daily 5–10 p.m. (to 11 p.m. Fri and Sat); lunch served Mon–Sat, 11:30 a.m.–2:30 p.m.*

Anthony's Pier 66, Bell Street Diner, and Fish Bar

$$$ **Waterfront** **SEAFOOD**

The three restaurants here, which are owned and operated by the same group, feature fresh, delicious seafood. Anthony's occupies the upper story of this bustling waterfront complex near the cruise ship terminal. Upscale, fresh seafood dishes are the stars at Anthony's, especially the salmon or halibut grilled on cedar planks (which impart a nice smoky flavor), and the Northwest Potlatch of shellfish. The restaurant boasts great views of Elliott Bay. The Bell Street Diner, at street level, offers a simpler seafood-intensive menu of salads, soups, and terrific, fresh fish tacos. The third venue in this culinary trinity is the walk-up Fish Bar, which sells fish and chips, Northwest chowder, and the like on the street in front of the complex. Kids usually enjoy meals at these restaurants.

2201 Alaskan Way at Pier 66. ☎ *206-448-6688. Reservations suggested at Anthony's Pier 66. Main courses: $8.95–$23.95. AE, MC, V. Open: Anthony's Pier 66 is open daily 5–9:30 p.m. (to 10 p.m. Fri and Sat, to 9 p.m. Sun); Bell Street Diner is open daily for lunch 11:30–3 p.m. and daily for dinner 3–10 p.m. (to 10:30 p.m. Fri and Sat, to 9 p.m. Sun); Fish Bar is open daily 11 a.m–5 p.m.*

Brasa
$$$$$ Belltown   CONTINENTAL

Enjoy one of Seattle's finest top-end meals from Tamara Murphy, formerly the executive chef at Campagne and one of most celebrated chefs in Seattle. Put yourself in Murphy's capable hands for dishes such as a roasted monkfish with gnocchi, or suckling pig served with chorizo and clams. Many dishes on the menu are cooked in the wood-fired oven (*brasa* is Portuguese for "live coals"). With co-owner Bryan Hill overseeing an eclectic wine list of hundreds of bottles from the Mediterranean region and pastry chef Valerie Mudry doing wonders with ice creams, brûlées, and chocolate creations, Brasa adds up to a memorable dining experience. One of Belltown's favorites, Brasa was named "Best Restaurant in Seattle" in *Food & Wine* magazine's 2000 Restaurant Poll.

2107 Third Ave., at Lenora Street. ☎ 206-728-4220. Reservations highly recommended. Main courses: $22–$30. AE, DC, DISC, MC, V. Open: Daily 5–10:30 p.m. (Fri–Sat to midnight).

The Brooklyn Seafood, Steak & Oyster House
$$ Downtown/Shopping District   SEAFOOD

This bustling businessmen's restaurant is a great place to try Northwest seafood, particularly oysters, which are served chilled on the half-shell and come from more than a dozen different producers, allowing you to taste the difference between a Quilcene and a Kumamoto. You also can't go wrong with the grilled fish or crab dishes. The restaurant is housed in one of the city's oldest buildings, giving it a historic, venerable look. The Oyster Bar is a great place for a happy-hour snack and microbrew.

1212 Second Ave., at University Street, near Benaroya Hall. ☎ 206-224-7000. Reservations not required. Main courses: $16–$34. AE, DC, DISC, MC, V. Open: Mon–Fri, 5–10 p.m. (to 10:30 p.m. Fri), Sat 4:30–10:30 p.m., Sun 4–10 p.m.; open for lunch Mon–Fri, 11 a.m.–3 p.m.

Buca di Beppo
$$ Lake Union   ITALIAN

I don't usually recommend chain restaurants, but I make an exception for Buca di Beppo, offshoots of which are springing up all over the country. Why? Because it's riotous fun, and the spaghetti-and-meatballs cuisine is done awfully well. Beppo's is a crowd-pleaser that kids adore, with kitschy decor and walls plastered with photos. The food comes in huge portions on platters, and if you order more than three dishes for six people, you end up taking food home — the meatballs are as big as softballs. Try the four-cheese pizza and linguine *frutti di mare*. For the ultimate experience, reserve the Pope's Room in advance (for parties of 8 or more), or the Kitchen Table, where you can watch the chefs cook.

701 Ninth Ave. N. at Roy Street. ☎ 206-244-2288. Limited reservations accepted, but call ahead to put your name on the seating list. Go early for the best chance for a short wait. Main courses: $15–$25, but they're made for 2 to 4 people each. AE, DC, DISC, MC, V. Open: Mon–Thurs, 5–10 p.m., Fri 5–11 p.m., Sat 4–11 p.m., Sun noon–10 p.m.

Cafe Juanita

$$$$ **Kirkland   NORTHERN ITALIAN**

I hesitate to send you across Lake Washington for food (the traffic can be brutal), but there's no denying that Chef Holly Smith is creating some of the most exquisite Italian food in town. You won't find a tomato on the menu most days, because Smith sticks to Northern Italian favorites like hand-cut tagliatelle pasta with local chanterelles, great risotto, and creamy fonduta cheese with bruschetta and white truffle oil. The ambience is warm and cozy, and the wine list is loaded with top bottles from the Piedmont region of Italy. Allow plenty of time for crossing the lake on the SR 520 bridge and plan to spend several hours eating your way through Smith's menu.

9702 NE 120th Place, Kirkland. Call for directions. ☎ 425-823-1505. Reservations required. Main courses: $15–$28. AE, DC, MC, V. Open Tues–Sun, 5–10 p.m. (Sun to 9 p.m.).

Campagne

$$$$ **Pike Place Market   COUNTRY FRENCH**

For 16 years, Campagne has been one of Seattle's favorite French bistros, making country French fare available to the whole family. As such, its fit in the Pike Place Market couldn't be better. Try the *tarte flamiche,* with leeks and bacon, or the three-course family dinners that may feature *poulet roti* (roast chicken) one night and steak frites another. The adjoining Café Campagne serves a bistro menu and packs them in for Sunday brunches of croque madames (ham and Gruyère on thick slices of fresh bread with a fried egg on top) and big bowls of coffee.

86 Pine St., at the Inn at the Market, between First Avenue and Pike Place. ☎ 206-728-2800. Reservations recommended. Main courses: $24–$30; prix fixe dinner: $45 per person. AE, DISC, MC, V. Open: Daily 5:30–10 p.m.

Canlis

$$$$ **Queen Anne   STEAK AND SEAFOOD**

One of Seattle's oldest fine-dining restaurants, Canlis was always the place to take Grandma out for a special dinner. Second-generation owners Chris and Alice Canlis have worked hard to bring the food and decor up to contemporary standards, and with the help of chef Greg Atkinson, they've succeeded. Views of Lake Union are memorable, and the service and wine list are impeccable. Come for filet mignon, Dungeness crabcakes, grilled salmon, or lamb chops, and finish things off with a fluffy soufflé.

2576 Aurora Ave. N., just before the Ship Canal Bridge, and reachable only on north-bound lanes. ☎ 206-283-3313. Reservations required; jackets advised for men. Main courses: $24–$41. AE, DC, DISC, MC, V. Open: Mon–Sat 5:30 p.m.–midnight.

Carmelita

$$$ **Fremont   VEGETARIAN**

Don't be frightened: The vegetarian menu here isn't just bean sprouts and lettuce leaves. The chefs at Carmelita fashion a thoughtful, interesting menu out of organic produce that is more about flavor than vegetarian dogma. Start out with a bowl of elephant-garlic potato soup served with truffled croutons and consider a homemade pizza topped with roasted eggplant or a red pepper tapenade. Entrees include pastas, gnocchis, and tofu dishes in generous portions. Set in two rooms that are elegantly decorated with paintings, Carmelita's is a vegetarian restaurant where you don't feel like looking for meat alongside the potatoes.

7314 Greenwood Ave. N., just past the west side of the zoo. ☎ 206-706-7703. Reservations recommended. Main courses: $13.95–$15.95. MC, V. Open: Tues–Sun 5–10 p.m. (to 10:45 p.m. on Fri and Sat).

Cascadia

$$$$$ **Belltown   CONTINENTAL/NORTHWEST**

This private venture by Aussie chef Kerry Sears and his hostess wife, Heidi Grathwol, gets it all right. The idea was to apply Kerry's "fine-dining" cooking skills to ingredients that come only from the Pacific Northwest. The result is a sensational series of tasting menus that may include baked mussels with leek sauce and stuffed mushrooms, an herb-baked partridge with blackberry reduction, or a perfect sage crêpe in a wine demiglaze. Whimsical touches like a "chocolate catch of the day" for dessert or the sensational mushroom soup served from a can (which Sears also designed) keep this place fun. The room is a cool, flowing space of hardwoods and cut glass. Cascadia has been one of the top tables in town since it opened in 1999, and it hasn't slipped an inch since. The prix fixe menus are the way to go, but feel free to mix and match from the many categories of food. Portions are small, and five courses just begin to satisfy big eaters. Early birds get great deals on a three-course meal.

2328 First Ave., between Bell and Battery streets. ☎ 206-448-8884. Reservations recommended. Main courses: $28–$30; 6- and 7-course tasting menus run $65–$90. AE, DC, DISC, MC, V. Open: Mon–Sat, 5–10 p.m. (to 10:30 p.m. Fri and Sat).

Seattle Dining — North & Northeast

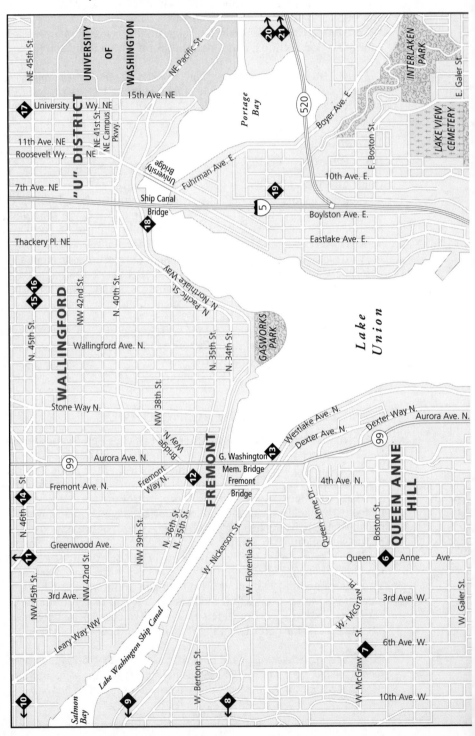

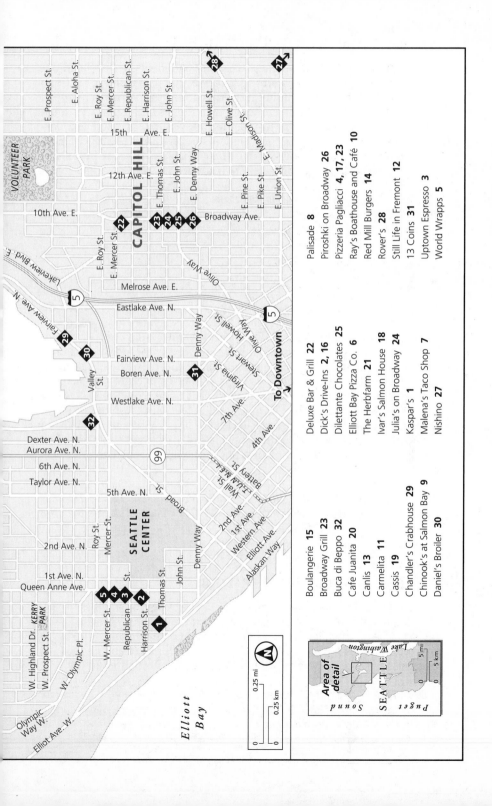

Palisade **8**
Piroshki on Broadway **26**
Pizzeria Pagliacci **4, 17, 23**
Ray's Boathouse and Café **10**
Red Mill Burgers **14**
Rover's **28**
Still Life in Fremont **12**
13 Coins **31**
Uptown Espresso **3**
World Wrapps **5**

Deluxe Bar & Grill **22**
Dick's Drive-Ins **2, 16**
Dilettante Chocolates **25**
Elliott Bay Pizza Co. **6**
The Herbfarm **21**
Ivar's Salmon House **18**
Julia's on Broadway **24**
Kaspar's **1**
Malena's Taco Shop **7**
Nishino **27**

Boulangerie **15**
Broadway Grill **23**
Buca di Beppo **32**
Cafe Juanita **20**
Canlis **13**
Carmelita **11**
Cassis **19**
Chandler's Crabhouse **29**
Chinook's at Salmon Bay **9**
Daniel's Broiler **30**

0.25 mi
0.25 km

Area of detail

Puget Sound
SEATTLE
Lake Washington
5 mi
5 km

Cassis

$$$ Capitol Hill COUNTRY FRENCH

French farmhouse cooking comes to a quiet corner of Capitol Hill in the form of this charming little bistro that serves up big, satisfying portions of classic French food. A different French country favorite is featured each weekday, such as a rich cassoulet on Sundays and rabbit with mustard on Wednesdays. The early-evening three-course prix fixe is a bargain at $24. The room is small and loud, and tables are close together, so be prepared to bump elbows with other diners as you tuck into steak frites, braised wild boar, or fragrant fish soup.

2359 Tenth Ave. East about a half-mile north of the Broadway retail district. ☎ 206-329-0580. Reservations recommended. Main courses: $17–$22; 3-course prix fixe 5–7 p.m: $24. AE, MC, V. Open: Daily 5–10 p.m. (Fri and Sat to 11 p.m.).

Chandler's Crabhouse

$$ Lake Union SEAFOOD

Great views of Lake Union and the yachts moored at Chandler's Cove are the draw at this venerable old place. Unfortunately, the food and decor leave something to be desired. The interior is rather dark and cramped, and the dishes aren't very imaginative. However, the whiskeyed crab soup is very good, and you can get a nice sampling of Northwest seafood like wild steelhead trout and several preparations of crab. This place is one of the few in town that bring in soft-shell crabs from the East Coast in season. Kids can choose from a good selection of fish and nonfish dishes; get them to finish their meal with the promise of a slice of banana cream pie for dessert. Crabby Hour Specials of drinks and appetizer-sized dishes are served in the renovated bar in the afternoons and after 9:30 p.m.

901 Fairview Ave. N. at the southeast end of Lake Union. ☎ 206-223-2722. Reservations suggested. Main courses: $16–$28. Open: Daily 11:30a.m.–10 p.m. (to 11 p.m. Fri & Sat). AE, DC, DISC, MC, V.

Chinook's at Salmon Bay

$$ Magnolia NORTHWEST/SEAFOOD

A working fishing-boat anchorage is the perfect setting for this bright, bustling restaurant that specializes in oyster stews, clam chowders, and big servings of fresh salmon and halibut that come on plates piled with roasted potatoes and vegetables. The fish and chips are among the best in town, and salads and sandwiches are available for lighter eaters.

1900 W. Nickerson St. at Fisherman's Terminal (exit Elliott Avenue W. just before the Ballard Bridge). ☎ 206-283-HOOK. Reservations not necessary. Main courses: $8–$15. Open: Daily from 4 p.m.; lunch served Mon–Fri, 11 a.m.–4 p.m. and Sat 11:30 a.m.–4 p.m.; breakfast served Sat and Sun, 7:30 a.m.–11:30 a.m. AE, MC, V.

The Crab Pot Restaurant and Bar
$$ Waterfront   SEAFOOD

For those who like to have their seafood dumped onto the table in a big mess of corn-on-the-cob, red potatoes, and chunks of sausage, this tourist spot at Pier 57 is your place. In fact, it's the only place in Seattle that offers this kind of butcher-block-paper East-Coast-fish-house presentation. You'll get better shellfish, halibut, and salmon elsewhere, but it's good, plentiful, and cheap here, and kids do love whacking crab claws with wooden mallets (doesn't everyone?). You can choose from a large selection of burgers and sandwiches, too.

Pier 57, Alaskan Way (next door to the Seattle Aquarium). ☎ *206-624-1890. Reservations not accepted. "Seafeasts": $12.45–$29.95/person for two or more. AE, MC, V. Open: Daily 11 a.m.–9 p.m. (to 10 p.m. Sat).*

Dahlia Lounge
$$$ Belltown   NORTHWEST FUSION

Local star Tom Douglas moved this, his first solo restaurant in Seattle (out of the three that he now operates), to a bigger, better space in Belltown in 2000, and the restaurant benefits greatly from the upgrade. The menu still features the most sensational crabcakes in town, along with Asian-influenced meat and fish dishes. The Sea Bar offers a variety of fresh seafood with interesting sauces. The coconut-cream pie is a local legend, with shavings of white chocolate and coconut cascading off the plate. If you need an extra fix of pie, it's now available at a bakery that Douglas opened alongside the restaurant.

2001 Fourth Ave. at Virginia Street. ☎ *206-682-4142. Reservations recommended. Main courses: $16–$31. AE, DC, DISC, MC, V. Open: Mon–Sat, 5:30–10 p.m. (to 11 p.m. on Fri and Sat); Sun 5–9 p.m.; lunch served Mon–Fri, 11:30 a.m.–2:30 p.m.*

Daniel's Broiler
$$$ Lake Union   STEAK

You can see fine views of Lake Union if you can tear yourself away from your huge slab of prime beef, which has been cooked to perfection under an 1800-degree broiler. This classic, locally owned steakhouse is all dark woods and fabrics. The meat is outstanding, and you can dress it up with peppercorn brandy sauce, bleu cheese sauce, or béarnaise sauce. Wine coordinator Michael Hanke can fix you up with the right bottle of Northwest wine from an outstanding list of more than 300 wines. If humanly possible, save room for warm chocolate cake at the end.

809 Fairview Pl. N. at the southeast end of Lake Union. ☎ *206-621-8262. Reservations recommended. Main courses: $26.95–$39.95. AE, DC, DISC, MC, V. Open: Daily 5 p.m.–10 p.m. (Fri & Sat to 11 p.m.).*

Dick's Drive-Ins

$ **Queen Anne, Ballard, and Wallingford   BURGERS**

Seattle's local hamburger joint competes with the national fast-food chains to offer cut-rate burgers, fries, and terrific milkshakes made with real milk. Try a Dick's Deluxe burger (a Big Mac by any other name) and a thick chocolate shake to fuel up for a day of sightseeing or revive after a night of dancing. Dick's does right by the locals: The kids who work here are eligible for college scholarships, so order an extra side of fries.

500 Queen Anne Ave. N., at Republican Street. ☎ 206-285-5155; 9208 Holman Rd. in north Ballard (15th Avenue NW becomes Holman above 90th Street). ☎ 206-783-5233; 111 NE 45th St., in Wallingford between 1st and 2nd avenues NE. ☎ 206-632-5125. Burgers and shakes under $3 each. No credit cards. Open: Daily 10:30 a.m.–2 a.m.

Earth & Ocean

$$$$$ **Downtown/Shopping District   CONTINENTAL**

If you tried this fancy place when it first opened at the W Seattle and vowed never to return, think again. Chef Johnathan Sundstrom turned it around, and it has become one of the top destinations for Seattle's most discriminating diners. Buying locally and thinking globally, Sundstrom creates dishes like seared foie gras with a salt-roasted white peach, exquisite sea urchin flan served in an eggshell, and a perfect New Zealand venison chop dusted with fennel pollen and served in a rich red-wine reduction. Pastry chef Sue McCown is known (and loved) locally for whipping up exotic desserts with funny names like "Snap Crackle Pop Cherry Pop Tart" (a pastry crust with sweet and sour cherry filling, served with lemon crème fraiche sorbet). It all adds up to a lavish, blow-the-budget meal.

1112 Fourth Ave. (at the W Hotel). ☎ 206-264-6060. Reservations recommended. Main courses: $19–$29. AE, DC, DISC, MC, V. Open: Breakfast 6:30 a.m.–10:30 a.m. Mon–Fri; 7:30 a.m.–11:30 a.m. Sat & Sun; Lunch 11:30 a.m.–2 p.m. Mon–Fri; Dinner: 5 p.m.–10 p.m. Mon–Thurs; to 10:30 Fri & Sat.

El Gaucho

$$$$ **Belltown   STEAK**

Seattle's favorite place to tuck into a slab of beef is this big, cavernous dining room in Belltown, featuring elegant waiters dressed in livery who attend to your every need. The meat is sensational, with classic cuts of sirloin, porterhouse, lamb, and veal chops. The tableside service of desserts, like bananas Foster or flaming Spanish coffees, are nearly worth the considerable price. Plan to eat big and spend big. The bar area is one of Belltown's liveliest for the after-work business crowd, and downstairs, the Pampas Room nightclub has live music and dancing most nights.

2505 First Ave. at Wall Street. ☎ 206-728-1337. Reservations recommended. Main courses: $13.50–$39. AE, DC, MC, V. Open: Daily 5 p.m.–2 a.m. (Sun to 11 p.m.).

Etta's Seafood
$$$ **Pike Place Market   SEAFOOD**

Named for chef/owner Tom Douglas's daughter, this one is the third in Douglas's triumvirate of excellent local restaurants. This place is devoted to seafood with an Asian flavor. Douglas's famous crab cakes are available, and other stars include a whole crisy tilapia served with edamame beans, and a spice-rubbed king salmon served with cornbread pudding. As always, the coconut cream pie for dessert is worth the price of parking.

2020 Western Ave., at the north end of the Pike Place Market. ☎ *206-443-6000. Reservations recommended. Main courses: $17–$26. AE, DC, DISC, MC, V. Open: Lunch 11:30 a.m. –4 p.m., Mon-Fri; Dinner daily 4 p.m.–9:30 p.m., (Sun to 9 p.m.; Fri & Sat to 10:30 p.m.).*

Fandango
$$$ **Belltown   LATIN**

Christine Keff, who made her name in Seattle with nearby Flying Fish, opened this bright, fun restaurant to bring a little needed culinary diversity to the local dining scene. The result is a menu of Latin dishes rarely seen in these parts, such as a Brazilian crab soup, oxtail stew served with plantains and yucca, and a rich vegetarian *posole* stew from Mexico. True to form, the locals are eating it up, solidifying Fandago's success on the Belltown restaurant scene.

2313 First Ave. between Bell and Battery streets. ☎ *206-441-1188. Reservations recommended. Main courses: $14.85–$18.95. AE, DC, MC, V. Open: Daily 5 p.m.–midnight.*

Fleming's Prime Steakhouse & Wine Bar
$$$$ **Downtown/Shopping District   STEAK**

A great location puts this urban steakhouse at the top of the heap of recent additions to the local steak scene. The handsome room in the Expediter building has comfortable booths, high ceilings, and large windows looking out over Madison Street. The filet mignon and strip steaks are perfectly broiled, and appetizers of Dungeness crab or sauteed scallops are a delicious way to whet your palate for the meat. A wine list with more than 100 wines by the glass allows you to easily explore Northwest wines.

1001 Third Ave. at Madison Street. ☎ *206-587-5300. Reservations recommended. Main courses: $17.50–$26.95. AE, DC, MC, V. Open: Daily 5–10 p.m. (to 11 p.m. Fri and Sat).*

Flying Fish
$$ **Belltown   SEAFOOD**

Northwest seafood meets Asian preparation styles in this chic, crowded restaurant. Flying Fish is practically the grande dame of Belltown's hot restaurant scene now, drawing a hip young Belltown crowd. Christine Keff brought her flair and considerable cooking talents to this, her first solo restaurant. People come for the ambience and dishes like a perfectly seared ahi tuna and Northwest steelhead spiced with Asian accents. An "Oyster Happy Hour" brings out the best shellfish in the region and accompanies the crustaceans with crisp, white wines. Desserts are worth waiting for. In the summer, the whole scene spills out onto sidewalk tables.

2234 First Ave. at Bell Street. ☎ *206-728-8595. Reservations recommended. Main courses: $9–$17. AE, DC, MC, V. Open: Daily 5 p.m.–1 a.m.*

The Georgian Room
$$$$ **Downtown/Shopping District   CONTINENTAL**

Under the tutelage of chef Gavin Stephenson, this fine-dining room at the Four Seasons Olympic delivers expert preparations of standards like grilled salmon, rack of lamb, and beef tenderloin. The room is everything you'd want from an urban oasis, all vaulted ceilings and high windows dressed in long drapes. If you want to impress your clients, book (well in advance) the chef's table in the kitchen, which gives a small group a close-up view of the cooks at work.

411 University St. at the Four Seasons Olympic Hotel. ☎ *206-621-7889. Reservations recommended. Main courses: $26–$38. Open: Mon–Sat, 5:30–10 p.m. (to 10:30 p.m. Fri and Sat); Sun brunch 7 a.m.–1 p.m. AE, DC, MC, V.*

The Herbfarm
$$$$$ **Woodinville   CONTINENTAL**

Have five hours to spend on dinner? This lavish restaurant in the eastside suburbs has long been a favorite of Seattle gourmands who like to linger over a long, expensive, delectable dinner. Sign up for a nine-course, five-wine feast prepared by resident genius Jerry Traunfeld, who dazzles with exotic preparations of foodstuffs you may never have heard of, like wild stinging nettles or fiddlehead ferns foraged locally or grown in the lovely gardens adjacent to the restaurant. Stagger to a bed in the Willows Lodge, across the parking lot, when you're done.

14590 NE 145th St., Woodinville. ☎ *425-485-5300. Reservations required. Nine-course prix fixe menus: $159–$189, including wine. AE, DC, MC, V. Open: Thurs–Sun at 7 p.m. (one seating only); Sun at 4:30 p.m.*

iCon Grill
$$$ **Downtown/Shopping District   REGIONAL AMERICAN**

The decor declares that the place is pure fun, with dozens of blown-glass balls hanging in nets and small lamps dotting nearly every available surface. Don't miss the hysterical treatments accorded the bathrooms, with dramatic music and video screens running clips of gushing waterfalls. And the food? It's an equally entertaining mix of comfort foods (even macaroni and cheese and meatloaf) and standards like broiled salmon and merlot-braised lamb shank.

1933 Fifth Ave. at Virginia Street. ☎ ***206-441-6330****. Reservations recommended. Main courses: $10–$27. AE, MC, V. Open: Daily 5:30–9 p.m. (to 10 p.m. Tues–Thurs, and to 11 p.m. Fri and Sat); lunch served Mon–Fri 11:30 a.m.–2 p.m.*

Ivar's Salmon House
$$ Lake Union   SEAFOOD

Ivar's fish and chips shops pop up all around the city, thanks to a local restaurateur who staked his clams (er, claim) here to inexpensive seafood. This flagship restaurant, located on a quiet stretch of Lake Union waterfront near Gasworks Park, is decorated to look like an American Indian longhouse, with totem poles, a long canoe, and an open-pit area where salmon is cooked on alderwood. Yes, the fish and chips are first-rate, and Ivar's has always made one of the best clam chowders in town — but it's the flavorful salmon that is the real hit here.

401 NE Northlake Way between Fremont and the University District on the north shore of Lake Union. ☎ ***206-632-0767****. Reservations recommended. AE, MC, V. Main courses: $12–$30. Open: Mon–Sat, 11 a.m.–10 p.m. (to 11 p.m. Fri and Sat); Sun 10 a.m.–2 p.m. for brunch and 3:30–10 p.m. for dinner.*

Julia's on Broadway
$$$ Capitol Hill   REGIONAL AMERICAN

Bare brick walls and oversized chandeliers give this Capital Hill restaurant a bluesy, urban, supper club atmosphere. Live jazz is featured on the weekends, and the menu shifts easily from sumptuous breakfasts of fresh juice and housemade muffins in the mornings to full lunches to dinners featuring pastas (the shrimp and ginger ravioli is particularly delightful), main course salads (try the Caesar with shrimp), and grilled fish and meats.

300 E. Broadway across from Broadway Market. ☎ ***206-860-1818****. Reservations recommended. AE, MC, V. Main courses: $12–$16. Open: Daily 8 a.m.–10 p.m.*

Kaspar's
$$$ Queen Anne   CONTINENTAL

A favorite of many locals, this homey place is situated on a quiet Queen Anne street. It's presided over by chef Kaspar Donier, who serves an eclectic continental menu that focuses on seafood and fresh, local products. Try Donier's chef's table in the kitchen for a very personal dining experience or hit the wine bar for excellent, low-priced bites and glasses of wine.

19 W. Harrison St. ☎ 206-298-0123. Reservations recommended. Main courses: $15–$23. AE, MC, V. Open: Tues–Sat, 5–9 p.m. (to 10 p.m. Fri and Sat).

Le Pichet
$$$ **Pike Place Market   FRENCH**

The perfect little French bistro has arrived in Seattle. This delightful *boite* opens up in the morning serving croissants and coffee and closes late at night after patrons have finished the last portions of mussels and fries. Try a slice of French farmhouse cheese to go with the little pitchers of wine for which the restaurant is named. For dinner, some star dishes include the excellent roasted chicken, the charcuterie plate, and the hearty bowl of onion soup. Chow down and thank the French for unassuming neighborhood restaurants where food is simple and delicious.

1933 First Ave. alongside the Pike Place Market. ☎ 206-256-1499. Reservations recommended for dinner. Main courses: $13–$30. AE, DC, MC, V. Open: Daily 8 a.m.–midnight (to 2 a.m. Fri and Sat).

Metropolitan Grill
$$$$ **Downtown/Shopping District   STEAK**

This downtown steakhouse is favored by businesspeople as well as local and visiting athletes. Huge slabs of 28-day aged beef are cooked to perfection over a mesquite grill. The Met also offers excellent preparations of halibut, wild king salmon, and jumbo prawns. A chateaubriand for two, carved tableside, makes for a romantic feast, and if you're in a martini mood, the bar stocks 41 different kinds of vodkas and a dozen gins.

820 Second Ave. at Marion Street. ☎ 206-624-3287. Reservations recommended. Main courses: $23.95–$42.95. AE, DC, DISC, MC, V. Open: Dinner daily 5 p.m.–11 p.m. (to 10 p.m. Sun); Lunch Mon–Fri 11 a.m.–3 p.m.

Nishino
$$$ **Madison Park   SUSHI**

A favorite of high-rollers and Microsofties (original vice president of sales Scott Oki is a co-owner), this is one of the top spots in town for sushi and Japanese food, thanks to the talents of Japanese chef Tatsu Nishino. Try the Arboretum Roll, named after the nearby park, for a pairing of avocado, rice, and the freshest fish. The $60 prix fixe *omakase* (chef's choice) meal makes a believer out of anyone who harbors doubts as to the splendors of Japanese cuisine. Expensive but exquisite.

3130 E. Madison St. near Lake Washington. ☎ 206-322-5800. Reservations required. Main courses: $4–$17; sushi $2.50–$7 a pair. AE, MC, V. Open: Daily 5:30–10:30 p.m. (Sun to 9 p.m.).

Oceanaire Seafood Room

$$$$ **Downtown /Shopping District   SEAFOOD**

This new and highly welcome addition to the local dining scene brings a "big steakhouse" concept to seafood, with a decor of dark wood and plush booths. Chef Kevin Davis exquisitely prepares fresh fish that's flown in daily from the four corners of the world. His jumbo lump crabcakes are unlike anything else in town, as are the excellent pink scallops with andouille sausage. Other superb dishes include halibut cheeks with a lemon piccata, as well as sesame-seared black cod. Don't miss the kobe-style melt-in-your-mouth beef served with crispy oysters. The wine list is not as extensive as you may expect, but it does include 20 wines by the glass.

1700 Seventh Ave. across from Pacific Place. ☎ *206-267-BASS. Reservations recommended. Main courses: $16.95–$34.95. AE, DC, DISC, MC, V. Open: Mon–Fri 11:30 a.m.–10 p.m. (to 11 p.m. Fri); Sat 5 p.m.–11 p.m., Sun 5 p.m.–10 p.m.*

Palace Kitchen

$$$ **Downtown   REGIONAL AMERICAN**

Local star Tom Douglas's base of operations is also his hippest restaurant, staying open late into the evening to serve an eager club-going crowd. The kitchen is open and bustling into the wee hours. Try Douglas's signature Burger Royale, the grilled salmon, or a plate of artisan cheeses. The big, horseshoe-shaped bar is a premier see-and-be-seen place in town. As you munch, check out the huge wall mural of a bustling, medieval palace kitchen.

2030 Fifth Ave. ☎ *206-448-2001. Reservations recommended. Main courses: $10–$23. AE, DISC, MC, V. Open: Daily 5 p.m.–2 a.m.*

Palisade

$$$ **Magnolia   SEAFOOD**

It's a bit hard to find, but this gorgeous, sprawling restaurant is well worth the drive to Elliott Bay Marina. Outside are views of the Olympic Mountains and ferries skimming Puget Sound; inside are slate floors and an enormous saltwater fishpond with anemones and trout. Seafood is the order of the day, and the kitchen frequently offers selections from all over the world, such as prawnlike Moreton Bay Bugs (a saltwater shellfish from Australia). Northwest salmon and oysters are always on the menu. Sunday brunches are a good buy, with a fruit (and chocolate) buffet to go with your breakfast entree.

2601 W. Marina Place at Elliott Bay Marina; exit Elliott Avenue for the Magnolia Bridge and follow the signs to the marina. ☎ *206-285-1000. Reservations recommended. Main courses: $15–$33. AE, DC, DISC, MC, V. Open: Mon–Sat 5:30–9:30 p.m. (to 10 p.m. on Fri and Sat), Sun brunch 10 a.m.–2 p.m. and dinner 4–9 p.m.; lunch Mon–Fri 11:30 a.m.–2 p.m., Sat 12–2 p.m.*

Ray's Boathouse and Cafe

$$$ **Ballard** **SEAFOOD**

A splendid view of Puget Sound and the Olympic Mountains draws flocks of diners to this popular seafood restaurant near the Ballard Locks. Downstairs is a fine-dining restaurant specializing in salmon, clams, and other seafood, all prepared exquisitely. The downstairs restaurant has a flair for tasty sauces (try the buttery black cod in a sake kasu sauce — it's a house specialty). Upstairs is a bit more casual and cheaper, with a menu that leans toward salmon burgers and lingcod fish and chips. The outdoor deck is a huge hit during the summer months. Waiting times can be long and service spotty, so I don't recommend this place for families with restless kids.

6049 Seaview NW, past the Ballard Locks. ☎ *206-789-3770. Reservations recommended; drop-in chances are better for the upstairs bistro. Main courses: $16–$45 (boathouse); $9–$17 (cafe). AE, DC, DISC, MC, V. Open: Daily 11:30 a.m.–10 p.m.*

Rover's

$$$$$ **Madison Park** **FRENCH**

This may well be the best restaurant in town, at least according to the readers and food editors of *Seattle Magazine.* I certainly wouldn't argue the point. Chef Thierry Rautureau, a transplanted Frenchman, gets national recognition for his exciting, classically based French cooking. The setting is a handsome frame house in an affluent neighborhood, and the excellent service and Rautureau's ready smile make you feel like part of the family. Some of his meals, such as the 11-course Halloween feast with chef and diners *en costume,* are legendary and sell out close to a year in advance. On any ordinary night, though, you select a prix fixe menu and watch as an array of wonders arrives at your table. Examples are spot prawns with foie gras and a celeriac puree, a perfect squab breast with caramelized turnips and Armagnac sauce, and scallops with foie gras in a chestnut puree — heavenly. Pair an eight-course chef's menu with Northwest and French wines for each course, and you'll reach dining Nirvana.

2808 E. Madison St. ☎ *206-325-7442. Reservations required. Main courses: Five-course tasting menu $69.50; eight-course menu $97.50. AE, DC, MC, V. Open: Tues–Sat, 5:30–9:30 p.m.*

Salty's on Alki Beach

$$$ **West Seattle** **SEAFOOD**

The food isn't the reason that people make the trek to this eatery in the bedroom community of West Seattle; it's the view. Seattle's downtown skyline is visible in full panoramic splendor from Salty's dining room and outdoor deck, and the basic menu of salmon, fish and chips, and steamed clams go down easily. This place is very popular in the summer months when the deck is open. Try to hold out for a table after dusk (which can be 9 p.m. or later in the middle of summer) for the best view of the city skyline.

1936 Harbor Ave. SW. Take the West Seattle Bridge exit on I-5 or Rte. 99 south and then the first exit in West Seattle to reach Alki Beach. ☎ *206-937-1085. Reservations recommended. Main courses: $17.50–$36. AE, DISC, MC, V. Open: Dinner daily 5–10 p.m. (Sat from 4–10 p.m. and Sun from 4–9 p.m.); lunch Mon–Fri 11 a.m.–2:30 p.m., Sat noon–3 p.m.; Sun brunch 9 a.m.–2 p.m. In summer, Salty's keeps later hours; call for times.*

Sazerac

$$$ Downtown/Shopping District   CAJUN

A San Francisco-style restaurant attached to the Hotel Monaco, Sazerac is a big, exuberant place with vivid murals, artful chandeliers, and an open kitchen that produces huge portions of Cajun-style comfort foods. Chefs Jan ("The Big Dog") Birnbaum and Jason McClure get it all just right: The jambalaya and fried catfish are terrific, and steak is presented in thick slabs smothered in a spicy sauce. The small bar area is a lively meeting place during happy hours. The restaurant is named after a New Orleans cocktail of whiskey and Pernod. Try one: It will put you in the festive, Sazerac mood.

1101 Fourth Ave. at Spring Street, adjacent to the Hotel Monaco. ☎ *206-624-7755. Reservations recommended. Main courses: $10–$25. AE, DISC, MC, V. Open: Dinner Mon–Thurs 5–10 p.m. (Fri and Sat 5–11 p.m.); lunch Mon–Sat 11:30 a.m.–2:30 p.m.; breakfast Mon–Fri 6:30–10 a.m., Sat and Sun 7–10:30 a.m.; Sun brunch 9 a.m.–2:30 p.m.*

Shiro's

$$ Belltown   SUSHI

Japanese chef Shiro Kashiba is the undisputed master of preparing fresh sushi in Seattle. He earned his stripes at the Nikko restaurant at the Westin before striking out on his own with this small, crowded Belltown restaurant that packs them in every night for exquisite sushi preparations. Get there early to avoid the masses, and if Shiro says, "Try the mackerel," don't think twice. The man has an eye for fresh fish, and his diners are the better for it.

2401 Second Ave. at Battery Street. ☎ *206-443-9844. Reservations recommended. Main courses: $16–$20.50. AE, MC, V. Open: Mon–Sat 5:30–10 p.m., Sun 4:30–9 p.m.*

Tia Lou's

$ Belltown   MEXICAN

Jumping to the top of the under-represented Mexican and Tex-Mex scene in town, this newish Belltown joint does fine work with green chile stews, homemade tamales, and a bracing *pozole* (a hominy and roasted pork stew). Named for the grandmother of the owners, the food is simple, spicy, and authentic, with fresh tortillas and pico de gallo and a raft of margaritas to wash it all down.

2218 First Ave. at Blanchard Street. ☎ *206-733-8226. Reservations recommended. Main courses: $9.95–$16.95. AE, D, MC, V. Open: Tues–Fri lunch 11:30 a.m.–2 p.m.; Tues–Sat dinner 5 p.m.–10 p.m.*

Tulio Ristorante
$$$ **Downtown Shopping District   NORTHERN ITALIAN**

Chef Walter Pisano named this place after his Italian father, and fittingly, Tulio's has the atmosphere of a warm, family gathering. Sometimes Tulio himself is on hand to greet guests. The fare is elegantly prepared Northern Italian, with some standout dishes that linger in the memory, such as smoked salmon ravioli and sweet-potato gnocchi. Service is top-notch. Larger parties should try to reserve the private banquet table located on the mezzanine above the somewhat crowded main dining room.

1100 Fifth Ave. at Seneca Street at the Hotel Vintage Park. ☎ *206-624-5500. Reservations recommended. Main courses: $12–$24. AE, DC, DISC, MC, V. Open: Daily 5–10 p.m. (to 11 p.m. Fri and Sat); lunch served Mon–Fri, 11 a.m.–2 p.m., Sat and Sun, noon–3 p.m.*

Waterfront
$$$$ **Waterfront   NORTHWEST FUSION**

This spacious and airy eatery at the north end of the commercial zone is an upscale restaurant situated among many tourist traps. The kitchen focuses on basic seafood fusion, with fish served in Asian preparations (such as a Thai seafood stew), but the menu offers something for everyone, including thick steaks patterned after the fare at sister restaurant El Gaucho. While the prices suggest something very special, you won't find it in the food; the real hit here is the view — a deck surrounding the restaurant and suspended over Elliott Bay offers wonderful, breezy walks. The long, curving bar is becoming a favorite meeting place.

2801 Alaskan Way at Pier 70 at the north end of the downtown waterfront. ☎ *206-956-9171. Reservations recommended. Main courses: $26.50–$39. AE, DC, MC, V. Open: Daily 5–10 p.m. (to 10:30 p.m. Fri and Sat).*

Wild Ginger
$$$ **Downtown/Shopping District   ASIAN**

Seattle's favorite Asian fusion restaurant didn't miss a beat when it moved to spacious new quarters near Benaroya Hall in 2000. People still flock to get their hands on delicious Thai satays, Seven Flavors Soup, and exquisite preparations of duck. It remains a tough reservation to get, and the service staff isn't any friendlier, but after you get in and get seated, you're bound to be satisfied with the flavors and artful presentations.

1401 Third Ave. at Union Street. ☎ *206-623-4450. Reservations recommended. Main courses: $8.50–$21. AE, DC, DISC, MC. Open: Mon–Sat 11:30 a.m.–1 a.m., Sun 4:30 p.m.–1 a.m.*

Serendipity in a savory bowl of soup

In this chapter, I barely scratch the surface of the extensive number of eating opportunities in Seattle. When it comes down to it, however, sometimes the most fun part of a trip is seeking out and finding your own favorite place. Serendipity in Seattle comes in many forms: in a savory bowl of soup at a plant-filled coffeehouse, in a basket of fish and chips at the Pike Place Market, or in a sexy little tapas bar along a side street. Check out the following neighborhoods, all of which offer plenty of opportunities to discover your own great place or simply to enjoy a quick bite as you look around.

On **Capitol Hill,** the food is mostly concentrated on the retail strip of Broadway between Pike Street and Roy Street. Pizza, great burgers, and ethnic food that includes good Thai, Mexican, and Mongolian barbecue are all available here.

The **Fremont** neighborhood has plenty of good places to grab a bite as you stroll around the kitschy antique shops and gaze at the public art. Look for the Still Life in Fremont coffeehouse for vegetarian fare, great soups, and homemade pastries and cookies. The area also boasts two good Thai places, a Greek spot, a Mexican spot, pizza places, and a restaurant solely devoted to desserts (and they are great desserts). Of course, the bars and brewpubs that cater to college students and neighborhood regulars all have good eats, too. At the top of the hill, a few blocks south of the zoo, the Marketime grocery store has great prepared sandwiches and salads.

The **Wallingford** shopping district on NE 45th Street houses a great variety of medium-priced restaurants. You find a stretch of ethnic restaurants in a five-block area, including a Pakistani place, curry houses, a Japanese noodle and sushi place, and a Spanish tapas restaurant. Look in the Wallingford Center shopping center, housed in a former public grade school, for several good choices. The grocery store on the corner of Wallingford Avenue has prepared foods (you can take them to the park a block south for a picnic), and the bakery on NE 45th has portion-size packages of cheese and pâtés to go with its bread and croissants.

In the **Queen Anne** neighborhood, look to both the lower and upper parts of Queen Anne Avenue N. for lots of inexpensive food shops. You have your choice of submarine sandwiches, wraps, Italian food, a Chinese buffet, and a place that brags about its New York-style bagels. The coffee shops here have terrific desserts, too.

On the Lighter Side: Top Picks for Breakfast, Snacks, and Meals on the Go

If you'd rather spend your time (and money) in Seattle on the go rather than sitting down to elaborate meals, you're in no way out of luck, nor do you have to resort to eating all your meals under the Golden Arches. Here are some worthy alternatives for finding quick bites and food on the run, including spots that sell foods that are specific to this region, and Park Place Market, one of the great grazing opportunities in the world. And lest I forget coffee, the favored snack food around here, here are some good tips on finding plenty of that famous Seattle brew.

Breakfast on the half-shell

The standard bacon, egg, and pancake breakfast gets a Northwest lift when you substitute the region's favorite local mollusk, the Puget Sound oyster, for the meat. Oysters and eggs, also called the "Hangtown Fry" on menus, makes for a delicious, briny breakfast with toast and hash browns. Look for it on the menu at the **Bay Cafe** (Fisherman's Terminal in Magnolia; ☎ 206-282-3435), a bustling diner with windows overlooking the Alaskan fishing fleet. In the Pike Place Market, check out **Lowell's** (1519 Pike Place; ☎ 206-622-2036), an aging institution with great views of Elliott Bay. You order breakfast from the cafeteria-style line, and servers then deliver the meal to you after it's cooked.

For more standard breakfast fare at good prices, try the **Salmon Bay Cafe** in Ballard (5109 Shilshole Ave. NW, just west of the Ballard Bridge; ☎ 206-782-5539) for wonderful stuffed French toast and workingman's portions, and **Donna's Diner** (1760 First Ave. S. near Safeco Field; ☎ 206-467-7359) for ridiculously cheap meat and egg breakfasts. If you're the kind of person who likes to have breakfast in the middle of the night, **13 Coins** (125 Boren Ave. N., just north of Denny Way; ☎ 206-682-2513) is a local institution that slings the hash 24 hours a day. For a breakfast treat that isn't cheap, **Café Campagne** (86 Pine St., at the Market; ☎ 206-728-2233) makes fabulous baked egg dishes, quiches, or simple baguettes and jams served with big bowls of caffe latte.

Living the high life in caffeine city

Speaking of coffee, a cuppa Joe and a baked good serve as a perfectly satisfying breakfast for many people, and you won't find a shortage of either in Seattle. Indeed, you may be overwhelmed by the sheer number of coffee possibilities in Caffeine City: Espresso carts on street corners; drive-through espresso shacks on major streets; quaint neighborhood coffee shops; and chain places, sometimes two or three on major retail corners, designed to look like little living rooms with fireplaces and easy chairs in which to sip your latte and nibble your muffin. The original **Starbucks** (1912 Pike Place Market; ☎ **206-448-8762**) is still doing business in the Market (with the original coquettish mermaid logo that has since been removed from the corporate identity), but many locals prefer to settle down at one of the numerous locations of **Tully's Coffee, Seattle's Best Coffee,** and **Caffe Ladro,** all of which make fine coffee and tea drinks and serve pies, bagels, and fresh muffins. If you're in the neighborhood, stop by **Cafe Bambino** (405 NW 65th St. in Ballard; ☎ **206-706-4934**), which is owned by artist Andhi Spath and displays his original paintings, and **Uptown Espresso** (525 Queen Anne Ave. N. in lower Queen Anne; ☎ **206-281-8669**), which makes terrific pies, scones, and muffins. In the Fremont retail district, **Still Life in Fremont** (709 N. 35th St.; ☎ **206-547-9850**) is a throwback coffeehouse with art on the walls, fresh baked goods, and excellent soups and vegetarian sandwiches.

Know your coffee lingo

A snotty Starbucks employee once said to a visitor from New York, "If you speak to me in my language, you'll get what you want." When ordering coffee in Seattle, try to follow these rules:

✔ State the size of drink you want — for example, short (which denotes small), tall (which is medium), or Grande (which is large).

✔ State the number of espresso shots you want in it (single or double).

✔ If you're ordering anything but full, caffeinated coffee, mention it now.

✔ State the type of drink you're ordering (latte, Americano, or mocha).

✔ Call the kind of milk you want: whole, 2 percent, or "skinny" (skim).

✔ Add any extras you may want, such as a hazelnut or vanilla flavoring.

So it goes like this: *"I'll have a short, single, half-decaf latte, 2 percent, with hazelnut."*

More tips: A regular cup of coffee is an Americano; order it with "room for cream" if you're going to add milk. Always get the whipped cream on a mocha (live a little; you're already getting plenty of extra calories and fat from the chocolate). And if somebody ever says, "If you speak to me in my language, you'll get what you want," turn around, walk out, and go to the next coffee place.

You saw it, you cook it

If you'd like to go home and dazzle your friends by preparing some authentic Pacific Northwest cuisine, pick up a copy of **Best Places Seattle Cookbook** (Sasquatch Books) by Cynthia Nims and Kathy Casey. The former is the food editor of *Seattle Magazine,* the latter a noted local chef. Together, they offer dozens of recipes that come straight from Seattle restaurants, from the Seattle cioppino at Anthony's Pier 66 to the coconut-cream pie from the Dahlia Lounge.

Doing a similar turn at the Pike Place Market is my friend Braiden Rex-Johnson, who writes the wonderful **Pike Place Market Cookbook** (Sasquatch Books), with lots of colorful inside information about market vendors and tons of recipes that can help you make meals out of the wealth of ingredients found in the Market.

Exploring the food stalls at Pike Place

It's no exaggeration to say that you can spend a week eating from the food vendors at the Pike Place Market and not taste the same thing twice. The Market is the epicenter of the local food scene, where farmers and grocers sell fresh fruits and produce, and dozens of stalls offer prepared foods and delicatessens. Most of the food stalls are open from the early morning hours to about 5 p.m., with restaurants open into the night. Explore the inner and outer reaches of the Market, and you encounter fresh cinnamon rolls, Greek specialties, Turkish delights, Filipino stir-fries, French bread, cookies, pastries, big Philadelphia-style cheese steak sandwiches, Chinese and Italian food, lots of coffee, and much more. You're sure to find a place that hits the spot for what you're craving, but do yourself a favor and don't miss **Piroshky, Piroshky** (1908 Pike Place; ☎ **206-441-6068**), which is run by Russian expats and makes tasty rolls filled with salmon, vegetables, or meat, plus wonderful desserts — the apple tarts are to die for. For seafood, **Jack's Fish Spot** (1514 Pike Place; ☎ **206-467-0514**) is not only a fish vendor, but it also has a stainless-steel counter where you can buy excellent fish and chips or Dungeness crab cocktails served with crunchy celery and homemade cocktail sauce. **World Class Chili** (1411 First Ave. inside the south arcade building; ☎ **206-623-3678**) serves the best chili in town, and **Biringer Farms** (1530 Post Alley; ☎ **206-467-0383**) sells generous slices of pies that include local favorites like fresh blackberries or huckleberries when the fruits are in season.

Asian snacks in the International District

Seattle's Asian neighborhood, called the International District, is just east of the new Seahawks Stadium. S. Jackson Street and S. King Street are the main thoroughfares. Although it's not as large or bustling as San Francisco or Vancouver's Chinatowns, the I.D. is a great place to find Asian restaurants and takeout food, frequently at rock-bottom prices. The first (and frequently the last) stop is **Uwajimaya Village** (600 Fifth Ave. S.; ☎ 206-624-6248). This complex features Seattle's largest Asian grocery store, Uwajimaya, and a splendid food court where you can find a dozen different cuisines represented, from Korean barbeque to Japanese noodles to Hawaiian plate lunches. For authentic Chinese dim sum, go to **House of Hong** (409 Eighth Ave. S.; ☎ 206-622-7997), which serves the delightful small bites that compose dim sum from 10 a.m. to 5 p.m. daily. The **Banh Mi 88 Deli** (1043 S. Jackson St., ☎ 324-9019) has Vietnamese sandwiches on fresh French rolls stuffed with pâté or ham, cilantro, and carrot for the unbelievable price of $1.50. Next door is a pan-Asian grocery store where you can try stinky durian fruits in season. (Don't eat them in your hotel; you'll stink the whole place up.) For delicious sponge cakes and bright-yellow egg custard tarts, stop at **A Piece of Cake** (514 S. King St.; ☎ 206-623-8284), which has tables where you can sit down and enjoy your cake and coffee.

Quick eats on the street

When food on the fly or cheap eats are the order of the day, find your way to one of these bargain places.

Bakeries

If loaves of fresh bread and artfully crafted pastries make you happy (they make me ecstatic), then seek out one of these bakeries, all of which have small areas in which to sit and devour your purchase. In Wallingford, try the **Boulangerie** (2700 N. 45th St.; ☎ 206-634-2211), a French bakery with baguettes, croissants, and lovely brioche baked around a circle of brie. Pioneer Square workers line up to get their bread and muffin fix at the **Grand Central Bakery** (214 First Ave. S.; ☎ 206-622-3644), which makes several varieties of artisan breads. At the Market, try the **Three Girls Bakery** (1514 Pike Place; ☎ 206-622-1045), which not only has a dozen varieties of bread but also sells fine Danish, cookies, and fresh macaroons. For exclusively Danish products from an old Ballard family, the **Larsen Brothers Danish Bakery** (8000 24th NW; ☎ 206-782-8285) fills the bill with buttery Danish pastries and breads. Just down the street, you'll find the **Tall Grass Bakery** (5907 24th NW; ☎ 206-706-0991), which has quickly become the best French bakery in town. People line up promptly at 6 p.m. to take home a hot baguette.

Burgers

Besides the fast-food **Dick's Drive-Ins** (see "Seattle Restaurants from A to Z," earlier in this chapter for listings), Seattle has a few burger places that stand out above the rest. Locals flock to the two locations of **Red Mill Burgers** (1613 W. Dravus, between Queen Anne and

Magnolia, ☎ **206-284-6363;** and 312 N. 67th St. in Greenwood, ☎ **206-783-6362**) for thick burgers and good, thin-cut fries. Order ahead over the phone, and they'll have your meal waiting for you to go, or drop in and sit at one of the tables. On Capitol Hill, the **Deluxe Bar & Grill** (625 Broadway E.; ☎ **206-324-9697**) is a sit-down restaurant that makes fine, oversize burgers. **Red Robin** (Northgate Mall, ☎ **206-365-0933;** and Seattle Waterfront, Pier 55, ☎ **206-623-1942**) is a sit-down chain restaurant that happily serves you a big, thick burger with numerous toppings.

Burritos and wraps

The craze of wrapping foods in a large tortilla that may be red from sun-dried tomatoes or green from spinach and pesto has hit Seattle's fast-food scene hard in recent years. **Taco del Mar** (numerous locations, including Ballard at 5431 Ballard Ave. NW, ☎ **206-706-9933,** and Pioneer Square at 90 Yesler Way, ☎ **206-467-5940**) is a good source for cheap, enormous, sloppy burritos made with whole or refried beans and either meats or fried fish. **World Wrapps** (numerous locations, including 528 Queen Anne Ave. N., ☎ **206-286-9727**) is another chain that does a good job stuffing Asian- or Mexican-style preparations into a big tortilla. For terrific, authentic Mexican burritos and tacos, get yourself to **Malena's Taco Shop** (620 W. McGraw St.; ☎ **206-284-0304**), in upper Queen Anne.

Fish and chips

Seattle's trademark fish and chips is made from fresh lingcod that comes out of Puget Sound, or flaky, white Alaskan halibut. Any shop worth its salt also offers fried oysters and excellent chowder. You can find a fine, cheap Northwest meal at any of the following locations. Opposite the Ballard Locks, tall, carved totem poles signal the location of the **Totem House Seafood & Chowder** restaurant (3058 NW 54th St.; ☎ **206-784-2300**). Take your catch back across the street to the park near the Locks or sit at the restaurant's outdoor picnic tables. You can find **Ivar's** restaurant (several locations), which are blue-and-white fast-food shops that sell fried fish and one of the best chowders in town, in most parts of town. Fisherman's Terminal between Queen Anne and Magnolia wouldn't be the same without **Little Chinook's** (Fisherman's Terminal; ☎ **206-283-HOOK**), a takeout fish and chips place with picnic tables overlooking the long piers where fishing boats tie up for the winter months.

Late night Broadway eats

If you're in the mood for a late-night nosh, head to Broadway on Capital Hill. **Piroshki on Broadway** (124½ Broadway E.; ☎ **206-322-2820**) serves delicious, handmade *piroshkies* (Russian calzones filled with mushrooms and potatoes, cabbage, or smoked salmon) until 11 p.m. (10 p.m. on Sundays). Down the street, the **Broadway Grill** (314 Broadway E.; ☎ **206-328-7000**) packs them into a lively room with a long stainless-steel counter and a kitchen that's open until 3 a.m. every night. Choose from a wide variety of salads, burgers, and grilled favorites like steak or lemon herb rotisserie chicken. To satisfy that late-night craving for sweets, **Dilettante Chocolates** (416 Broadway E.; ☎ 206-329-6463) has cases of chocolate truffles, as well as a gorgeous selection of cakes that you can buy by the slice and eat at their cafe tables. Dilettante Chocolates is open until 1 a.m. on Friday and Saturday nights and until midnight during the rest of the week.

Packing up for a picnic

Eat inside on a beautiful summer day? No way! say Seattleites, who know only too well how fleeting fine weather can be and take every opportunity to be outside. The perfect way to enjoy one of the city's many parks is armed with a basket of food, of course. The Pike Place Market has everything you need. For Italian fare, go to **DeLaurenti's Specialty Food Market** (1435 First Ave.; ☎ 206-622-0141) for a great selection of breads, meats, and cheeses. In the upstairs room, you find Italian wines at good prices. Farther down Pike Place, **Cucina Fresca** (1904 Pike Place; ☎ 206-448-4758) has gorgeous prepared Italian foods, including mozzarella and tomato salads, grilled chicken, roasted vegetables drowning in olive oil, and specialty pizzas. Local chef and author Kathy Casey opened **Dish D'Lish** (1505 Pike Place; ☎ 206-223-1848) selling delights like a big four-cheese macaroni casserole that warms up nicely in the microwave, mini-meatloaves, blue cheese scalloped potatoes, and a nine-layer chocolate cake for dessert. Round out your meal with fresh fruits or desserts from the Market's vendors and then head to the north end of the waterfront and Myrtle Edwards Park to enjoy it.

Pizza

Pizzeria Pagliacci gets consistently high marks for quality pizza; its "Brooklyn Bridge" pie is loaded with pepperoni, sausage, mushrooms, and vegetables. It delivers throughout the city (☎ 206-726-1717) and has sit-down restaurants in lower Queen Anne (550 Queen Anne Ave. N.; ☎ 206-285-1232), Capitol Hill (426 Broadway E.; ☎ 206-324-0730) and the University District (4529 University Way NE; ☎ 206-632-0421). On upper Queen Anne, the **Elliott Bay Pizza Co.** (2115 Queen Anne Ave. N.; ☎ 206-285-0500) sells by the slice or the pie and makes hearty grinder-style sandwiches. **Zeek's Pizza** has a nice sit-down restaurant near the zoo in the upper Fremont/Greenwood neighborhood (6000 Phinney Ave. N.; ☎ 206-789-0089).

Index of Restaurants by Price

$

Dick's Drive-Ins
Fish Bar
Tia Lou's

$$

Bell Street Diner
The Brooklyn Seafood, Steak & Oyster
House

Buca di Beppo
Chandler's Crabhouse
Chinook's at Salmon Bay
The Crab Pot Restaurant and Bar
Flying Fish
Ivar's Salmon House
Shiro's

$$$

Anthony's Pier 66
Carmelita
Cassis
Dahlia Lounge
Daniel's Broiler
Etta's Seafood
Fandango
iCon Grill
Julia's on Broadway
Kaspar's
Le Pichet
Nishino
Palace Kitchen
Palisade
Ray's Boathouse and Cafe
Salty's on Alki Beach

Sazerac
Tulio Ristorante
Wild Ginger

$$$$

Andaluca
Cafe Juanita
Campagne
Canlis
El Gaucho
Fleming's Prime Steakhouse &
    Wine Bar
Metropolitan Grill
Oceanaire Seafood Room
Waterfront

$$$$$

Brasa
Cascadia
Earth & Ocean
The Georgian Room
The Herbfarm
Rover's

Index of Restaurants by Neighborhood

Ballard

Dick's Drive-Ins
Ray's Boathouse and Cafe

Belltown

Anthony's Pier 66, Bell Street Diner &
    Fish Bar
Brasa
Cascadia
Dahlia Lounge
El Gaucho
Fandango
Flying Fish
Shiro's
Tia Lou's

Capitol Hill

Cassis
Julia's on Broadway

Downtown/Shopping District

Andaluca
The Brooklyn Seafood, Steak &
    Oyster House
Earth & Ocean
Fleming's Prime Steakhouse &
    Wine Bar
The Georgian Room
iCon Grill
Metropolitan Grill
Oceanaire Seafood Room
Palace Kitchen
Sazerac
Tulio Ristorante
Wild Ginger

Fremont

Carmelita

Kirkland
Cafe Juanita

Lake Union
Buca di Beppo
Chandler's Crabhouse
Daniel's Broiler
Ivar's Salmon House

Madison Park
Nishino
Rover's

Magnolia
Chinook's at Salmon Bay
Palisade

Pike Place Market
Campagne
Etta's Seafood
Le Pichet

Queen Anne
Canlis
Dick's Drive-In
Kaspar's

Wallingford
Dick's Drive-In

Waterfront
The Crab Pot Restaurant and Bar
Waterfront

West Seattle
Salty's on Alki Beach

Woodinville
The Herbfarm

Index of Restaurants by Cuisine

Asian
Wild Ginger

Burgers
Dick's Drive-Ins

Cajun
Sazerac

Continental
Brasa
Cascadia
Canlis
Earth & Ocean
The Georgian Room
The Herbfarm
Kaspar's

Country French
Campagne
Cassis
French

Le Pichet
Rover's
Italian
Buca di Beppo

Latin
Fandango

Mediterranean
Andaluca

Mexican
Tia Lou's

Northern Italian
Cafe Juanita
Tulio Ristorante

Northwest
Cascadia
Chinook's at Salmon Bay

Northwest Fusion
Dahlia Lounge
Waterfront

Regional American
iCon Grill
Julia's on Broadway
Palace Kitchen

Seafood
Anthony's Pier 66, Bell Street Diner &
    Fish Bar
The Brooklyn Seafood, Steak & Oyster
    House
Canlis
Chandler's Crabhouse
Crab Pot Restaurant and Bar
Chinook's at Salmon Bay
Etta's Seafood
Flying Fish
Ivar's Salmon House

Oceanaire Seafood Room
Palisade
Ray's Boathouse and Cafe
Salty's on Alki Beach
Waterfront

Steak
Canlis
Daniel's Broiler
El Gaucho
Fleming's Prime Steakhouse & Wine
    Bar
Metropolitan Grill

Sushi
Nishino
Shiro's

Vegetarian
Carmelita

Part IV
Exploring Seattle

The 5th Wave   By Rich Tennant

"We've seen where they filmed parts of 'Sleepless in Seattle,' the TV show 'Twin Peaks,' and several documentaries on Sasquatch. I'm not sure why, but I feel like just going back to the hotel room and watching TV."

In this part . . .

You've arrived in Seattle, you've settled in to your hotel, and you're ready to see the sights. In this part, I describe the city's top attractions — giving advice on what to see and what to avoid — and offer an insider's look at other cool things to see and do. I offer advice on the best places to take kids and teens and where to go to enjoy Seattle's glorious natural spaces. In addition, I outline several specific city itineraries as well as day trips to the surrounding areas. For shoppers, I give a breakdown of Seattle's great shopping neighborhoods and where to find items that are uniquely Pacific Northwest. Finally, the nightcrawler in you should appreciate the chapter on Seattle nightlife, which covers everything from performing arts to theater to bars and clubs with attitude.

Chapter 15

Seattle's Top Sights and Cool Things to Do

In This Chapter

▶ Finding the best things to see and do in Seattle

▶ Enjoying museums and a theater made just for kids

▶ Scoping out cool places for even the most jaded teens

▶ Taking advantage of special spots for the blissfully romantic

▶ Exploring a wealth of parks

▶ Touring Seattle by air, bus, rail, underground, or duck

Don't feel bad if all you want to do during your first days in Seattle is walk the streets, sit at a sidewalk cafe sipping lattes and eating pie, and stroll a waterfront path at sunset. Those activities are all intrinsic parts of the Seattle experience. After you soak up the atmosphere of the city — and Seattle has loads of it — you may want to visit some of the unique attractions that the city has to offer. Just be sure to build in plenty of time for relaxing, too, because this town has as pleasant a cafe society as you're likely to encounter anywhere.

The Top Attractions from A to Z

In this section, I cover the details of Seattle's must-see attractions.

Benaroya Hall
Downtown

The $118-million home of the Seattle Symphony, built in Beaux Arts-style in the heart of downtown, was funded in large part by private donors that included several Microsoft millionaires. The hall opened in 1998 and has been the center of the city's cultural scene ever since. The acoustics have been compared to Carnegie Hall's for sheer, crystal-clear brilliance, and in 2000, a state-of-the-art concert organ was added to the hall, broadening the symphony's range even more. Book your tickets early; this is a perennial sellout. If you'd like to tour the hall, meet in the Grand Lobby on the Third Avenue and University Street side, Monday through Friday at noon or 1 p.m.

200 University St. at Second Avenue, near the Seattle Art Museum. ☎ *206-215-4747. Internet:* www.seattlesymphony.org *for a calendar and online purchase option. Admission: $10–$77 for concerts; tours are free. No children under 5 allowed into concerts.*

Boeing Plant
Everett

Here's a neat doubleheader to impress your kids. At Boeing's largest assembly plant, they can see how airplanes are built and also stand inside the single largest building under one roof in the world. (For extra credit, tell your kids that all of Disneyland fits into the building.) Cool! Despite heavy layoffs over the last few years, Boeing remains the single largest employer in Washington. The guided tour, which utilizes raised catwalks to traverse the massive space, is an impressive inside look at great sections of airplanes coming together.

Boeing Tour Center on SR 526 in Everett, 30 miles north of Seattle. Take I-5 north and then head west on 526; give yourself at least an hour from downtown Seattle. ☎ *800-464-1476 or 206-544-1264. Internet:* www.boeing.com/companyoffices/aboutus/tours/. *Open: One-hour tours are first-come first-served and run Mon–Fri from 9 a.m.–11 a.m. and 1 p.m.–3 p.m. Admission: $5 adults, $3 seniors and children under 16. Children must be at least 4 feet, 2 inches tall.*

Experience Music Project
Seattle Center

It started out as a small museum to house Paul Allen's collection of Jimi Hendrix memorabilia and mushroomed into a $100-million shrine to rock-and-roll music. People either love or hate the curving, multihued building by architect Frank Gehry that sits like a basket of dumped laundry under the Space Needle. The admission fee is steep, but once inside, grown-ups appreciate the galleries with artifacts like Janis Joplin's feather boa and Elvis's motorcycle jacket, while kids love playing instruments in the Sound Lab, riding a motion-simulator into the heart of a James Brown concert, or performing "Wild Thing" karaoke-style before a simulated crowd. Skip the MEGs (CD-ROM devices that provide running commentary on the exhibits) for smaller children; they're bulky and ponderous. The Turntable restaurant and Liquid Lounge bar are fine hangouts.

2901 Third Ave., at Seattle Center (adjacent to the Space Needle and Monorail). ☎ *206-770-2700. Internet:* www.emplive.com. *Open: Sun–Thurs 10 a.m.–6 p.m. (galleries open to 11 p.m. on Fri and Sat); call for restaurant and lounge hours. Admission: $19.95 adults, $15.95 seniors and teens 13–17, $14.95 children 7–12, children 6 and under free.*

Downtown Seattle Attractions

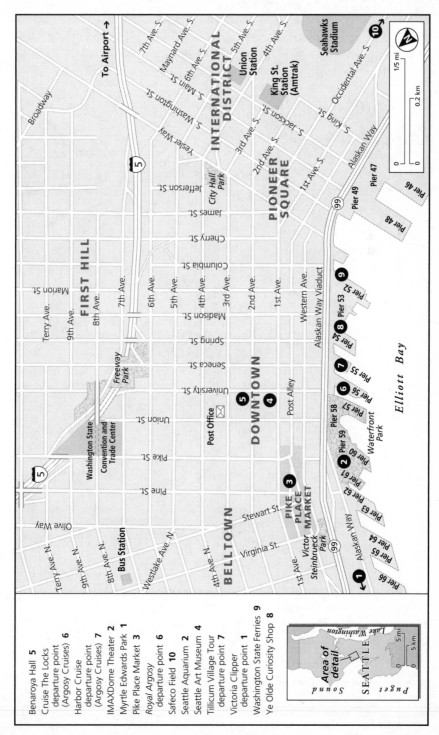

Benaroya Hall **5**
Cruise The Locks
 departure point
 (Argosy Cruises) **6**
Harbor Cruise
 departure point
 (Argosy Cruises) **7**
IMAXDome Theater **2**
Myrtle Edwards Park **1**
Pike Place Market **3**
Royal Argosy
 departure point **6**
Safeco Field **10**
Seattle Aquarium **2**
Seattle Art Museum **4**
Tillicum Village Tour
 departure point **7**
Victoria Clipper
 departure point **1**
Washington State Ferries **9**
Ye Olde Curiosity Shop **8**

Seattle Attractions—North & Northeast

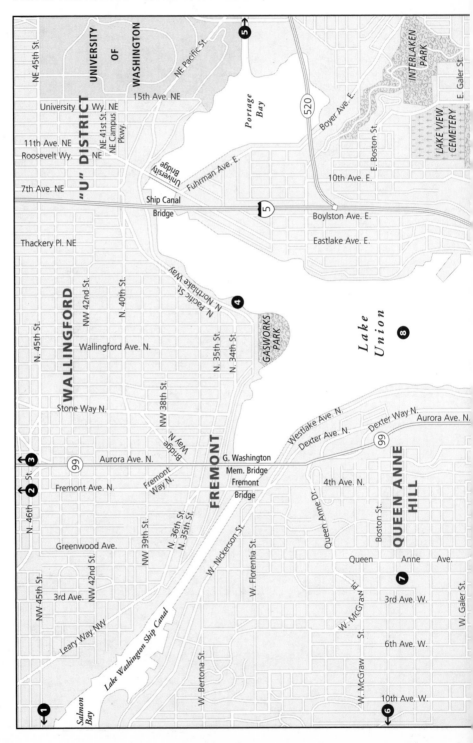

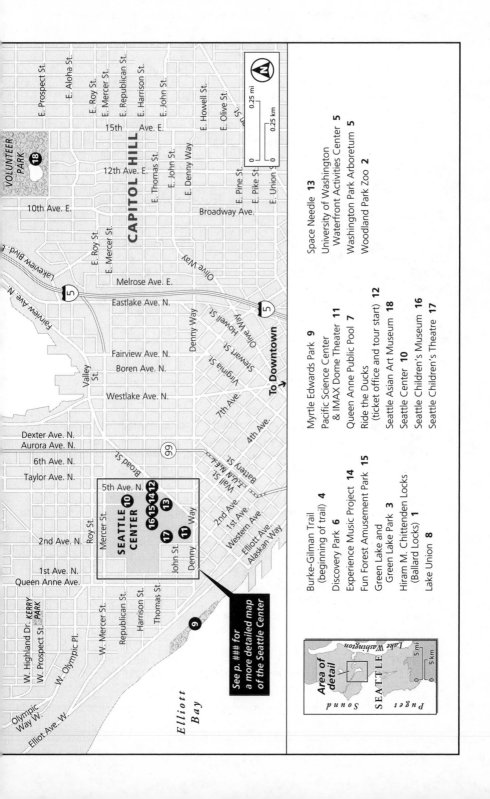

Space Needle **13**
University of Washington
Waterfront Activities Center **5**
Washington Park Arboretum **5**
Woodland Park Zoo **2**

Myrtle Edwards Park **9**
Pacific Science Center
& IMAX Dome Theater **11**
Queen Anne Public Pool **7**
Ride the Ducks
(ticket office and tour start) **12**
Seattle Asian Art Museum **18**
Seattle Center **10**
Seattle Children's Museum **16**
Seattle Children's Theatre **17**

Burke-Gilman Trail
(beginning of trail) **4**
Discovery Park **6**
Experience Music Project **14**
Fun Forest Amusement Park **15**
Green Lake and
Green Lake Park **3**
Hiram M. Chittenden Locks
(Ballard Locks) **1**
Lake Union **8**

See p. ### for
a more detailed map
of the Seattle Center

0.25 mi
0.25 km

Area of
detail
SEATTLE
Puget Sound
Lake Washington
5 mi
5 km

VOLUNTEER PARK
CAPITOL HILL

E. Prospect St.
E. Aloha St.
E. Roy St.
E. Mercer St.
E. Republican St.
E. Harrison St.
E. John St.
E. Howell St.
E. Olive St.
15th   Ave. E.
12th Ave. E.
E. Thomas St.
E. John St.
E. Denny Way
Broadway Ave.
10th Ave. E.
E. Pine St.
E. Pike St.
E. Union St.

Lakeview Blvd. E.
Fairview Ave. N.
E. Roy St.
E. Mercer St.
Melrose Ave. E.
Eastlake Ave. N.
Fairview Ave. N.
Boren Ave. N.
Westlake Ave. N.

Olive Way
Denny Way
Howell St.
Virginia St.
Stewart St.
To Downtown

Dexter Ave. N.
Aurora Ave. N.
6th Ave. N.
Taylor Ave. N.
5th Ave. N.
2nd Ave. N.
1st Ave. N.
Queen Anne Ave.

SEATTLE CENTER

Valley St.
Broad St.
Mercer St.
Roy St.

John St.
Denny Way

7th Ave.
4th Ave.
Wall St.
Battery St.
2nd Ave.
1st Ave.
Western Ave.
Elliott Ave.
Alaskan Way

W. Highland Dr.
W. Prospect St.
W. Olympic Pl.
W. Mercer St.
W. Republican St.
W. Harrison St.
W. Thomas St.
KERRY PARK
Olympic Way W.
Elliot Ave. W.

Elliott Bay

Celebrating at the Seattle Center

Seattle Center's grounds and buildings (see the listing for Seattle Center later in this chapter) get turned into an enormous, groovin' street party three times a year for major festivals that attract hundreds of thousands of visitors over the course of three- and four-day weekends. **Bite of Seattle,** the city's homage to local food and drink, takes place every July, with more than 90 food vendors representing the city's restaurants. Live music and beer gardens (where you can wash down all the treats that you bought from the food vendors) add to the festivities. Labor Day weekend is the time for **Bumbershoot,** an enormous arts festival of music, dance, fine arts, and literature performed simultaneously in a dozen different Seattle Center venues, with one admission price buying access to everything. The earlier **Northwest Folklife Festival,** held over Memorial Day weekend, is devoted to folk music and performances. Food is served at each event, and the people-watching and entertainment values are unsurpassed. Go early to beat the crowds and try to pick up advance tickets whenever possible to avoid the enormous lines to get in. **Bite of Seattle:** ☎ **206-232-2982;** Internet: www.biteofseattle.com; admission is free; $2–$5 for samples of food items. **Bumbershoot:** ☎ **206-281-8111;** Internet: www.bumbershoot.org; admission varies. **Northwest Folklife Festival:** ☎ **206-684-7300;** Internet: www.nwfolklife.org; admission varies.

Hiram M. Chittenden Locks
Ballard

Also known as the Ballard Locks, this little park and engineering feat created by the U.S. Army Corps of Engineers is one of the most pleasant diversions in the city on a nice day. The Locks were built to allow boats to navigate through the different water levels of Lake Union and Puget Sound, and it's fun to watch everything from canoes and dinghies to yachts and commercial barges tie into a lock, have a door close behind them with a clang, and then ascend or descend on a pillow of water. It's also interesting to visit the fish ladders on the south side of the waterway (reached by walking over the dam that holds back Lake Union) with viewing windows that allow you to see full-grown salmon fighting their way upstream to return to their spawning grounds. Most salmon runs take place from June to September, but the timing varies each year. The combination of technology and nature is a hit with every age I've taken there, and the Locks are always on the itinerary when friends and relatives come to town.

3015 NW 54th St. (in Ballard; continue west on Market Street; it passes the Locks about 1 mile past the main commercial district). ☎ *206-783-7059. Open: All daylight hours; boat traffic is heaviest on weekends. Admission: Free.*

Lake Union
Downtown

For a quintessential Seattle experience, spend some time on or around Lake Union, the teardrop-shaped body of water just north of downtown. Sailboats and pleasure craft ply the waters, rowers do their thing in canoes and kayaks, and seaplanes take off and land with a roar of engines. Big, family-friendly restaurants with outdoor patios offering great views line the eastern shore. For the best experience, head to the Northwest Outdoor Center and rent big, steady kayaks (doubles and triples are great for taking kids along) with foot-controlled rudders and spray skirts that keep the water off your clothes and paddle among the communities of dollhouse-like houseboats on either shore, with the city's buildings providing a backdrop. Boat lovers will love to browse the docks of the Center for Wooden Boats, which collects historic craft and lets you take everything from old canoes and dinghies to handsome sailboats out for a spin around the lake.

North of Mercer Street in downtown Seattle. **Northwest Outdoor Center:** *2100 Westlake Ave. N., on the west side of the lake in the commercial strip of buildings.* ☎ *206-281-9694. Internet:* www.nwoc.com. *Fees: Single kayak $10 per hour; double $15 per hour. Canoes and kayaks also available from the* **Center for Wooden Boats,** *1010 Valley St., at the north end of the lake just west of the Burger King (*☎ *206-382-BOAT), and the* **University of Washington Waterfront Activities Center,** *just behind Husky Stadium on Lake Washington (*☎ *206-543-9433).*

Museum of Flight
South Seattle

Seattle loves its airplanes, and this imposing steel-and-glass museum is a fine way for kids and aviation buffs to immerse themselves in aircraft. The museum is on the grounds of one of Boeing's main plants, and part of it is the little Red Barn that was the company's original factory back in 1910. Inside is a range of aircraft (many of them built by Boeing), including a DC3 and a Blackbird suspended from the ceiling, a biplane, and an Apollo space capsule that you can peer into. A small area of toy planes allows younger children to get some of their climbing and interactive energy satisfied. A snackbar is on the premises. Allow a half-day for getting to the museum and exploring the galleries.

9404 E. Marginal Way S. on the west side of Boeing Field. Take I-5 South to exit 158. ☎ *206-764-5720. Internet:* www.museumofflight.org. *Admission: $11 adults, $7 seniors, $6.50 ages 5–17, children 4 and under free; first Thurs also free from 5–9 p.m. Hours: Daily 10 a.m.–5 p.m.; until 9 p.m. on Thurs.*

Pike Place Market
Downtown

City officials have worked overtime to ensure that the Pike Place Market, begun in 1907 and one of Seattle's most enduring institutions, remains true to its roots. A big push was made a few years ago to add more tourist-friendly T-shirt and souvenir shops, but the Market fought to keep the emphasis on food and flowers. The Market remains the single best place in the city to find fresh produce and seasonal specialties like Rainier cherries, Washington asparagus, fresh king salmon, and Northwest hazelnuts. The food grazing is unsurpassed: Don't leave without trying a Dungeness crab cocktail, a fresh-baked piroshky or cinnamon roll, and, of course, coffee from any number of vendors, including the original Starbucks (with the original randy mermaid sign that you won't see at worldwide McStarbucks outlets). Explore below the main floor to find wonderful specialty shops, including one of the best stores devoted to magic and old magic posters in the country, a fragrant store dedicated to spices, and an exotic bird store where the parrots squawk in your face. A 90-minute Market Heritage Tour is offered Wednesday through Sunday at 11 a.m. and 2 p.m., beginning at the Market Heritage Foundation Visitor Center on Western Avenue. At night the vendors clear out, but the several excellent restaurants, bars, and theater in the Market keep on hopping.

Do not, repeat *do not,* drive into Pike Place itself, unless you want to get stuck in a jam of delivery trucks and hordes of pedestrians. You will never find parking at the Market; the vendors occupy all the parking spaces beginning at the crack of dawn. Park instead in the lot on Western Avenue adjacent to the Market, where the first hour is free.

Seattle's favorite meeting place is Rachel the Pig, the life-size brass piggybank in the crook of Pike Place under the big clock. Kids love to sit on Rachel and pose for pictures, and frequently musicians and clowns making balloon animals entertain the crowds.

Pike Place, which starts at First Avenue and Pike Street, with shops spread out in several buildings on First Avenue and Western Avenue between Union Street and Virginia Street. ☎ *206-682-7453. Internet:* www.pikeplacemarket.org. *Hours: Mon–Sat 9 a.m.–6 p.m.; Sun 11 a.m.–5 p.m. Admission: free. Market Heritage Tours are $7 for adults and $5 for seniors (60 and over) and kids under 18.*

Safeco Field
Downtown

The Seattle Mariners ballpark was the most expensive ever built, at $517 million, when it opened in July 1999. A large portion of the cost was for the retractable roof that closes after every home game while the P.A. system plays "Flight of the Valkyries." It's a truly wonderful place to watch a ballgame. The seats in the upper deck on the first base line have the best views of the Space Needle and downtown skyline. Feel free to wander about and check out the playground for kids behind centerfield and the food venues that offer such goodies as Northwest chowder, salmon, sushi, and microbrews. Artwork and decorative touches are everywhere, including posters of famous ballplayers from around the world that decorate the upper deck concourse. Stand near the bullpens in centerfield when the relievers are warming up, and you'll get a gut feeling for the speed of a major-league fastball. Tours are offered daily, and when the team is out of town these tours include visits to the dugouts and locker rooms.

First Avenue S. at S. Atlantic Street, just south of Pioneer Square. ☎ 206-622-HITS for ticket information and schedules. Internet: www.seattlemariners.com. *Admission: $6–$45; box offices are located on the south side of the stadium, and a Mariners team store with complete merchandise is located on the First Avenue S. side. Admission for tours is $7 adults, $5 children (tour information: ☎ 206-346-4000).*

Seattle Aquarium
Downtown

God knows that Puget Sound is too cold to swim or snorkel in, but you can get an eel's-eye perspective on the teeming life in the Sound at this waterfront aquarium. The Puget Sound tank features bizarre wolf eels, lingcod and rockfish, and a giant Pacific octopus named Neah. A shark tank has plenty of action to excite the kids, and they can pet a starfish (not exactly a cuddly experience) in the hands-on tank. The Aquarium also houses the IMAXDome Theater, with films that unfold in a giant panorama overhead.

Pier 59 on the Waterfront, a few blocks south of the Edgewater Hotel. Take the elevator or steps from the Pike Place Market to Alaskan Way and then walk or catch the waterfront streetcar heading north. ☎ 206-386-4320. Internet: www.seattle aquarium.org. *Open: Daily 10 a.m.–7 p.m. Admission: $11 adults, $7 children 6–12, $5 children 3–5. Extra charges and package rates for the ImaxDome films.*

Seattle Art Museum and Seattle Asian Art Musuem
Downtown and Capitol Hill, respectively

Sculptor Jonathon Borofsky's enormous *Hammering Man* points the way to the Seattle Art Museum's (SAM) new location downtown near the Market. Major traveling exhibitions stop here, and the permanent collections, with Native American art and Northwest contemporary art, provide a good orientation to the region's art history. One downfall of the museum is that it offers everything under the sun, from African art to European masters, but little of any one thing. The positive aspect of this, however, is that visitors are bound to find something here to interest them. In Volunteer Park on Capitol Hill, the Seattle Asian Art Museum is as tranquil a setting as you can find in the city. Located in SAM's former Art Deco digs, the musuem boasts a fine collection of pan-Asian art with an emphasis on Japanese and Chinese exhibits.

Be sure to get a personal CD-ROM headset for yourself and each child at SAM (they're free). The museum has programs geared to all age levels, and it's a great way to keep kids occupied and involved with the museum tour, which they can do at their own pace while you linger over your favorite works.

Seattle Art Museum: 100 University St., on First Avenue. ☎ 206-654-3100. Internet: www.seattleartmuseum.org. *Open: Tues–Sun 10 a.m.–5 p.m. (to 9 p.m. Thurs); closed Mon. Admission: $7 adults, $5 seniors, children 12 and under free. Free first Thurs of the month.*

Seattle Asian Art Museum: Volunteer Park, 14th Ave. E. and E. Prospect Street. Find street parking anywhere on the perimeter of the park and enjoy the walk to the museum. ☎ 206-654-3100. Open: Summer Tues–Sun 10 a.m.–5 p.m. (to 9 p.m. Thurs); closed Mon. Fall, winter and spring Wed–Sun 10 a.m.–5 p.m. (to 9 p.m. Thurs); closed Mon. Admission: $3 adults, children 12 and under free. Free first Thurs of the month.

Seattle Center
Seattle Center

At some point in your trip, you're bound to wind up at Seattle Center: This multiblock complex, located just north of downtown in the Queen Anne neighborhood, is not only home to many of the city's arts venues, such as the Pacific Northwest Ballet, Seattle Children's Theatre, and Seattle Opera, but it also houses crowd-pleasing attractions including the Space Needle, the Experience Music Project, and the Pacific Science Center. Seattle Center is a great place to blow off steam with the younger set. The computerized fountain is a huge hit on warm days for kids who don't mind getting wet, and an amusement park offers rides and a videogame parlor. The Center House stages dances and exhibitions such as Winterfest, provides games, activities, and hands-on exhibitions for children, and houses several inexpensive fast-food-type vendors. Be sure to call ahead for information on festivals and events: During the three major festivals of the year, the place gets incredibly crammed.

305 Harrison St. is the official location, but the entire area is within the boundary of First Avenue N. and Fifth Avenue, and Denny and Mercer streets. Parking lots are more abundant on the Fifth Avenue side; Monorail from Westlake Center goes directly to Seattle Center's Center House. ☎ 206-684-7200 for program information. Internet: www.seattlecenter.com. *Admission: free. Hours vary with programs.*

Space Needle
Seattle Center

Still the most beloved symbol of Seattle, the Space Needle continues to be a must-see landmark. Built for the 1962 World's Fair, it has been spruced up of late, with a new visitor center and gift shop on the lower levels. At 520 feet, the observation deck has nice signage pointing out what you can see in all directions (on a sunny day), and just enough

Seattle Center

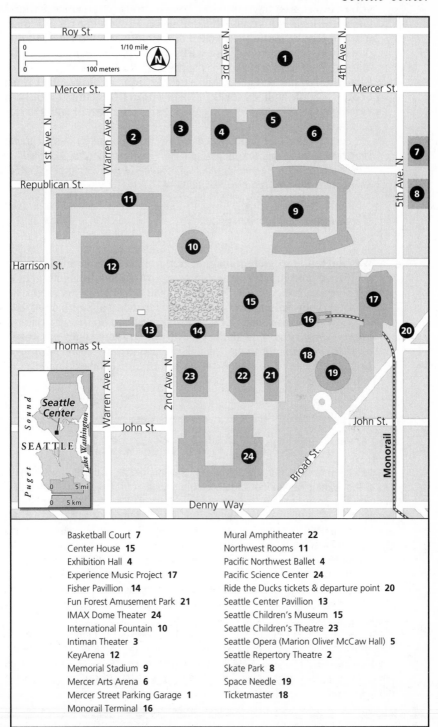

Basketball Court **7**

Center House **15**

Exhibition Hall **4**

Experience Music Project **17**

Fisher Pavillion **14**

Fun Forest Amusement Park **21**

IMAX Dome Theater **24**

International Fountain **10**

Intiman Theater **3**

KeyArena **12**

Memorial Stadium **9**

Mercer Arts Arena **6**

Mercer Street Parking Garage **1**

Monorail Terminal **16**

Mural Amphitheater **22**

Northwest Rooms **11**

Pacific Northwest Ballet **4**

Pacific Science Center **24**

Ride the Ducks tickets & departure point **20**

Seattle Center Pavillion **13**

Seattle Children's Museum **15**

Seattle Children's Theatre **23**

Seattle Opera (Marion Oliver McCaw Hall) **5**

Seattle Repertory Theatre **2**

Skate Park **8**

Space Needle **19**

Ticketmaster **18**

space through the railings to give you a chilling *Vertigo* look down. If you're too scared to go outside, you can shop in the Observation Deck's gift shop for a souvenir. The lounge and revolving restaurant can be fun, but they're generally packed and expensive, and the food definitely doesn't match the views. Fireworks here on New Year's Eve are the best in town. For views and pictures of the Needle, head to Kerry Park on West Highland Avenue in Queen Anne or take your photographs from a ferry boat. Expect long lines for the Observation Deck elevator, but a nearby video-game parlor can occupy the kids while a parent waits in line.

219 Fourth Ave. N. at Seattle Center. Take the monorail to Seattle Center from Westlake Center, or park on lots off Fifth Avenue. ☎ *206-443-2100. Internet:* www.spaceneedle.com. *Open: Daily 9 a.m.–11 p.m. Admission: $12.50 adults, $11 seniors, $10 children 11–17, $5 ages –4–10.*

Washington State Ferries
Downtown

Washington State maintains one of the most extensive ferry systems in the world, and much of it is centered around Seattle. For a scenic, inexpensive way to see Puget Sound, you can't beat standing on the top deck of a ferry crossing from downtown Seattle to Bainbridge Island or Bremerton. Go at sunset for the best views, and on the way back you can admire the city skyline as the downtown buildings light up. Keep an eye out for dolphins and sea lions. The outdoor areas on the bow can get pretty chilly, but the upper-deck outdoor area is heated and there is less wind chill in the stern.

Viewing Mount Rainier

Seattle's favorite sight, the one that evokes a collective sigh from its citizenry, is of 14,410-foot Mount Rainier looming above the city on a clear day 100 miles south of the city. The postcard view from the city is at Kerry Park (3rd Avenue W. and Highland Drive, in the Queen Anne neighborhood), where a small strip of grass perched on a hilltop looks south over the city's buildings and Elliott Bay, with the big mountain in the background. Otherwise, keep your camera ready for Rainier sightings when you head south on Aurora Avenue toward downtown, crossing Lake Washington in either direction on the I-90 and SR520 bridges, or from numerous viewpoints on the University of Washington campus. For a closer look, head south to the mountain itself, which has numerous hiking trails to explore and fields of wildflowers that pop up in July and August. The best approach is from the visitor center located at Paradise, at the 5,400-foot level of the mountain in Mount Rainier National Park. Mountain Rainier National Park is located 110 miles from downtown Seattle on SR706 (☎ 360-569-2211). Admission is $10 per vehicle, $5 per person, cyclist, or motorcyclist. Call ahead in the winter months to be sure the roads are open.

Car decks on the boats are first-come, first-served, so if you're going to drive onto the ferry, particularly at the beginning or end of a holiday weekend, plan to get to the terminal early and bring some reading material, because the parking lots get packed and you may have to wait up to two hours to get onto a boat. If you can avoid driving onto the ferry during rush hours, do so at all costs, or you'll encounter considerable commuter traffic.

Pier 52 on the Waterfront, just north of Pioneer Square. Pedestrian walkway directly to terminal from First Avenue and Columbia Street. ☎ *206-464-6400. Internet:* www.wsdot.wa.gov/ferries. *Numerous daily departures and returns. Fees: Foot passengers pay $5.40 westbound only (free to return to Seattle); $9.50 for car and driver ($12 during peak tourist months in the summer) each way to Bainbridge Island.*

Woodland Park Zoo
Fremont

A number of exhibits have been added in recent years, including a Komodo dragon exhibit, a jaw-dropping look at gorillas, which have produced offspring here, and an equally stunning exhibit of black bears. The experience of watching the bears swimming in their pond inches away from where you stand, with trout dodging their huge legs, is unforgettable. Habitats are big and as natural as possible, from an African savannah to a tropical rain forest. Don't miss the Nocturnal House, a dark, quiet place where creatures of the night zip by the viewing windows, and have a look at the collection of snakes and spiders. The zoo also has a petting zoo and pony rides for the little ones. In the summer, the zoo offers a concert series that is quite popular and sells out quickly.

5500 Phinney Ave. N. in Fremont; main parking area on Fremont Avenue N. & N. 50th Street Drive north on Aurora Avenue, exit at Green Lake Way, turn left onto N. 46th Street and right on Fremont Ave. N. to reach the main gate and parking area. ☎ *206-684-4800. Internet:* www.zoo.org. *Open: Daily 9:30 a.m.–6:30 p.m. Admission: $10 adults, $9.25 seniors, $7.50 children 6–17, $5.25 children 3–5.*

More Cool Things to Do and See

Ever the magnanimous one, I say a rousing "To each his own" to my multifaceted readers who, after meeting atop the Space Needle and snapping pictures, scatter to all parts of the city to pursue their diverse interests. In the following sections, I detail some attractions geared toward specific ages and interests. Parents with children can expect a full slate of museums and attractions geared specifically to the younger set, with visits to parks and pools to burn off energy. Teens who make it out of the Experience Music Project with time and money to spare can take unusual tours into unexpected corners of the city and find great places to hang out with their own kind. The blissfully romantic (you can spot them by their serial hand-holding and sappy grins) can stroll through charming neighborhoods and find world-class places for bonding, and outdoor lovers can get their fill of the city's parks and biking trails.

Seattle just for kids

Spend a few days in Seattle with your kids and you may see why all of those Californians moved up here for quality-of-life issues. You can utilize the whole city to keep the children happy and entertained, from visits to the downtown museums and attractions to trips to neighborhood parks that are equipped with wading pools and playground apparatus, to breaks at the indoor public pools that are dotted around the city.

Enchanted Village and Wild Waves
Federal Way

The biggest and best amusement park in the state is located some 20 miles south of the city. The Enchanted Village side has rides, including merry-go-rounds and a big roller coaster, and the water park section has lots of fast slides and tubes, and spraying stations to keep all ages happy and cool on hot summer days. Keep in mind that despite the high prices, the park gets utterly jammed by locals who are thrilled by the sunny weather.

36201 Enchanted Pkwy. S., Federal Way. Take I-5 South to Exit 142-B (direction Puyallup). ☎ *253-661-8000. Internet:* www.sixflags.com/parks/enchanted village/index.asp. *Open mid-May to Sept; call for hours. Admission: $29.99 adults and children over 4 feet tall; $24.99 all other children and seniors.*

Fun Forest Amusement Park
Seattle Center

Seattle Center's amusement park is smaller than Enchanted Village's, but it's also a heck of a lot closer and cheaper. It has a log-flume ride and a smallish roller coaster, as well as a fun house of horrors and a couple of those upside-down rides that only teenagers can stomach. You get lots of cotton candy, popcorn, and carnival games of chance, too. Next door is a huge video-game parlor.

Adjacent to the Monorail and Experience Music Project. ☎ *206-728-1585. Open noon–7 p.m. in summer (to 11 p.m. Fri and Sat; to 8 p.m. Sun); hours vary during the winter. Admission charged per ride; purchase ride tickets at kiosks.*

Pacific Science Center
Seattle Center

Seattle's science museum is a big, sprawling building with several wings and a courtyard that features a pond with replicas of dinosaurs bathing.

Everything is hands-on and interactive, and kids learn about physics and natural sciences without even knowing it. A cool dinosaur exhibit has life-size animatronic models that move and roar, and a technology center allows you to play virtual basketball against a 7-foot-tall pro. The center is geared to grade-school ages and below, but teenagers enjoy the IMAX theater on the premises (see the section "Seattle just for teens," later in this chapter).

200 Second Ave. N. ☎ 206-443-2001. Internet: www.pacificsciencecenter. org. *Open daily 10 a.m.–6 p.m. Admission: $9 adults, $6.50 ages 3–13 and seniors.*

Playgrounds

The city has lots of neighborhood playgrounds that are equipped with swings, slides, merry-go-rounds, and, in many cases, wading pools that are filled up in the summer and provide hours of entertainment for toddlers. If sightseeing and city-scouring gets to be a bit too much for your youngsters, and everyone needs a break, head to a park to let them play while you sit on a bench and gather yourself. Ask your hotel's front desk or concierge to recommend a playground close by, or give one of the ones in the following listing information a try.

Green Lake Park, *Green Lake Drive N., at the north end of the lake, just west of the community center. Unnamed playground in Wallingford at Woodlawn Avenue N. and N. 43rd Street, two blocks south of the Wallingford commercial district.* ☎ *206-386-4320 for Seattle Parks and Recreation. Open: Daylight hours. Admission: free.*

Ride the Ducks
Seattle Center

This land/sea tour on a refurbished military amphibious craft is a riot for kids, because everyone is handed a duck-bill-shaped "quacking" noise-maker to honk early and often throughout the narrated tour. For more details, see "And on Your Left: Seeing Seattle by Guided Tour," later in this chapter.

Tickets at Seattle Center kiosk adjacent to the Space Needle. ☎ *206-441-3825. Internet:* www.ridetheducksofseattle.com. *Multiple tours throughout the day. Admission: $22 adults, $12 kids.*

Seattle Children's Museum
Seattle Center

In the basement of the Seattle Center's Center House, this museum is a hands-on buffet of attractions for younger children, from toddlers to grade-school age. Kids can enjoy a great bubble station and kinetic sculptures, as well as an enormous carved volcanic mountain with stations for sliding, touching, and learning about trees and nature.

The Center House. ☎ *206-441-1768. Internet:* www.thechildrensmuseum.org. *Open –Mon–Fri 10 a.m.–5 p.m., Sat. & Sun. 10 a.m.–6 p.m. Admission: $6 adults and children; $5.50 seniors.*

Seattle Children's Theatre
Seattle Center

One of the best children's theaters in the country, this place is dedicated solely to producing works for children. The spiffy new theater presents both old classics and world premieres, with a repertory that goes beyond kiddie entertainment to explore issues of self and society that speak to children. It's well-attended by local grade schools and the public, so inquire into ticket availability early in your trip planning.

The Charlotte Martin Theatre, 2nd Ave. N. at Thomas Street. ☎ *206-441-3322. Internet:* www.sct.org. *Open Sept–June, with public shows and matinees on weekends only. Admission varies with each production.*

Swimming pools

It is the hardy child indeed who would brave a swim in frosty Puget Sound, which never gets above 55 degrees, even on the hottest summer days. Instead, take your kids to an indoor swimming pool for a family swim. Pools are located near community centers around the city and are equipped with locker rooms with keyed lockers and showers, and, in some cases, saunas or whirlpool baths.

Ballard pool, *1471 NW 67th St., just north of Ballard High School;* ☎ *206-684-4094.* ***Queen Anne pool,*** *1920 1st Ave. W., atop the hill and across from McClure Middle School;* ☎ *206-386-4282. Call ahead for hours for family and public swims. Admission: $2.50 adults, $1.75 children.*

The Waterfront
Downtown

Not so much a neighborhood as a commercial strip, this section of Alaskan Way in downtown Seattle is a fun attraction for families with kids. The old-fashioned streetcar plies a railroad track from one end of the strip to the other, competing with horse-drawn carriages for your transportation buck. In between are lots of souvenir shops, hot dog stands, restaurants, and terminals for pleasure cruises and ferries. In summer, one of the piers turns into an outdoor concert venue that presents national acts. A big, new cruise-ship terminal docks megaliners every week during the summer. This is a glitzy part of Seattle that kids enjoy, and the views of Puget Sound and the Olympic Mountains are terrific.

Downtown Seattle on Alaskan Way from Myrtle Edwards Park to Pioneer Square.

Ye Olde Curiosity Shop
Downtown

This souvenir store on the Seattle waterfront ups the gawking factor considerably with authentic shrunken heads and real mummies on display in glass cases alongside T-shirts and tacky tourist items. The gross-out aspect is high; kids love it.

Pier 54, Alaskan Way on the Seattle Waterfront (just north of the ferry terminal). ☎ *206-682-5844. Open daily 9:30 a.m.–6 p.m. (weekends 9 a.m.–6 p.m.). Admission: free.*

Seattle just for teens

Sure, I know what teens want. They want to be around kids their own age doing cool things. And when I figure out what things are cool all of the time to every teen, I'll issue a special bulletin and let you know. In the meantime, here are a few activities around Seattle that your older kids might enjoy. Keep in mind, too, that they might appreciate being handed a fistful of dollars and being left to their own devices for a few hours at the Pike Place Market or Experience Music Project. In that vein, a night off from the family to catch a movie in one of Seattle's many theaters could go a long way toward maintaining family harmony.

Fremont

Seattle's funkiest neighborhood is a great place to explore. Teens appreciate the kitschy stores that sell vintage clothing, pop culture paraphernalia and knick-knacks, and the public art that ranges from an enormous bronze sculpture of Lenin that was hauled over from a Russian fire sale to the hammered-tin Fremont rocket that is propped up on the side of a commercial building. On weekends, an open market sells crafts and handmade goods, and at night, the parking lot clears out and classic movies are screened on the side of a building, with people arriving with their own folding chairs and coolers to enjoy the show. A pleasant footpath on the north side of the ship canal makes for peaceful walks.

Begins just after the Fremont Bridge on Fremont Avenue N. and N. 35th Street.

GameWorks
Downtown

The video-game parlor by Steven Spielberg's DreamWorks company is far and away the best electronic entertainment in the city. The multilevel space boasts all the top, state-of-the-art video games, including simulated jet-ski and skiing games and an incredible electronic version of shoot-'em-up that has you strapped into a seat that rises and falls some 30 feet — great french fries and pizza, too. Buy your kid a pass card and turn him or her loose while you shop at the nearby stores. After 10 p.m., it's only open to people ages 18 and older.

1511 Seventh Ave. at Pike Street ☎ *206-521-0952. Internet:* www.gameworks. com. *Open Mon–Thurs 11 a.m.–midnight; Fri 11 a.m–1 a.m.; Sat 10 a.m.–1 a.m.; Sun 11 a.m.–midnight. Admission: Free. Games cost $1–$3 each. Ask about special weekday and weekend promotions.*

Gasworks Park
Fremont/Wallingford

This very urban park between the Fremont and Wallingford neighbor-hoods is more about happenings than playing on kiddie swings and slides. Named for the rusty, Gothic-looking old boilers and machinery that constituted the city's power source way back when, it's a hilly expanse overlooking downtown and Lake Union. On most days, it's a great place to fly kites and hang out, and it frequently hosts outdoor con-certs and festivals throughout the summer, including a huge Fourth of July bash that culminates in a fireworks show over the lake.

N. Northlake Way and Meridian Avenue N. Take the Fremont Bridge from down-town and turn right, then right on Stone Way, and stay on it as it turns into N. Northlake Way.

IMAX Dome Theater
Seattle Center

The impressive, six-story IMAX movie screen at Pacific Science Center presents stellar new films, including the breathtaking *Everest,* which was made by Seattle climbers and photographers. Don't miss the 3-D pre-sentations when they're offered; the images pop off the screen and hover before your eyes with the best 3-D effects I've ever seen. They've lately begun to screen feature films like the latest *Star Wars*, too. A movie here is a great way to soak up some cultural and natural history in a crowd-pleasing format that impresses even the most jaded teens.

Pacific Science Center at Seattle Center. Ticket kiosk for IMAX films is located behind the museum on the 2nd Avenue N. and John Street side. ☎ *206-443-2001. Internet:* www.pacificsciencecenter.org. *Showtimes throughout the day. Admission: $6.75–$8.50 adults, $5.75–$7.50 ages 3–13 and seniors.*

University of Washington
University District

The stately, classical buildings of UW (universally pronounced U-Dub) and the stellar views of Mount Rainier in the distance make this tree-lined campus a great place to stroll, particularly if your teenager wants a taste of the college atmosphere. Red Square, in the center of campus, is a paved redbrick area surrounded by libraries and classroom buildings where students rollerblade, skateboard, and play Frisbee. It's well worth a visit if college is starting to enter the family conversation. Adjacent University Avenue NE features a great strip of cheap food places and student-oriented shops.

Main entrance at 15th Avenue NE and NE 45th Street; take I-5 north to first exit after bridge (NE 45th and 50th streets) and turn right. ☎ 206-543-2100. Best to visit during daylight hours. No admission; campus parking lots fill up early, so find parking on nearby streets.

Seattle for romantics

With its ever-present water views, drawbridges, green tree-filled parks, and ubiquitous coffee shops, Seattle is a great place for exploring with your sweetheart. Combine some of these attractions with a romantic dinner for two in a cozy Belltown boite to keep the old heartstrings twanging.

The bridges of King County

Seattle's downtown is connected to the north-side neighborhoods by several bridges, three of which are lovely little drawbridges that go back decades. They all have pedestrian walkways and offer nice views of the canal, with pleasure craft and commercial barges slowly traveling to and from Lake Union and Puget Sound. The lowest, the Fremont Bridge, is the most-opened drawbridge in the country.

__Ballard Bridge__ on Elliott Avenue W. as it becomes 15th Avenue W. __Fremont Bridge__ at Westlake Avenue and Fremont Avenue N. __University Bridge__ on Eastlake Avenue as it becomes Roosevelt Way N.

Emerald Downs
Auburn

Seattle's new, state-of-the-art horse-racing track makes for a grand afternoon out. Even if you don't like to wager, it's fun to watch the thoroughbred horses parade in the paddock before each race, the jockeys in silks boosted onto their backs. The competition is first-rate, and there are plenty of opportunities for wining and dining.

2300 Emerald Downs Dr., about 40 minutes southeast of the city. Take Rte. 167 from I-405 S. to 15th Ave. NW exit. ☎ 888-931-8400 or 253-288-7711. Internet: www. emeralddowns.com. Daily post times during April–Sept season. Admission fee: $4; children 17 and under free.

Golden Gardens Park
Ballard

Seattle's idea of a beach is this rocky point on a tip of land on the edge of the Ballard neighborhood. A paved path leads past the chilly beach and a restroom station to a natural wetlands where you can see water-fowl and starfish that wash up in the tidal flats. Sea lions bark from the rocky areas alongside the adjacent marina, and the views of water, islands, and mountains are stellar. Dog lovers can climb the steep stairs up the adjacent hill to find a large fenced area where dogs come to play leash-free.

Seaview Avenue NW in Ballard, past the Chittenden (Ballard) Locks. Plenty of free parking at the park.

Myrtle Edwards Park
Downtown

This strip of the downtown waterfront is north of all the shops and attractions, and it receives far less traffic than most of the city's parks, which is a pity, because it has great views of Puget Sound, ferryboats crossing to Bainbridge Island, and the towering Olympic Mountain range, plus a paved path for walkers and cyclists and strips of green grass dotted with park benches. On the Fourth of July, the park hosts a huge festival that culminates in a dramatic fireworks show.

Alaskan Way, north of Pier 70 and the cruise ship terminal. Free parking available.

Seattle Center dances
Seattle Center

Known around town as "the old people's dance," the ballroom dances held weekly at Seattle Center attract an adorable crowd of seniors, couples, and kids on dates. Musical combos that invariably consist of three or four elderly gents produce a smooth sound to which you can foxtrot, Lindy hop, and even jitterbug. The dance floor at the Seattle Center House is smooth and spacious. It's very sweet entertainment, and free to boot.

Seattle Center House, adjacent to the monorail station. ☎ 206-684-7200. Dances most Saturdays 8–10 p.m. and occasional matinees. Admission: Free; dance lessons usually offered at 7 p.m. for $5.

Seattle for nature and outdoors lovers

Want to immerse yourself in trees and nature without even leaving the city? It's easy, because Seattle is graced with an abundance of parks that preserve the Northwest's natural setting of tall cedars and pines. The following suggestions offer some great options for getting outside and exploring.

Burke-Gilman Trail

This terrific urban bike trail was born when an old, abandoned railroad bed that ran through several northside neighborhoods was paved over.

The Burke-Gilman stretches from Fremont past the University district and all the way up to the top of Lake Washington, with extensions on the way that connect it to Ballard and the Locks. Walkers and joggers enjoy the pedestrian-only path and views of Lake Union and Lake Washington, while cyclists whiz past. Skaters can rent wheels for the path at **Urban Surf** (2100 N. Northlake Way; ☎ **206-545-9463**), opposite Gasworks Park.

Best place to park and begin trail is at Gasworks Park, N. Northlake Way and Meridian Avenue N. between Fremont and Wallingford. Free parking. Continue east on trail toward UW and points north.

Carkeek Park
Ballard

The salmon are returning to Piper's Creek after careful reclamation efforts in this wild, rugged park on a chunk of hillside in north Ballard. Park the car at an unassuming lot off NW 105th Street and leave all urban sights and sounds behind in this tree-filled natural wonderland. The creek meanders past the footpath as you make your way to a small, rocky beach on Puget Sound. In the fall, the whole place is blanketed in large red and yellow oak leaves. Look for salmon from various viewpoints along the creek.

8th Avenue NW and NW 105th Street in north Ballard. Look for trailheads and parking behind big shopping center. Cars can also continue to parking lot near the beach from Carkeek Park Road, but walking the path from the hilltop down is more fun.

Discovery Park
Magnolia

Visit this mammoth, 513-acre park to pack a variety of Northwest experiences into one long day of exploring. A rocky beach reached by a steep path is studded with driftwood and tidal pools that reveal all sorts of Puget Sound critters, from mussels to bright starfish. Walk the length of the beach to discover a working lighthouse. The upper sections of the park have big meadows of wildflowers and swaying grasses, as well as paths that lead through stands of tall, native trees. The park is so big that you may want to spend a half-day on one side of it and then drive to the other side to begin anew. Guided nature tours are offered on weekends.

3801 W. Government Way in the Magnolia neighborhood; several entrances to the park. Call ☎ 206-386-4236 for programs and information.

Green Lake
Fremont

The best place in the city for jogging and roller-skating is the three-plus-mile paved path around this smallish, manmade lake. Seattleites of every shape and size use the path for exercise on all but the gloomiest days.

Rent skates from **Gregg's Green Lake Cycle** (7007 Woodlawn Ave. NE; ☎ 206-523-1822). You can rent bikes there, too, but the path is generally too crowded for cyclists, so stick to the roads that circle the lake and the path or head south to the Burke-Gilman Trail (see the listing earlier in this section) for cycling.

W. Green Lake Way N., just east of Woodland Park and the zoo. Ample parking is available at the south end of the lake.

Cougar Mountain Regional Wildland Park
Eastside

This park encompasses the foothills of the Cascades Mountains (known as the Issaquah Alps). At 3,000 acres, the park is one of the largest designated urban wilderness areas in the country. Miles and miles of hiking trails traverse the dense forests, and thanks to local hiking clubs, the trails are well marked and maintained. Look for the signage and markings of the turn-of-the-century mine shafts that left this area with communities named Newcastle and Coal Creek.

From Seattle, take I-9 east to Exit 13 and proceed south five miles to park entrance. The Issaquah Alps Trail Club (Internet: www.issaquahalps.org) provides information and guided hikes.

University of Washington Waterfront Activities Center
Lake Washington/University District

This shop, adjacent to the university's Husky Stadium, is a prime spot to rent canoes and kayaks for exploring the marshy areas of Lake Washington and the ship canal. Paddle in the peaceful, reedy areas where the lake meets the canal and look for otters and waterfowl, and then cross under the Route 520 bridge (don't forget to snicker at the motorists above who are no doubt stuck in traffic) toward little islands near the Washington Park Arboretum. It's an idyllic paddle, and if you want to turn it into serious exercise, you have 30-mile-long Lake Washington before you.

Montlake Boulevard NE behind Husky Stadium in the University District. ☎ 206-543-9433. Open daily. Various fees for renting watercraft.

Washington Park Arboretum
Washington Park

This 200-acre park has walking trails that lead past hundreds of trees, many of which are identified by signs. Inside is a gorgeous Japanese garden, as well as thousands of cultivated plant and flower varietals. The best time to come is in the spring, when the cherry trees and rhododendrons are flowering and the park is fairly bursting with color and life. The grounds can get pretty mushy during wet seasons, so wear appropriate footwear.

2300 Arboretum Dr. E. at Lake Washington Boulevard across the ship canal from the University of Washington. ☎ 206-543-8800.

And on Your Left, the Space Needle: Seeing Seattle by Guided Tour

Seattle is a very manageable city to explore on your own, which is to say that the core areas are not so big that you get lost, nor are there crime-ridden areas that are best to avoid. Still, you may prefer the comfort and convenience of a guided tour, especially if you're pressed for time or would like a fast orientation to the city so that you can decide which spots you want to focus on. In Seattle, guided tours are also the only way to see certain inaccessible places (such as Bill Gates's house or an uninhabited San Juan island), unless by chance you bring along your own boat, seaplane, or World War II amphibious landing craft (more on that later).

The downside of guided tours? You have to come and go on someone else's schedule, not your own, and chances are that you have to reboard the bus just when you find the perfect cafe for an espresso. You also travel in a pack with other tourists, so you usually don't enjoy much interaction with the locals.

Touring Seattle on land

The mode of travel for land tours of Seattle run the gamut, from big buses to trains to walking shoes. Here are some of the best of the bunch:

✔ The major tour operator in town is **Gray Line of Seattle** (☎ 206-626-5208 or 800-426-7532; Internet: www.graylineofseattle.com), which operates sightseeing tours on big, comfortable buses. Gray Line's **Seattle City Tour** ($29 adults, $14.50 children) is a three-hour spin that takes in the downtown shopping district and waterfront, the Space Needle, Pioneer Square, and the Chittenden (Ballard) Locks. You see the same sights on the **Double Decker Bus Tour** ($21 adults, $11 children), which puts you in an open-topped bus for your drive around town. You get more time to linger during the six-hour **Grand City Tour** ($39 adult, $19.50 children), which spends a bit more time at the previously mentioned places and adds a visit to the Pike Place Market. A self-guided option is the company's **Seattle Trolley Tours** ($17 adult, $9 children), which are offered in the summer and consist of an all-day pass to a hop-on, hop-off open-air trolley bus that winds its way around the city and offers narration on the attractions and neighborhoods. You get off the trolley at an attraction that you like and then reboard when it swings back around. Gray Line also ventures out to all points in the Northwest, and they can package up combinations of tours that take in Mount Rainier or head to Victoria, British Columbia (see Chapter 5).

✔ **See Seattle Walking Tours** (☎ **425-226-7641;** Internet: www. see-seattle.com) leads you through the major stops in downtown Seattle, including Pioneer Square, the International District, and the Market. Tours are split into two groups and are contingent on six or more people signing up. The cost is $20 per person.

✔ The **Pike Place Market** offers daily 90-minute, guided Market Heritage Tours at 11 a.m. from Wednesday through Sunday throughout the year. The tours offer a lively walk around the Market, with good, behind-the-scenes stories and glimpses of the Market's many buildings and shops. Tours all begin at the Market Heritage Foundation Visitor Center at 1531 Western Ave. (☎ **206-682-7453,** ext. 653 for information; www.pikeplacemarket.org); admission is $7 adults; $5 seniors and children under 18.

✔ Want to really get under the skin of Seattle? A popular and highly unusual tour in Pioneer Square explores a section of the city that has long been out of commission. The **Seattle Underground Tour** (☎ **888-608-6337** or 206-682-4646; Internet: www.underground tour.com; $9 adults, $7 college students and children 13–17, $5 kids 6–12) literally goes beneath the city to show you turn-of-the-century storefronts and alleys that were once at street level and were buried when Seattle raised itself up a story or two to get away from the mud bogs that the streets had become. The tour is anything but dull: Tour guides jazz up the script with a rapid-fire patter of jokes and gags that are a riot to some people and an annoyance to others. Don't try this one if you have a bad back: You may have to bend over or skitter through a few narrow openings in the old underground passages.

✔ For a pleasant rail tour of the eastside communities of Renton, Bellevue, and Woodinville, the **Spirit of Washington Dinner Train** (☎ **800-876-RAIL** or 206-227-RAIL. Internet: www.spiritof washingtondinnertrain.com) is a set of renovated antique railroad cars that make tours from the train depot in Renton, WA (a half-hour's drive southeast of Seattle), and chug slowly through the woodsy communities of Seattle's eastside suburbs. Dinner is served on starched white linens, with vintage wines, and you end up at a winery in Woodinville for browsing and shopping before turning around and heading back. Lunchtime tours are also offered on weekends. More a wining and dining opportunity than a bona-fide tour, it does offer some narration and information along the route. Tours are October through May Tuesday to Saturday at 6:30 p.m., Saturday at noon, and Sunday at 11 a.m. and 5:30 p.m.; June through September Monday to Saturday at 6:30 p.m., Saturday at noon, and Sunday 11 a.m. and 5:30 p.m. Admission is $59.99 to $74.99, including dinner and dessert.

Touring Seattle by air

Just as a ferryboat trip across Puget Sound is a quintessentially Northwest experience, taking a tour on a seaplane that takes off and lands on the water is a unique local attraction. Several companies use Lake Union and Lake Washington as their bases of operations, flying the same solid, reliable DeHavilland Beaver floatplanes with pontoons that Alaskan bush pilots use. The planes seat six passengers and are operated by a single pilot. Get the copilot's seat, and you have an unsurpassed view of the city and the islands of Puget Sound.

Here are a few of the companies that can take you up, up, and away over Seattle:

✔ In Seattle, **Seattle Seaplanes,** 1325 Fairview Ave. E. (☎ **800-637-5553** or 206-329-9683;) flies from Lake Union and offers 20-minute flight tours of the city for $42.50. It can also accommodate charters of up to six passengers to fly to the San Juan Islands or Canada's Gulf Islands. The small terminal is at the southeast corner of Lake Union, just north of Chandler's Cove.

✔ **Kenmore Air,** 950 Westlake Ave. N., just south of the Northwest Outdoor Center (☎ **800-543-9595** or 425-486-1257; Internet: www.kenmoreair.com) is a scheduled-service floatplane operator that flies directly to Victoria and the San Juan Islands, with several departures per day. Kenmore acts as a mini airline, boarding passengers on docks adjacent to its modest terminal on the lake, but the service provides the same opportunity for flight-seeing as a charter, with a route that heads directly up Puget Sound and over Whidbey Island and the San Juans. The cost is $150 roundtrip for adults and $135 for children to the San Juans, and the same fare is applicable for a one-day round-trip excursion. The company has another terminal on the north end of the lake in the community of Kenmore.

✔ In Renton, **Sound Flight,** 243 W. Perimeter Road on the southern shore of Lake Washington (☎ **800-825-0722**) is a charter service that offers two-hour flight-seeing tours to the San Juans or Mount Rainier for $269 per person. If you have a group, you can save money by chartering the whole plane for $717, and the pilot can land wherever you like, such as in a deserted cove on an uninhabited island for a picnic lunch.

Touring Seattle by water

Seattle is unsurpassed for touring opportunities on the water, whether you make a short crossing to Bainbridge Island or ride for several hours to the San Juan Islands or Victoria, British Columbia. Make sure that you schedule some time in your vacation to get on the water; the views and environment are sensational on Puget Sound as you cruise among islands with the city perched on one shore, Mount Rainier to the south, snowcapped Mount Baker to the north, and the jagged Olympic Mountain range looming to the west. Sailboats, yachts, and huge commercial ships share the waterways with you, and seagulls gracefully ride the airstreams trailing the big ferryboats, hoping for a handout. You may even see dolphins or a rare pod of killer whales swimming by.

Here is a sampling of the many tour operators that cruise the local waters:

✔ The least expensive option for getting on the water is to take a **Washington State ferry** (☎ 206-464-6400; see the description earlier in this chapter and Chapter 17 for more information) from Pier 52 on the Waterfront, just north of Pioneer Square. These aren't guided tours, but you get plenty of great Puget Sound views. Boats leave two or three times an hour bound for Bainbridge Island or the town of Bremerton, and foot passengers pay only $5.40 for a round-trip fare (it costs more for cars).

✔ **Argosy Cruises** (☎ 800-426-7505 or 206-623-4252; Internet: www.argosycruises.com), which is affiliated with Gray Line of Seattle, has a number of packages available on big, double-decker tour boats. A popular one-hour harbor cruise ($16 adults, $7 children 5 to 12) departs from Pier 55 in the center of the Seattle waterfront and offers some nice views of the city from Elliott Bay. A **Cruise the Locks** package gives you the rare opportunity to navigate the Chittenden (Ballard) Locks from Puget Sound to Lake Union ($29 adults, $10 children). For the "Who Wants to Be a Millionaire" crowd, Argosy also offers tours of Lake Washington that depart from Lake Union's Chandler's Cove and make their way past the magnificent mansions that are perched on the eastern shore of the grand lake, including Bill Gates's modest waterfront estate (which includes a fishpond where Bill raises and releases his own salmon).

Located on the waterfront at Pier 56, the *Royal Argosy* (☎ 206-674-3500) is a harbor cruise ship that offers lunch, dinner, and party cruises throughout the day, frequently including live music. Fares usually begin at $36 for lunch and $69 for dinner.

✔ Pier 69 is the terminal for **Victoria Clipper** (☎ 800-888-2535 or 206-448-5000; Internet: www.victoriaclipper.com), whose high-speed and very comfortable cruising catamarans shoot to Victoria, British Columbia, in under three hours, passing the San Juan Islands on the way. You could conceivably make the round-trip in a day if you wanted to see a lot of water all at once. Fares are $68 to $113 for adults and $34 to $56.50 for children 1 to 11, with discounts and land tour options available. These very popular cruises are frequently sold out during the summer months, so reserve your seats well ahead of time.

✔ For a taste of Northwest Native American culture, the **Tillicum Village Tour** is an interesting dinner cruise that leaves daily from Pier 55 on the Seattle waterfront, bound for Tillicum Village on tiny Blake Island, which is opposite West Seattle and just north of Vashon Island. The tour includes narration, a Northwest salmon dinner cooked on an open fire and served in a decorated long-house, and Native American dances and entertainment. A little time is built in for you to explore the remote shores of the island, which is a state park (☎ **206-443-1244;** Internet: www.tillicum village.com. $59.74 adults; $22.98 children 5–12; $54.23 seniors).

Touring Seattle by Duck

"By land or by sea? I just can't decide!" you wail. You obviously need **The Duck,** a novel tour of Seattle and Lake Union that is conducted on board a renovated WWII amphibious landing craft (the same kind you saw in *Saving Private Ryan* landing soldiers on the beaches of Europe). This is a covered, open-air vehicle that plies the streets of downtown Seattle showing you the sights while, equipped with duck-billed noise-makers, you quack at any and all passersby. The driver doubles as narrator and chief quacker. Making its way to Fremont and the northern edge of Lake Union, it plops into the water and chugs along by propeller as it tours houseboat communities and the shores of Gasworks Park before clambering, dripping wet, back onto the road and returning to its Seattle Center base. The 90-minute tours begin and end near the Space Needle (☎ **800-817-1116** or 206-441-DUCK; $22 adults, $12 kids).

Chapter 16

A Shopper's Guide to Seattle

• •

In This Chapter

▶ Tuning in to the local shopping scene

▶ Browsing the big names in Seattle retailing

▶ Getting a smart shopping guide to the Pike Place Market and other outdoor markets

▶ Hitting the stores, neighborhood by neighborhood

▶ Discovering Seattle's stores from A to Z

• •

Seattle has a long and storied history as a shopping mecca, starting with the Alaskan gold-rushers who came to town to load up on supplies before heading north. Seattle is still a fantastic place to find rugged outerwear for active lifestyles, but in recent years, the shopping scene has grown to include major retailers and international and specialty shops. In this chapter, I acquaint you with the city's broad spectrum of shopping opportunities.

Making the Shopping Scene

Ever tried shopping in downtown Los Angeles or Phoenix? Not much there, huh? But while other Western cities have abandoned their downtown shopping cores, Seattle has managed to maintain a vibrant downtown shopping scene. Most of the action is centered downtown, so it's easy to hit many of the hot spots from a hotel that's in this area. In this section, I provide tips on finding exactly what you want and concentrating your shopping in certain zones of the city.

Store hours vary and change seasonally, so it's best to call ahead. Plan on most department stores opening between 9 and 10 a.m. and closing between 5 and 6 p.m., with 11 a.m. to 5 p.m. being the standard on Sunday and later hours offered during the holiday buying season. The downtown shopping malls (**Pacific Place, City Centre,** and **Westlake Center**) stay open until 9 p.m., and some stores, such as bookstores and music shops, are open as late as 11 p.m. Don't plan on arriving late at the **Pike Place Market,** however: The stalls are deserted by 6 p.m. (though restaurants and bars here are open late). Conversely, don't rush out the door after breakfast to go shopping at boutiques and independent stores, which frequently don't open until 11 a.m.

Seattle has a rather hefty 8.8% sales tax, which consists of the 6.5% charged in the rest of the state of Washington plus a surcharge tacked on for the sheer pleasure of it. If you tour the Northwest and plan on making any large purchases, you should consider (as Seattleites often do) waiting to buy the item in Oregon, which has no sales tax.

The Big Boys (and Girls) of Retailing

Seattle has its share of big-name stores, many of which originated here and continue to be major draws for shoppers:

- ✔ **Eddie Bauer:** 1330 Fifth Ave. at Union Street (☎ 206-622-2766); also in University Village. Eddie was a Seattle boy with a fondness for designing rugged clothes for fishing and hiking. Who knew he'd grow up to be the godfather of casual chic?

- ✔ **Fred Meyer:** 915 NW 45th St., Ballard (☎ 206-297-4300) and 417 Broadway E., Capitol Hill (☎ 206-328-6920); open until 11 p.m. The Northwest equivalent of Target or an upscale Woolworth's, this discount department chain originated in Seattle. It's the locals' favorite choice for toys, housewares, sundries, and casual clothes.

- ✔ **Niketown:** 1500 6th Ave. at Pike Street (☎ 206-447-6453). Lovers of the swoosh can find their favorite gear here, at astonishing prices, in a store that's a shrine to mega-athletes. Browsers like the autographed gear and nonstop video entertainment of Nike athletes in action.

- ✔ **Nordstrom:** 500 Pine St. at Fifth Avenue (☎ 206-628-2111). Seattle's locally owned upscale department store practically saved downtown in 1998 by moving into a vacant space in the center of town. It boasts the best service in the city and an unrivaled shoe department.

- ✔ **REI:** 222 Yale Ave. N. at Thomas Street, just north of Denny Way (☎ 206-223-1944). The name stands for Recreational Equipment, Inc., which has long been Seattle's co-op of choice for gearing up for the great outdoors. The store is now located in a cavernous flagship space with its own climbing wall, mountain bike track, and waterfalls.

Prowling the Market (s)

The **Pike Place Market** is a great place to eat, drink coffee, and purchase fresh vegetables, fruit, and fish (see Chapter 14 for my gushing review of the eating opportunities), but it's also a very cool place to shop, with lots of little stores peppering the Market's buildings and alleys. Be sure to go below the main level of the market to the **"Down Under"** shops to find all kinds of interesting things. Also hit **Western Avenue** on the waterfront side of the Market, which has, among other things, an exotic spice store and a shop that sells live parrots and macaws. At the end of the main arcade of produce vendors, crafts merchants hawk handmade flutes, jewelry, silk-screened T-shirts, tie-dyed dresses, and more.

Tourist-at-the-market syndrome: Don't let this happen to you!

It's funny at first, and then it quickly becomes downright annoying, to see a group of tourists fresh off the bus standing in a clump at the Pike Place Market and staring at the fish on sale as if at any moment they might spring to life and dance the Macarena. They take pictures of the fish, they have their pictures taken with the fish, and then they move on to do the same with meats, cheeses, and produce. People who actually come to buy the stuff (as opposed to being entertained by it) get shut out or stuck behind groups of gawkers, which sort of defeats the purpose of a working food market. Do me a favor, folks, and keep it moving — don't clog the aisles and buy a few things to separate yourself from the mobs.

The success of the Pike Place Market has spawned a number of smaller markets around the city. In Fremont, the **Fremont Sunday Market** (600 N. 34th St., just west of the Fremont Bridge) is a major center for arts and crafts, with dozens of vendors who set up tables and booths for their handmade furniture, jewelry, pottery, and clothing. It's outdoors in the summer but moves into a covered space the rest of the year. In the summer and fall months, farmers and food vendors come to the U-District every weekend for the **University Market** (corner of University Way NE and NE 50th St.), a neighborhood event that is a good way to find produce in season from nearby farms. If antiques are your passion, the **Antiques at Pike Place** market (92 Stewart St. near the Pike Place Market) is a collection of as many as 80 vendors who gather to display and sell their antiques and collectibles.

The exotic **Market Magic** (Down Under shops; ☎ 206-624-4271) has wonderful, wall-size posters of great magicians and a large selection of gags and books on performing magic tricks; **Sur La Table** (84 Pine St. on Pike Place; ☎ 206-448-2244), a serious kitchenware shop for the gourmet cook, has a huge selection of utensils and heavy-duty cookware, as well as an impressive array of cookbooks and gift items like dish towels and serving dishes; **Made in Washington** (Post Alley; ☎ 206-467-0788) is great for souvenirs from the Northwest; **Isadora's Antique Clothing** (1915 First Ave. between Pine and Lenora streets; ☎ 206-441-7711) has exquisite replicas of 1930s and '40s gowns and tuxedoes; and **The Great Wind-Up** (Economy Market Atrium; ☎ 206-621-9370) carries a broad selection of clever wind-up toys (some are antiques) and other oddities.

Seattle's Great Shopping Neighborhoods

Seattle's best shopping zones are scattered around the city, with a great deal of the action taking place downtown. As in other discussions of the downtown area (such as restaurants and lodgings), I divide downtown into smaller sections here.

Belltown

Seattle's trendiest downtown neighborhood is home to designer boutiques and interesting shops selling home furnishings and accessories. Be warned that the neighborhood is in constant flux these days, with retail space prices going through the roof, so stores tend to come and go quickly. Check out **Great Jones Home** (1921 2nd Ave; ☎ 206-448-9405) for furnishings and accessories. (The vanilla candles look like they've been plucked from classic old farmhouses.) Sturdy outdoor wear is the stock in trade of **Patagonia** (2100 First Ave.; ☎ 206-622-9700), which has its own line of weather-resistant shells and parkas (practically evening wear in casual Seattle). Shoe lovers hoof it to **J. Gilbert Footwear** (2025 First Ave.; ☎ 206-441-1182) for handsome fashions that mostly hail from European shoe designers. Further down First Avenue, near the Market, you'll find **Watson Kennedy Fine Home** (1022 First Ave.; ☎ 206-652-8350), with a gorgeous collection of home decor items foraged largely from France and Italy by owner/aesthete Ted Watson Kennedy.

Capitol Hill

When the dress code calls for leather chaps and retro T-shirts, Seattle's gays head to this neighborhood, just east of downtown, and cruise the shops on Broadway. The boutique shops sell the cattiest greeting cards and the most outrageous T-shirts in town. For fancy party clothes for glam girls, check out **Rockin' Betty's** (401 Broadway E. in the Broadway Market; ☎ 206-709-8821); cool bowling shirts and vintage duds are available nearby at **Red Light** (312 Broadway E.; ☎ 206-329-2200). **Twice Sold Tales** (905 E. John St., a block from Broadway; ☎ 206-324-2421) has a fine selection of used books. For retro furniture from the '60s and '70s, make your way to **Area 51** (401 E. Pine St.; ☎ 206-568-4782), which turns kitschy items like old gym lockers into home decor fashion statements.

The Shopping District

There's no other way to describe this section in the heart of downtown, home to Seattle's biggest and grandest stores, with **Nordstrom** (500 Pine St. at Fifth Avenue; ☎ 206-628-2111) serving as its epicenter. Within just a few blocks are **The Bon Marche** (3rd Avenue and Pine Street; ☎ 206-506-6000), another major department store; national chain retailers like **Eddie Bauer** (1330 Fifth Ave. at Union Street; ☎ 206-622-2766) and **Old Navy** (601 Pine St.; ☎ 206-264-9341), and three major indoor shopping centers (okay, urban malls). These malls are **Pacific Place** (600 Pine St. at 6th Avenue), the newest downtown shopping area, which houses the most upscale retailers, such as Seattle's first **Tiffany & Co.** (☎ 206-264-1400); **City Centre** (6th Avenue and Union Street), which is home to major chain retailers like **Ann Taylor** (☎ 206-652-0663) and **FAO Schwarz** (☎ 206-442-9500) and has gorgeous displays of handblown glass by Seattle artist Dale Chihuly; and **Westlake Center** (400 Pine St.), which houses a load of specialty shops and a food court, as well as the downtown station for the Seattle Center monorail.

Pioneer Square

Seattle's oldest district (Yesler Way was the original "Skid Row," so named because loggers skidded their cut timber down the steep hillside to the waterfront) is now an artsy area of galleries and shops. Among the standouts are **Bud's Jazz Records** (102 S. Jackson St.;

☎ **206-628-0445**), with one of the greatest selections of jazz in the country, and the **Elliott Bay Book Company** (101 S. Main St.; ☎ **206-624-6600**), which is widely regarded as Seattle's best bookstore. Just south of Pioneer Square, Safeco Field houses the **Seattle Mariners Team Shop** (1250 First Ave. S.; ☎ **206-346-4287**), with everything from baseball caps to replica jerseys. You can find clever toys at **Magic Mouse** (603 First Ave.; ☎ **206-682-8097**), which carries hand-crafted toys from Europe and a great selection of plush stuffed animals.

The Waterfront

Starting just south of the Pike Place Market and continuing to Myrtle Edwards Park to the north, the **Seattle Waterfront** on Alaskan Way is loaded with souvenir shops and amusements. You don't find much of substance here, but you do find the bizarre and indeed curious **Ye Olde Curiosity Shop** (1001 Alaskan Way at Pier 54; ☎ **206-682-5844**), which hawks genuine oddities like real shrunken heads and a mummy alongside the T-shirts and Space Needle pencil sharpeners.

Queen Anne

The neighborhood that encompasses Seattle Center has a few retail strips worth perusing. At KeyArena, basketball fans can find their favorite hoop gear at the **Sonics Team Shop** (312 First Ave. N.; ☎ **206-269-SHOP**), where a great bite of your paycheck can procure a Seattle SuperSonics jersey with a player's name stitched onto the back. **Tower Records** (500 Mercer St.; ☎ **206-283-4456**) continues to be a major supplier of music and videos, and has a Ticketmaster outlet inside. For an unusual activity that kids love, check out the **Paint 'n Place** ceramics studio (2226 Queen Anne Ave. N.; ☎ **206-281-0229**) at the top of the hill, where you can paint your own designs on plates, mugs, or pottery, and have your creations fired in the on-site kilns.

Neighborhoods north of downtown

The neighborhoods just north of the ship canal that connects Lake Union and Lake Washington to Puget Sound have plenty of distinctive character, which is apparent in their shopping opportunities. The neighborhood of **Fremont** in particular, which likes to jokingly bill itself as "the center of the universe," is well worth a visit. Fremont boasts a great concentration of antique stores that lean toward the artful kitsch side of retro goods. **Deluxe Junk** (3518 Fremont Place N.; ☎ **206-634-2733**), offers lots of kidney-shaped tables, retro clothes, and knick-knacks that hail from the 1950s and 1960s. Across the street is **Fritzi Ritz** (3425 Fremont Place N.; ☎ **206-633-0929**), which concentrates on antique clothes and accessories. **GlamOrama** (3414 Fremont Ave. N.; ☎ **206-632-0287**) plays it strictly for laughs with pop culture kitsch like lunch boxes interspersed with retro clothes. The **Fremont Antique Mall** (3419 Fremont Place N.; ☎ **206-548-9140**) has a little bit of everything in its cavernous basement space. **Dusty Strings** (3406 Fremont Ave. N.; ☎ **206-634-1662**), is well worth a visit for musical instrument aficionados. The store houses the work of fine craftsmen who make beautiful dulcimers and folk instruments, as well as acoustic guitars, mandolins, and banjos. **Shorey's Bookstore** (1109 N. 36th St.; ☎ **206-633-2990**) specializes in rare editions and has an enormous inventory of hard-to-find books to peruse.

The **Ballard** neighborhood to the west of Fremont is known for its Scandinavian roots, which are reflected in **Olsen's Scandinavian Foods** (2248 NW Market St.; ☎ **206-782-8288**), where you can find house-pickled herring, cookies, and lingonberries to take home to your Swedish grandma. Another Olsen, craftsman **Sten Olsen,** runs a violin-repair shop that sells high-quality used violins and cellos (6508 8th Ave. NW; ☎ **206-783-7654**). Ballard is also home to the city's greatest collection of novelty items, gags, punching nun puppets, plastic Martians whose eyes pop out when you squeeze them, and tons of other goodies at **Archie McPhee** (2428 NW Market St.; ☎ **206-297-0240**), which is great fun to browse and is a hit with kids. Record lovers may want to make the pilgrimage to **Bop Street Records & Tapes** (5512 20th Ave. NW; ☎ **206-783-3009**), which has hung around a long time, with a huge collection of used records, to take advantage of the rebirth of vinyl. To see items that have been salvaged from Seattle's old mansions, check out **The Restore** (1440 NW 52nd St.; ☎ **206-297-9119**), which collects and resells everything from claw-footed bathtubs to chandeliers and window frames from tear-down homes.

The **U-District** at the very eastern end of the ship canal, bordering Lake Washington, is home to **University Village** (NE 45th Street and 25th Avenue NE), a big urban shopping center with a **Barnes & Noble** bookstore (☎ **206-517-4107**), an **Eddie Bauer** outlet, and lots of clothing and accessory stores that are geared to college students. Adjacent to the UW campus is the **University Book Store** (4326 University Way NE; ☎ **206-634-3400**), which has a fine selection of contemporary books and hosts frequent author visits. It has a good selection of UW souvenir gear, too. A few blocks away, **Half-Price Books** (4709 Roosevelt Way NE; ☎ **206-547-7859**) is a big, spacious store where you can buy many of your favorite books used; they have a great selection of used software, too.

Seattle Stores by Merchandise

Here is a breakdown of stores sorted by the kind of merchandise they carry.

Antiques and retro wares

Antiques at Pike Place: 92 Stewart St.; ☎ 206-441-9643.

Deluxe Junk: 3518 Fremont Place N.; ☎ 206-634-2733.

Fremont Antique Mall: 3419 Fremont Place N.; ☎ 206-548-9140.

Fritzi Ritz: 3425 Fremont Place N.; ☎ 206-633-0929.

GlamOrama: 3414 Fremont Ave. N.; ☎ 206-632-0287.

Isadora's Antique Clothing: 1915 First Ave.; ☎ 206-441-7711.

Books and music

Barnes & Noble: University Village; ☎ 206-517-4107.

Bop Street Records & Tapes: 5512 20th Ave. NW; ☎ 206-783-3009.

Bud's Jazz Records: 102 S. Jackson St.; ☎ 206-628-0445.

Dusty Strings: 3406 Fremont Ave. N.; ☎ 206-634-1662.

Elliott Bay Book Company: 101 S. Main St.; ☎ 206-624-6600.

Half-Price Books: 4709 Roosevelt Way NE; ☎ 206-547-7859.

Olsen's Violins: 6508 8th Ave. NW; ☎ 206-783-7654.

Shorey's Bookstore: 1109 N. 36th St.; ☎ 206-633-2990.

Tower Records: 500 Mercer St.; ☎ 206-283-4456.

Twice Sold Tales: 905 E. John St.; ☎ 206-324-2421.

University Book Store: 4326 University Way NE; ☎ 206-634-3400.

Fashion

Ann Taylor: City Centre; ☎ 206-652-0663.

Betsey Johnson: 1429 5th Ave.; ☎ 206-624-2887.

Bon Marche: 3rd Avenue and Pine Street; ☎ 206-506-6000.

Eddie Bauer: 1330 Fifth Ave. (also in University Village); ☎ 206-622-2766.

J. Gilbert Footwear: 2025 First Ave.; ☎ 206-441-1182.

Niketown: 1500 6th Ave. at Pike St.; ☎ 206-447-6453.

Nordstrom: 500 Pine St.; ☎ 206-628-2111.

Old Navy: 601 Pine St.; ☎ 206-264-9341.

Red Light: 312 Broadway E.; ☎ 206-329-2200.

Rockin' Betty's: 401 Broadway E.; ☎ 206-709-8821.

Home decor

Area 51: 401 E. Pine St.; ☎ 206-568-4782.

The Best of All Worlds: 523 Union St.; ☎ 206-623-2525.

Great Jones Home: 1921 2nd Ave.; ☎ 206-448-9405.

The Restore: 1440 NW 52nd St.; ☎ 206-297-9119.

Sur La Table: 84 Pine St.; ☎ 206-448-2244.

Watson Kennedy Fine Home: 1022 First Ave.; ☎ 206-652-8350.

Outdoor clothing and gear

Patagonia: 2100 First Ave.; ☎ 206-622-9700.

REI: 222 Yale Ave. N.; ☎ 206-223-1944.

Salmon and specialty food items

DiLaurenti Specialty Food Market: 1434 First Ave.; ☎ 206-622-0141.

Jack's Fish Spot: 1514 Pike Place; ☎ 206-467-0514.

Olsen's Scandinavian Foods: 2248 NW Market St.; ☎ 206-783-8288.

Pike Place Fish: 86 Pike Place; ☎ 206-682-7181.

Wild Salmon Seafood Market: Fisherman's Terminal; ☎ 206-283-3366.

Souvenirs and collectibles

Archie McPhee: 2428 NW Market St.; ☎ 206-297-0240.

Made in Washington: Post Alley; ☎ 206-467-0788.

Mariners Team Shop: Safeco Field; ☎ 206-346-4287.

Market Magic: Pike Place Market; ☎ 206-624-4271.

Paint 'n Place: 2226 Queen Anne Ave. N.; ☎ 206-281-0229.

Sonics Team Shop: 312 First Ave. N. at Key Arena; ☎ 206-269-SHOP.

Tiffany & Co: Pacific Place; ☎ 206-264-1400.

Ye Olde Curiosity Shop: 1001 Alaskan Way; ☎ 206-682-5844.

Toys

FAO Schwarz: City Centre; ☎ 206-442-9500.

The Great Wind-Up: 93 Pike Place; ☎ 206-621-9370.

Magic Mouse: 603 First Ave.; ☎ 206-682-8097.

Top Ten Toys: 104 N. 85th St.; ☎ 206-782-0098.

Chapter 17

Five Great Seattle Itineraries and Three Dandy Day Trips

. . . .

In This Chapter

▶ Seeing the sights in three days

▶ Enjoying the Emerald City's natural pleasures

▶ Sipping and snacking in Seattle

▶ Hanging out with the cool crowd

▶ Touring Seattle with kids

▶ Exploring the San Juan Islands

▶ Hiking in Mount Rainier National Park

. . . .

*T*his chapter gives you some itineraries to help organize your time in Seattle, and several different day trips that explore the area around Seattle.

Great Itineraries

If you really want to experience Seattle, take it easy. Don't run around like a maniac. The Space Needle isn't going anywhere, and if your only option for visiting it today means making a mad dash across the city in rush-hour traffic, see it tomorrow. Start your day with a simple plan: Include a few top attractions and/or areas of the city that you want to see; try to plot your schedule so that you're not spending too much of the day driving from one end of the city to another; and most importantly, be flexible. If the kids decide they want to spend twice the allotted time at the Children's Museum, don't try to cram everything else into half the time. Simply scratch something off the list or reschedule.

Keep in mind that you won't be the only one who wants to get to the top of the Space Needle on a sunny summer day — so be sure to budget time for waiting in lines at the most popular attractions, or try to get to those places early to beat the crowds.

Seattle Excursions

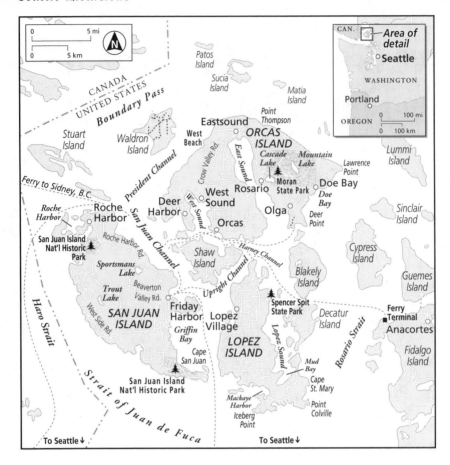

Give yourself some time to gather yourself and rest up if you have dinner plans. Enjoy a leisurely meal at a fine restaurant. Also, keep in mind that during the summer months, when daylight savings time is in effect, it frequently stays light outside until well after 9 p.m., so you may find that you can see everything without rushing, even if you have a busy schedule.

When you're planning your journeys around the city, remember that it's a lot easier and faster to go north and south in Seattle than it is to go east and west. You can move quickly and smoothly from, say, Pioneer Square to the Pike Place Market to Belltown to Queen Anne, but getting from the waterfront to Madison Park or the eastside communities of Bellevue and Kirkland can be a long, slow journey.

Following are some suggested itineraries for discovering Seattle on your own or with kids in tow. In setting up these routes, I tried to give you a good, overall view of the city and hit the highlights while keeping your travel and transfer time between attractions down to a minimum. For more details on the attractions and top sights listed here, see Chapter 15.

Seattle in Three Days

Three days? Are you kidding? It takes three days for some Seattleites to finish a large cup of latte and eat a bagel! Actually, in three days you can get a good, quick overview of the city's top spots and then spend the rest of your trip either going back for quality time at your favorites or moving in ever-widening circles to see more parts of the city.

Day one

If you're staying at a hotel downtown, leave the car parked and head on foot or by bus to the **Pike Place Market.** If you get there early, you can watch the flower vendors setting up blossoms at their stalls and the crafts merchants receiving their daily stall assignments. Have breakfast in one of the Market's many restaurants or from a take-out vendor and spend some time perusing the unusual shops on the lower levels of the market. Now walk a few blocks south on First Avenue to the **Seattle Art Museum** (except on Mondays, when it's closed) and spend the rest of the morning perusing its galleries and special exhibits. If you prefer street life and art galleries, continue farther south to the **Pioneer Square** district to explore the wealth of art galleries and shops. For lunch, frequent one of the restaurants in the area or head back to the Market, where you can pick up a basket full of goodies and have a picnic overlooking Elliott Bay at **Victor Steinbrueck Park** (at the north end of Pike Place Market, on Western Avenue at Virginia Street). Afterward, go down to the waterfront on Alaskan Way and consider taking a ferry ride to **Bainbridge Island** and back, or a cruise on a tour boat. Make your way north to the **Seattle Aquarium** and the adjoining **Seattle IMAX Dome,** and then leisurely stroll alongside Puget Sound at **Myrtle Edwards Park** before heading uphill two blocks to First Avenue for an evening of exploring **Belltown**'s restaurants and pubs.

Day two

Get yourself to **Seattle Center** by either taking a cab, riding the monorail from **Westlake Center,** or heading out on foot, and spend the better part of the morning and early afternoon enjoying the views from atop the **Space Needle** and strolling the Seattle Center grounds. A visit to **Experience Music Project,** the **IMAX theater,** and/or the **Pacific Science Center** would be in order, and you can buy lunch from one of the take-out vendors in the **Seattle Center House** or at the many restaurants on nearby Queen Anne Avenue N. Take some time to peruse the **Queen Anne** neighborhood by making the arduous walk halfway up the steep hill to Highland Avenue N., where great views of the city and Mount Rainier are seen from **Kerry Park.** Continue to the top of the hill for more shopping and restaurants or head back downtown for shopping at **Pacific Place** and the **shopping district.** (See Chapter 16 for shopping info.)

Day three

Get out of downtown and explore some of the neighborhoods that make Seattle unique. Start with a visit to **Ballard** and the **Hiram M. Chittenden Locks** (also called the "Ballard Locks"), where salmon might be running and viewable from windows in the fish ladder. Funky **Fremont** is worth several hours of strolling and stopping to shop or have coffee, and **Wallingford** has a lively retail district as well as interesting homes on the streets leading down to **Gasworks Park.** For a uniquely Seattle experience, rent kayaks on **Lake Union** and paddle among the houseboat communities on either shore, or take a sightseeing tour of the city by floatplane.

Seattle for Nature Lovers

This itinerary maximizes the opportunities to see Seattle's marvelous outdoor landscapes, trees, and parks. Start with a visit to the neighborhood of **Magnolia** and **Discovery Park** for an early hike on the bluffs above Puget Sound. You can walk down the steep trail to a rocky beach or get back in the car and drive to the **Ballard Locks** to see whether the salmon are running; then continue west to **Golden Gardens Park** for great views of the Sound, islands, and tidepools. Next stop is **Green Lake,** the manmade lake in the neighborhood of the same name, for a jog or stroll on the paved path that encircles the lake. Next, make your way south to **Gasworks Park** for great views of the city and Lake Union. You can rent skates here and navigate the **Burke-Gilman Trail** through the U-District and the University of Washington, or consider crossing the **Fremont Bridge** on foot, walking down the eastern shore of **Lake Union** to rent kayaks at the **Northwest Outdoor Center** or canoes or sailboats at the **Center for Wooden Boats.** You can paddle or sail the lake and explore the communities of dollhouse-like houseboats.

Make sure to include a visit to **Volunteer Park** in Capitol Hill in your travels. Volunteer Park boasts a greenhouse conservatory with a lovely flower and botanical collection. Also make time to walk among the themed gardens and towering trees at the **Washington Park Arboretum.** If you can't get enough of paddling, rent canoes from the **University of Washington Waterfront Activities Center.** 30-mile-long **Lake Washington** will provide you with all the canoe-friendly water you could possibly want.

Seattle for Coffee and Snack Lovers

Want to spend most of your time enjoying Seattle's cafe society, lingering over coffee and a newspaper or good book, and taking rambling walks around the city's neighborhoods? Go ahead, I won't tell! Put your finger on the caffeinated pulse of the city at one of these coffee zones.

The **Pike Place Market** is heaven for browsers and snackers. Be sure to check out the coffee bars on **Post Alley** for large, delicious cups of latte and baked goods. You could easily while away a morning moseying through the Market, visiting all of the shops and vendors, and stopping every hour or so to enjoy a cuppa Joe and a snack. Or tear yourself away from the Market and head a few blocks south to **Pioneer Square** for more cafes, as well as great bookstores and art galleries.

The neighborhoods of **Fremont, Wallingford,** and **Capitol Hill** are also perfectly suited for browsing, strolling, and sipping. Check out the public art and kitschy antique shops in **Fremont** and take a walk along the quiet, shaded **Ship Canal** in between stops for coffee and homemade cookies at, among others spots, the **Still Life in Fremont** coffee shop. **Wallingford**'s commercial strip has a wonderful teahouse and bakery among its many espresso vendors, and handsome houses line its broad streets. **Capitol Hill**'s Broadway is a lively, ultra-urban thoroughfare where Seattle's pierced and leather set hangs out. Within two blocks of this hip street, you find tree-lined boulevards with some of the oldest and stateliest homes in the city, plus some great coffee shops, particularly in the south part of the neighborhood near Pike and Pine streets.

Seattle for the Tragically Hip

The grunge scene may have long departed the city, but Seattle is still a pretty cool place to be. If art and culture are your thing, try including the following in your schedule.

The hip Seattle neighborhood these days is **Belltown,** that section of upper First through Third avenues that is loaded with new restaurants, clubs, and bars. During the summer, the party atmosphere goes up a notch or two when the restaurants open up their sidewalks and patios to diners. **Capitol Hill** is another scenemaker's nabe, with the artery of Broadway fueling Seattle's gay and alternative scenes and boasting Seattle's hottest dance clubs. **Pioneer Square** has the largest concentration of art galleries in the city, along with fine book and music stores. Venues for live music and concerts are scattered among all three of these neighborhoods.

For culture's sake, don't miss a symphony performance at **Benaroya Hall** and visit the **Seattle Art Museum,** a few blocks away from the Hall. Combine your trip to Capitol Hill with a stop at the **Seattle Asian Art**

Museum in Volunteer Park, and the **Frye Art Museum** for 19th-century American painting. **Dale Chihuly**'s stunning glasswork is on display at the **City Centre** shopping arcade downtown, as well as at the **Foster/White Gallery,** which has branches in City Centre and Pioneer Square.

Seattle is known in opera circles for its stagings of Wagner's *Ring Cycle*, and tickets sell out as early as a year in advance of a new production. Try to snag tickets to the **Seattle Opera,** which performs in **Seattle Center** (in the newly renovated Opera House). The **Pacific Northwest Ballet** is also based at Seattle Center, as are two of Seattle's biggest and most vital theaters, the **Seattle Repertory Theater** and **Intiman Theatre.** Lovers of the stage should also check out **A Contemporary Theater (ACT),** located downtown near the convention center. Broadway-style shows and musicals are performed at the lavishly renovated **Fifth Avenue Theater** and at the **Paramount Theater.** For half-price tickets to any of these venues, check out the **Ticket/Ticket** kiosks at the Pike Place Market and in Capitol Hill's Broadway Market.

Seattle with Kids

Kids have a great time in Seattle when parents plan vacation days to combine equal parts playing and running with sightseeing. If you can, try to avoid long, boring stretches in the car. You can find plenty of parks and kid-friendly attractions (not to mention cotton candy and ice-cream cones) to keep everyone happy.

Make a deal with the younger set as you make your way to **Seattle Center,** your first stop on the city tour: You get to do things you like (such as go to the top of the **Space Needle** or visit an art gallery), and then they can choose from a whole host of amusements. Younger children will love to play and splash in the huge, computerized fountain in the heart of Seattle Center or ride the merry-go-round and log flume at the **Fun Forest Amusement Park** (cotton candy and hot dogs available). The **Seattle Children's Museum** is great for toddlers, and the **Pacific Science Center** has lots of hands-on exhibits that are great for older children. Teens will love the **Experience Music Project.** Shell out the extra 15 bucks for them to appear "live" before an audience playing "Wild Thing," with a photograph to prove it, and you'll have the all-time best souvenir of adolescence. By midday you'll be ready to take a city tour on board the fun, raucous **Ride the Ducks** amphibious tour, which departs from a location near the Space Needle and offers a unique tour on both the city streets and Lake Union. Afterward, head to the Seattle Waterfront for souvenir shopping and consider taking the whole gang on to **Tillicum Village,** an authentic Native-American dinner and show that's a short boat ride away on Blake Island.

On another day, head to huge **Discovery Park** in the Magnolia neighborhood. The south side entrance is closest to a beach and sand dune walk; the north side has trees and a cool play structure of slides and swings. The Interpretive Center, also on the north side, offers guided nature walks. Stop for lunch at **Fishermen's Terminal** for fish-and-chips or chowder and check out the fishing boats that moor in the marina. Then cross the **Ballard Bridge** and spend the afternoon in the Ballard neighborhood, where you can watch boats in the **Ballard Locks** and maybe even view salmon running through windows set in a fish ladder. Nearby, on Market Street, visit **Archie McPhee's,** the best souvenir shop in the city for funny, kitschy toys and amusements. Watch the sunset from **Golden Gardens Park** and don't miss the tidepools and wetlands that are accessible via boardwalks on the park's western-most edge. Head back downtown for dinner and set your teens loose in **GameWorks** for the best videogaming in the city.

The Best Day Trips

After you've had time to explore the city, head out of town to see first-hand why people fall so much in love with the Pacific Northwest. The following day trips, using Seattle as a base, show off some of the marvels of western Washington, from the high mountains that bracket the city, to the water and islands of Puget Sound.

Day trip #1: The Mountain Loop — The North Cascades Highway

The North Cascades mountain range provides the spectacular scenery for this driving tour, which begins and ends in Seattle and takes 6 to 8 hours, depending on how often you stop. Bring lots of film for this trip; the vistas are incredible. You can drive this route only from May through the end of September; during winter months the road past Newhalem is generally snowed in and impassable.

Begin by leaving **Seattle** headed north on I-5 through the towns of **Everett** and **Marysville,** which is the home of the **Tulalip** Native American reservation. Exit at **Hwy 20** in Burlington, headed east, and make your first stop at the **Mount Baker Ranger District** headquarters and visitor center (2105 Hwy 20; ☎ 425-775-9702) in nearby Sedro Woolley. Continue east on Hwy 20, and if you'd like an early hike or a dip in a lake on a hot day, take the Baker Lake Highway to lovely **Baker Lake,** which boasts awesome views of looming **Mount Baker**. Return to Hwy 20 and continue east through the small village of Marblemount to **Newhalem,** where you find the **North Cascades Visitor Center** (☎ 360-856-5700), a handsome, chalet-style lodge with interpretive information on the local forest and great hiking trails to explore, including the Trail of the Cedars, a marked trail that winds between towering, old-growth trees.

Continuing east on Hwy 20, alongside the Skagit River, you pass the three dams that provide the bulk of Seattle's electrical energy. Be sure to stop at the **Diablo Dam,** a cool, Art Deco slab of concrete with street lamps that glow orange. You can stop the car and walk across the dam, pausing to stand before an incredible gush of water roaring through the spillway into the twisting river. The **Ross Dam** is a few miles further up the road on **Ross Lake. Seattle City Light** (☎ 206-684-3030) offers guided and self-guided tours of the dams and power plants during the summer (though some of the dams are closed to the public at press time due to heightened security; call ahead). After passing Ross Lake, you have a long, winding drive on the **North Cascades Scenic Highway,** with gorgeous alpine views, particularly in September when the leaves change. The highway ends in the charming, Old West-style town of **Winthrop,** in the rugged Okanogan region, which is composed of rolling hills and forests. Head south on Rte 153 and 97 through semi-arid, desertlike terrain to the town of **Wenatchee,** the capital of Washington's apple industry, where you can buy fresh fruit from side-of-the-road stalls. Head west on Hwy 2 through **Leavenworth,** a tourist village with a Bavarian theme, and then cross back over the mountains over 4,000-foot **Stevens Pass,** rejoining I-5 just north of Everett.

Day trip #2: The San Juan Islands

There's something magical about the San Juan Islands, that string of pearl-like islands off the northwest tip of the U.S. mainland. People love the rolling pastures, the beaches and parks, the artistic communities, and the frequent sightings of eagles, orca whales and deer. Even the weather lends a Brigadoon-esque aspect to the San Juans, which lie in a rain shadow that shunts much of the drizzly weather north to Vancouver or south to Seattle. Situated northwest of Seattle, the San Juans are an island-hopper's dream, with ferries or floatplanes connecting the string of peaceful little islands, which are wonderful for strolling, biking, or shopping in quaint, small towns. You can do this trip in a long 8- to 10-hour day or plan for an overnight visit.

Your day should begin very early in the morning with a drive to the town of **Anacortes** in northern Washington, an hour and a quarter's drive from downtown Seattle. Going early gives you a shot at catching an early ferry for this very popular passage, which is often jammed during the summer months. The car and passenger ferries operated by **Washington State Ferries** (☎ 800-84-FERRY or 888-808-7977 in Washington, or 206-464-6400; Internet: www.wsdot.wa.gov/ferries) link Anacortes with four of the hundreds of islands that make up the San Juan chain: **Lopez, Shaw, Orcas,** and **San Juan.** If you don't have a car and it's summer, you also have the option of taking the passenger-only private ferry operated by **Victoria Clipper** (☎ 800-888-2535 or 206-448-5000; Internet: www.victoriaclipper.com) from downtown Seattle to San Juan or Orcas Island.

If you're short on time or want to see more of the islands than you can by ferry, you can fly to the San Juans. **Kenmore Air,** 950 Westlake Ave. N. (☎ **800-543-9595** or 425-486-1257; Internet: www.kenmoreair.com), offers floatplane flights that take off from Lake Union (and also from the north end of Lake Washington).

Contact the **San Juan Island Chamber of Commerce,** P.O. Box 98, Friday Harbor, WA 98250 (☎ **360-378-5240;** Internet: www.sanjuan island.org); or the **Orcas Island Chamber of Commerce,** P.O. Box 252, Eastsound, WA 98245 (☎ **360-376-2273;** Internet: www.orcas island.org). For information on Lopez Island, contact the **Lopez Island Chamber of Commerce,** P.O. Box 102, Lopez, WA 98261 (☎ **360-468-4664;** Internet: www.lopezisland.com).

On the Internet, also check out the following: www.sanjuanweb.com, www.orcasisle.com, and www.thesanjuans.com.

Orcas Island

Shaped like a horseshoe, Orcas Island has long been a popular summer-vacation spot and is the most beautiful of the San Juan Islands. Orcas is a particular favorite of nature lovers, who come to enjoy the green rolling pastures, forested mountains, and fjordlike bays. Others come for the pottery made and sold on the island. **Eastsound** is the largest town on the island and has several interesting shops and good restaurants.

Around the island are several interesting pottery shops. A few miles west of Eastsound off Enchanted Forest Road is **Orcas Island Pottery** (366 Old Pottery Rd; ☎ **360-376-2813;** Internet: www.orcasisland pottery.com), the oldest pottery studio in the Northwest. At the end of this same road, on West Beach across from the West Beach Resort, you find **The Right Place Pottery Shop** (☎ **360-376-4023**). Between Eastsound and Orcas on Horseshoe Highway is **Crow Valley Pottery** (2274 Orcas Rd.; ☎ **360-376-4260;** Internet: www.crowvalley.com), housed in an 1866 log cabin. On the east side of the island in the community of Olga, you find **Orcas Island Artworks** (Horseshoe Highway; ☎ **360-376-4408**), which is full of beautiful work by island artists and craftspersons, and shares a space with Café Olga, one of the better restaurants in town.

Moran State Park (☎ **360-376-2326;** Internet: www.parks.wa.gov), which covers 5,252 acres of the island, is the largest park in the San Juans and the main destination for most island visitors. If the weather is clear, you can get great views from the summit of Mount Constitution, which rises 2,409 feet above Puget Sound. The park also has 5 lakes, 32 miles of hiking trails, and an environmental learning center. Fishing, hiking, boating, mountain biking, and camping (campsite reservations through **Washington State Parks** ☎ **888-226-7688;**

Internet: www.parks.wa.gov/reserve.asp) are all popular park activities. The park is off Horseshoe Highway, approximately 12½ miles from the ferry landing.

South of the community of Olga, on the east arm of the island, you find a great ½-mile trail through **Obstruction Pass Park.** This trail leads to a quiet little cove that has a few walk-in/paddle-in campsites. The park is at the end of Obstruction Pass Road.

The best way to see the Orcas Island coast is by sea kayak. Located at the Orcas Island ferry landing, **Orcas Outdoors** (☎ 360-376-4611; Internet: www.orcasoutdoors.com) offers guided sea-kayak tours lasting from 1 hour ($25) to overnight ($220). Three-hour guided tours ($45) are offered by **Shearwater Adventures** (☎ 360-376-4699; Internet: www.shearwaterkayaks.com). Two-hour paddles ($25) are offered by **Spring Bay Inn** (☎ 360-376-5531; Internet: www.springbayinn.com), which is located on the east side of the island near the village of Olga. These trips are in an area where bald eagles nest in the summer.

If you want to see some of the orca whales for which the San Juans are famous, you can take a whale-watching excursion with **Deer Harbor Charters** (☎ 800-544-5758 or 360-376-5989; Internet: www.deerharborcharters.com), which operates out of both Deer Harbor and Rosario Resort and charges $47 for adults and $32 for children; or with **Orcas Island Eclipse Charters** (☎ 800-376-6566; Internet: www.orcasislandwhales.com), which operates out of the Orcas Island ferry dock and charges $46.50 for adults and $30 for children.

Located at the Orcas ferry landing, the country-style **Orcas Hotel** (P.O. Box 155, Orcas, WA 98280; ☎ 888-672-2792 or 360-376-4300; Fax: 360-376-4399; Internet: www.orcashotel.com), is an attractive old Victorian hotel that is a good choice for anyone coming over without a car. Set on an open hillside above the spectacular Deer Harbor inlet, the luxurious cottages of the casual **The Resort at Deer Harbor** (P.O. Box 200, Deer Harbor, WA 98243; ☎ 888-376-4480 or 360-376-4420; Fax: 360-376-5523; Internet: www.deerharbor.com) look across the water to a forested cliff and offer the best views on the island. The **Starfish Grill,** the resort's casual and moderately priced bistro, is one of the best restaurants in the San Juans. **Rosario Resort & Spa** (1400 Rosario Rd., Eastsound, WA 98245; ☎ 800-562-8820 or 360-376-2222. Fax: 360-376-2289; Internet: www.rosarioresort.com) is the most luxurious lodging on Orcas Island. **Spring Bay Inn** (P.O. Box 97, Olga, WA 98279; ☎ 360-376-5531; Fax: 360-376-2193; Internet: www.springbayinn.com) is a waterfront B&B that has fun and interesting innkeepers (both are retired park rangers).

San Juan Island

Although neither the largest nor the prettiest of the islands, San Juan is the most populous and touristy of the San Juan Islands. **Friday Harbor,** is home to numerous shops, restaurants, motels, and bed-and-breakfast inns that cater to visitors. With its large, well-protected marina, it's one of the most popular places in the islands for boaters to drop anchor.

You can stroll around town admiring the simple wood-frame shop buildings constructed in the early 20th century, which now house art galleries and other interesting shops. One of your first stops should be the tasting room at **Island Wine Company,** Cannery Landing (☎ **360-378-3229**), which is the only place you can buy wine from San Juan Cellars (which makes its wine with grapes from eastern Washington). You'll find the wine shop on the immediate left as you leave the ferry. Also in town, stop by the **Whale Museum,** 62 First St. N. (☎ **800-946-7227** or 360-378-4710; Internet: www.whale-museum.org) to see whale skeletons and models of whales and learn all about the area's pods of orcas (also known as killer whales).

You can see most of the island's main attractions by driving a long loop around the perimeter of the island. The island has a lot of rolling pas-tureland and farms, including one place that raises dozens of llamas and alpacas. Start the drive by following Roche Harbor signs north out of Friday Harbor (take Spring Street to Second Street to Tucker Avenue). In about 3 miles, you come to **San Juan Vineyards,** 2000 Roche Harbor Rd. (☎ **360-378-9463;** Internet: www.sanjuanvineyards.com), which makes wines both from grapes grown off the island and from its own estate-grown Siegrebbe and Madeline Angevine grapes.

A little farther north, you come to **Roche Harbor Resort,** once the site of large limestone quarries that supplied lime to much of the West Coast. Amidst the abandoned machinery stands the historic Hotel de Haro, a simple whitewashed wooden building with verandas across its two floors. The deck of the hotel's lounge is one of the best places on the island to linger over a drink. The **Westcott Bay Reserve (☎ 360-370-5050),** a new sculpture park that includes more than 45 works of art set in grassy fields and along the shores of a small pond, occupies an old pasture on the edge of the resort property. Back in the woods near the resort you'll find an unusual **mausoleum** that was erected by the founder of the quarries and the Hotel de Haro.

English Camp is located south of Roche Harbor, on West Valley Road. Set amid shady trees and spacious lawns, the camp is the picture of British civility. There's even a formal garden surrounded by a white picket fence. You can look inside the reconstructed buildings and imag-ine the days when this was one of the most far-flung corners of the British Empire. If you're full of energy, hike up to the top of 650-foot **Mount Young** for a panorama of the island. An easier hike is out to the end of **Bel Point.**

South of English Camp, watch for the Bay Road turnoff. This connects to the Westside Road, which leads down the island's west coast. Along this road is **San Juan County Park,** a great spot for a picnic. A little far-ther south is **Lime Kiln State Park,** the country's first whale-watching park and a great place to spot these gentle giants in summer.

At the far south end of the island is the windswept promontory that housed the **American Camp** during the Pig War. A visitor center and a few reconstructed buildings are located here. **Hiking trails** here lead along the bluffs and down to the sea. One trail leads through a dark forest of Douglas firs to **Jackle's Lagoon,** a great spot for bird-watching. Keep your eyes peeled for bald eagles, which are relatively plentiful around here.

The winding country roads on San Juan are ideal for leisurely bike trips. If you didn't bring your own wheels, you can rent from **Island Bicycles,** 380 Argyle St., in Friday Harbor (☎ **360-378-4941**).

Two- to four-hour **sea-kayak tours** ($39 to $49) are offered by **San Juan Safaris** (☎ **800-450-6858** or 360-378-1323; Internet: www.sanjuan safaris.com) at Roche Harbor Resort, **Leisure Kayak Adventures** (☎ **800-836-1402** or 360-378-5992; Internet: www.leisurekayak.com), and **Crystal Seas Kayaking** (☎ **877-SEAS-877** or 360-378-7899; Internet: www.crystalseas.com). Most of these companies also offer full-day and overnight trips.

Three- and four-day trips are offered by **San Juan Kayak Expeditions** (☎ **360-378-4436**; Internet: www.sanjuankayak.com).

When it's time to spot some whales, you have two choices. You can take a whale-watching cruise, or you can head over to the excellent **Lime Kiln State Park**, where a short trail leads down to a rocky coast-line from which orca whales, minke whales, Dall's porpoises, and sea lions can sometimes be seen. The best months to see orcas are June to September, but it's possible to see them throughout the year.

Whale-watching cruises lasting from 4 to 6 hours are offered in the summer by **San Juan Excursions** (☎ **800-80-WHALE** or 360-378-6636; Internet: www.watchwhales.com), which operates out of Friday Harbor. Three-hour whale-watching trips from Roche Harbor Resort, on the north side of the island, are offered by **San Juan Safaris** (☎ **800-450-6858** or 360-378-1323; Internet: www.sanjuansafaris.com).

Friday Harbor House (130 West St. (P.O. Box 1385), Friday Harbor, WA 98250; ☎ **360-378-8455;** Fax 360-378-8453; Internet: www.fridayharbor house.com) is a luxurious little boutique hotel that brings urban sophistication to Friday Harbor. The dining room is one of the best on the island, serving Northwest cuisine. Located at the north end of the island, **Roche Harbor Village** (248 Reuben Memorial Dr. (P.O. Box 4001), Roche Harbor, WA 98250; ☎ **800-451-8910** or 360-378-2155; Fax 360-378-6809; Internet: www.rocheharbor.com) is steeped in island his-tory, with the historic Hotel de Haro, established in 1886, serving as the resort's centerpiece. Although the rooms in the Hotel de Haro are quite basic, the building has loads of atmosphere. The best accommodations here are the four new luxury McMillin suites in a restored home adjacent to the historic hotel. Also on the property, the modern condominiums are good bets for families.

Lopez Island

Lopez maintains more of its agricultural roots than either Orcas or San Juan, and likewise has fewer activities for tourists. If you just want to get away from it all and hole up with a good book for a few days, Lopez may be the place for you. Lopez Islanders are particularly friendly — they wave to everyone they pass on the road.

Lopez Village is the closest thing this island has to a town, and here you find almost all of the island's restaurants and shops, as well as the **Lopez Island Historical Museum** (☎ **360-468-2049**), where you can learn about the island's history and pick up a map of historic buildings. In July and August, the museum is open Wednesday through Sunday from noon to 4 p.m. In May, June, and September, it's open Friday through Sunday from noon to 4 p.m.

Lopez Island Vineyards (☎ **360-468-3644**), on Fisherman Bay Road between the ferry landing and Lopez Village, makes wine from fruit grown here in the San Juans.

Because of its size, lack of traffic, numerous parks, and relatively flat terrain, Lopez is a favorite of cyclists. You can rent bikes from **Lopez Bicycle Works & Kayaks** (2847 Fisherman Bay Rd.; ☎ **360-468-2847**; Internet: www.lopezbicycleworks.com), at the marina on Fisherman Bay Road.

Eight county parks and one state park provide plenty of access to the woods and water on Lopez Island. Over on the east side of the island you'll find **Spencer Spit State Park** (☎ **360-468-2251**), which has a campground. Here, the forest meets the sea on a rocky beach that looks across a narrow channel to Frost Island. You can hike the trails through the forest or explore the beach. Down at the south end of the island, you'll find the tiny **Shark Reef Sanctuary,** where a short trail leads through the forest to a rocky stretch of coast that is among the prettiest on all the ferry-accessible islands. This is a great spot for a picnic.

If you want to explore the island's coastline by kayak, contact **Lopez Island Sea Kayaks** (☎ **360-468-2847**; Internet: www.lopezkayaks.com), which is located at the marina on Fisherman Bay Road and is open May through October.

Located right in Lopez Village, **Edenwild Inn** (132 Lopez Rd. (P.O. Box 271), Lopez Island, WA 98261; ☎ **800-606-0662** or 360-468-3238; Fax: 360-468-4080; Internet: www.edenwildinn.com), a modern Victorian

B&B, is a good choice if you've come here to bike. Set on 30 acres of pastures, old orchards, and forest between the ferry landing and Lopez Village, the modern cottages at **Lopez Farm Cottages and Tent Camping** (555 Fisherman Bay Rd., Lopez Island, WA 98261; ☎ **800-440-3556;** Internet: www.lopezfarmcottages.com) are tucked into a grove of cedar trees on the edge of a large lawn.

Day Trip #3: Mount Rainier National Park

Mount Rainier and 235,625 acres surrounding it are part of **Mount Rainier National Park,** which was established in 1899 as the fifth U.S. national park. From downtown Seattle, the easiest route to the mountain is via I-5 south to exit 127. Then take Wash. 7 south, which in some 30 miles becomes Wash. 706. The route is well marked. Allow yourself about 2½ hours to reach the park's Paradise area.

Before you leave, contact the park for information: **Mount Rainier National Park,** Tahoma Woods, Star Route, Ashford, WA 98304-9751 (☎ **360-569-2211,** ext 3314; Internet: www.nps.gov/mora). Keep in mind that the Henry M. Jackson Memorial Visitor Center at Paradise is open only on weekends and holidays during winter. Park entrances other than the Nisqually entrance are closed throughout the winter.

Just past the **main southwest entrance (Nisqually),** you'll come to Longmire, site of the National Park Inn; the **Longmire Museum** (exhibits on the park's natural and human history); a **hiker information center** that issues backcountry permits; and a **ski-touring center** where you can rent cross-country skis and snowshoes in winter.

The road then climbs to **Paradise** (elevation 5,400 ft.), the aptly named mountainside aerie that affords a breathtaking close-up view of the mountain. Paradise is the park's most popular destination, so expect crowds. During July and August, the meadows are ablaze with wildflowers. In March, you see climbers gearing up for summit attempts. The circular **Henry M. Jackson Memorial Visitor Center** provides 360° panoramic views, and a short walk away is a spot from which you can look down on Nisqually Glacier. Many miles of **trails** lead out from Paradise, looping through meadows and up onto snowfields above timberline. It's not unusual to find plenty of snow at Paradise as late as July. In summer, you can continue beyond Paradise to the **Ohanapecosh Visitor Center,** where you can walk through a forest of old-growth trees, some more than 1,000 years old.

Continuing around the mountain, you reach the turnoff for **Sunrise.** At 6,400 feet, Sunrise is the highest spot in the park accessible by car, and a beautiful old log lodge serves as the visitor center. From here you can see not only Mount Rainier, seemingly at arm's length, but also Mounts Baker and Adams. Some of the park's most scenic trails begin here at Sunrise. This area is usually less crowded than Paradise.

At both Paradise and Sunrise, hikers can choose from a good variety of outings, from short, flat nature walks to moderately difficult loops to long, steep, overnight hikes.

If you want to see a bit of dense forest or hike without crowds, head for the park's **Carbon River entrance** in the northwest corner. A long day hike in this area provides an opportunity not only to come face to face with the Carbon Glacier but also to enjoy superb alpine scenery. This is the least visited region of the park because it only offers views to those willing to hike several miles uphill. The road into this area is in very bad shape, however, and a high-clearance vehicle is recommended. Be sure to call the park for a road-condition update before heading this way.

Mount Rainier National Park has several **campgrounds.** Two of the park's campgrounds — Cougar and Ohanapecosh — take reservations, which you should make several months in advance for summer weekends. To make reservations, contact the **National Park Reservation Service** (☎ **800-365-2267;** Internet: http://reservations.nps.gov). Located in Longmire, in the southwest corner of the park, **National Park Inn** (Mount Rainier National Park, Ashford, WA 98304; ☎ **360-569-2275;** Internet: www.guestservices.com/rainier), is a rustic lodge with a view of Mount Rainier from its front veranda. High on the flanks of Mount Rainier, in Paradise, **Paradise Inn** (Mount Rainier National Park, Ashford, WA 98304; ☎ **360-569-2275;** Internet: www.guest services.com/rainier) is the quintessential rustic mountain retreat and should be your first choice of accommodations in the park (book early). The inn is the starting point for miles of trails that wander through flower-filled meadows in summer.

Chapter 18

Living It Up After the Sun Goes Down: Seattle Nightlife

. . . .

In This Chapter

▶ Finding out what's playing and how to get tickets

▶ Exploring Seattle's vibrant theater scene

▶ Enjoying great classical music, opera, and ballet

▶ Partying into the night: clubs, bars, and hangouts

. . . .

*F*ew groups benefited more from Seattle's technology-fueled pros-
perity than the city's performing-arts community. The Seattle
Symphony moved into gorgeous Benaroya Hall, theater companies
flourished and brought expensive new productions to the city, and
the Seattle Opera broke ground on a complete renovation of its Opera
House. Seattle's cultural scene continues to thrive. In this chapter,
I give you the lowdown on the local arts-and-entertainment scene and
tell you where to find out what's going on and how to get tickets.

What's Happening: Getting the News

The best sources for finding out what's playing in town are the city's
free weekly newspapers — the *Seattle Weekly* and *The Stranger* —
both of which are available in coffeehouses and news boxes around the
city. For online information, look to seattle.citysearch.com or consult the online editions of the *Seattle Times* (www.seattletimes.com)
or the *Seattle Post-Intelligencer* (www.seattlep-i.com).

Where to Get Tickets

Most of the big entertainment venues in town, including Benaroya Hall
and other theaters, have their own box offices where you can procure
advance or day-of-show tickets. The major ticket seller in town is

Ticketmaster Northwest (☎ 206-628-0888), which charges a sliding fee for its services but is frequently the only place in town to obtain tickets for big shows. The company has kiosks in Westlake Center and at Tower Records (5th Avenue and Roy Street), where you can look at seating charts for shows. For discounted tickets, go to the **Ticket/Ticket** booths (☎ 206-324-2744) at the Pike Place Market or the Broadway Market shopping center on Capitol Hill. They have a list of all shows that offer discounted seats; you pay half-price of the top ticket price plus a small service charge (cash only), receive a voucher, and then pick up your tickets at the event itself.

The Play's the Thing: The Local Theater Scene

Seattle is a great town for live theater. It must be the constant drizzle outside that makes people want to huddle together in cozy theaters and watch live dramas played out before their eyes. Whatever the reason, the city is rewarded for its hearty support of theater with world premieres of new plays that are bound for New York and London, as well as top touring productions of lavish Broadway musicals.

Just as New York has Broadway, off-Broadway, and off-off-Broadway, Seattle's theater tends to break down into similar classifications, giving patrons a full range of plays, musicals, and fringe theater to explore.

For Broadway-style shows that are all pomp and music, with dazzling costumes and lively choreography, look to the **Paramount Theatre** (911 Pine St.; ☎ 206-443-1744; box office on the 9th Avenue side of the building), which is housed in a historic old downtown building that received a much-needed major renovation and is now a great venue for big touring productions of Broadway shows like *The Producers*. In a similar vein, located in the center of downtown, is the **5th Avenue Theatre** (1308 Fifth Ave.; ☎ 206-625-1900), another venue that devotes itself to Broadway-style touring shows in a grand space with a splendid Chinese-themed decor that's reminiscent of the great theaters of New York and Los Angeles.

Seattle's off-Broadway would be the three major theater companies in town that premiere world-class work and stage top theatrical repertory during their seasons. Actors like Richard Gere and Alan Arkin have put in time on these boards, and it's not unusual to find stars like Lily Tomlin polishing up their acts in Seattle before taking them to London or New York. The theaters to focus on are the **Intiman Theater** (Intiman Playhouse at Seattle Center; ☎ 206-269-1900), whose season runs from May through October; the **Seattle Repertory Theatre** (Bagley Wright Theatre at Seattle Center; ☎ 206-443-2222), with a season that runs from October through May; and **A Contemporary Theater** (ACT) (700 Union St.; ☎ 206-292-7676), which offers productions from April to November and usually mounts a splendid production of *A Christmas Carol* to top off the year. The ACT complex also houses a cabaret for late-night music.

You may enjoy the works presented at the **Seattle Children's Theatre** (Charlotte Martin Theatre at Seattle Center; ☎ 206-441-3322), just as much as your kids do. The company takes its children's theater very seriously, including world premieres and specially commissioned works in its repertoire, such as the recent *Mask of the Unicorn Warrior*, which was inspired by the medieval tapestries that hang in the Cluny Museum in Paris. The theater is handsomely supported by the community and returns the favor with shows that are staged during weekdays for school groups and presented as weekend matinees and evening performances for the general public.

For off-off-Broadway-type plays that are simpler in execution and often more daring in theme and content, check out the **Empty Space Theatre** (3509 Fremont Ave. N.; ☎ 206-547-7500) in Fremont. If you love good improvisational comedy, try the shows mounted by Unexpected Productions every weekend at the **Market Theater** (Post Alley in the Pike Place Market; ☎ 206-781-9273).

Music, Dance, and More: The Performing Arts

Seattle's cultural calendar is filled throughout the year with performances by a top-notch symphony and ballet, as well as an opera company that receives international recognition. Read on to see how you can get your fill of highbrow entertainment in the Emerald City.

The Seattle Symphony

Under the able baton of conductor and musical director Gerard Schwarz, the Seattle Symphony plays its repertoire of classical music in gorgeous new Benaroya Hall (200 University St.; ☎ 206-215-4747), which was largely funded by local philanthropists. With acoustics that have been compared to those of Carnegie Hall, Benaroya is a great place to brush up on your Mozart or Beethoven or, if you're lucky enough to snag a ticket, to catch soloists like violinist Itzhak Perlman on one of his annual visits. Of interest is the addition of a $4-million concert organ, a rarity in most concert halls, which allows for full-throated concerts of baroque organ music that fill every corner of Benaroya Hall with sound.

The Seattle Opera

Opera fans the world over flock to the city every other year to witness the spectacle of Wagner's *Ring Cycle,* the Seattle performances of which set the standard for international productions. Tickets are tough to come by for those shows, but you have a good chance of catching one of the opera's many repertory productions during the August-through-May season. This is grand opera at its best, with lavish sets and costumes to match the big voices. The Seattle Opera House, in the Seattle Center (☎ 206-389-7676), was completely renovated in 2002.

The Pacific Northwest Ballet

Seattle's resident dance company has been reaching out to the whole family in recent years with productions that are great for introducing kids to classical dance. The company's repertoire has included new works choreographed by codirector Kent Stowell and classical gems like Tchaikovsky's *The Sleeping Beauty.* For many locals, the highlight of the cultural season (September through June) is the ballet's gorgeous production of *The Nutcracker* in December, with Maurice Sendak–designed sets that are one of the ballet's many treasures (Seattle Center; ☎ 206-292-2787).

Hitting the Bars and Clubs

If contemporary live music and hitting the local nightlife scene are more to your taste, you can find plenty happening in Seattle's bars and clubs, particularly during the summer months and on weekends. Don't come expecting a grunge music scene, however — it left town years ago — but Seattle still has plenty of lively music and dancing to go around.

Live! Music and dancing

For dancing and listening to national touring acts as well as local bands that prefer their music loud and raw, you have several options in Seattle. Downtown regulars go to the **Showbox** (1426 First Ave., across from the Pike Place Market; ☎ 206-628-3151), a cavernous techno-space that attracts lots of big-name national acts. In Belltown, the **Crocodile Cafe** (2200 2nd Ave.; ☎ 206-441-5611) is a dark, atmospheric room where rock-and-roll is played late into the night. You often find top musicians jamming there in the wee hours after they've played their shows at the mega-concert venues such as KeyArena or Memorial Stadium. In the quiet neighborhood of Ballard, two clubs in particular attract dancin' fools: **The Tractor Tavern** (5213 Ballard Ave. NW; ☎ 206-789-3599), which programs everything from good rockabilly bands to swing ensembles to Irish groups, and the **Ballard Firehouse** (5429 Russell Ave. NW; ☎ **206-784-3516**), which, true to its name, is an old firehouse that now pulses with R&B-based rock music. Swing dancers do their thing at Capitol Hill's **Century Ballroom** (915 E. Pine St.; ☎ **206-324-7263**), an old dowager of a hall where your '50s party dress and dinner jacket fit right in. The most technologically happening club in town has got to be Experience Music Project's **Sky Cathedral** (Seattle Center; ☎ **206-770-2700**), where live acts play against the backdrop of an enormous synchronized video screen and light show that comes straight from the deep pockets of billionaire founder Paul Allen.

Party time: Bars with attitude

College kids and those who like a loud, raucous scene head to the many bars in Pioneer Square, several of which present music that strives to rise above the din of people slamming beer and shots. Ancient drinking establishments include **Doc Maynard's Public House** (610 First Ave. S.; ☎ **206-682-4646**) and **J&M Cafe and Cardroom** (201 First Ave. S.; ☎ **206-292-0663**). A few of the clubs and bars in Pioneer Square participate in a joint cover-charge promotion that allows you to access any and all participating places for $8 to $10. More genteel drinkers who like to rub elbows with Seattle's cool set make their way to the **Cyclops** bar (2421 First Ave.; ☎ **206-441-1677**), which anchors the nightlife scene in Belltown, or **Tini Big's Lounge** (100 Denny Way; ☎ **206-284-0931**), which serves outlandishly large and varied martinis in lower Queen Anne. Seattle and the Pacific Northwest have developed a deserved reputation for their fine micro-brews; drink them at the source at the **Trolleyman Pub** (3400 Phinney Ave. N. in Fremont; ☎ **206-548-8000**), which pours wonderfully crafted ales from the Red Hook Brewery, and at the **Pyramid Alehouse & Brewery** (1201 First Ave. S.; ☎ **206-682-3377**), which opens an outdoor beer garden before every Mariners game, serving its own smooth lagers and Hefeweizens to large crowds.

Social magnets: Restaurant and hotel bars

Seattle's restaurant and hotel bars are also magnets for social life. Each has its own crowd, style, and character, and many offer light bites to go with the drinks. Here are a few of the hot spots:

- ✔ **El Gaucho:** For a sophisticated crowd in suits and dresses who sip cocktails before heading off to dinner.

- ✔ **Oliver's:** At the Mayflower Park Hotel. Makes the best martinis in the city and usually proves it every year by winning an impartial Martini Challenge contest.

✔ **Waterfront:** An exciting new venue on Elliott Bay with a long, curving bar that is fast becoming a favorite singles scene.

✔ **Hunt Club:** A dark and atmospheric bar at the Sorrento Hotel that is a great secret hideaway for romantics.

✔ **Palace Kitchen:** Lines up a hip Belltown crowd around its horse-shoe-shaped bar for sturdy drinks late at night after the theaters and cultural venues have emptied out.

Seattle's music festivals

For sheer selection and nonstop entertainment, you can't beat Seattle's two big arts festivals, both held every year at Seattle Center. The **Northwest Folklife Festival** (☎ 206-684-7300) brings hundreds of ethnic music, dance, and storytelling acts to the dozens of stages set up on the grounds of Seattle Center. Held over Memorial Day weekend, it makes for a dizzying orgy of entertainment as you careen from an Appalachian fiddle concert to a demonstration of Eastern European line-dancing. Labor Day weekend, at the end of the summer, brings **Bumbershoot** (☎ 206-281-8111), the extraordinary arts festival that features contemporary entertainment of every stripe and color, from literary readings and modern dance exhibitions to concerts by national touring acts. *Be warned:* Both of these festivals attract hundreds of thousands of people, so if big crowds are not for you, either go very early in the day or don't go at all.

Part V
Discovering Olympic National Park

The 5th Wave   By Rich Tennant

"Yes, sir, our backcountry orientation programs are held at the Footblister Visitor Center, the Lostwallet Ranger Station, or the Cantreadacompass Information Pavilion."

In this part . . .

This part gives you the lowdown on what to see and do in that vast chunk of mountainous real estate known as Olympic National Park. I tell you the best ways to get to the Park, some tips on not seeing more tourists than trees, and where to find the best places to eat and sleep in the Park. I also steer you to places where you can find more information to help you maximize your time by taking in the best scenery and sites.

Chapter 19

Getting to Know Olympic National Park

In This Chapter

▶ Introducing three parks in one

▶ Exploring the must-see attractions in the park

*W*hen you've finished exploring Seattle to your heart's content and want to escape the city for the simpler pleasures of nature, it's time to travel west to a gigantic slice of Northwest real estate that seems to have it all. Olympic National Park is the answer for people who can't decide where to head on vacation and pose that classic question: "Should I go to the beach this year, or should I head to the mountains?" Relax . . . you can have it all. Within its 922,653 acres, Olympic National Park offers three totally different experiences. The only problem you face is packing for three different vacations.

Olympic National Park: Beaches, Glaciers, Mountains, Lakes, and Rainforest

Interested in mountains and glaciers? Olympic is capped by a range of sky-scraping, snow-capped mountains that support the lowest elevation glacier system in the Lower 48. In roughly 40 miles, the park's terrain runs from sea level to peaks nearly 8,000 feet high. Topped by 7,965-foot-tall Mount Olympus, the park's roof features alpine and subalpine areas that you can hike through in summer on multiday backpacking treks or kick-and-glide through in winter on cross-country skis. The park even has a small downhill ski area with tows, which is open on weekends in the winter.

Olympic National Park

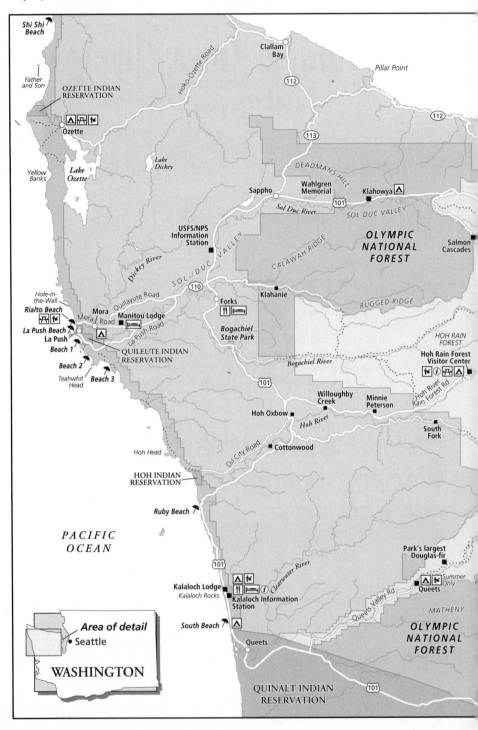

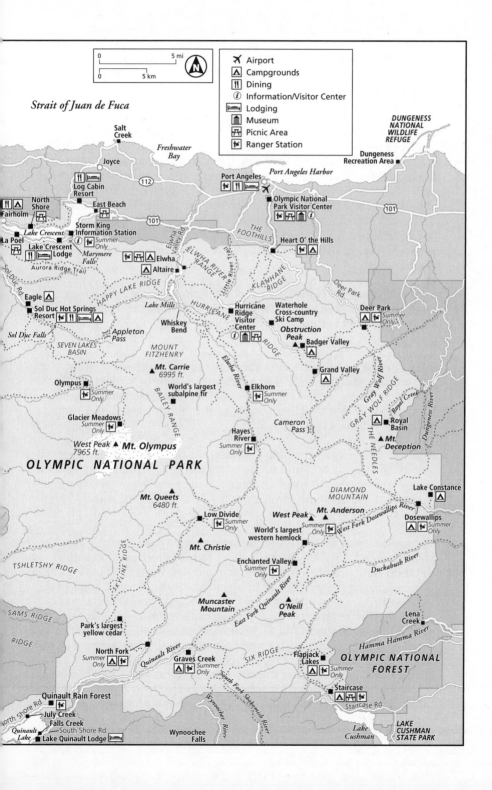

✈	Airport
⛺	Campgrounds
🍴	Dining
ⓘ	Information/Visitor Center
🛏	Lodging
🏛	Museum
⛱	Picnic Area
🏚	Ranger Station

Strait of Juan de Fuca

DUNGENESS NATIONAL WILDLIFE REFUGE

Dungeness Recreation Area

Freshwater Bay

Salt Creek

Joyce

Port Angeles Harbor

Port Angeles

Log Cabin Resort

North Shore
Fairholm

East Beach

Olympic National Park Visitor Center

THE FOOTHILLS

Heart O' the Hills

Storm King Information Station

Lake Crescent

La Poel

Lake Crescent Lodge

Marymere Falls

Aurora Ridge Trail

Elwha
Altaire

KLAHHANE RIDGE

Deer Park Rd

HAPPY LAKE RIDGE

Lake Mills

HURRICANE

ELWHA RIVER RANGE

Eagle

Sol Duc Hot Springs Resort

Sol Duc Falls

Appleton Pass

SEVEN LAKES BASIN

Whiskey Bend

MOUNT FITZHENRY

Hurricane Ridge Visitor Center

Waterhole Cross-country Ski Camp

Obstruction Peak

Badger Valley

Deer Park

RIDGE

Mt. Carrie
6995 ft.

World's largest subalpine fir

Grand Valley

Olympus

BAILEY RANGE

Elwha River

Elkhorn

GRAY WOLF RIDGE

Gray Wolf River

Royal Creek

Dungeness River

Glacier Meadows

Cameron Pass

Hayes River

Royal Basin

West Peak
7965 ft.

Mt. Olympus

OLYMPIC NATIONAL PARK

Mt. Deception

THE NEEDLES

Mt. Queets
6480 ft.

DIAMOND MOUNTAIN

Lake Constance

SKYLINE RIDGE

Low Divide

West Peak

Mt. Anderson

West Fork Dosewallips River

Dosewallips

World's largest western hemlock

TSHLETSHY RIDGE

Mt. Christie

Enchanted Valley

Duckabush River

SAMS RIDGE

RIDGE

Muncaster Mountain

O'Neill Peak

East Fork Quinault River

Lena Creek

Park's largest yellow cedar

North Fork

Quinault River

Graves Creek

SIX RIDGE

Flapjack Lakes

Hamma Hamma River

OLYMPIC NATIONAL FOREST

South Fork Skokomish River

Staircase

Staircase Rd

Quinault Rain Forest

North Shore Rd

July Creek
Falls Creek

South Shore Rd

Quinault Lake

Lake Quinault Lodge

Wynoochee River

Wynoochee Falls

Lake Cushman

LAKE CUSHMAN STATE PARK

Love to roam wave-pounded beaches? Olympic boasts 63 miles of some of the most scenic coastline anywhere, with towering *sea stacks* — rock monoliths left behind when the coastline receded under the relentless pounding of the waves — that rise above the foaming surf. Thick coniferous forests run up to the edge of the sand-and-cobble beaches, hiding them from the roads and lending some solitude. These beaches are not the pristine, white-sand-and-suntan-lotion ones of southern California. They're big, rugged stretches of Northwest coastline littered with amazing varieties of driftwood, black and gray sand and pebbles, and a huge variety of native wildlife. Although this stretch of Pacific Ocean is probably too cold for you to enjoy anything but a brief swim on a dare, the water teems with marine life ranging from whales and sea lions to colorful sea stars (starfish). If that's not enough, on clear days you're guaranteed spectacular sunsets thanks to the surf and sea stacks. People love to wander these beaches for hours, admiring the driftwood and enjoying the solitude and the steady sound of pulsing surf and crashing waves punctuated by the cries of gulls.

Thankfully, you won't find any beachfront homes or seaside burger joints along the park's coast, which is one of the largest sections of wilderness coast in the continental United States.

If neither snow-capped peaks nor surf-swept beaches sound appealing, head into the Northwest's largest remaining undisturbed old-growth and temperate rain forests. The park's muggy forests, soaked by 12 to 14 feet of rain a year and often cloaked in low-lying clouds or drizzle, wrap around you with thick, mossy-green walls of vegetation. You can almost feel the forest growing.

In addition to rugged mountains, wilderness beaches, and lush rain forests, the park boasts meadows strewn with wildflowers, deep valleys, shimmering lakes, soothing hot springs, and cascading waterfalls tossed in between the coastline and the peaks. Three unique choices — one park, one trip.

You need at least three days to explore Olympic National Park. Frankly, your choice of when to visit boils down to how much you like wet weather. Spring can be on the raw side and wet, but it does have its own magic. For starters, the wetness enhances the emerald color of the rain forests. And you often see gray whales cavorting along the coastline while they migrate north. Summers can't be beat. July and August are the driest months in the park, and September can be quite nice, too. The threat of the forests growing moldy disappears because rain is relatively minimal this time of year. Fog banks often roll in from the Pacific in the mornings, but the mist usually burns off by midday to reveal mostly blue skies. Like spring, fall can also be wet and raw, but this season has its high points, too. The rain forests become extra lush, and in early fall, you can often spot sea lions lounging along the coast. Crowds are sparse in Olympic during winter, the onset of the rainy season — the year's heaviest rains fall in December and January. At this time, the park's upper elevations become buried in snow — on average, the park's high country receives 15+ feet of snow each winter.

Must-See Attractions

Where to go, where to go, where to go? That's the dilemma with a park of Olympic's diversity. So let me give you some suggestions for a wonderful sampling of all the different landscapes — and seascapes — that this national park has to offer:

- ✔ **Hoh Rain Forest:** This pocket of humidity, with its moss-covered trees, bushy ferns, and slimy banana slugs, is a perfect example of the world's temperate rain forests.

- ✔ **Hurricane Ridge:** You can easily reach the park's highest point by car, and its views of the Strait of Juan de Fuca and Mount Olympus and the rest of the Olympic mountains are riveting. The wind howls as you stand on top of the world and gaze out over miles and miles of pristine wilderness, with a Switzerland-like array of craggy mountain peaks towering all around. A visitor center provides shelter and information, and many hiking and cross-country skiing tours depart from here.

- ✔ **Lake Crescent:** Anglers appreciate this glacier-carved lake for its rare Beardslee and Crescenti trout species, while romantics are happy just to pull up a lakefront chair at Lake Crescent Lodge. Cold, long, and deep, with few cottages on its shores, the lake is, for many people, the quintessential secluded alpine lake. The shores are a great spot for camping. For those who like to swim, the water is appreciably warmer than the waters of Puget Sound or the Pacific Ocean, making this lake a great place to stop for a summer dip.

- ✔ **Marymere Falls:** This 90-foot waterfall cascades out of the forest and nourishes a moss community that blankets the cliffside and the boulders at the falls' base.

- ✔ **Ruby Beach:** Sea stacks — rocky outposts that are remnants of a coastline that was eroded by Pacific storms long ago — make this nook of the park a favorite with photographers, rock hounds, and kids who've never seen sea stars or anemones (small, colorful, spineless creatures with tentacles) revealed in a tidal pool during low tide. The area has great driftwood, too, and lots of secluded places to sit down with a picnic and admire nature at its most rugged.

- ✔ **Sol Duc Hot Springs:** Most parks have a commercial side, and this spot is Olympic's. But its pools are kid magnets and are wonderful for older folk to ease into, too, particularly after a long day on the trail.

Chapter 20

Planning Your Visit
to the Park

. . . .

In This Chapter

▶ Figuring out the best ways to get to the park

▶ Planning and packing for your trip

▶ Finding information on the park

▶ Staying safe

. . . .

*N*ow that your appetite is whet for a visit to the Park, here is the low-down on the essentials that can help your visit go smoothly. In this chapter, I include all the nitty-gritty details about getting to the Park, what to bring, and how to stay safe in the wilderness.

Getting There

Reaching Olympic National Park is easy, thanks to the international airport near Seattle, which is a relatively short car ride — or shuttle flight — from the park. By relatively short, I mean that you can be admiring the outskirts of the park about two hours after you've pick up your luggage at baggage claim.

If you happen to be coming from Victoria, B.C., you can reach the park from the sea, thanks to the ferries that arrive at the docks at Port Angeles from Victoria.

Driving in

Seattle is the closest major gateway to Olympic National Park, which anchors Washington State's peninsula in the Pacific. From the city, you can reach the park either by taking a ferry across Puget Sound or by heading south on Interstate 5 to Tacoma and then taking Washington 16 north to Bremerton and Washington 3 north to U.S. 101 to reach the east side of the park. Alternatively, you can drive west from Olympia on

Washington 8 to Aberdeen and then north on U.S. 101 along the Park's western side.

If you take the ferry across the sound from Seattle to either Bainbridge Island or Winslow, you find park entrances along U.S. 101 at Port Angeles, Hurricane Ridge, Elwha, Lake Crescent, and Sol Duc.

If you're looking at a map, it seems much quicker to get to the park as the crow flies, which means that you would take a ferry from downtown Seattle, cross Bainbridge Island and then make your way to Highway 101 bound for Port Angeles. However, keep in mind that during the summer, you're bound to wait in the ferry terminal's holding lot for up to two hours before getting on a boat, you must pay a hefty $12 crossing fee just for the car and driver (more for passengers), and then you have to deal with steady traffic all the way to the Hood Canal bridge that leads to 101. If you're heading to the park's western side or you're starting from SeaTac airport, you're better off driving south to Tacoma on I-5 and then heading west on Hwy 16 across the Tacoma Narrows Bridge.

Traveling up U.S. 101 from Aberdeen, you have the choice of entering the park in the Quinault or Queets valleys, or at Kalaloch Beach, the Hoh Rain Forest, or Mora. You reach Ozette in the northwestern corner via a road off Washington 112. From spur roads off U.S. 101 on the east side of the park, you can reach Staircase and the park's entrance at Dosewallips. You find an entrance to Hurricane Ridge on the southern border of Port Angeles, and you can reach Deer Park via a road that heads south off U.S. 101 just east of Port Angeles.

Some of these entrances may close in the winter, so check with the park visitor center at ☎ **360-565-3130** before setting out for Olympic.

For Puget Sound ferry schedules, contact **Washington State Ferries** (☎ **206-464-6400**). For ferries arriving in Port Angeles from Victoria, British Columbia, contact **Black Ball Transportation** (☎ **360-457-4491**) in Port Angeles for year-round ferry service or **Victoria Express** (☎ **800-633-1589** or 360-452-8088), for seasonal walk-on ferry service.

Flying in

If you want to fly to the park, **Horizon Air** provides service to **Fairchild International Airport** (☎ **360-457- 8527**) in Port Angeles from Seattle Tacoma International Airport and Victoria, British Columbia. **Budget Rent-A-Car** has an outlet at Fairchild. (See Appendix B for the toll-free number for Horizon and Budget.)

The closest major airport is the **Seattle Tacoma International Airport** (☎ **800-544-1965** or 206-431-4444), known as Sea-Tac, located 15 miles south of Seattle on Interstate 5. Most of the major airlines and car-rental agencies are here; see Appendix B for their toll-free numbers. For bus service from the airport, see the next section, "Busing in."

Busing in

Olympic Bus Lines (☎ 360-417-0700; Internet: www.olympicbus lines.com) offers twice daily service to and from Seattle and Seattle Tacoma International Airport to Port Angeles. **Pennco Transportation** (☎ 360-582-3736; Internet: www.penncoshuttle.com) makes nine trips daily between the airport and Port Angeles. Other bus companies on the peninsula include **Clallam Transit** (☎ 800-858-3747 or 360-452-4511), which operates Monday through Saturday within Port Angeles with commuter services to Sequim, Joyce, Lake Crescent, Forks, Neah Bay, and La Push; **Jefferson Transit** (☎ 360-385-4777), which is based in Port Angeles and serves Brinnon and connects with Clallam Transit in Sequim; **Grays Harbor Transit** (☎ 800-562-9730 or 360-532-2770), which operates from Olympia and Aberdeen with service to Lake Quinault; and **Mason County Transit** (☎ 800-374-3747 or 360-427-5033), which runs between Shelton, Olympia, Bremerton, and Brinnon.

On the peninsula, **Olympic Tours** (☎ 360-457-3545) offers park tours for groups as large as 30 people and can shuttle you to and from trail-heads for backpacking treks.

Planning Ahead

For information prior to your trip, write Superintendent, 600 East Park Avenue, Port Angeles, WA 98362; call ☎ 360-565-3130; or check the park's Web site at www.nps.gov/olym.

Reserving a room or a campsite

A lead time of several weeks to a month is usually sufficient for reserving a room at many of the motels and hotels in the Port Angeles area, but several months would be more appropriate for such resort locations as Lake Crescent and Quinault Lake. I offer recommendations on local lodging in Chapters 24 through 26; for lodging inside the park, see Chapter 22.

Due to the park's popularity with backpackers, some backcountry sites — Ozette Coast, Grand and Badger valleys, Royal Basin, Lake Constance, Flapjack Lakes, and the Sol Duc/Seven Lakes Basin — operate under a quota system. You can reserve one of the designated sites in these areas for trips between May and September by calling the **Wilderness Information Center** (☎ 360-565-3100) up to 30 days before your trip. However, you won't necessarily be without a campsite if you can't make an advance reservation, because half of the spots are held back and are available on a first-come, first-served basis at the ranger stations.

Packing for the park

Don't forget your rain gear when packing for Olympic National Park. You may be able to sneak in a multiday trip in summer without needing it, but better to have it and not need it than need it and not have it, right? Trust me, rain gear almost always comes in handy. During the spring months, it's very rare to get through a whole day without at least one good rain shower. Also, keep in mind that temperatures can vary significantly during the day, and it's not unusual for nighttime temps to drop into the 40s during late-spring cold snaps. Stay warm by always packing a sweater or, even better, a lightweight down- or synthetic-filled vest.

If you're going to be camping, make sure that your tent has a good rain fly. I highly recommend testing this setup in your backyard with your garden hose before you find out the hard way that your tent doesn't like rain. Waterproof sleeping pads can also make many a wet night much more bearable when you're trying to sleep on soggy ground. Extra tarps come in handy, too, if you can manage the weight.

Figuring Out the Lay of the Land

Olympic National Park is a veritable island of wilderness in the heart of the Olympic Peninsula. In fact, 95% of the park is officially designated wilderness. Surrounded on three sides by water — the Pacific Ocean to the west, the Strait of Juan De Fuca to the north, and the Hood Canal to the east — the park offers sanctuary to a rich animal population and an escape from civilization for those who visit.

No roads loop through the park. Instead, a highway, **U.S. 101,** hooks and crawls around the park's west, north, and east sides, and a few smaller roads make relatively short forays into the park from the highway. None of these roads is longer than 17 miles, which usually means a quick trip to your destination.

The one destination that is difficult to reach is **Ozette.** Getting there requires a 40-mile side trip from Sappho, near the park's western border, down Washington **Highways 113** and **112,** which lead you through the Olympic National Forest to the coast and Ozette.

Park headquarters and the biggest (and best) visitor center are both located on the north side of the park in **Port Angeles.** From the visitor center, **Hurricane Ridge** — with its smaller visitor center, picnic area, hiking trails, and panoramic views of the Strait of Juan de Fuca, the Olympics and their glaciers — lies 17 miles south via **Hurricane Ridge Road.** Stemming off from this road are hiking trails and a dirt road leading to Obstruction Peak.

Following are other side roads that dash into the park and a list of the destinations that they reach:

- ✔ **Elwha Valley Road** leads to Altaire Campground, Elwha picnic area, and Lake Mills, just below the northern edge of the park.

- ✔ **Sol Duc Road** leads to the Sol Duc campground, Sol Duc Hot Springs Resort, and several popular trailheads in the park's northwestern corner.

- ✔ **Hoh River Rain Forest Road** leads to the Hoh Rain Forest and its visitor center and campground on the west side of the park.

- ✔ **Queets Valley Road** leads from Hwy 101 to the Queets campground near the park's southwestern corner.

- ✔ **North Shore Road** runs along the north side of Quinault Lake to the Quinault Rain Forest and the North Fork and Graves Creek campgrounds.

- ✔ **South Shore Road** runs along the south side of Quinault Lake to the North Fork and Graves Creek campgrounds.

- ✔ **Staircase Road** in the park's southeastern corner runs to the Staircase campground and several trailheads that lead you to breathtaking alpine vistas and thick forests.

- ✔ **Deer Park Road** leads from Hwy 101 to the Deer Park campground on the northeastern corner.

Although physically separated from the alpine heart of the park, the 63 miles of **coastline** are indeed part of Olympic National Park. This rugged stretch of sand and rock runs from Kalaloch Beach just above the Quinault Indian Reservation all the way north to Shi Shi Beach, which borders the Makah Indian Reservation. **U.S. 101** runs 10 miles along the coast between South Beach and Ruby Beach, and **Washington 110** runs to Rialto Beach and La Push, midway along the coastline. The only other coastal access in the park is via the **Hoko-Ozette Road,** which runs about 20 miles from Washington 112 to Ozette Lake.

When exploring the park, remember to be patient. Like other park road systems, Olympic's is nothing like a freeway system. U.S. 101 has a few straight stretches, but for the most part, it winds and bends and creeps over and around the mountainous landscape. After you leave this main road for one of the spur roads, the number of bends and turns seems to double.

Arriving in the Park

When you enter the park, you are handed a copy of the park's newspaper, *Bugler,* a great source for discovering what's happening during your visit. For more information, head to one of the visitor centers or ranger stations.

Finding information

The park has three visitor centers that offer exhibits, maps, guides, and information, plus smaller ranger and information stations (open only in summer) that are located at popular trailheads.

Olympic National Park Visitor Center (☎ 360-565-3130), on the southern edge of Port Angeles, is the park's largest visitor center and offers great exhibits on Olympic's Native American history and wildlife, as well as a good selection of park books, posters, videotapes, and postcards. The center is open year-round; hours vary by season. If you're in a hurry to be outdoors, try the marked loop trail into the forest near the visitor center or eat at a nearby picnic table. The trail is easy to manage and crosses a gushing creek; it's a good place for kids to burn off some energy before getting back into the car for the drive up to Hurricane Ridge.

A 45-minute drive from the main visitor center brings you to one of the most popular spots in the park, the **Hurricane Ridge Visitor Center.** Here you find free telescopes for spying on distant peaks and glaciers, as well as a snack bar, interpretive exhibits, and trails. The center is open daily from 10 a.m. to 5 p.m.

The **Hoh Rain Forest Visitor Center,** on the west side of the main part of the park, is some 15 miles down a turnoff from U.S. 101. This tiny center offers a good explanation of rain forests and their climate, as well as a primer on glaciers. You can pick up wilderness trip permits here if you plan to take the Hoh River Trail 18½ miles to Glacier Meadows. The center is open daily; hours vary seasonally. Smaller information centers include the **Storm King Information Station,** on Lake Crescent in the northern section of the park, and the **Kalaloch Information Station,** on the south end of the beach section of the park. You can get food and some supplies near the **Sol Duc Ranger Station** at the Hot Springs Resort.

For maps and updated trail conditions, stop at the nearest ranger station or at the **Wilderness Information Center** (☎ 360-565-3100), located just behind the main visitor center in Port Angeles.

Paying fees

Entrance into the park for up to a week costs $10 per vehicle, or $5 per individual hiking or biking. Annual passes cost $30. If you have a park pass, you don't need to pay the entrance fee; see Chapter 8 for information on the National Park Pass and Chapter 4 for the lowdown on Golden Age and Golden Access passports. Parking at Ozette costs $1 per day; parking in all other areas is free.

All overnight hiking trips require a $5 registration fee for a permit that is good for two weeks and covers up to a dozen people, as well as an individual nightly fee of $2 per person for every night out. (Hikers 16 and younger are exempt from the nightly fee.) Permits are available at the **Wilderness Information Center** (☎ **360-565-3100**) in Port Angeles.

Getting around

To get around Olympic National Park, you need a car. The park doesn't have a public transportation system. Cyclists had better be in excellent condition and able to climb severe hills.

Remembering Safety

If you plan to head off into the park's backcountry, keep in mind these pointers to ensure a safe trip:

- ✔ **Hypothermia:** This condition is a real danger with Olympic's generally wet, cool climate. Protect yourself by having rain gear with you and by dressing in layers of synthetic clothing, which dries much more quickly than cotton clothing.

- ✔ **Food and water:** Hikers should always carry extra food, water, clothing, and a firestarter with them. If you get lost, wet, or stranded by a weather system, these supplies can save your life.

- ✔ **Cougars:** They roam the park's backcountry, and although you most likely won't spot one, if you do, don't turn your back on it or try to run away. These actions can encourage the cougar to attack. If the big cat seems aggressive and begins to stalk you, try to scare it off by waving your arms and shouting or by throwing rocks or sticks at it. Make yourself as large and loud as possible. Always keep small children within sight distance on trails and in campgrounds.

- ✔ **Black bears:** These animals also call the park home and are much more visible than cougars. If you see a bear down the trail, either give it a wide berth or backtrack until it leaves. If a bear comes into your camp, make some noise to scare it off. Also, be sure to hang your food high above the ground from a bear wire, where available, or store the food in an animal-resistant food container, which are available for a $3 per trip donation from the **Wilderness Information Center** (☎ **360-565-3100**) and any staffed ranger station.

If you plan to make a trip to the beach, keep the following in mind:

✔ **Coastal hiking:** This activity can be dangerous because tides can trap you. Never hike around headlands unless you know how high tides can get and when they come in. Detailed maps, showing safe routes around headlands, as well as tide tables, are available from visitor centers, the Wilderness Information Center (☎ **360-565-3100**), and staffed ranger stations.

✔ **Swimming:** Along the coast, swimming can be hazardous because of logs in the surf. Felled by storms and washed into the ocean by streams, they can easily knock a swimmer unconscious. Also, the cold water and strong currents make swimming a risky proposition here. If kids insist on playing in the water, find a calm spot and let them splash around in the shallow water.

✔ **Raccoons:** Believe it or not, these critters can be troublesome for campers on the beach near Ozette. Park officials suggest that you store your food in animal-resistant food containers to thwart these masked marauders.

Chapter 21

Enjoying the Park

· ·

In This Chapter

▶ Exploring Olympic National Park's top attractions

▶ Finding the best hikes

▶ Spotting wildlife

▶ Taking advantage of ranger programs

· ·

*H*ere are some tips for maximizing your time in the park and getting the most out of its varied landscapes and recreational opportunities. In other words, when that herd of Roosevelt Elk crosses your path, I hope that your nose won't be buried in the guidebook!

Enjoying the Park

Although the vast majority of Olympic National Park is rugged backcountry that you need a horse or a pair of hiking boots to reach, you can get a strong impression of the park from several readily and easily accessible areas.

Before you walk out across the rocks during low tide at any of the beaches in the Park, make sure to check the tide table for the day and keep an eye on the incoming water — if you don't, you can quickly find yourself stranded.

The rules of most national parks state that taking anything out of the park is illegal, but in Olympic you're allowed to collect a handful of stones or empty shells from the beaches. So you don't have to look nervously over your shoulder as you pocket a few.

Exploring the top attractions

In this section, I cover the very best natural attractions that Olympic National Park has to offer, from rainforest to beaches to glacial lakes to waterfalls.

Hoh Rain Forest

Overload your senses here. Your nose fills with the rich scent of the earth that nurtures the forest while your eyes try to decipher the varying hues of green that tint this emerald cathedral. Sitka spruce trees 8 feet thick climb skyward for 200 to 300 feet, mossy curtains droop from vines and big-leaf maples, and blankets of Oregon oxalis and waist-high Sword ferns cover the forest floor.

As you walk the forest's trails, be careful not to squish the Banana and European Black slugs, which are oversized snails traveling without their shells. These slimy critters are various sizes and colors. The Banana Slug is the biggest (up to a foot long) and the most colorful, coming in greens, browns, and yellows. While looking for the slugs, you may spot large tracks left by the elk that live in the forest.

For my recommended hikes in the rain forest, see Hall of Mosses Trail and Spruce Nature Trail in the section "Taking a hike," later in this chapter.

The rain forest is at the end of Hoh River Rain Forest Road, which is roughly 10 miles south of Forks off U.S. 101.

Hurricane Ridge

If you visit Hurricane Ridge during any season but winter, you won't find much solitude. The ridge is immensely popular, and the drive there during warm-weather months is often done in convoy. But where else can you stand in one place and see both the ocean and a nearly 8,000-foot-tall peak covered with snow and glaciers?

On the 17-mile drive up to the ridge along Hurricane Ridge Road, you're quickly pulled out of the muggy lowlands and deposited near the roof of this corner of the world. On a clear day, from the trails that scamper across the ridge, you can gaze north to the Strait of Juan de Fuca and beyond to Canada. (See High Ridge and Alpine Hills, in the section "Taking a hike," later in this chapter.) To the south, snowy Mount Olympus and her sister peaks, which are home to 60 glaciers, tear at the horizon. As you stand on Hurricane Ridge under the summer sun, you may find yourself longing for a little shade.

If you abhor crowds, plan either an early-morning or late-afternoon trip to the ridge top.

For similar views and fewer people, go to nearby Deer Park, located at the end of the serpentine 15-mile-long Hurricane Ridge Road, which begins outside the park just east of Port Angeles. What's the catch? The steep gravel road is off-limits to recreational vehicles and rigs hauling trailers. Plus, negotiating this road takes a lot longer than driving the paved Hurricane Ridge Road.

Hurricane Ridge is 17 miles south of Port Angeles on Hurricane Ridge Road.

Lake Crescent

You may think that you've been transported to New York's Adirondack region when you reach Lake Crescent, in the north end of the park. Dense forests surround this glacial lake, and the shorefront Lake Crescent Lodge features the same dark paneling and stone fireplace that you would find in an Adirondack lodge. You can even settle into a lawn chair with a view of the lake.

Lake Crescent is a great place to rent a canoe or rowboat to ply the waters in search of the Beardslee or Crescenti trout that lurk far beneath the surface. This is a "catch-and-release" fishery, so pack your camera to record your catch. See the section "Keeping active," later in this chapter, for details on boating.

Near the Lake Crescent Lodge are the Storm King Ranger Station and a 1¼-mile trail that leads to **Marymere Falls,** a beautiful, feathery 90-foot waterfall. Along the trail, mosses, lichens, and ferns clutter the forest floor and climb up into the canopy. Narrow, single-log bridges cross Barnes Creek twice just before the falls. (These bridges aren't difficult to cross, unless they're wet and slippery.) Just after you begin a steep climb up the hillside toward the top of the falls, a shortcut breaks off to the left and follows a more level, less strenuous path to an overlook opposite the falls. At the most, plan on a 90-minute round-trip, but if you're in a hurry, you can visit the falls and get back to your car in half that time.

Lake Crescent is roughly 21 miles west of Port Angeles on U.S. 101.

La Push Beach

Although it's not as accessible as Ruby Beach, **La Push** (located just south of Rialto Beach), has an even larger collection of sea stacks than Ruby Beach. The beach is wide and long and very remote, with a smattering of vacation cottages that you can rent.

La Push is at the end of Washington 110.

Rialto Beach

This is the most accessible beach in the park, because the Mora Road runs to a parking lot just above it. The beach makes a good starting point for hikes along the park's coastline and is a great place for kids who like to search for wave-polished stones or peer into tide pools in search of sealife. One-and-a-half miles north of the parking lot lies Hole-in-the-Wall, a jutting piece of headland through which the surging surf has chiseled a tunnel that you can explore during low tide. There is a picnic area at the beach, and camping is available in nearby Mora.

Rialto Beach is at the end of Mora Road off Washington 110.

Ruby Beach

Having spent some time in Hawaii, I'm something of a connoisseur of beaches. But Ruby Beach is nothing like the smooth, sandy beaches of my childhood. Towering stacks of basalt stand at the mouth of Cedar Creek, which pours into the ocean here. The stacks are remnants of cliffs that were slowly, but steadily, pounded into sand by the waves.

A short trail winds down from the parking lot to the beach, where you have some great photo ops of these stacks. But don't immediately turn around and head back to your car after snapping a few pictures. Stroll along this beachcomber's dream, which boasts polished agates, tangles of drift logs, and other flotsam tossed up by the waves. Pockets of water on the beach are alive with marine life; spend some time searching in the small pools for green anemones, sea urchins, shellfish, and brightly colored sea stars, also known as starfish.

Most people congregate near the stacks at the creek mouth; if you walk 10 minutes north or south along the beach, you leave most of humanity behind. The best time to visit Ruby Beach is at low tide, because the dropping water level reveals more water pockets full of marine life.

If you're determined (and foolhardy enough) to dash into the surf for a dip, watch for rogue logs that were washed out to sea by rivers after being toppled by storms. Waves toss these around like toothpicks, and you can't win a collision with them.

Ruby Beach is along U.S. 101 almost 8 miles north of the Kalaloch Information Station.

Sol Duc Hot Springs

Although the Sol Duc area has hot, spring-fed swimming pools, these pools aren't the main reason to visit this area — although the watery diversion is good for subduing any troublesome kids in your car. The real reason to come here is for the roughly 1½-mile round-trip hike to Sol Duc Falls (see the description in the section "Taking a hike," later in this chapter). Although less than half as tall as Marymere Falls, these falls have more water volume and plunge into a rectangular flume that the Sol Duc River has cut through the bedrock. A wooden bridge just below the falls is a great spot for photographs.

Secluded beaches

If you're worried about running into crowds at Rialto or Ruby beaches, try one of the six beaches along the coast between Ruby Beach and South Beach. Known simply as **Beach 1, Beach 2, Beach 3**, and so on, you reach these beaches via footpaths across from small pullouts on U.S. 101. Some of these beaches have tide pools to explore; others are great for beachcombing or clamming during the season. (Clamming season varies depending on the beach and type of clam. For more details, check with the nearest ranger station.) The beaches on the coast between Ruby and South Beach are along U.S. 101.

The trail to the falls also provides access into the backcountry. From here, you can hike to the High Divide for stunning views of the Hoh Valley and Mount Olympus, explore the Seven Lakes Basin, or trek to the headwaters of the Bogachiel River.

Sol Duc Hot Springs is 40 miles west of Port Angeles via U.S. 101 and the Sol Duc Road.

Taking a hike

With its coastlines, dense rain forests, and alpine terrain, Olympic offers so many great hiking opportunities that it would be a crime just to drive through the park and stay in your car. You have beaches to comb, rain forests to explore, and high country trails to hike. In all, more than 600 miles of marked trails and 955 designated campsites exist in the park. Following are just some of the hiking possibilities.

See "Arriving in the park," in Chapter 20, for information on backcountry hiking and fees.

Bogachiel River

Your energy level determines how far you can hike on this trail, which features a rain forest setting similar to that of the Hoh Rain Forest but without the crowds. The trail runs about 21½ miles from the park boundary to the junction of the Mink Lake and Little Divide trails. The first few miles wind through thick rain forest with towering Douglas firs, Sitka spruce, Western cedar, and big-leaf maples all draped in mosses. Along the way are several stream crossings. The Bogachiel Shelter, 6 miles from the trailhead, is a good destination for an overnight, round-trip hike. Of course, heartier hikers may want to go further.

Distance: 43¼ miles round-trip. Level: Easy to moderate in the lowlands, steeper as you head inland. Access: 5 miles south of Forks, turn onto Undie Road and drive 5 miles to the trailhead.

Cape Alava/Sand Point Loop

This excellent three-legged loop trail begins at Ozette ranger station and offers ocean views, beach camping, petroglyphs (prehistoric rock art), and an easy return hike back to your car. The trail begins on a cedar-plank boardwalk that winds about 3 miles through coastal marsh and grasslands to the beach and Cape Alava, the westernmost point in the Lower 48. As you make your way 3 miles south on the beach, be sure to look for the petroglyphs on the rocks along the shore next to the high-tide mark. The end of this leg is marked by the Sand Point Trail, another boardwalk stretch that runs 3 miles back to the ranger station at Ozette.

Before you embark on this trek, check the tide charts posted at the trailhead. Take care on the boardwalks, which can get slippery when wet.

Distance: 9¼ miles round-trip. Level: Easy. Access: Ozette Ranger Station.

Glacier Meadows

This route is one that's taken by climbers heading to Mount Olympus. Early on, the hiking is easy and captivating as you pass through the rain forest, with its dense vegetation and towering trees. If you're alert, you may be able to spot the Roosevelt elk that live in the area. The trail's first 12 miles follow the Hoh River Valley and are easy to walk. Beyond the intersection with the Hoh Lake Trail, you enter a deep gorge and hike past Elk Lake and on to Glacier Meadows and the toe of Blue Glacier on Mount Olympus. Plan this hike carefully. Snowmelt from the glaciers picks up in late July and can make travel tricky. Hiking this trail round-trip can take several days; most people take four days.

Distance: 37 miles round-trip. Level: Easy early on and then moderate as you begin to climb into the high country and encounter stream crossings, most over foot logs or bridges. Access: Hoh Rain Forest.

Hall of Mosses Trail

If you have time for only one hike in the Hoh Rain Forest, this trail should be it. Hiking the loop takes about 40 minutes. The trail winds through a green kingdom of lush vegetation. It's not steamy, like a tropical rain forest, but you can feel the humidity. Along the trail, *epiphytes* — plants that grow on other plants, in this case in the form of spongy club mosses, lichens, liverworts, and licorice ferns — scramble across tree trunks and limbs and up into the leafy canopy where they manage to block most of the sun's rays from reaching the floor. Scattered here and there on the ground are toppled trees and rotting stumps that serve as nurseries for the next generation of trees. Shallow, crystal clear creeks flow through the forest.

Distance: ¾ miles round-trip. Level: Easy. Access: Hoh Rain Forest Visitor Center.

High Ridge and Alpine Hills

The short, paved, 1-mile High Ridge Route is great for kids: It's short enough so that it won't tire them out, offers great views of Mount Olympus and her sister peaks to the south, and contains interpretive exhibits to teach them something. If you're up for more, follow the unpaved looping trail to Sunrise Ridge, which, on clear days, serves up sweeping views of the Strait of Juan de Fuca and Port Angeles to the north.

Distance: 1–8 miles round-trip. Level: Easy to moderate. Access: Hurricane Ridge Visitor Center.

Sol Duc Falls

Although it's short, this picturesque forest hike offers great photo opportunities, a refreshing waterfall, and kid-friendly hiking. Streams jumping through moss-covered boulders, the dense emerald forest, and the cascading waterfall along the Sol Duc River are perfect photo backgrounds. Just below the falls, a bridge spanning the river provides a great vantage point to see how the river has cut a channel through the bedrock.

Distance: 1½ miles round-trip. Level: Easy. Access: Near Sol Duc Ranger Station.

Spruce Nature Trail

This trail through the Hoh Rain Forest takes about an hour to negotiate round-trip. Because this section of forest is younger, the route is not as densely packed with vegetation as the Hall of Mosses Trail. A highlight, however, includes a side trail to the Hoh River where you can see *glacial flour,* finely ground sediment that the Hoh Glacier scraped from the bedrock as it inched its way down below the snowfields beneath Middle and East peaks. The flour gives the Hoh River its milky appearance.

Distance: 1¼ miles. Level: Easy. Access: Hoh Rain Forest Visitor Center.

One-day wonder

The only way to cross Olympic National Park is on foot. Although U.S. 101 wraps around three sides of the park, its route runs through the Olympic National Forest, not the park. To get into the park, you need to shoot down spur roads that can run up to 17 miles in length. As a result, if you're determined to see as much of the park as possible, you're going to have to drive quite a bit and pack and unpack your bags every day.

But don't despair. You can get a surprisingly good feel for the park in one day. It'll be a long day, for sure, but you'll come away having sampled its three main environments. (Unless otherwise indicated, see

"Exploring the top attractions," earlier in this chapter, for more information on all the attractions mentioned in this itinerary.)

The best place to start this journey is in **Port Angeles.** After rising early and eating a good breakfast, leave for **Hurricane Ridge** in time to get there by 8 a.m. (If weather allows: Heavy rains and/or high winds will slow the trip considerably, or even close the road temporarily.) On a clear day, you'll be rewarded with eye-popping views of Mount Olympus and the Strait of Juan de Fuca.

A good, quick hike on Hurricane Ridge is the High Ridge route. After an initial 1-mile walk along a paved trail that offers good interpretive panels, you can continue to Sunrise Ridge, with its killer views of the strait to the north and the glacier-coated peaks to the south.

By 10 a.m., you should be ready to head back down to Port Angeles and the **Olympic National Park Visitor Center.** Here you can load up on any brochures or additional guidebooks that strike your fancy and also get a sense of the region's cultures and natural history.

Your next stop is the **Hoh Rain Forest,** 91 miles and roughly two hours away by car. It'll probably be approaching midafternoon by the time you near the rain forest, so stop at the **Hard Rain Café and Mercantile** for lunch. The two-beef-patty Mount Olympus Burger and an order of fries will keep you going for the rest of the afternoon.

After lunch, continue to the rain forest, where a hike through the **Hall of Mosses** (see the "Taking a hike" section, earlier in this chapter) is mandatory. The hike doesn't take long, and the route leads you through some of the park's best rain forest. Following the hike, you can either continue down the nearby Spruce Nature Trail, which leads along the fringe of the rain forest and out to the Hoh River, or spend some time in the visitor center's tiny museum, with its solid information on rain forests.

If you manage to stay fairly on schedule, you can make it from the Hoh Rain Forest to **Ruby Beach,** roughly 30 miles away, in time to enjoy a stroll along the beach and get some great sunset photographs. Take a short stroll whether it's a clear day or raining — walking through mists can be just as interesting as walking in sunshine, plus you can get some beautiful photographs of the sea stacks laced with fog.

A great way to end your day is with dinner and a room at the **Lake Quinault Lodge,** which is 40 miles from Ruby Beach, just outside the park's southwestern corner (345 South Shore Rd., Quinault; ☎ **800-562-6672** or 360-288-2900; Internet: www.visitlakequinault.com/lake_quinault_lodge.htm; see Chapter 22). President Franklin Delano Roosevelt visited this gorgeous lakefront log lodge in October 1937 during a trip that he conducted to determine whether a national park should be established here.

If you have more time

Although it's not as big as Yellowstone and some other sprawling Western parks, Olympic National Park requires more than a day or two if you're determined to see it all. (Well, really seeing it all could take years.)

If you have a few extra days, consider a trip to **Lake Ozette** on the coast. Although Lake Ozette can be crowded, a visit is well worth your time. The focal point of this area is the 7,787-acre freshwater lake, but you're also close to the coast, which boasts tide pools, old-growth coastal rain forest, and, if you look hard enough, petroglyphs. (Hint: You can find them on Wedding Rocks, located halfway between Cape Alava and Sand Point.) The lake's campground has only 14 sites, so if you're lucky enough to get one, you enjoy relative solitude at night. The area also has backcountry lake sites that you can reach by boat and other coastal backcountry sites.

For a hike in the area, see Cape Alava/Sand Point Loop in the section "Taking a hike," earlier in this chapter. The 9¾-mile hike from Cape Alava to Shi Shi Beach is another good option, if you don't mind getting wet. The trail crosses the Ozette River, which can be waist deep at times.

Ranger programs

Campfire talks, guided walks through the rainforest and subalpine meadows, and beachcombing are some of the usual ranger-led activities in the park.

Definitely plan to accompany one of the rangers on the tidepool beach walks that they lead daily during the summer months from Mora and Kalaloch. Kids and adults alike love these 2½-hour hikes, which investigate the marine life of tide pools. Meeting times vary according to the tides. Check the *Bugler,* the newspaper that you receive upon entering the park, or park bulletin boards, for exact times.

Another great family outing is stargazing atop Hurricane Ridge. Rangers occasionally lead stargazing parties, so consult the park's newspaper for dates.

Although you can guide yourself along the trails through the Hoh Rain Forest, ranger-led hikes held daily provide background on the forest's plant and animal dynamics, as well as on the nearby Hoh River.

For families with small children, the ubiquitous campfire talks — featuring lectures on everything from bears to cougars to the park's trees — are held regularly at various locations around the park; check the *Bugler* for dates and times. You can also pick up information on the Junior Ranger Program, for kids ages 5 to 13, at the main park visitor center in Port Angeles.

Spotting the local wildlife

With its vast array of wildlife, Olympic National Park offers incredible opportunities to see animals in their natural habitats. Where else can you see both whales and black bears on the same day? Even more fascinating is that the glaciations that once isolated the peninsula from the rest of the continent led to the evolution of at least 18 unique types of animals, including the **Olympic snow mole,** the **Olympic short-tailed weasel,** and the **Olympic marmot.**

Tidepools along the coast are the best places to spot a variety of the park's wildlife in one place. In these shallow pools, you usually can find **green anemones** (small, colorful, spineless creatures) with their tentacles floating in the water. You may also spot **sea stars** (starfish) and **hermit crabs** in these pools, as well as a variety of **mussels.**

While you're searching tide pools, remember to take a look out at the ocean from time to time. If you're lucky, you may spot a **California sea lion** or perhaps a **harbor seal.** These furry critters enjoy sunning themselves on off-shore rocks when they're not frolicking in the water. A good time to look for them is in late summer and early fall when they migrate up the coastline toward the Strait of Juan de Fuca and Puget Sound. Harder to spot are **Northern fur seals,** which prefer the waters off Cape Flaherty on the peninsula's northwestern tip.

East Coasters usually need to board a boat to spot whales, but in Olympic National Park all you need to do is be on the right beach at the right time of year. If you visit in the spring or fall, head to the coast to look for waterspouts made by passing **gray whales.** These guys like to feed just off the beaches where the Hoh and Quillayute rivers pour into the Pacific. Another good place to look for them is from the bluffs of Beach 6 along U.S. 101 north of Kalaloch Lodge. Rangers at the **Kalaloch Ranger Station** (☎ 360-962-2283) can provide information on the whale migrations.

Moving inland, you may cross paths with **Roosevelt elk.** Slightly bigger than their Rocky Mountain cousins, the park was almost named after these animals. They're easiest to spot in the early morning or evening browsing in old clearcuts in the Olympic National Forest that surrounds the park. The Hoh and the Quinault valleys are also good places to look for elk. Just as visible are **Columbia black-tailed deer,** which prefer Hurricane Ridge during the early morning or late-afternoon.

Black bears are not so easily spotted, but they're out there. In early summer along Hurricane Hill, you may see them munching on the lush vegetation.

If you head into the high country, you may spot a **mountain goat** clattering along a rocky ridge. These animals aren't native to the park.

Harder to spot, but park residents just the same, are **cougars, bobcats, weasels, river and sea otters, beavers, marmots, flying squirrels, two varieties of skunk,** and **coyotes.**

In the park's rivers and lakes, and in the ocean off the coast, are five types of **salmon,** four **trout** species (including the Beardslee and Crescenti trout species native to Lake Crescent), three kinds of **char,** as well as **whitefish, shiners, lampreys, bass, suckers, perch, Northern pikeminnow,** and **sculpin.**

If you're lucky, as I was, you may see a **bald eagle** hoisting one of these fish out of the park's waters. Dozens of bird species travel through Olympic at various times of the year, taking advantage of its fisheries and forests for food and shelter. Along with the more common **blackbirds, finches, ravens,** and **sparrows,** you can spot various **shorebirds, woodpeckers, pelicans,** and **loons.**

Perhaps the park's most comical-looking bird is the **tufted puffin.** Their bodies are covered with black feathers, and they have large, bright-orange bills and heads covered with white feathers that sweep back into yellowish tufts. Unfortunately, you probably won't spot any of them because they avoid people and spend most of their time on off-shore islands, although people who have visited Cape Flattery, which is outside the park's boundaries, have seen them.

Keeping active

In addition to hiking, Olympic National Park offers several opportunities for outdoor fun.

Boating

Although large and often windy, glacier-carved Lake Crescent is a beautiful place to do a little paddling. Lush, green forests rise straight up from the shores of this 624-foot deep lake. If you have access to an inflatable kayak, you can bring it and pump it up on the spot before setting off to explore the lake's forested coastline. Alternately, you can rent canoes at **Fairholm General Store and Cafe** (☎ **360-928-3325**) at the west end of the lake or at the **Log Cabin Resort,** 3138 E. Beach Rd. (☎ **360-928-3325**), on the lake's northeast shore. Lake Crescent Lodge rents rowboats (☎ **360-928-3211**). If you've brought your own boat, you can find boat ramps on U.S. 101 at Storm King (near the middle of the lake) and at Fairholm (at the west end of the lake). The Log Cabin Resort, on East Beach Road on the lake's northeast shore, has a private boat ramp.

If you're paddling, be careful not to stray too far out from shore because midday winds can quickly whip up the lake, making for an arduous paddle back.

Fishing

If you love to fish, you've come to the right park. However, most fish caught in the park's freshwater streams and lakes must be released. Because fishing regulations can change from year to year, to keep track of what you can and can't take home, pick up a copy of the fishing regulations from any ranger station or visitor center.

You don't need a Washington state fishing license inside the park, but if you plan to go surf fishing in the ocean or clamming, you need to stop by a sporting goods store to get the requisite state licenses. In Port Angeles, stop by **Swain's General Store** (602 E. First St.; ☎ **360-452-2357**); license prices vary depending on the type of fishing that you will do.

Snowshoeing and cross-country skiing

You can have a satisfying winter trek on any of the snow-covered roads leading into the mountains. However, if you want great views, head to Hurricane Ridge with the rest of the winter crowd and set out on any of the area's trails. Cross-country and downhill ski rentals and snowshoe rentals are available from the ski shop on the lower level of the **Hurricane Ridge Visitor Center** (no telephone).

White-water rafting, scenic floating, and kayaking

In and around the park, you can white-water raft, enjoy a scenic float, or go sea kayaking. Guided trips generally last a half-day, and canoe and kayak rentals are available. For details, contact **Olympic Raft & Kayak**, 123 Lake Aldwell Rd., Port Angeles (☎ **888-452-1443** or 360-452-1443; Internet: www.raftandkayak.com).

Escaping the rain

On a rainy day, a good place to take your kids is the visitor center at park headquarters in Port Angeles. Not only does this center have top-notch displays on Native Americans and wildlife, but younger kids also enjoy the Discovery Room, where they can play in a miniature log ranger station, learn about ecology, and build a totem pole with felt stick-on pieces. Older kids are kept busy in the main visitor center with the virtual scavenger hunt that requires them to study the exhibits so that they can answer questions about the park.

Hark! What grows there?

From 200-foot-tall **Sitka spruce trees** to hard-to-find **calypso orchids,** the vegetative side of Olympic National Park can be just as dazzling as its wildlife. The rain forests are heavy with **spruce** and **big-leaf maples** draped in mosses and lichens, and the somewhat drier lowland forests feature **Douglas fir, Western hemlocks, Western red cedar, red alder,** and, in especially dry areas, **Pacific madrone,** a red-barked tree that peels its outer layers.

In the high country of Hurricane Ridge and above are twisted and gnarled sub-alpine **fir trees** contorted by the winds and heavy snows, as well as dainty **white avalanche** and yellow **glacier lilies, marigolds, paintbrushes,** and **buttercups** that burst into color when the snows melt.

Chapter 22

Deciding Where to Stay and Eat in the Park

In This Chapter

▶ Staying at hotels and cabins in the park

▶ Finding a place for a quick bite or a full, sit-down dinner

▶ Camping in Olympic National Park

*W*ithin the boundaries of Olympic National Park, you don't have an overwhelming number of choices when it comes to eating and sleeping. The good news is that the park's environment stays pristine and natural, but the bad news is that you won't find many opportunities for food on the fly once you've entered the park. In this chapter, I give you the lowdown on the various choices for lodging and dining within the park. Use the suggestions here if you want to stay within the confines of the park. Make plans and reservations for lodging well in advance, because rooms in the park are quite popular.

However, don't be discouraged if your choices inside the park aren't available, because many inns, motels, full-service hotels, and restaurants are located in the towns surrounding the Park. The accommodations and restaurants outside the Park are detailed in Part VI, which profile the major towns of the region and offer suggestions on where to stay, where to eat and drink, and what to do after you've visited the Park.

Where to Stay in Olympic National Park

Awfully big park, awfully few pillows. Traditional hotel or motel lodging options are pretty few and far between within the boundaries of the Park itself, and those lodgings — particularly the nicer ones — tend to get snapped up quickly or be reserved months in advance. If it's a bed you're looking for, you're more likely to find it in one of the towns adjacent to the Park (see Chapters 24 through 26).

However, if you've come to camp or you don't mind bedding down in a cabin that will never make those "100 Most Fabulous" lists, you should be happy with the array of camping options that Olympic National Park offers.

Lodging in the park

The park offers only a few options when it comes to putting a roof over your head. Two lodgings are at Lake Crescent, the third is just south of there, and the fourth is along the coast.

Winter offers the year's best lodging rates. You can usually find a bargain at Kalaloch Lodge during the winter months.

Kalaloch Lodge
$$$

The lure of this cedar-shingled lodge and its cabins is the sea-front location. This place is the only lodging on the coast within the park's boundaries. But be careful when making reservations; although the lodge and some of the cabins perch on a bluff above the mouth of Kalaloch Creek and the sandy coast, some cabins are across the highway and lack ocean views. Also, some cabins offer wood-burning stoves, while others do not. Ask about the views and the stoves when you book. The cabins accommodate between four to seven people. Despite the Kalaloch Lodge's coastal location, Lake Crescent Lodge (see the next entry) and the gorgeous Lake Quinault Lodge (located just south of the park; see Chapter 21) offer more romantic accommodations.

If you reserve a cabin with a kitchenette, you need to bring your own cookware and utensils. Although you're wise to make a reservation at least four months ahead of your arrival, the lodge does hold back five rooms for walk-in business.

157151 U.S. 101, north of South Beach. ☎ ***360-962-2271****. Fax: 360-962-3391. Internet:* www.visitkalaloch.com*. Rates: $135–$258. AE, MC, V.*

Lake Crescent Lodge
$$

Located in a wonderful, peaceful area in the park's north end, this lodge and group of cabins are just minutes from Marymere Falls and less than an hour from Hurricane Ridge. Although the historic lodge is picturesque, I recommend the fireplace-equipped cabins. Located along the lakeshore, these cabins offer better views than the lodge rooms, have their own bathrooms (some lodge rooms don't), and are simply more comfortable.

In the lodge, motel-style rooms with their own bathrooms are also available, though only some of them have lake views.

416 Lake Crescent Rd. ☎ *360-928-3211. Internet:* www.lakecrescentlodge. com. *Rates: $43–$205. AE, DISC, DC, MC, V.*

Log Cabin Resort

$$

This turn-of-the-century resort on the north shore of Lake Crescent offers some of the cheapest lodging in the park. The four lodge rooms are the best deal, featuring lake and mountain views, a private bathroom, and a queen bed and a queen futon. The resort also has chalets on the shoreline with lake and mountain views. The chalets have bathrooms and showers and sleep up to six people. You also find an assorment of cabins, ranging from those with kitchenettes and bathrooms to simple cabins without indoor plumbing (a communal bathroom is nearby). If you opt for a no-plumbing cabin, note that you need to supply your own bedding.

Lake Crescent, 3183 E. Beach Rd. ☎ *360-928-3325. Fax: 360-928-2088. Internet:* www.logcabinresort.net. *Rates: $59–$140. DISC, MC, V.*

Sol Duc Hot Springs Resort

$$

These cabins are nothing fancy, but the hot springs are nearby, so if a good soak is what matters, stay here. But if the heavy traffic of campers, day trippers, and other resort guests is likely to spoil your vacation, head elsewhere. If you want to handle your own meals, opt for the higher end cabins, because they include kitchens. You won't find any phones, radios, or televisions in the cabins, though the lodge has payphones, along with a decent restaurant, a pool-side deli, an espresso bar, and a grocery store. You can arrange a massage, but they're pretty pricy, starting at $45 for 30 minutes.

Sol Duc Road near Eagle. ☎ *360-327-3583. Fax: 360-327-3593. Internet:* www. northolympic.com/solduc. *Rates: $112–$132. AE, DISC, MC, V.*

Campgrounds

The camping options in the park are as varied as the scenery, with everything from developed campgrounds to primitive backcountry sites available in the rain forests, along the coast, and in the high country. Even with 15 developed campgrounds and more than 900 primitive sites inside the park, lining up a spot to pitch your tent or park your camper can be tricky. The weather, lack of an all-inclusive reservation system, and restrictions against RVs and trailers can conspire against you. Although both RVs and trailers are allowed at most campgrounds, the recommended length is 21 feet, and the campgrounds at Deer Park, Graves Creek, North Fork, and Queets don't allow RVs or trailers at all. Check with park headquarters to make sure that your rig is allowed.

Campground reservations are restricted to the group sites at Kalaloch and Mora. Everywhere else is first-come, first-served. Lining up your campsite early in the day is always wise. This practice is mandatory on nice weekends when the weather lures more people to the park.

If you want to camp in the off-season, your only options are the campgrounds at Elwha, Heart o' the Hills, Hoh, Kalaloch, and Mora. Other campgrounds are open seasonally or closed during low-use periods. Because weather can keep some campgrounds closed longer than you may expect, call **park headquarters** (☎ 360-565-3130) to see what's open before you make plans.

So, what are the tricks to landing a campsite? Simply put, knowing the territory and the trends. To enhance your odds and improve your selection, arrive early in the day and in midweek, if possible. If you're traveling with friends, it's not a bad idea to send someone ahead early in the morning to stake out and reserve a great campsite that the whole group can enjoy later.

Although Olympic's campgrounds are scattered around the park, the crowds aren't. The Sol Duc and Kalaloch campgrounds usually fill first, followed by Hoh and Altaire. **Sol Duc Hot Springs,** with its 80 sites, is also popular because of the pools there.

Although **Lake Ozette** is remote, it's a favorite among many and can be crowded. Fifteen campsites are on the lake and accessible by car. More sites are available in the backcountry; you can reserve them by phone (☎ 360-565-3100). The **Ericsons Bay** site on the lake promises solitude because you can reach it only by boat — it's well worth the effort.

Another not-as-crowded spot is the Deer Park campground. Close to Port Angeles, **Deer Park** has 18 sites accessible only by a narrow gravel road, which winds its way from sea level to 5,400 feet. RVs and trailers are prohibited on the road.

The park offers many options for **backcountry camping.** Reservations are available in a few spots, too. All the sites on the Ozette Coastal Loop require advance reservations; other popular wilderness camp areas, including Grand Valley and the Seven Lakes Basin, also offer reservations. To make reservations and obtain camping permits for the park's backcountry wilderness, contact the park's **Wilderness Information Center** (☎ 360-565-3100).

As far as facilities and options go, the campgrounds are all fairly similar. As a ranger pointed out, there are no playgrounds, hookups, or showers at any of the sites, and they all have nearby hiking trails. If flush toilets are important to you, keep in mind that the campgrounds at Deer Park, Graves Creek, and Queets are equipped only with pit toilets. Nearly all the others have accessible facilities for those with limited mobility; check with park headquarters to be sure.

Where to Eat

The park has few dining options. The dining rooms at Lake Crescent Lodge and the Log Cabin Resort, both on Lake Crescent, are open seasonally. Dining rooms at Kalaloch Lodge on the coast, and in the Lake Quinault Lodge on the eastern shore of Lake Quinault, are open year-round. If you're in the northeastern end of the park, head into Port Angeles for a better variety of eateries.

Kalaloch Lodge

$ CONTINENTAL/SEAFOOD

With the ocean a stone's throw from the kitchen, it's no surprise that seafood dominates the dinner menu here. Delectable dishes may include a grilled salmon filet served with lemon-dill butter or a full pound of peel-and-eat shrimp. Vegetarian dishes and chops are also on the menu. Near the front of the lodge is a coffee shop where you can order breakfast or a sandwich for lunch.

157151 U.S. 101. ☎ *360-962-2271. Reservations recommended. Main courses: $6–$23. Open: Daily 7 a.m. to 4 p.m; dinner served Sun–Thurs 5 p.m.–8 p.m. and Friday and Saturday 5 p.m.–8:30 p.m. AE, MC, V.*

Lake Crescent Lodge

$ CONTINENTAL/SEAFOOD

The picturesque view of the lake through this restaurant's two walls of windows lends great atmosphere to your meals. The dinner menu offers creative seafood dishes like "Triple Fins" — an entree of salmon, mahi-mahi, and halibut, plus pastas and steaks. Seafood omelets, traditional egg dishes, fresh fruit crêpes, and "Candy Apple French Toast" hold down the breakfast menu. A corner lounge in the lobby serves up drinks that you can enjoy in front of the fireplace or out on the veranda.

416 Lake Crescent Rd. ☎ *360-928-3211. Reservations required for dinner and recommended for Sunday brunch. Main courses: $6–$25. Open: Daily 7:30 a.m.–10 a.m., noon–2:30 p.m., and 6:00 p.m.–8:30 p.m; Sunday brunch 11 a.m.–2 p.m. AE, DC. MC, V.*

Log Cabin Resort
$ **CONTINENTAL/SEAFOOD**

This all-day restaurant at the Log Cabin Resort is open to the public and starts the day off with hearty breakfasts, some of which are named after park rangers. (The Ranger Laurie is eggs, potatoes, fruit, and toast.) Lunch consists of salads, burgers, and sandwiches, and the dinner menu is built around seafood favorites like halibut, salmon, and Idaho Lake Trout. Steak and chicken dishes are also popular, and vegetarians have a variety of options, including tofu added to rice and pasta dishes.

3183 E. Beach Rd. ☎ *360-928-3325. Reservations required for dinner. Main Courses: $4.95–$18.95. Open: Daily 8 a.m.–8 p.m. DISC, MC, V.*

Part VI
Exploring the Olympic Peninsula

The 5th Wave   By Rich Tennant

AFTER HIKING TO THE HEART OF THE OLYMPIC NATIONAL PARK, FRANK AND MONA MOVE ON TO THE LUNGS AND KIDNEY.

LUNGS ⇒
3.8 km
OLYMPIC NAT'L PARK

In this part . . .

The Olympic Peninsula is a great place to explore even after you've had your fill of the enormous park that occupies its midsection. If the tourist traffic gets too overwhelming at places like Hurricane Ridge and the Hoh Rainforest, you can chill out and find a beach all to yourself in charming towns like Sequim and Port Townsend. In this section, I offer myriad tips on exploring the vast rural area that constitutes the northwesternmost part of the Pacific Northwest. I give the lowdown on excellent places to eat, great places to stay, and wonderful beaches and lakes to explore.

Chapter 23

The Olympic Peninsula

• •

In This Chapter

▶ Orienting yourself on the Olympic Peninsula

▶ Finding information

• •

*1*f, on your way to Olympic National Park's Hurricane Ridge, you find yourself in a traffic jam that seems to consist of all five million annual visitors to Olympic National Park at once, don't despair. A simple turnoff away from the mountains and toward the coast will open up whole new worlds to explore, where you won't have to compete with heavy crowds. Like the park at its center, the Olympic Peninsula is a vast and varied place that has endless opportunities for recreation, activities and sightseeing. If you enjoy walking on beaches, strolling through quaint, funky towns, paddling canoes or kayaks, and keeping your eyes peeled for waterfowl, seals, and killer whales, you'll have a great time here.

The coastline of the Olympic Peninsula is dotted with intriguing small towns that are well worth exploring. The main drags in many of the Olympic Peninsula's towns can be described as "Main Street, U.S.A" without a hint of irony. These towns are home to a population of artists, timber workers, and others who pride themselves on having escaped the big city for a more relaxed setting and lifestyle, which they're happy to share with visitors. The communities here sponsor some of the best festivals and cultural gatherings in the state, and the downtown areas of the towns often boast interesting shops and restaurants. As you drive between towns, you're treated to a backdrop of lush rural meadows where horses and cows graze. I give you the lowdown on what to do and where to go in Port Ludlow, Port Townsend, Sequim, and other Olympic Peninsula towns.

Because lodgings and campsites within the Olympic National Park itself are so scarce, you may wind up making one of the towns on the Olympic Peninsula your base of operations during your visit. You can find plenty of interesting lodgings here, from simple condo rooms and motels to beautifully appointed Victorian B&Bs to rustic cabins to full-resort hotels. I detail the accommodations offerings in the following three chapters.

Orienting Yourself on the Olympic Peninsula

To get a good idea of this region, which encompasses approximately 5,000 square miles, imagine the Olympic Peninsula as an island roughly the size and topography of Kauai that drifted up to the continental U.S. and attached itself to the northwest corner.

With the massive and largely impenetrable Olympic National Park dominating its center, the Olympic Peninsula's inhabited areas occupy a coastline that is bordered on the west side by the Pacific Ocean; on the north by the Strait of Juan de Fuca, which separates Vancouver Island from Washington; and on the east by the long finger of the Hood Canal, which separates the Olympic Peninsula from the neighboring Kitsap Peninsula. The coastlines have long been the home of this region's residents, from the Native American tribes who fished the waters off the coast to the timber and shipping barons who built their towns on the water's edge with hopes of gaining vast riches.

Washington's new National Scenic Byway

Although U.S. 101, the main artery that carries traffic around the Olympic Peninsula, is itself wonderfully scenic, don't neglect some of the lesser traveled backroads of the region. In 2001, Washington State 112 was named a National Scenic Byway by the Federal Highway Administration. The route begins eight miles west of Port Angeles off of U.S. 101 and meanders along the northernmost shoreline of the Olympic Peninsula for 61 miles to Cape Flattery, the northwesternmost point in the continental U.S.

Services are spotty on the route, so begin your trip with a stop at the Joyce General Store, which dates back to the early-1900s and is an old-time emporium where you can stock up on snacks and drinks while admiring a collection of mounted hunting trophies and antiques. A few miles northeast of Joyce is Salt Creek County Park, where you'll find interesting tidepools, a pebbly beach, campsites and hiking trails, and views across the Strait of Juan de Fuca to Vancouver Island. Farther west, Pillar Point, at the mouth of the Pysht River, is an imposing, rocky cliff that stands sentry in the cold channel waters; its driftwood-studded beach is fun to explore. The Merrill & Ring Pysht Tree Farm, which dates back to the 1880s, is nearby and has a self-guided tour that explains forestry management. Continue north all the way to Neah Bay, the tribal home of the Makah Indians; the offshore sea stacks that you'll see from the road are called Sail and Sea Rocks and are feeding grounds for gray whales.

The Olympic Peninsula

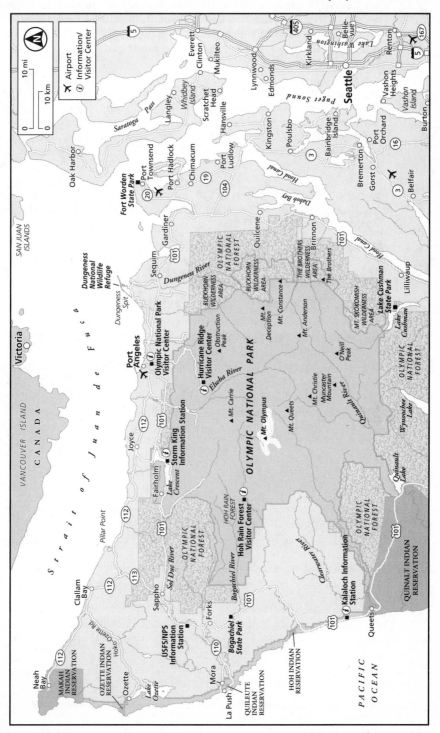

The Peninsula is circumnavigated by U.S. 101, which begins at Olympia, swings north along the Hood Canal almost to Port Townsend, turns due west past Port Angeles and Lake Crescent, meanders south near Forks, and then lingers briefly alongside the ocean at Kalaloch before swinging back inland and passing logged-out forests and rolling headlands on its way to Aberdeen.

If you were to drive the whole Peninsula in a day, you would pass through several climate zones, from the warm and dry weather in Sequim (pronounced *Skwim*), which has become a retirement haven thanks to its sheltered location in a "rain shadow" of the mountains, to the wet Hoh Rain Forest, which receives more than 130 inches of rain a year.

For information on getting to the Olympic Peninsula via car, plane and public transportation, see the information on getting to the Olympic National Park in Chapter 20.

Obtaining Visitor Information on the Olympic Peninsula

For information on lodging, restaurants, and activities, contact the North Olympic Peninsula Visitor & Convention Bureau, 338 W. First St., #104, Port Angeles, WA, 98362 (☎ **800-942-4042;** Internet: www.olympic peninsula.org). The Port Angeles Chamber of Commerce also has visitor information at its offices at 121 E. Railroad Ave. (near the ferry terminal; ☎ **360-452-2363**).

Chapter 24

Port Ludlow to Port Hadlock

In This Chapter

▶ Exploring the resort area of Port Ludlow

▶ Discovering a gem of a restaurant in tiny Port Hadlock

▶ Chowing down on Chimacum's perfect piece of pie

*T*his chapter gives you the lowdown on the beautiful resort town of Port Ludlow, the tiny town of Chimacum (with its incredible pies), and a fun and lively restaurant in the funky seaside town of Port Hadlock.

Port Ludlow

Port Ludlow is a former sawmill site that is now one of the few full-service resorts in the region. Here you find a woodsy landscape that is home to vacation houses and a sparkling New England-style inn that's located alongside the blue-green tidal waters of Ludlow Bay. Views of Puget Sound, Whidbey Island, and distant Mt. Baker make for excellent scenery. The resort area has two restaurants, a marina with slips for 300 pleasure-craft, and a 27-hole golf course that is rated as one of the toughest in the state.

Getting there

If you've taken the car ferry from Seattle to either Bainbridge Island or Bremerton (see Chapter 21 on getting to the Olympic Peninsula by car) and braved the traffic through Poulsbo and over the Hood Canal Bridge, you can get off the beaten path by turning off onto state Hwy 19 rather than heading for Hwy 101. Once on Hwy 19, continue until you reach Port Ludlow.

Visitor information

For information on lodging, restaurants, and activities, contact the **North Olympic Peninsula Visitor & Convention Bureau,** 338 W. First St., #104, Port Angeles, WA, 98362 (☎ **800-942-4042;** Internet: www. olympicpeninsula.org).

Exploring the area

Port Ludlow has half a mile of **beaches** to explore, as well as numerous **hiking and biking trails** that weave through the neighboring forests. Sightings of wildlife such as blue heron, raccoons, otters, and deer are frequent. The resort's **marina** (☎ **800-308-7991;** Internet: www.portludlowresort.com) rents bikes ($3 to $6 per hour) and provides maps of biking trails. It also rents kayaks ($10 to $15 per hour) and 14-foot watercraft ($20 per hour), which are both excellent for exploring **Ludlow Bay.** Be sure to ask about tide changes before you embark on a water tour. Northwest golf architect Robert Muir Graves designed the three nine-hole layouts at the **golf course** (☎ **800-455-0272).** The courses occupy the headland opposite the marina and are quite hilly and narrow, calling for accurate shot placement.

Staying in style

The Resort at Port Ludlow (1 Heron Rd.; ☎ **877-805-0868** or 360-437-0411; Internet: www.ludlowbayresort.com) is a handsome yellow-trimmed inn alongside the bay that appears to have been transplanted directly from Cape Cod. Those who remember a rental program for the resort's condos are out of luck: The resort discontinued overnight condo rentals in 2003, leaving the Inn (formerly known as the Heron Beach Inn) as the only bed in town for short-stay overnight guests. The 37 rooms are large, plush, and lovingly appointed with fireplaces, deep tubs, and thick duvets. The common room is a fine place to play chess or sip wine. The restaurant (see the next section) is first-rate. Families with kids are out of luck, as there is no swimming pool on the property and the setup is not particularly conducive to family lodging. The price is also the steepest on the Olympic Peninsula, with rooms starting at $189 per night.

Dining out

The Harbormaster Restaurant at the resort has been recently redubbed **Harbormaster Seafood and Spirits** (☎ **877-805-0868** or 360-437-0411). Located in the building above the marina, it has nice water views and a menu that is strong on basic seafood dishes such as steamed clams, and halibut and chips. The selection of burgers and salads should satisfy nonfish eaters.

The fare at the **Fireside Room** at the Inn (see more information on the resort in the preceding section; ☎ **877-805-0868** or 360-437-0411) is more upscale and ambitious, with tenderloins of beef and hazelnut-crusted oven-roasted salmon emerging from the kitchen of chef Steve Head. Get a table on the verandah on a balmy summer night for a romantic dinner for two.

Chimacum and Port Hadlock

Continuing north from Port Ludlow on Hwy 19 leads you past pasture-lands and farms to tiny Chimacum, which boasts the **Chimacum Cafe** (9253 Rhody Dr.; ☎ **360-732-4631**), a modest diner-style restaurant that is known for its terrific homemade pies. Try the rhubarb, a refreshingly tart (meaning "not gooey-sweet") fruit filling in a flaky crust. Then, think about working your way through the other two dozen or so pies on the menu. Burgers and hearty breakfasts are good, too. Breakfast, lunch, and dinner are served.

Just north of Chimacum, a turn-off from Hwy 19 leads to the seaside town of **Port Hadlock,** whose false-front Old West-style buildings have all been painted in lurid hot pinks, blues, and purples. The main attraction here is the handsome old wooden **Ajax Café** (271 Water St.; ☎ **360-385-3450**; Internet: www.ajaxcafe.com), a fun, festive restaurant where seaplanes and pleasure craft tie up to the dock outside. The restaurant is only open for dinner. The menu features fresh seafood, including halibut and salmon. On summer weekends, the restaurant offers live blues, jazz, and folk music and attracts a lively local crowd that likes to drink beer and wine and dig into ribs cooked with Jack Daniels.

Chapter 25

Port Townsend

. . . .

In This Chapter

▶ Exploring Washington's Victorian seaport town

▶ Touring Port Townsend's uptown district and parks

▶ Staying in former officers' housing at Fort Worden

▶ Taking in zany festivals and a museum devoted to wooden boats

. . . .

*P*ort Townsend is the one "don't miss" town on the Olympic Peninsula, a place with great architecture, beautiful natural landscapes, excellent shopping and dining, and plenty of activities for everyone in the family. Make sure that you leave space in your itinerary to spend a solid day or two exploring the town; you may well find that you don't want to leave.

Perhaps the best thing about the town, which is perched on a little round knob of land at the entrance to Puget Sound, is its lively, vibrant 8,000 residents. To say that the citizenry of Port Townsend marches to the beat of a different drummer is an understatement that doesn't do justice to the town. In the summer and fall months, when the town's calendar is loaded with festivals, it can seem like the locals march to an altogether different percussion section.

Port Townsend has plenty to enjoy, beginning with the striking Victorian buildings and homes that rival the architecture in any place on the West Coast for turn-of-the-century (that other century) charm. Several historic homes have been turned into bed-and-breakfasts and decorated with antiques and period decor. A restaurant and shopping scene downtown enlivens Water Street, and live music is presented practically every night of the week. Add to these activities a vivid outdoor landscape that is framed on one side by Olympic National Park and on the other by Puget Sound. The town offers beaches and hiking trails, quiet waters to paddle, and rural roads to cycle, all under skies that receive about half the annual rainfall of Seattle.

It's almost as if Port Townsend is trying mightily to overcome a past that was very serious and high-minded indeed. Founded in 1851 and quickly built up, the seaport town had high hopes and the massive backing of shipping and timber interests who envisioned a great commercial center alongside Puget Sound. But then — oops! — the state's business and politics all moved down-Sound to Seattle and Olympia, leaving Port Townsend high and dry, albeit with enough wonderful, ornate homes and commercial buildings that the town is now recognized as a National Historic Landmark District.

Artists and merchants came to the rescue, restoring vitality to the flagging local economy, turning Water Street's vacant buildings into shops and galleries, transforming decommissioned Fort Worden into a living museum and festival center, and infusing the Victorian town with a mischievous spirit of fun. The tourists followed and have found plenty to enjoy.

Getting There

Continuing north from Chimacum, Hwy 19 merges into Hwy 20 seven miles south of Port Townsend. Hwy 20 leads directly into town and deposits you on Water Street, the main thoroughfare in Port Townsend. If you're driving on Hwy 101, turn off onto Hwy 20, 14 miles south of Port Townsend.

If you're coming from Vancouver, British Columbia, or northern Washington, you can bypass the Seattle metropolitan region by approaching Port Townsend from Whidbey Island. Pick up Hwy 20 west at Burlington, Washington, and make your way to the Keystone ferry terminal, where boats can take you across the narrow channel to downtown Port Townsend. For Puget Sound ferry schedules, contact **Washington State Ferries** (☎ 206-464-6400).

To arrive by bus or at the airport in nearby Port Angeles, see Chapter 20 for details.

Finding Information

For information before you go or once you get to Port Townsend, contact the **Port Townsend Chamber of Commerce Visitor Information Center,** 2437 E. Sims Way, Port Townsend, WA 98368 (☎ 888-365-6978 or 360-385-2722; Internet: www.ptguide.com), which has all sorts of information on everything from the arts scene to a range of accommodations.

As a tourist town, Port Townsend schedules quite a few annual festivals throughout the year. The last week of March, the town celebrates its Victorian heritage with the **Victorian Festival** (☎ 888-698-1116; Internet: www.victorianfestival.org). The **Jazz Port Townsend** festival is held toward the end of July. The **Wooden Boat Festival,** the largest of its kind in the United States, is on the first weekend after Labor Day. To see inside some of the town's many restored homes, schedule a visit during the **Historic Homes Tour** on the third weekend in September.

The **Olympic Music Festival** (☎ 206-527-8839; Internet: www.olympic musicfestival.org), held nearby in an old barn near the town of Quilcene, is the area's most important music festival. This series of weekend concerts takes place between mid-June and mid-September.

One of the town's most popular festivals is the **Kinetic Sculpture Race** held annually in mid-October. Racers compete in handmade contraptions, and the goal is to reach the finish at the bottom of Water Street dead in the middle of the pack. The jockeying for middle-of-the-pack position is hysterical. Afterward, a Kween is Krowned, and everyone repairs to a big costume ball for an evening of dancing and more hilarity.

Because parking spaces are hard to come by in downtown Port Townsend on weekends and anytime in the summer, **Jefferson Transit** (☎ 360-385-4777; Internet: www.jeffersontransit.com), the local public bus service, operates a shuttle into downtown Port Townsend from a park-and-ride lot on the south side of town. Jefferson Transit also operates other buses around Port Townsend. Fares are 50 cents to $1. If you need a taxi, call **Peninsula Taxi** (☎ 360-385-1872).

Exploring the Area

You certainly won't be bored here. You can stroll in the historic district and take in the Victorian homes, shop around the town's art galleries, beachcomb, bike, explore the old military structures at Fort Worden State Park, see the town from a sailboat, and more.

Exploring the town

With its abundance of restored Victorian homes and commercial buildings, Port Townsend's most popular activity is simply walking or driving through the historic districts. The town is divided into the waterfront commercial district and the residential Uptown Port Townsend, which is atop a bluff that rises precipitously only 2 blocks from the water. Uptown Port Townsend developed in part so that proper Victorian ladies wouldn't have to associate with the "riffraff" that frequented the waterfront. At the Port Townsend Visitor Information Center, you can pick up a map with a self-guided tour of the town's many historic homes and commercial buildings.

Before exploring the town, stop by the **Jefferson County Historical Museum and Library** (540 Water St.; ☎ 360-385-1003; Internet: www.jchsmuseum.org), where you can learn about the history of the area. Among the collections here are regional Native American artifacts and antiques from the Victorian era. It's open Monday through Saturday from 11 a.m. to 4 p.m. and Sunday 1 to 4 p.m. (In January and February, it's open Saturday and Sunday only.) Admission is $2 for adults and $1 for children under 12.

Water Street is the town's main commercial area. Restored 100-year-old brick buildings, many of which have ornate façade, line the street for several blocks. Within these buildings are dozens of interesting shops and boutiques, several restaurants, and a handful of hotels and inns. To discover a little more about the history of this part of town and to gain a different perspective, walk out onto **Union Wharf,** at the foot of Taylor Street, which has interpretive plaques covering topics ranging from sea grass to waterfront history.

The town's noted Victorian homes are in Uptown Port Townsend, atop the bluff that rises behind the waterfront's commercial buildings. This area is known for its stately homes and great views and is home to the city's favorite park, Chetzemoka Park. To reach Uptown, either drive up Washington Street (1 block over from Water Street) or walk up the stairs at the end of Taylor Street, which start behind the Haller Fountain. Walk or drive "uptown" (up the steep cliff that Washington Street climbs) and spend the morning admiring Victorian architecture at, among many other places, the **James House** (1238 Washington St.; ☎ 800-385-1238), which functions as a B&B; the massive **U.S. Customs House/Post Office** (at Washington, Harrison, and Van Buren streets.), which was completed in 1893; and the **F.W. Hastings House** (313 Walker St.; ☎ 800-300-6753), which was once the residence of the German Consul and is now an inn.

The most fascinating Uptown home open to the public is the **Ann Starrett Mansion** (744 Clay St; ☎ 360-385-3205), Port Townsend's most astoundingly ornate Queen Anne Victorian home. Currently operating as a bed-and-breakfast inn, this mansion is best known for its imposing turret, ceiling frescoes, and unusual spiral staircase. The house is open for guided tours daily from noon to 3 p.m. Tours cost $2.

Also here in Uptown, at the corner of Garfield and Jackson streets, is **Chetzemoka Park,** which was established in 1904 and is named for a local S'Klallum Indian chief. The park perches on a bluff overlooking Admiralty Inlet and provides access to a pleasant little beach. However, it's the rose garden, arbor, and waterfall garden that attract most visitors.

Shopping is just about the most popular activity in Port Townsend's old town, and of the many stores in the historic district, several stand out. **Earthenworks Gallery** (702 Water St.; ☎ 360-385-0328) showcases colorful ceramics, glass, jewelry, and other American-made crafts; **Ancestral Spirits Gallery** (701 Water St.; ☎ 360-385-0078) is a large space with a great selection of Northwest Native American prints, masks, and carvings; and **Artisans on Taylor** (236 Taylor St.; ☎ 360-379-8098) is a small boutique that specializes in blown glass and pottery by local craftspeople. Women enamored of Port Townsend's Victorian styling will want to visit the **Palace Emporium** (1002 Water St.; ☎ 360-385-5899), a dress shop specializing in modern Victorian fashions. Lovers of old cars and garages will flip over **Bergstrom's Classic Autos** (809 Washington St.; ☎ 360-385-5061), a restored garage that houses vintage autos and memorabilia.

Exploring Fort Worden State Park

Plan to spend a good part of a day at **Fort Worden State Park** (200 Battery Way; ☎ 360-344-4400). The fort, a former U.S. army base that guarded the mouth of Puget Sound, is north of the historic district and can be reached by turning onto Kearney Street at the south end of town, or onto Monroe Street at the north end of town, and following the signs. Built at the turn of the century, the fort is now a 360-acre state park that boasts a wide array of attractions. The park consists of restored barracks, parade lawns, campsites, a restaurant, and handsome military houses (many of which you can rent; see the section "Staying in Style," later in this chapter). Now a home to numerous festivals and events, the Fort also houses museums that kids and adults alike will enjoy. The park is a great place to beachcomb or ride bikes, and you can enjoy a picnic at any number of waterside beach spots. For many people, the main reason to visit the park is to hang out on the beach. Scuba divers also frequent the park, which has an underwater park just offshore. If you're here in spring, don't miss the colorful blooms in the Rhododendron Garden.

At the **Commanding Officer's Quarters Museum** (☎ 360-344-4452; Internet: www.olympus.net/ftworden/museums.htm), you can see what life was like for a Victorian-era officer and his family. The home has been fully restored and is filled with period antiques. In June, July, and August it's open daily from 10 a.m. to 5 p.m.; from September through October and April through May it's open on weekends from noon to 4 p.m. The museum is closed November through February. Admission is $2 for adults and free for children under 12.

You can find out about life below the waters of Puget Sound at the park's **Port Townsend Marine Science Center** (532 Battery Way; ☎ 360-385-5582; Internet: www.ptmsc.org). This excellent kid-geared hands-on museum and aquarium boasts touch tanks and nature exhibits. From June 15 through Labor Day, the center is open Wednesday through Monday from 11 a.m. to 5 p.m. From September 4 to October 31, it's open 11 a.m. to 4 p.m. On weekends and from April 7 through June 14, it's open from noon to 4 p.m. Admission is $3 for adults, $2 for children 6 to 17, and free for children under 6.

Throughout the year, the **Centrum** (☎ **800-733-3608** or 360-385-5320; Internet: www.centrum.org) presents a wide variety of concerts and other performances.

Exploring Port Townsend from the water and air

If you'd like to explore the town from the water, you've got several options. **Brisa Charters** (☎ **877-41-BRISA** or 360-385-2309; Internet: www.olympus.net/brisa_charters) and **Bryony Charters** (☎ **360-481-0605;** Internet: www.sailbryony.com) both offer three-hour sailboat tours ($65), though Bryony Charters operates only between April and October. In the spring and fall, **Port Townsend Marine Science Center** (☎ **360-385-5582;** Internet: www.ptmsc.org) operates educational boat tours ($45) to nearby Protection Island, a wildlife refuge that is home to more than 70% of Puget Sound's nesting seabirds. May through September, cruises ($52.50 per adult) through the San Juan Islands are offered by **Puget Sound Express** (431 Water St.; ☎ **360-385-5288;** Internet: www.pugetsoundexpress.com), which also offers passenger ferry service to Friday Harbor. During the summer, you're almost certain to see orca whales on these trips. If you'd like to try your hand at paddling a sea kayak around the area's waters, contact **Kayak Port Townsend** (435 Water St.; ☎ **800-853-2252** or 360-385-6240; Internet: www.kayakpt.com), which offers two-hour ($30), half-day ($40), and full-day tours ($76) and also rents sea kayaks.

Staying in Style

Bishop Victorian Hotel (714 Washington St.; ☎ **360-385-6122** or 800-824-4738; Internet: www.bishopvictorian.com) is one of many Victorian-built and decorated lodgings in town. This handsome brick building is a block off Water Street and has comfortable suites with kitchenettes, as well as a lovely garden that is a perfect place to sit and read the Sunday paper. Suites here are $99 to $199 per night.

The Tides Inn (1807 Water St.; ☎ **360-385-0595** or 800-822-8696; Internet: www.tides-inn.com) should be called "The Tubs Inn" for the big soaking tubs that are steps from the bed and offer views of Port Townsend Bay. Parts of the movie "An Officer and a Gentleman" were filmed in this waterfront lodging's older motel-style units. Rooms range from $68 to $269 from March to mid-October and $60 to $189 from mid-October through February.

Several of the former **officers' houses at Fort Worden State Park** (200 Battery Way; ☎ **360-344-4434**; Internet: www.olympus.net/ftworden) are now available for rental, and with up to six bedrooms each, they're a great bargain for groups of friends or large families. Each house is equipped with a full kitchen and linen service. Book well in advance during popular festivals.

Built in 1889 for $6,000 as a wedding present for Ann Starrett, **Ann Starrett Mansion** (744 Clay St.; ☎ **800-321-0644** or 360-385-3205; Fax 360-385-2976; Internet: www.starrettmansion.com) is a Victorian jewel box that is by far the most elegant and ornate bed-and-breakfast in Port Townsend (and the entire state for that matter). The rose and teal mansion is a museum of the Victorian era: A three-story turret towers over the front door, and every room is exquisitely furnished with period antiques. If you aren't staying here, you can still have a look around during one of the afternoon house tours ($2). Breakfast is an extravaganza that can last all morning and will certainly make you consider skipping lunch. This B&B is all about pampering amid Victorian elegance. Regular rooms range from $115 to $185, except from the honeymoon suite, which can go up to $225.

Built in 1892 by a wealthy baker, **Manresa Castle** (7th and Sheridan streets; ☎ **800-732-1281** or 360-385-5750; Fax 360-385-5883; Internet: www.manresacastle.com) is a reproduction of a medieval castle that later became a Jesuit retreat and school. Today, traditional elegance pervades Manresa Castle. Of all the hotels and B&Bs in Port Townsend, this castle offers the most historic elegance for the money. The guest rooms have a genuine vintage appeal that manages to avoid the con-trived feeling that so often sneaks into the room decor of B&Bs. The best deal in the hotel is the tower suite during the off season. For $135 a night, you get a huge room with sweeping views from its circular seat-ing area. An elegant lounge and dining room further add to the "Grand Hotel" feel of this unusual accommodation. In winter, rooms range from $75 to $90, and suites range from $95 to $150. In summer, rooms range from $85 to $100, and suites range from $150 to $175.

Dining Out

The Otter Crossing Café (130 Hudson St.; ☎ **360-379-0952**), with local art decorating the walls, is a great spot for breakfast, serving delicacies such as Dungeness crab omelettes and Swedish lingonberry French toast. The cafe is located on the edge of Point Hudson Marina and offers great views of the Puget Sound and the boats at the marina.

The Salal Café (634 Water St; ☎ **360-385-6532**) is another great spot for breakfast. It wins local awards for its lavish menu, which boasts such items as blueberry crêpes, homemade biscuits and gravy, and an oyster scramble. Main course prices range from $6.50 to $8.95.

The dining room at **Manresa Castle** (7th and Sheridan streets; ☎ **360-385-5750**), the imposing Victorian hotel reviewed earlier in the chapter, is run by a Swiss chef who brings a continental flair to formal dining. The Sunday brunch is the best in town. You may wish that you were wearing your Sunday finest and had brought Grandma along with you to enjoy the classical dining room and elegant service. Main course prices range from $18 to $24.

The location is a bit out of the way (across the street from the Boat Haven marina south of downtown Port Townsend), but romantic, low-key **Lonny's Restaurant** (2330 Washington St.; ☎ **360-385-0700;** Internet: www.lonnys.com) is one of the best restaurants in the Northwest. The Mediterranean menu of chef/owner Lonny Ritter is long and always features plenty of daily specials. Whether you come for lunch or dinner, be sure to start with the oyster stew, which is made with pancetta and fennel; it's heavenly. At both lunch and dinner, you can choose from a wide variety of interesting pasta dishes — the rigatoni Gorgonzola is especially delicious. Traditional Spanish paella is another tasty dish. Local oysters, mussels, and clams show up frequently on the fresh sheet and are hard to resist. Interesting wines are usually available by the glass. Be sure to call well in advance for a weekend dinner reservation. Main course prices range from $11.95 to $21.95.

Works by local artists, lots of plants, and New Age music on the stereo set the tone at **Silverwater Café** (237 Taylor St.; ☎ **360-385-6448;** Internet: www.silverwatercafe.com), a casually chic restaurant. Though the menu focuses on Northwest dishes, it also includes preparations from around the world. You can start your meal with an artichoke-and-Parmesan pâté and then move on to ahi tuna with lavender pepper, prawns with cilantro-ginger-lime butter, or smoked chicken with brandy and apples. The oysters in a blue cheese sauce are excellent. If you're a vegetarian, you'll find about half a dozen options. Main courses range from $10 to $18.

Provisions for a picnic are available at **The Cellar Market** (940 Water St.; ☎ **360-385-7088**), which sells deli sandwiches and wines, and at **Aldrich's Market** (940 Lawrence St.; ☎ **360-385-0500**), an uptown grocery store with a salad bar and deli.

Chapter 26

Sequim and Port Angeles

. . . .

In This Chapter

▶ Hiking the Dungeness Spit

▶ Staying in waterfront lodgings in Sequim and Port Angeles

▶ Exploring lavender farms and a park devoted to exotic animals

. . . .

*O*n the northern coast of Washington, on the thin strip of coastal plain that gives way to the towering Olympic mountains, are the towns of Sequim and Port Angeles, which make very nice bases of operation for exploring Olympic National Park and the entire Olympic Peninsula.

The quiet coastal town of **Sequim** (pronounced *skwim*) has been discovered by active retirees who love the views of the water and mountains, the proximity to the park, and the fact that the mountains cast a "rain shadow" over the area that ensures over 300 sunny days a year. A town of neat houses and quiet streets, Sequim is home to good family restaurants, pick-your-own farms, and produce vendors. Lavender is a popular local product, and an annual **Lavender Festival** in July draws more than 20,000 visitors. Lavender farms (see the section "Exploring the Area," later in this chapter) are open all year, with gift shops that sell all sorts of items scented with the fragrant plant.

Seafood lovers should instantly recognize the name Dungeness, which is the title of the bay that Sequim sits along, as well the name of the long sand spit that constitutes the Dungeness National Wildlife Refuge (described later in this chapter in the section "Exploring the Area"). This bay is indeed the home of sweet Dungeness crabs, and seafood restaurants are eager to serve you this local specialty.

Port Angeles is the gateway to Olympic National Park, and it's through here that most of the park's five million visitors are funneled. (See Chapter 21 for park information.) The ferry terminal on the north end of town, with service to Victoria, British Columbia, across the Strait of Juan de Fuca, anchors an active waterfront complex that contains hotels, restaurants, a playground for children, and a fine, paved waterfront trail that serves as an evening promenade for locals and visitors alike.

Getting There

Sequim and Port Angeles lie on the U.S. 101 corridor on the north end of the Olympic Peninsula. Port Angeles is the transportation hub of the region and is easily accessible by car, bus and commuter plane. (See Chapter 21 for details.)

Finding Information

You can find information for both towns on the Web site of the **North Olympic Peninsula Visitor and Convention Bureau** (www.olympic peninsula.org), with separate links to the **Sequim Dungeness Valley Chamber of Commerce** (1192 E. Washington, P.O. Box 907, ☎ 800-737-8462 or 360-683-6197; Internet: www.visitsun.com) and the **Port Angeles Chamber of Commerce** (121 E. Railroad Ave., ☎ 877-456-8372 and 360-452-2363; Internet: www.portangeles.org).

Exploring the Area

On the northwest side of Sequim, you'll find **Dungeness Spit and the Dungeness National Wildlife Refuge** (☎ 360-457-8451), a remarkable sand spit. At seven miles long, this narrow strip of sand and gravel is the longest natural sand spit in the United States. It juts into Dungeness Bay and provides a haven for hundreds of species of birds. If you're up for the 14-mile round-trip hike, you'll find a lonely lighthouse at the end of the spit, but be sure to check tide tables to make sure that you don't get stuck out there. Note that pets aren't allowed on the spit because of its wildlife refuge status.

The **Museum & Arts Center** (175 West Cedar St., Sequim, ☎ 360-683-8110; Internet: sequimmuseum.org) is a small museum devoted to the area's culture and history. It's most notable for the Manis Mastodon Exhibit, a collection of Ice Age artifacts found during a nearby excavation of an ancient mastodon.

Olympic Game Farm (1423 Ward Rd., Sequim; ☎ 360-683-4295; Internet: www.olygamefarm.com) grew from the work of wild animal trainers Lloyd and Catherine Beebe, who trained exotic animals for years for Hollywood productions. The farm houses dozens of animals, from a rare white rhinoceros to zebras, wolves, and Kodiak and grizzly bears, to tame elk and buffalo. Driving tours are available year-round, and in the summer months, you can take a guided walking tour that includes contact with some of the friendlier residents of the park.

Jardin du Soleil Lavender (3932 Sequim-Dungeness Way, Sequim; ☎ **877-527-3461** or 360-582-1185; Internet: www.jardindusoleil.com) is an organic lavender farm where you can see thousands of lavender plants in bloom and purchase numerous lavender-scented products in the gift shop. Pick your own lavender bouquet or take home a plant to begin your own lavender patch.

Although Sequim's pastoral farmland is quickly giving way to residential developments and new golf courses, **Graysmarsh Farm** (6187 Woodcock Rd., Sequim; ☎ **360-683-5563;** Internet: www.graysmarsh.com) continues to operate as a pick-your-own farm and gift center. The season starts in mid-June with pick-your-own strawberries and continues throughout the summer with raspberries, lavender, loganberries, and blueberries. A great selection of jams and preserves are available in the gift shop.

For those who like gaming and nightclub entertainment, the **7 Cedars Casino** (270756 U.S. 101; ☎ **800-4LUCKY7**) is a handsome tribal casino run by the S'Klallam tribe. The longhouse-style building has a good, inexpensive restaurant and entertainment by musicians, comedians, and other national touring acts.

Arthur D. Fiero Marine Life Center (Port Angeles City Pier; ☎ **360-452-3940**) is a hands-on museum with touch tanks that display 80 species of sea creatures collected from the waters around Port Angeles. The museum sits at the end of a pier that has a playground and a public beach.

Port Angeles Fine Arts Center, (1203 E. Lauridsen, Blvd., Port Angeles; ☎ **360-457-3532;** Internet: www.portangelesartscenter.com) has collections of contemporary art and a five-acre "Art Outside" sculpture garden, which is located on a lovely trail system through forests that blend into nearby Olympic National Park.

Enjoying Outdoor Adventures

In this section, I give details on the abundant opportunities for outdoor activity that this region offers.

Bicycling

If you're interested in exploring the region on a bike, you can rent one at **Sound Bikes & Kayaks** (120 E. Front St., Port Angeles; ☎ **360-457-1240;** Internet: www.soundbikeskayaks.com), which can recommend good rides in the area and also offers bicycle tours. Bikes are $30 per day or $9 per hour.

Camping

Klallam County Parks operates the **Dungeness County Park** (554 Voice of America West, Sequim; ☎ 360-683-5847), which is located near the entrance to the Dungeness Spit. The park has 68 campsites, all of which you can reach by car or on foot, which are available on a first-come, first-served basis. The campsites don't have electric or water hookups, but the park has shared modern bathroom facilities and a playground for kids. Wildlife sightings are frequent: When I last visited, I saw four deer in the first five minutes.

Llama trekking

If you want to take an overnight trip into the backcountry of the Olympic National Park but don't want to carry all the gear, consider letting a llama carry your stuff. **Kit's Llamas** (P.O. Box 116, Olalla, WA 98359; ☎ 253-857-5274; Internet: www.northolympic.com/llamas) offers llama trekking in the Olympic Mountains. They'll bring the animals to you and meet at a designated trailhead. Prices, based on a group of six to eight adults, are $35 to $75 per person for day hikes and $75 to $150 per person per day for overnight and multiday trips, with special rates for children. **Deli Llama** (17045 Llama Lane, Bow, WA 98232; ☎ 360-757-4212; Internet: www.delillama.com), which is based near Burlington, also does llama treks ranging from four to seven days in Olympic National Park ($125 to $145 per person per day).

Sea kayaking and canoeing

Guided sea-kayaking trips on nearby Lake Aldwell, at Freshwater Bay, and at Dungeness National Wildlife Refuge are offered by **Olympic Raft & Kayak** (123 Lake Aldwell Rd., Port Angeles; ☎ 888-452-1443 or 360-452-1443; Internet: www.raftandkayak.com), which charges between $42 and $99 per person. Tours are available for all experience levels — the company will choose the site to match your comfort level. Sea-kayak rentals are available at **Sound Bikes & Kayaks** (120 E. Front St., Port Angeles; ☎ 360-457-1240; Internet: www.soundbikeskayaks.com), which charges $12 per hour or $40 per day.

Whale-watching

Puffin Adventures (Neah Bay Marina, Neah Bay; ☎ 888-305-2437; Internet: www.puffinadventures.com) offers whale-watching and wildlife cruises for $50 per person. The cruises explore the waters of the Strait of Juan de Fuca and the Olympic Coast National Marine Sanctuary outside of Neah Bay.

Staying in Style

Not so much a motel in the traditional sense as a collection of roomy cottages, **Dungeness Bay Motel** (140 Marine Dr., Sequim; ☎ 888-683-3013 or 360-683-3013; Internet: www.northolympic.com/dungeness bay) enjoys a lovely setting across the street from Dungeness Bay, with a private beach with picnic tables and chairs. The cottages have full kitchens and cable-equipped TVs, plus sweeping views of mountains and cow pastures out back.

Another cluster of cottages across from the beach and near Dungeness Spit, **Juan de Fuca Cottages** (182 Marine Dr., Sequim; ☎ 866-683-4433 or 360-683-4433. Internet: www.juandefuca.com) boasts whirlpool tubs and fireplaces in every cottage, as well as a 250-title video library that guests have unlimited access to.

Red Lion Inn (221 N. Lincoln, Port Angeles; ☎ 800-733-5466 or 360-452-9215; Internet: www.redlion.com) is a chain hotel that's well-situated on the waterfront at Port Angeles, just steps away from the municipal pier, beach, and ferry terminal. The outdoor pool makes this place kid-friendly, and the outdoor hot tub is popular with adults. A paved walkway alongside the bay is great for evening strolls for the whole family.

The prime attraction of **BJ's Garden Gate** (397 Monterra Dr., Port Angeles; ☎ 800-880-1332 or 360-452-2322; Internet: www.bjgarden. com), a lovely waterfront estate, is the extensive garden, which bursts with flowers in the summer and spring. The Victorian home has five bedrooms decorated with antiques and amenities like double Jacuzzi baths, sitting places or fireplaces and water views, with the lights of Victoria sparkling in the distance at night.

Choosing Where to Dine

Breakfast is the big attraction at **Oak Table Cafe** (3rd and Bell streets, Sequim; ☎ 360-683-2179; Internet: www.oaktablecafe.com), a family restaurant with wonderful items that you rarely see on standard menus, such as eggs benedict with mushroom sauce, German and Swedish pancakes, and the house specialty, a baked apple pancake that is the size of a pie, served with homemade apple syrup and a caramelized topping. Lunch and dinner fare is standard family-style food served in large portions.

If you've come to Dungeness Bay looking for seafood, **The 3 Crabs** (11 Three Crabs Rd., Sequim; ☎ 360-683-4264) is your place. This waterfront family restaurant specializes in local crabs and shellfish.

Besides whole Dungeness crabs served with butter, you can order crab cakes, crab burgers, halibut sandwiches, and oyster stew.

Bella Italia (118 East First St., Port Angeles; ☎ **360-457-5442**) is a friendly Italian restaurant that prides itself on fresh ingredients, from produce to seafood, that contribute to a light and flavorful northern Italian cuisine. An extensive wine list features more than 300 Northwest and Italian wines.

A casual eatery on the main drag of Sequim, **The Buzz** (128 North Sequim Ave., Sequim; ☎ **360-683-2503**) is the place to stop in for a cup of espresso in the morning, fresh cinnamon rolls and baked goods all day, and ice-cream cones at night.

Part VII
The Part of Tens

The 5th Wave   By Rich Tennant

"Being in Seattle, we had the first grunge IS dept. Then we were a techno-Pop dept., and now we're sort of a neo-50's-Lou Reed IS dept."

In this part . . .

In this part, I provide fun, quirky tips on visiting Seattle and the Olympic Peninsula that are guaranteed to make your visit all the richer.

Chapter 27

Ten Northwest Taste Treats You Simply Can't Miss

* *

In This Chapter

▶ Tasting local treats that are indigenous to the Northwest

▶ Sampling Seattle and the Olympic Peninsula's tastiest dishes

* *

1 don't know about you, but I find that when I travel, a great way to get into the local scene quickly is through my palate. I review and discuss Seattle and the Olympic Peninsula's restaurants elsewhere in this book; this chapter is where I get down to the specifics and write about ten things I could eat over and over, and the best places to get them.

Crab Cocktails

Shrimp cocktail might be good — exotic even — but it pales in comparison to a Northwest Dungeness crab cocktail, which consists of chunks of sweet, fresh crab over a small layer of chopped celery with a dollop of piquant cocktail sauce dropped over the top. Crab cocktails are served at many fine restaurants, but the best place to eat one is at the unpretentious, stainless-steel lunch counter at **Jack's Fish Spot** (1514 Pike Place; ☎ 206-467-0514) at the Pike Place Market.

Piroshky!, Piroshky!

Russian *piroshky,* also known as pierogies in many places, are often fairly basic pockets of dough filled with various ingredients. However, at the Pike Place Market's **Piroshky, Piroshky** (1908 Pike Place; ☎ 206-441-6068), they reach an unheard-of level that approaches an art form. Savory piroshkies (which I must eat as a main course before allowing myself to hit the dessert piroshkies hard) are filled with creamy smoked salmon spread or fragrant cabbage and onions. You can also order open-faced apple tarts, which are perfectly baked and redolent of cardamom and cinnamon. Another treat is Moscow Rolls, turnovers filled with a sweetened cream cheese. Piroshkies are a must-stop treat on every single visit I've ever made to the Market.

Copper River Salmon

In Seattle, all salmon is not created equal. There is a big difference between a chum salmon and a king salmon, but the most treasured fish of them all is the Copper River salmon, which arrives in May, fresh from the Alaskan river of its origin. This salmon is rich in oil and even darker in color than most kings, and its flavor is robust. It becomes the special at most seafood restaurants and is snapped up at grocery stores. If you see it on a menu, it's definitely worth the premium price charged. The opening of Copper River season, when the first fish are flown in from Alaska, is practically a city holiday, with great fanfare.

Pie at the Dahlia Lounge

For those travelers who have scoured the world for the best coconut-cream pie, it may come as a surprise that the paramount pie doesn't come from a fancy restaurant in Hawaii, but from Tom Douglas's **Dahlia Lounge** (2001 Fourth Ave. at Virginia St.; ☎ 206-682-4142) in Seattle. This is a pie to be reckoned with — a pile of rich coconut cream on a flaky crust, with shavings of white chocolate cascading over the top. It's also available by the whole pie at the restaurant's takeout bakery, as well as at Douglas's other restaurants, **Palace Kitchen** (2030 5th Ave.; ☎ 206-448-2001) and **Etta's Seafood** (2020 Western Ave.; ☎ 206-443-6000).

Kerry Sears' Oysters

A platter of freshly shucked oysters on the half shell nestled on beds of cracked ice is a welcome sight at any fine restaurant, but these shellfish are taken up a notch at **Cascadia** (2328 First Ave., between Bell and Battery streets; ☎ 206-448-8884), Kerry Sears' fine-dining restaurant in Seattle's Belltown. Sears picks only the tiniest, most delicate morsels of oyster from Puget Sound growers and then serves them with a rack full of test tubes that contain delicious dressings for the shellfish. It's the most exotic oyster presentation in the city and kicks off one of Sears' seven-course meals perfectly.

A Darn Fine Cuppa Joe

Is there any other city in the country that is as passionate about coffee as Seattle? I don't think so. This city is the only place I know where people take sides over who roasts their beans the best, Starbucks or Tully's, and whether you should grab a cup of caffe latte on the fly at a drive-through espresso booth or park at your favorite neighborhood coffee shop. I head to my friend Andhi Spath's **Café Bambino** (405 NW 65th St.; ☎ **206-706-4934**) for great coffee and good company every time.

Apple Pancakes in Sequim

I had heard that the apple pancakes served at the **Oak Table Cafe** (3rd and Bell streets, Sequim; ☎ **360-683-2179**) in Sequim were special. I knew that something wonderful was going on when the waitress brought a cruet of house-made apple syrup to pour on my pancake. But when the thing arrived, as big and high as a pie, with layers of apples baked into a custardy filling, topped with a thick cinnamon/brown sugar glaze, I nearly gasped in admiration. This pancake is worth traveling for, and the only one I've ever had that I couldn't finish and was happy to take home in a carton.

Jumbo Lump Crab Cakes

The nearly year-round availability of excellent Dungeness crab has caused Seattleites to become accustomed to a certain high level of crab cake excellence. Any restaurant worth its salt produces a decent crab cake, lightly breaded with Panko and fried to a golden brown. But when Chef Kevin Davis of the **Oceanaire Seafood Room** (1700 Seventh Ave. across from Pacific Place, ☎ **206-267-BASS**) presented me with his jumbo lump crab cakes, made from East Coast crab, I had to agree that there was a new sheriff in town. Big, juicy pieces of crab delicately held together by the lightest of egg batters makes for a sensational crab cake.

Halibut and Chips

I wouldn't take a chance on fish and chips at most vacation destinations (with the possible exception of London), but the dish is a must-try in Seattle. Forget about fish sticks and the cheap, oily stuff that is served as fish in other places; here, they take fresh lingcod or halibut flown in from Alaska, dip it in Panko, and fry to a golden brown. With a mound of fries, it's a delicious and cheap fast-food treat. A fine fish and chips is served at Seattle's **Little Chinook's at Salmon Bay** (Fisherman's Terminal; ☎ 206-283-HOOK), which has picnic tables that offer views of the Alaska fishing fleet tied up at long docks.

Larsen's Danish

It's pretty hard to find fault with a good Danish pastry anywhere, but how often can you buy one at an authentic Danish bakery? Seattle's Scandinavian heritage in the Ballard neighborhood is evident in the unusual food items found there (though I wouldn't wish lutefisk on anyone but the staunchest Swedes), including a terrific Danish at the **Larsen Brothers Danish Bakery** (8000 24th Ave. NW at NW 80th Street; ☎ 206-782-8285).

Chapter 28

Ten Quintessentially "Northwest" Things to Do

In This Chapter

▶ Experiencing essential Northwest sights and attractions

▶ Partying in Seattle and the Olympic Peninsula: Local celebrations and festivals

Clean lakes and rivers in the middle of an urban environment. Salmon fighting their way upstream past viewing windows. A ferryboat ride at sunset with views of towering, snowcapped mountains. Many wonderful things about the Pacific Northwest make it stand out from other parts of the country. If your time is limited, or you just want to soak up some pure Pacific Northwest ambience, go straight to these attractions or activities.

Ride a Ferry across Puget Sound

Crossing Puget Sound on a Washington State ferry is an experience that is not to be missed. Boats leave from downtown Seattle loaded with cars and passengers on their way to Bainbridge Island and Bremerton. Grab a cup of coffee from the snack bar and head outside to one of the observation decks to see the striking tableau of city, water, sailboats, gulls, and islands unfold. See Chapter 15 for more information.

Go to the Top of the Space Needle

Seattle's landmark, rising up from Seattle Center like a giant exclamation point, was built in 1962 for the World's Fair and still has a magnetic attraction for visitors. Ride the elevators to the top to get a great panoramic view of the entire region, and be sure to snap some pictures of the Needle itself to prove without a doubt that you've been to Seattle. See Chapter 15 for details.

Watch the Salmon, Eat the Salmon

Wild salmon, so long a symbol of the Northwest, are in danger of becoming a historic relic. Salmon runs have been declining over the years, and local salmon breeding grounds are dwindling. If you're lucky, however, you can still see wild salmon, as well as farm-hatched salmon that were released into the wild, fighting their way upstream through underwater viewing windows at the Hiram M. Chittenden Locks in Seattle (see Chapter 15). Hopefully the experience won't diminish your appreciation of a perfectly prepared salmon dinner at a local restaurant. The salmon served here, by the way, come from fisheries in Alaska, where the noble species is still thriving.

Have a Latte at the Pike Place Market

Coffee culture is alive and well in the Northwest, and you find plenty of opportunities to indulge in fresh-brewed espresso drinks at numerous shops, drive-through stands, and kiosks in Seattle and the Olympic Peninsula. The best caffe latte experience can be had at the small vendors in Pike Place Market, itself a Northwest landmark and well worth exploring. Sitting at a sidewalk table in the Market on a pleasant morning with a cuppa Joe and a croissant is an experience that lingers in memory for many visitors. See Chapter 14 for more info.

Children don't have to be left out of the coffee-shop experience. Any espresso stand worth its salt also offers a top-notch hot chocolate or chocolate milk, topped with whipped cream, for the younger set.

Paddle a Kayak

Paddling the smooth waters of Lake Union in Seattle or Port Townsend Bay are great ways to see parts of the Northwest that landlocked visitors miss. Kayak rental shops in both places offer safe, stable kayaks with foot-operated rudders and spray skirts that keep you warm and dry. In Seattle, you paddle among communities of dollhouse-like houseboats in the shadow of the Space Needle. Port Townsend offers quiet paddles past wildlife refuges. Kayaking in both places takes you instantly out of the urban noise and bustle into peaceful corners. See Chapters 15 and 25 for more info.

If you're going paddling, you need a light, water-resistant jacket or shell and a hat. Your legs and lower body will stay dry thanks to the enclosed kayak hulls and spray skirts, but you're likely to drip water from your paddles onto your head and upper body.

Children can also participate in paddling when you rent double and triple kayaks, with compartments for each rider that are secure and dry. Everyone wears life jackets, of course, and kids can do as much or as little paddling as they want from their positions in the front of the boat. You control the steering and the movement from the back of the boat.

Soak in the Panorama at Hurricane Ridge

The most breathtaking views in Olympic National Park are from this visitor center high up in the mountains. Before you is a landscape that encompasses the jagged peaks of the Olympics, sweeping valleys, and miles of trees. See Chapter 21 for info.

Take a Peek at Bill Gates's House

It says something about Seattle that the world's richest man continues to live here (as does his former sidekick, Paul Allen, who is also no slouch in the personal-wealth department). Gates built his own Xanadu on the shores of Lake Washington, in the eastern suburb of Bellevue, and tour boats routinely cruise past the property to give visitors a good look at this vivid symbol of Northwest opulence. Seeing the Gates manse up close (or spotting Bill at his infrequent public appearances) is a reminder of the high-tech wealth that has transformed Seattle over the last decade (see Chapter 15).

Ride a Floatplane to the San Juan Islands

The San Juan Islands of northwest Washington are idyllic little pearls an hour away from Seattle. People flock here in the summer months to get a good, strong dose of rural life, uncrowded roads, forest hikes, and peaceful little beaches. You can take a ferry to the main islands, but the greatest way to experience the San Juans is to take a floatplane from Lake Union in downtown Seattle that flies over many of the islands and lands at deserted coves of uninhabited islands for some unique beach-combing and exploration. If you're on a tight schedule, a two-hour flightseeing tour gives you terrific views (and photo ops) of the islands (see Chapter 17).

Snap Pictures of Mount Rainier

Call them the pillars of Seattle society: Mount Rainier and Mount St. Helen (in southern Washington) are the most formidable symbols of the Northwest landscape. Mount Rainier appears to the south of Seattle like a giant, snow-covered beacon. Look to Chapter 15 for tips on the best places for mountain sightings and Chapter 17 for information on hiking at Mount Rainier National Park.

Attend Bumbershoot and the Lavender Festival

Seattle and the Olympic Peninsula love their annual festivals, and you can really capture the exuberance and feel of each place by attending their biggest events. You can also get up close and personal with a sizable chunk of each town's population, because these events draw upwards of 100,000 people each. In Seattle, Labor Day weekend sees the celebration of Bumbershoot, an arts and entertainment festival where visitors are treated to performances by everyone from major touring rock bands to chamber musicians and literary figures. Sequim's Lavender Festival in July is a great opportunity to see fields of blooming lavender, and take home any number of lavender-scented gifts. See Chapter 2 for details.

Appendix A

Quick Concierge: Seattle

● ●

Fast Facts

AAA Washington

General information: ☎ 206-448-5353. Emergency Road Service (24 hrs.): ☎ 800-222-4357.

American Express

Travel agency (6450 Southcenter Blvd.; ☎ 206-246-7661). To report lost or stolen cards: ☎ 800-992-3404. For information on traveler's checks: ☎ 800-221-7282.

ATMS

Widely available throughout downtown and on most retail strips. Ask your hotel for the location of the nearest one, or ask any store-keeper where to find one.

Baby sitters

Ask your hotel to recommend one. Other-wise, **Best Sitters** (☎ 206-682-2556) or **The Seattle Nanny Network** (☎ 206-374-8688).

Camera Repair

Ballard Camera (1836 NW Market St.; ☎ 206-783-1121); **Ken's Camera** (1327 2nd Ave.; ☎ 206-223-5553).

Convention Centers

Washington State Convention & Trade Center (8th Ave. and Pike Street; ☎ 206-461-5840). Convention Center stop on downtown bus tunnel.

Dentists

Ask your hotel or call **Dentist referral service** (509 Olive Way; ☎ 206-448-CARE).

Doctors

Call **911** for urgent situations. Go to a hospital emergency room for immediate care (see Hospitals) or call the **Doctor referral service** (☎ 206-448-CARE). If your child is sick and you're not sure if he or she needs care, call the **Children's Hospital Nurse Consultation** line (☎ 877-526-2500 or 206-526-2500).

Emergencies

For **police, fire,** and **ambulance,** call **911.**

Hospitals

Harborview Medical Center (325 9th Ave.; ☎ 206-731-3000) is the major trauma center. **Swedish Medical Center** (747 Broadway; ☎ 206-386-6000); **Swedish Medical Center/ Ballard** (5300 Tallman Ave. NW; ☎ 206-782-2700).

Hotlines

HIV/AIDS/STD Hotline (☎ 206-205-7837). **King County Children's Crisis Team** (☎ 206-461-3222). **Rape Relief Crisis Line** (☎ 206-632-7273). **Suicide-Survivors of Suicide Crisis Clinic** (☎ 206-587-4010). **Better Business Bureau** (☎ 206-431-2222).

Information

Seattle-King County Convention & Visitors Bureau Visitor Information Center (Washington State Convention & Trade Center, 800 Convention Place at 8th Avenue and Pike Street; ☎ 206-461-5840). Internet: www.seattleinsider.com. Also, the *Seattle Times* Web site (www.seattle times.com).

Internet Access

Many hotels offer Internet access in guest rooms or business centers. Otherwise, **Kinko's** many locations are wired for high-speed access (735 Pike St.; ☎ 206-467-1767; 1335 2nd Ave., ☎ 206-292-9255; 1740 NW Market St., ☎ 206-784-0061).

Liquor Laws

The legal drinking age in Washington is 21. Beer and wine are sold at grocery stores and convenience stores. Hard liquor is only sold at state liquor stores (2105 6th Ave.; ☎ 206-464-7841; 515 1st Ave. N.; ☎ 206-298-4616), which are closed Sundays and holidays.

Maps

Available from the **Visitors Bureau** (see Information). Street maps generally available free from hotels and car-rental agencies. Great selection of local and international maps sold at **Metsker Maps of Seattle** (702 First Ave.; ☎ 206-623-8747) and **Wide World Books & Maps** (4411 Wallingford Ave. N.; ☎ 206-634-3453).

Newspapers

The *Seattle Post-Intelligencer* and the *Seattle Times* are both morning papers; they publish a joint Sunday paper. *The Seattle Weekly* and *The Stranger* are free, arts-and-entertainment weekly newspapers. There is a major newsstand selling local and international newspapers and magazines at the **Pike Place Market** on the corner of First Avenue and Pike Place.

Pharmacies

Major pharmacies are **Bartell Drug Stores** (☎ 877-227-8355 for locations), **Rite Aid Pharmacies** (☎ 800-748-3243), and **Walgreens**, which operates 24-hour prescription service at its Ballard (5409 15th Ave. NW; ☎ 206-781-0056) location.

Police

Call **911** for emergencies.

Radio Stations

NPR is carried by **KUOW** at the University of Washington (**94.9** on the FM dial). **KJR-AM (950)** is an all-sports station, and **KIRO-AM (710)** is good for local news.

Restrooms

Hotels and restaurants have restrooms that are available to the public. You also find public restrooms at the **Pike Place Market** (one level below Pike Place), **Westlake Center, Pacific Place,** and **Seattle Center.**

Safety

Seattle has long enjoyed a sterling reputation for street safety, but recent events have tarnished the city's image. Avoid **Pioneer Square** late at night, particularly when the bars are letting out and during major celebrations. The area is completely safe during the day and early evening hours. Be wary of events that draw huge crowds onto the streets; these have grown increasingly violent in recent years.

Smoking

Smoking is not allowed in most restaurants, bars, or public buildings, and it's generally frowned upon in public gatherings. Look for designated smoking areas or confine it to your car or smoking-allowed hotel room if you can.

Taxes

Washington's sales tax is 8.8%. Hotel rooms within the Seattle city limits get hit with an additional 7%, and car rentals have an 18.3% rental surcharge and yet another 10% if you pick up the car at the airport.

Taxis

You can find taxis at most major hotels; otherwise, you need to call one (see Chapter 12 for info). Rates are $1.80 for the flag drop and $1.80 per mile.

Time Zone

Pacific Standard Time, which is three hours behind New York. Daylight Savings Time is observed in the summer.

Transit Information

Call **Metro** for 24-hour information (☎ 800-542-7876 or 206-553-3000) on buses. For ferry information and schedules, call the **Washington State Ferries** (☎ 800-84-FERRY or 206-464-6400).

Appendix B

Quick Concierge: The Olympic Peninsula and Olympic National Park

• •

Fast Facts

Area Code

☎ 360.

ATMs

None in the park, but you can find them in Port Angeles, Port Townsend, Sequim, and Forks.

Doctors and Dentists

Call **911** for urgent situations. Go to a hospital emergency room for immediate care (see Hospitals); call hospitals for referrals to doctors.

Emergency

☎ 911

Entrance Fees at Olympic National Park

$10 per vehicle per week; $5 for walk-ins.

Fishing License

Not required within the park, but stop by ranger and visitor centers for regulations.

Hospitals and Doctor Referrals

Olympic Memorial Hospital, 939 Caroline St., Port Angeles, WA (☎ 360-417-7000); and

Forks Community Hospital, 530 Bogachiel Way, Forks, WA (☎ 360-374-6271). **Jefferson General Hospital**, 834 Sheridan Ave., Port Townsend (☎ 800-244-8917).

Information

Olympic National Park, Visitor Center, 600 East Park Ave., Port Angeles, WA 98362; ☎ 360-565-3130; Internet: www.nps.gov/olym. **North Olympic Peninsula Visitor & Convention Bureau**, 338 W. First St., #104, Port Angeles, WA, 98362; ☎ 800-942-4042; Internet: www.olympicpeninsula.org. **Port Angeles Chamber of Commerce**, 121 E. Railroad Ave. (near the ferry terminal); ☎ 360-452-2363; Internet: www.portangeles.org.

Lost and Found at Olympic National Park

☎ 360-565-3000.

Pharmacies

Rite Aid Pharmacies, 110 Plaza St., Port Angeles (☎ 360-457-3456); and **Safeway**, 110 E. 3rd St., Port Angeles (☎ 360-457-0788).

Police

Call ☎ **911**.

Post Office

424 E. First St., Port Angeles; 1322 Washington St., Port Townsend, and East Division Street, Forks.

Road Conditions and Weather

☎ 360-565-3131 (recorded) or ☎ 360-565-3132 (visitor center).

Taxes

Lodging and meal rates vary depending on location.

Time Zone

Pacific standard time.

Making Dollars and Sense of It

Expense	Daily cost	x	Number of days	=	Total
Airfare					
Local transportation					
Car rental					
Lodging (with tax)					
Parking					
Breakfast					
Lunch					
Dinner					
Snacks					
Entertainment					
Babysitting					
Attractions					
Gifts & souvenirs					
Tips					
Other					
Grand Total					

Fare Game: Choosing an Airline

When looking for the best airfare, you should cover all your bases — 1) consult a trusted travel agent; 2) contact the airline directly, via the airline's toll-free number and/or Web site; 3) check out one of the travel-planning Web sites, such as www.frommers.com.

Travel Agency_____ Phone_____

    Agent's Name_____ Quoted fare_____

Airline 1_____ Quoted fare_____

    Toll-free number/Internet_____

Airline 2_____ Quoted fare_____

    Toll-free number/Internet_____

Web site 1_____ Quoted fare_____

Web site 2_____ Quoted fare_____

Departure Schedule & Flight Information

Airline_____ Flight #_____ Confirmation #_____

Departs_____ Date_____ Time_____ a.m./p.m.

Arrives_____ Date_____ Time_____ a.m./p.m.

Connecting Flight (if any)

Amount of time between flights_____ hours/mins

Airline_____ Flight #_____ Confirmation #_____

Departs_____ Date_____ Time_____ a.m./p.m.

Arrives_____ Date_____ Time_____ a.m./p.m.

Return Trip Schedule & Flight Information

Airline_____ Flight #_____ Confirmation #_____

Departs_____ Date_____ Time_____ a.m./p.m.

Arrives_____ Date_____ Time_____ a.m./p.m.

Connecting Flight (if any)

Amount of time between flights_____ hours/mins

Airline_____ Flight #_____ Confirmation #_____

Departs_____ Date_____ Time_____ a.m./p.m.

Arrives_____ Date_____ Time_____ a.m./p.m.

Going "My" Way

Day 4

Hotel_____ Tel._____

Morning_____

_____

Lunch_____ Tel._____

Afternoon_____

_____

Dinner_____ Tel._____

Evening_____

_____

Day 5

Hotel_____ Tel._____

Morning_____

_____

Lunch_____ Tel._____

Afternoon_____

_____

Dinner_____ Tel._____

Evening_____

_____

Day 6

Hotel_____ Tel._____

Morning_____

_____

Lunch_____ Tel._____

Afternoon_____

_____

Dinner_____ Tel._____

Evening_____

_____

Going "My" Way

Day 7
Hotel_____ Tel._____

Morning_____

_____

Lunch_____ Tel._____

Afternoon_____

_____

Dinner_____ Tel._____

Evening_____

_____

Day 8
Hotel_____ Tel._____

Morning_____

_____

Lunch_____ Tel._____

Afternoon_____

_____

Dinner_____ Tel._____

Evening_____

_____

Day 9
Hotel_____ Tel._____

Morning_____

_____

Lunch_____ Tel._____

Afternoon_____

_____

Dinner_____ Tel._____

Evening_____

_____

Your Cruise & Ferry Schedule

Travel Agency_____ Phone_____

Agent's Name_____

Web Site_____

Cruise Information & Departure Schedule

Cruise Line_____ Ship Name_____

Port of Embarkation_____ Date_____

Boarding Time_____ a.m./p.m. Departure Time_____ a.m./p.m.

Ports of Call_____

Return Cruise Information

Port_____ Date_____ Time_____ a.m./p.m.

Ferry Information & Departure Schedule

Ferry Line_____ Ship Name_____

Departure Port_____ Date_____

Boarding Time_____ a.m./p.m. Quoted Fare_____

Departure Time_____ a.m./p.m. Arrival Time_____ a.m./p.m.

Ferry Information & Departure Schedule

Ferry Line_____ Ship Name_____

Departure Port_____ Date_____

Boarding Time_____ a.m./p.m. Quoted Fare_____

Departure Time_____ a.m./p.m. Arrival Time_____ a.m./p.m.

Ferry Information & Departure Schedule

Ferry Line_____ Ship Name_____

Departure Port_____ Date_____

Boarding Time_____ a.m./p.m. Quoted Fare_____

Departure Time_____ a.m./p.m. Arrival Time_____ a.m./p.m.

Notes

Index

See separate Accommodations and Restaurant Indexes following this index.

General Index

• A •

AAA, 29, 30, 54, 61, 70
AARP, 30, 35, 70
accommodations. *See also*
　Accommodations Index; hotels
　amenities, 61, 62
　apartment houses, 59
　bed-and-breakfast, 24, 59, 65, 66, 100
　budget for, 24–25
　choosing, 79–80, 105–106
　cost, 24, 25, 58, 64
　cottages (log-cabin), 24
　discounted rates, 18, 30, 61, 64–65
　high season, 17, 30, 64
　hostels, 24, 35, 36, 58, 95, 104–105
　inns, 25, 59
　Internet access, 94, 103, 290
　kid-friendly, 91, 94, 97, 98, 99, 101,
　　103, 106, 277
　kitchenettes in, 59, 95
　local, 84–85
　low season, 18, 30, 64
　maps, 88–89, 92–93
　money-saving tips, 25, 30–31
　motels, 24, 57–58
　by neighborhood, 107
　non-smoking, 58
　Olympic National Park, 249–253
　Olympic Peninsula, 65, 257
　package deals, 30, 48, 64
　parking, 58, 112
　pet-friendly, 91
　Port Angeles, 277
　Port Ludlow, 262
　Port Townsend, 270–271
　by price, 60–62, 106–107
　rack rates, 61, 63
　reservations for, 64–66
　tax on, 27, 122
　without reservations, 66–67
airlines. *See also* airports
　airfares, 49–51
　bankruptcy, 50
　choosing, 49
　contact information, 49
　frequent-flier programs, 30, 49, 51
　missed flights, 53
　money-saving tips, 51
　package tours, 47–48
　reservations, 50–51, 52
　tickets, 50, 52
　Web sites, 47, 49, 50
airports. *See also* airlines
　arrival time, 52, 53
　bus services, 56, 111
　check-in, 52–53
　children at, 52
　Fairchild International Airport,
　　55–56, 230
　getting through, 51–53
　luggage, 45, 52
　Sea-Tac Airport, 49, 56, 110–111,
　　230–231
　security, 51–53
　transportation from, 110–111
　Web site, 49
Allen, Paul (Microsoft billionaire),
　13, 162, 219
Amtrak, 54, 112
amusement parks, 174
antiques, 191, 196
apartment houses, 59
aquarium, 169
Arkin, Alan (actor), 216
Atkinson, Greg, 135
ATMs, 27–28, 29, 110, 121

attractions. *See also* markets;
   museums; parks; Seattle Center;
   Space Needle
Benaroya Hall, 161–162, 217
budget for, 26
downtown Seattle, 161, 163
Experience Music Project, 13, 26,
   36, 162
Hiram M. Chittenden Locks, 166, 286
IMAX Dome Theater, 169, 175, 178
kid-friendly, 167, 168–169, 169
Lake Union, 12, 19–20, 167
maps, 163–165
Mount Rainier, 172
for nature and outdoor lovers,
   180–183
north and northeast Seattle, 164–165
Port Townsend, 266–270
for romantics, 179–180
Safeco Field, 16, 168–169
Seattle Aquarium, 169
University of Washington Waterfront
   Activities Center, 182
Washington State Ferries, 172–173
Woodland Park Zoo, 173
attractions for kids. *See also* swimming
ballet and, 218
Discovery Park, 181, 204–205
The Duck (amphibious landing craft),
   175, 187, 204
Enchanted Village and
   Wild Waves, 174
Fort Worden State Park, 269–270
Fun Forest Amusement Park, 174
kid-friendly, 162
Pacific Science Center, 170, 174–175
playgrounds, 175
Rachel the Pig, 168
Seattle Center fountain, 26, 170
Seattle Children's Museum, 175–176
Seattle Children's Theatre, 217
Tillicum Village, 187, 204
The Waterfront, 80, 176, 194
Ye Old Curiosity Shop, 177
attractions for teens. *See also*
   swimming
Fremont, 177
GameWorks, 177–178

Gasworks Park, 178
IMAX Dome Theater, 169, 175, 178
University of Washington, 178–179

• *B* •

baby-sitting services, 34, 289
Bainbridge Islands, 14
Ballard Locks (Hiram M. Chittenden
   Locks), 166, 286
Ballard neighborhood, 195
ballet, 13–14, 218
banks, 121
Bargain Alert icon, 6
bars and clubs, 27, 219–220
baseball, 16, 169
basketball, 27
Bauer, Eddie (clothing merchant), 13
The Beatles (rock group), 96
bed-and-breakfast, 24, 59, 65, 66, 100
Beebe, Lloyd and Catherine
   (animal trainers), 274
Belltown, 80, 124, 192, 203
Benaroya Hall, 161–162, 217
Best Places Seattle Cookbook (Nims,
   Cynthia and Casey, Kathy), 152
Better Business Bureau, 47
biking, 118, 180, 182, 211, 275
Birnbaum, Jan "The Big Dog"
   (chef), 147
Bite of Seattle festival, 19, 166
Black Ball Transportation (ferry), 55
Black, Tom (chef), 124
black travelers, 38–39
boating, 19, 21–22
Boeing (aircraft company), 1, 162, 167
Boeing Field, 111
books and music, 195, 196
Borofsky, Jonathon (sculptor), 169
breakfast, 150
bridges of King County, 179
Brown, James (musician), 162
bucket shops (consolidators), 51
budget for trip
  accommodations, 24–25
  ATM fees, 28
  attractions, 26

credit cards, 29
entertainment, 26–27
hidden expenses, 27
meals, 25–26
money-saving tips, 30–31
parking, 25
petty cash, 28
rental car, 25, 27, 31
shopping, 26
taxes, 27
transportation, 25
worksheet, 23
Bumbershoot, 20, 73, 166, 220, 288
Burke-Gilman Trail, 118–119, 180–181
bus service
  airport, 56, 111
  Double Decker Bus Tour, 183
  electric Kool-Aid bus system, 116
  escorted tours, 45–47
  fares, 56, 115
  guided tours, 183–184
  Olympic National Park tours, 56, 231
  Ride Free Zone, 112, 115–116
  from Sea-Tac airport, 111
  Seattle, 56, 115
  tickets, 115

• C•

calendar of events, 19–22, 73–74
Canlis, Chris and Alice
    (restaurant owners), 134–135
canoes, 167, 182, 276
Capitol Hill, 37, 193, 203
car rental
  budget, 25, 27, 31
  discounts, 61, 70
  Fairchild International Airport, 56
  liability insurance, 71
  money-saving tips, 31, 70–71
  pros and cons, 69–70, 112
  rates, 25, 31, 70
  reservations, 70–71
  from Sea-Tac airport, 111
  taxes, 27, 70, 112, 122, 291
Carkeek Park, 181
carry-on luggage, 45, 52–53, 75

Cascade Mountains, 12, 205–206
Casey, Kathy (chef), 152, 155
cash advance, 29, 121–122
casinos, 28
Centrum's Winter Chamber Musical
    Festival, 20
Chef's Table (dining experience), 127
children. *See also* attractions for kids
  coffee shops and, 286
  cost-cutting tips, 31
  dining with, 34
  itineraries for, 204–205
  kayaking, 287
  learning-vacations, 35
  traveling with, 33–35
  video-game parlor, 177
Chimacum, 14, 263
climate. *See* weather
Clinton, Bill (former president), 103
clothing. *See also* dress code
  casual, 74
  local scene, 26
  outdoor, 197
  overview, 13
  rain, 74
  spring, 17
  umbrellas, 18, 74
  winter, 18
coffee shops
  breakfast and lunch at, 127, 150
  lingo of, 151
  locating, 126, 127, 150–151, 283
  at Pike Place Market, 203, 286
Colbert, Claudette (actor), 23
consolidators, 51
A Contemporary Theater, 217
cookbooks, 152
cottages (log-cabin), 24
Cougar Mountain Regional Wildland
    Park, 182
courtesy vans, 111
credit cards
  buying airlines tickets with, 50
  cash advance, 29
  Collision Damage Waiver (CDW), 71
  emergency 800-number, 122
  frequent-flier programs, 51

cuisine. *See also* seafood
  apple pancakes, 283
  Asian, 152–153
  bakeries, 153
  breakfast, 150
  burgers, 140, 153–154
  burritos and wraps, 154
  coconut cream pie, 141, 282
  cookbooks, 152
  danish, 284
  dessert, 124, 141, 155, 282
  northwest, 135, 281–284
  overview, 12
  piroshky, 281–282
  pizza, 155
  restaurants by, 157–158
  soup, 149
  steak, 123–124, 133, 140, 141
  vegetarian, 135

• *D* •

dance
  ballet, 13–14, 218
  ballroom, 180
  live, 218–219
Davis, Kevin (chef), 145
day trips
  Mount Rainier National Park, 212–213
  North Cascades Highway, 205–206
  Olympic National Park, 243–244
  San Juan Islands, 206–212
daylight savings, 17, 200, 291
debit cards, 121–122
dining. *See* Restaurant Index
disabilities, travelers with
  Golden Access Passport, 36–37
  planning trip and, 36–37
  transportation, 36
  travel agencies and, 37
Discovery Park, 181, 204–205
dogs, 40, 180
dolphins, 172, 186
Donier, Kaspar (chef), 143–144
Douglas, Tom (chef/owner), 124, 139, 141, 145, 282
Downtown Seattle
  Belltown, 80, 124, 192, 203
  maps, 81–83, 88–89

The Market, 80
  restaurant maps, 130–131, 136–137
  Ride Free Zone, 112, 115–116
  The Shopping District, 80, 114, 193
  street car, 117, 176
  The Waterfront, 80, 176, 194
dress code
  local, 26
  restaurants, 74, 126
  symphony and opera, 74
driving. *See also* car rental; parking; traffic
  around Seattle, 112–113
  highway recommendations, 113
  to Olympic National Park, 55, 229–230
  to Olympic Peninsula, 55
  parking, 25, 112, 117
  to Port Ludlow, 261
  to Port Townsend, 266
  to Seattle, 54, 111
  tips, 113–114
The Duck (amphibious landing craft), 175, 187, 204
Dungeness crab
  cost of, 125
  crab cakes, 283
  crab cocktail, 281
  home of, 273
  where to buy, 125, 127
Dungeness Crab & Seafood Festival, 22, 273

• *E* •

Elderhostel, 36
Emerald Downs, 179
emergencies
  hospitals, 289, 293
  lost credit cards, 122
  medical, 289
Empty Space Theatre, 217
Enchanted Village and Wild Waves, 174
escorted tours, 45–47
event calendars, 19–22, 73–74
Expedia (online travel agency), 49, 65
Experience Music Project, 13, 26, 36, 162

• F •

Fairchild International Airport,
    55–56, 230
fall, 18
family itinerary, 33–35. *See also*
    attractions for kids; attractions
    for teens
Familyhostel, 35
farmer's markets, 126, 152
ferries
  Black Ball Transportation, 55, 230
  cost, 25
  dogs on, 40
  fares, 117
  Puget Sound ferry, 55, 266
  to San Juan Islands, 206
  Victoria Express, 55, 230
  Washington State Ferries, 35, 54, 55,
    117, 172–173, 186
festivals
  Bite of Seattle, 19, 166
  Bumbershoot, 20, 73, 166, 220, 288
  Centrum's Winter Chamber Musical
    Festival, 20
  Dungeness Crab & Seafood Festival,
    22, 273
  Fourth of July, 19–20
  Irrigation Festival, 21
  Juan de Fuca Festival, 21
  Labor Day, 166, 288
  Lavender Festival, 21, 273, 288
  Northwest Folklife Festival, 19, 73,
    166, 220
  Port Townsend, 266–267
  RainFest, 21
  reservations, 73
  Seafair festival, 19
  Seattle International Film Festival, 19
  Spring Carnival at Hurricane
    Ridge, 21
  Wooden Boat Festival, 21–22, 266–267
fireworks, 19–20, 172
Fisherman's Terminal, 154
floatplanes, 185, 206, 207, 287
Food & Wine magazine, 133
Fort Worden, 20
Fort Worden State Park, 269–270

Fourth of July, 19–20
Fremont, 177, 191, 194–195
frequent-flier programs, 30, 49, 51, 70
*Frommer's Family Vacations in
    the National Parks* (Wiley
    Publishing), 35
Frommer's Fly Safe, Fly Smart
    (Wiley Publishing), 51
Fun Forest Amusement Park, 174

• G •

GameWorks, 177–178
Gasworks Park, 19–20, 178
Gates, Bill (Microsoft executive), 13,
    183, 287
gay or lesbian travelers
  planning trip, 37–38
  shopping, 193
Gehry, Frank (architect), 162
Gere, Richard (actor), 216
Golden Access Passport, 36–37
Golden Age Passport, 35–36
Golden Gardens Park, 179–180
Grathwol, Heidi (hostess), 135
Gray Line buses, 111, 183, 184
Green Lake park, 175, 181–182
Greyhound, 54–55
guided tours
  by air, 185
  Boeing Plant, 162
  cost, 183
  The Duck (amphibious landing craft),
    175, 187, 204
  on land, 183–184
  Pike Place Market, 168, 184
  Safeco Field, 169
  by water, 185–187

• H •

Halloween feast, 73
Hammering Man (sculpture), 169
Hanke, Michael
    (wine coordinator), 139
Harborview Medical Center, 71, 72
Heads Up icon, 6

health issues
　health-care facilities, 71–72
　Medic Alert Identification Tag, 72
　medical insurance, 45, 72
　pharmacies (all-night), 72, 290
　prescription medications, 72, 75
　water quality, 71
Hendrix, Jimi (musician), 162
high season, 17, 30, 64
highways
　Interstate 5, 113
　Interstate 90, 113
　North Cascades Highway, 205–206
　Route 99/Aurora Avenue, 113
hiking, 12–13, 236, 241–243
Hill, Bryan (restaurant owner), 133
Hiram M. Chittenden Locks
　　(Ballard Locks), 166, 286
holidays
　Fourth of July, 19–20
　Labor Day, 166, 288
　Memorial Day, 166
　New Year's Eve, 20, 172
horse-drawn carriages, 176
horse-racing track, 179
hospitals, 71, 72, 289
hostels
　cost, 24
　described, 58
　Elderhostel, 36
　Familyhostel, 35
　Seattle locations, 95, 104–105
hotels. *See also* accommodations;
　　Accommodations Index
　all-suite, 24
　bars, 219–220
　boutique, 60, 96
　chain, 57–58
　choosing, 24–25
　concierge services, 73
　corporate, 59–60
　reservations, 64–65
　seasonal rates, 30, 61
　swimming pools, 33
　taxes, 27, 122, 291
　upper-crust, 60
　Victorian-era, 24
　Web sites, 30, 64

How to Take Great Trips with Your Kids
　　(The Harvard Common Press), 35
Hurricane Ridge, 13, , 227, 238, 287

• I •

icons in this book, 6–7
IMAX Dome Theater, 169, 175, 178
insurance
　car rental, 71
　lost-luggage, 45
　medical, 45, 72
　tour cancellation, 46
　travel, 44, 45, 50
　trip-cancellation, 44
International District, 152–153
Internet access, 94, 103, 290
Intiman (theater company), 13, 216–217
Irrigation Festival, 21
itineraries
　art and culture, 203–204
　for children, 204–205
　coffee and snacks lovers, 203
　day trips, 205–213
　family, 33–35
　nature lovers, 202
　planning, 199–201
　three-day, 201–202

• J •

jaywalking, 119
Joplin, Janis (musician), 162
Juan de Fuca Festival, 21

• K •

Kashiba, Shiro (chef), 147
kayaking
　for children, 287
　Lake Union, 167
　Lake Washington, 182
　overview, 286–287
　Port Angeles, 276
　San Juan Islands, 208, 210, 211
Keff, Christine (chef/owner), 124,
　　141–142

Kennedy, Ted Watson
(shop owner), 192
Kid Friendly icon, 6

• L •

Labor Day, 166, 288
Lake Union, 12, 19–20, 167, 178
Lavender Festival, 21, 273, 288
Lenin (sculpture), 177
Llama trekking, 276
Lodging. *See* accommodations;
Accommodations Index
London, Jack (writer), 13
Lopez Island, 211–212
low season, 17, 18, 30, 64
luggage
carry-on, 45, 52–53, 75
checked, 53
lost-luggage insurance, 45
packing, 72, 75
Lynch, David (film director), 100

• M •

Magnuson Park, 40
Makah Days, 21
maps
accommodations, 88–89, 92–93
attractions, 163–165
Downtown Seattle, 81–83, 88–89,
130–131, 136–137
Greater Seattle, 81
neighborhoods, 81–83
north & northeast Seattle, 136–137
Olympic National Park, 224–225
Olympic Peninsula, 259
purchasing, 113, 290
restaurants, 130–131, 136–137
San Juan Islands, 200
Seattle Center, 171
markets. *See also* Pike Place Market
farmer's, 126, 152
Fremont Sunday Market, 191
The Market, 80
shopping at, 191–192
supermarkets, 122, 127, 128, 153
University Market, 191

Marymoor Park, 40
McClure, Jason (chef), 147
McCown, Sue (pastry chef), 140
Medic Alert Identification Tag, 72
Memorial Day, 166
Metro bus system, 115
Metro (street car), 117, 176
Microsoft campus, 13
monorail, 117, 170
motels, 24, 57–58
Mount Rainier, 12, 288
Mount Rainier National Park, 172, 173,
212–213
Mudry, Valerie (pastry chef), 133
Murphy, Tamara (chef), 124, 133
museums
Museum of Flight, 167
Pacific Science Center, 170, 174–175
Port Townsend Marine Science
Center, 269
Seattle Art Museum, 169–170
Seattle Asian Art Museum, 169–170
Seattle Children's Museum, 175–176
music. *See also* Seattle Symphony
Centrum's Winter Chamber Musical
Festival, 20
Experience Music Project, 13, 26,
36, 162
live jazz, 143
Northwest Folklife Festival, 19, 73,
166, 220
overview, 13–14
Seattle Opera, 13, 204, 218
shopping, 190, 196
Myrtle Edwards Park, 20, 180

• N •

Nashino, Tatsu (chef), 144
Neah Bay, 21
neighborhoods. *See also* Downtown
Seattle
accommodations, 107
Ballard, 195
Fremont, 177, 191, 194–195
International District, 152–153
local Seattle, 84–85
maps of, 81–83

neighborhoods *(continued)*
parking, 114
Queen Anne, 73, 84, 194
restaurants, 149
shopping, 192–195
The Shopping District, 80, 114, 193
University District, 84, 195
New Year's Eve, 20, 172
newspapers, 73, 128, 213, 215, 290
nightlife
bars and clubs, 27, 218–220
information, 215
performing arts, 217–218
theaters, 216–217
Nims, Cynthia *(Best Places Seattle Cookbook)*, 152
North Cascades Highway, 205–206
North Olympic Peninsula Visitor & Convention Bureau, 65, 74
Northwest Folklife Festival, 19, 73, 166, 220
Northwest icon, 7
Northwest Outdoor Center, 167

• O •

Oki, Scott (restaurant owner), 144
Olsen, Sten (violin shop owner), 195
Olympic National Park
accommodations, 249–253
attractions, 227, 237–241
bus tours, 56, 231
driving to, 55, 229–230
entrance fees, 235
fast facts, 293–294
hiking, 12–13, 241–243
Hurricane Ridge, 13, 287
Lake Ozette, 245
maps, 224–225
one-day itinerary, 243–244
outdoor activities, 247–248
overview, 12, 232–233
packing for, 232
rainfall, 15
rainy day activities, 248
ranger programs, 245
reservations, 231–232
restaurants, 253–254

safety issues, 235–236
side roads, 233
transportation, 55–56, 229–231
trees, 248
visitor centers, 232–233, 234
Web site, 231
wildlife, 235–236, 246–247
Olympic Peninsula
accommodations, 65, 257
described, 14, 253–254
fast facts, 293–294
map, 259
National Scenic Byway, 258
North Olympic Peninsula Visitor & Convention Bureau, 65, 74, 260
orientation to, 258–260
transportation to, 55–56
visitor information, 260
weather, 15, 260
Web sites, 65, 260
Olympic Tours, 56, 231
opera, 13, 74, 218
Orbitz (online travel agency), 49
Orcas Island, 207–208

• P •

Pacific Northwest Ballet, 13–14, 218
Pacific Science Center, 170, 174–175. *See also* IMAX Dome Theater
package tours
accommodations and, 30, 48, 64
airlines and, 47–48
choosing, 47–48
hidden expenses, 48
single travelers and, 47
packing luggage
carry-on, 45, 52–53, 75
for Olympic National Park, 232
prescription medications, 72, 75
restrictions, 52–53, 75
what to take, 74
Paramount Theatre, 216
parking, 25, 58, 112, 114–115, 117
parks. *See also* Olympic National Park
amusement parks, 174
Carkeek Park, 181
children at, 34

Cougar Mountain Regional Wildland Park, 182
Discovery Park, 181, 204–205
Fort Worden State Park, 269–270
Gasworks Park, 19–20, 178
Golden Gardens Park, 179–180
Green Lake park, 175, 181–182
Magnuson Park, 40
Marymoor Park, 40
Moran State Park, 207–208
Mount Rainier National Park, 172, 173, 212–213
Myrtle Edwards Park, 20, 180
Washington Park Arboretum, 182–183
Perlman, Itzhak (concert violinist), 217
pets, 40, 91, 180
pharmacies (all-night), 72, 290
picnic, 155
Pike Place Market
  coffee shops, 203, 286
  disabled travelers and, 36
  food stalls, 152
  guided tours, 168, 184
  hours, 190
  overview, 12, 126, 168
  parking garage, 115, 168
  Rachel the Pig, 168
  shopping at, 191
  traffic congestion, 168
  Web site, 168
Pike Place Market Cookbook (Rex-Johnson, Braiden), 152
Pioneer Square, 72, 112, 193–194, 203
Pisano, Walter (chef), 148
planning trip. *See also* budget for trip
  black travelers, 38–39
  calendar of events, 19–22, 73–74
  with dogs, 40
  family itinerary, 33–35
  gay or lesbian travelers, 37–38
  itineraries, 199–201
  seasons, 15–18, 30
  seniors, 35–36
  travelers with disabilities, 36–37
  traveling alone, 39–40
playgrounds, 175
Port Angeles
  accommodations, 277
  attractions, 275

described, 14, 273
driving to, 274
Fairchild International Airport, 55–56, 230
Juan de Fuca Festival, 21
kid-friendly activities, 275
outdoor activities, 275–276
restaurants, 278
visitor information, 274
Port Hadlock, 263
Port Ludlow, 14, 261, 262–263
Port Townsend
  accommodations, 270–271
  attractions, 266–270
  community center, 22
  described, 14, 265–266
  driving to, 266
  festivals, 266–267
  Fort Worden State Park, 269–270
  Marine Science Center, 269
  restaurants, 271–272
  shopping, 268–269
  transportation, 267
  visitor information, 266
  Wooden Boat Festival, 21–22, 266–267
Port Townsend Arts Guild Holiday Crafts Fair, 22
prescription medications, 72, 75
Presley, Elvis (musician), 162
Priceline (online reservations), 50–51, 65, 71
public transportation, 25
Puget Sound, 12, 14, 17
Puget Sound ferry, 55, 266

• *Q* •

Queen Anne, 73, 84, 194
quick concierge, 289–291, 293–294

• *R* •

rack rates, 61, 63
RainFest (festival), 21
Rautureau, Thierry (chef), 146
reservations
  accommodations, 64–66
  airline, 50–51, 52

reservations *(continued)*
  car rental, 70–71
  cost-cutting tips, 30–31
  festivals, 73
  hotel, 64–65
  Olympic National Park, 231–232
  online, 49–51, 65–66, 71
  restaurant, 73, 126–127
  showing up without, 66–67
  sporting events, 73
  Web sites, 65, 66
restaurants. *See also* cuisine;
     Restaurant Index
  Asian, 152–153
  bars, 219–220
  budget for, 25–26
  Chef's Table experience, 127
  cost of, 26, 129
  by cuisine, 157–158
  dress code, 74, 126
  kid-friendly, 133–134, 138, 139, 140,
     277, 278
  kids' menus, 34
  late night Broadway eats, 154–155
  maps, 130–131, 136–137
  money-saving tips, 31, 127–128
  by neighborhood, 149, 156–157
  Olympic National Park, 253–254
  picnic, 155
  Pike Place Market, 152
  Port Ludlow, 262–263
  Port Townsend, 271–272
  by price, 155–156
  reservations, 73, 126–127
  Sequim and Port Angeles, 277–278
  tips, 129
  valet parking, 115
Rex-Johnson, Braiden (*Pike Place
     Market Cookbook*), 152
roller skating, 181–182

• S •

Safeco Field, 16, 168–169
safety. *See* security
sales tax, 27, 122, 190, 291
salmon
  Copper River, 282
  season, 16, 125, 166, 181, 286

Sekiu Winter Salmon Derby, 20–21
  shopping for, 198
San Juan Islands
  day trips, 206–212
  floatplanes to, 206, 207, 287
  Lopez Island, 211–212
  map, 200
  Orcas Island, 207–208
  overview, 14
  San Juan Island, 208–211
  transportation to, 206–207
  Web site, 207
Schwarz, Gerard (symphony
     conductor), 217
sea lions, 172, 180
Seafair festival, 19
seafood. *See also* salmon
  crab, 22, 125, 127, 273, 281, 283
  Dungeness Crab & Seafood Festival,
     22, 273
  fish and chips, 138, 154, 283–284
  Kerry Sears' oysters, 282
  restaurants, 124, 125
Sears, Kerry (chef), 124, 135, 282
seasons, 15–18, 30
Sea-Tac Airport
  contact information, 49, 56
  getting through, 110
  to Olympic National Park, 230–231
  traveling from, 110–111
Seattle Aquarium, 169
Seattle Art Museum, 169–170
Seattle Arts Festival. *See* Bumbershoot
Seattle Asian Art Museum, 169–170
Seattle Center. *See also* Space Needle
  dances, 180
  described, 84, 170
  Experience Music Project, 13, 26,
     36, 162
  festivals, 166
  fountain, 26, 170
  map, 171
  Pacific Science Center, 170, 174–175
  Ride the Ducks (amphibious
     tour), 175
  Web sites, 20, 166, 170
Seattle Children's Museum, 175–176
Seattle Children's Theatre, 176, 217
Seattle International Boat Show, 19
Seattle International Film Festival, 19

Seattle Magazine, 146, 152
Seattle Mariners (baseball team), 16
Seattle Monorail, 117
Seattle Opera, 13, 74, 218
Seattle Post-Intelligencer (newspaper), 73, 128, 215
Seattle Rep (theater company), 13
Seattle SuperSonics (basketball team), 27
Seattle Symphony, 13–14, 74, 161–162
Seattle Tacoma International Airport. *See* Sea-Tac Airport
Seattle Times (newspaper), 215
Seattle Weekly (newspaper), 73, 215
Seattle-King County Convention & Visitors Bureau, 74, 113, 128
security
  airport, 51–53
  crime, 29, 72
  lost wallet, 122
  Olympic National Park, 235–236
  Pioneer Square and, 72, 112
  wildlife and, 235–236
Sekiu Winter Salmon Derby, 20–21
senior travelers, 35–36
Sequim
  accommodations, 277
  attractions, 274–275
  dining, 277–278
  driving to, 274
  Irrigation Festival, 21
  John Wayne Marina, 22
  kid-friendly activities, 274
  Lavender Festival, 21, 273, 288
  outdoor activities, 275–276
  restaurants, 277–278
  visitor information, 274
shopping
  big name stores, 190
  budget for, 26
  gay or lesbian traveler, 193
  markets, 191–192
  by merchandise, 196–198
  by neighborhood, 192–195
  overview, 189–190
  Port Townsend, 268–269
The Shopping District, 80, 114, 193
SideStep (online travel agency), 49
single travelers, 39–40, 47
Smith, Holly (chef), 134

souvenirs, 198
Space Needle
  cam views from, 73
  crowds at, 199
  described, 84, 170, 172
  New Year's Eve event, 20
  sightseeing, 285
Spath, Andhi (coffee shop owner), 283
Spielberg, Steven (film director/ producer), 177
spring, 16–17
Spring Carnival at Hurricane Ridge, 21
Stadium Exhibition Center, 19
Starbucks (coffee house), 1, 126, 151, 168, 283
Stephenson, Gavin (chef), 142
Stowell, Kent (ballet director), 218
street car, 117, 176
Sturges, Preston (writer), 23
summer, 17, 200
Sundstrom, Johnathan (chef), 124, 140
supermarkets, 122, 127, 128, 153
swimming
  community center pools, 176
  hotel pools, 33
  Pacific Ocean beach and, 34
  Puget Sound and, 17
  safety issues, 236
symphony, 13–14, 27, 74, 161–162

• *T* •

taxes
  car rental, 27, 70, 112, 122, 291
  hotel, 27, 122, 291
  sales, 27, 122, 190, 291
taxi
  fares, 116, 291
  getting around Seattle, 116–117
  from Sea-Tac airport, 110
teens. *See* attractions for teens
temperatures, 15, 16, 17
theaters
  A Contemporary Theater, 217
  Empty Space Theatre, 217
  IMAX Dome Theater, 169, 175, 178
  Intiman, 13, 216–217
  overview, 216–217
  Paramount Theatre, 216

theaters *(continued)*
  Seattle Children's Theatre, 176
  Seattle Rep, 13
tickets
  agents, 65–66, 73
  airline, 50, 52
  bus, 115
  Experience Music Project, 162
  money-saving tips, 27
  Museum of Flight, 167
  purchasing, 73, 215–216
  Seattle SuperSonics (basketball
    team), 27
  symphony, 27, 162
  Web sites, 73
Tillicum Village, 187, 204
Tip icon, 6
Tomlin, Lily (comedian), 216
tours. *See also* guided tours
  cancellation policies, 46
  escorted, 45–47
  for families, 35
  package, 30, 47–48, 64
town car, 110–111, 117
toys, 198
traffic
  congested, 2, 109, 113, 168
  driving into Seattle, 111
  highway recommendations, 113
  laws, 113–114
  Pike Place Market and, 168
  for Washington State Ferries, 173
train travel
  Amtrak, 54, 112
  guided tours, 184
transportation. *See also* airlines; bus
    service; car rental; driving; ferries
  biking, 118, 182, 211, 275
  budget for, 25
  disabled travelers, 36
  driving, 54, 55
  floatplanes, 185, 206, 207, 287
  horse-drawn carriages, 176
  monorail, 117
  to Olympic Peninsula, 55–56
  public transportation, 25
  Ride Free Zone, 112
  to Seattle, 48–51, 54

street car, 117, 176
taxis, 110, 116–117, 118, 291
town car, 110–111, 117
train travel, 54, 112, 184
trolley, 183
walking, 118–119
Transportation Security
    Administration (TSA), 52–53
Traunfeld, Jerry (chef), 142
travel agents
  online, 47, 49, 65–66
  travel packages, 30
  using, 43–44
travel insurance, 44, 45, 50
travel magazines, 48
traveler's checks, 28–29, 122
Travelocity (online travel agency), 49,
    65–66
TravelWeb (online travel agency), 66
trolley, 183
Tully's Coffee (coffee shop), 126, 151

• *U* •

University District, 84, 195
University of Washington, 84, 178–179
University of Washington Waterfront
    Activities Center, 182
U.S. National Park Service, 35, 36–37

• *V* •

Vallee, Rudy (actor), 23
Vashon Islands, 14
Victoria Express (ferry), 55, 230
visitor information
  Mount Rainier National Park, 212
  North Olympic Peninsula Visitor &
    Convention Bureau, 65, 74
  Olympic National Park, 232–233, 234
  Olympic Peninsula, 260
  Port Ludlow, 262
  Port Townsend, 266
  Seattle-King County Convention &
    Visitors Bureau, 74, 113, 128
  Wilderness Information Center, 235

• *W* •

walking
  Burke-Gilman Trail, 118–119, 180–181
  with children, 34
  dogs, 40, 180
  jaywalking, 119
  tours, 184
Washington lake, 12
Washington Park Arboretum, 182–183
Washington State Convention and
    Trade Center, 113
Washington State Ferries
  commuter traffic, 173
  contact information, 54, 55, 117,
    173, 230
  described, 172–173
  senior discount, 35
  sightseeing, 186, 285
  Web site, 173
water tours, 185–186
The Waterfront, 80, 176, 194
Waterfront streetcar, 117
weather
  fall, 18
  information, 294
  Olympic Peninsula, 15, 260
  rainfall, 15, 16
  spring, 16–17
  summer, 17
  temperature, 15, 16, 17
  winter, 18
Web sites
  AARP, 35
  airlines, 47, 49, 50
  ATMs, 27, 28
  Better Business Bureau, 47
  calendar of events, 19–22, 73–74
  disabled travelers, 37
  escorted tours, 46
  family vacation advice, 35
  gay or lesbian traveler, 38
  Mount Rainier National Park, 212
  newspapers, 73, 215
  Olympic Peninsula, 65, 260
  online reservations, 49–51, 65–66, 71
  package tours, 47–48
  Sea-Tac Airport, 49

Seattle Symphony, 162
Seattle-King County Convention &
    Visitors Bureau, 128
ticket services, 73
Transportation Security
    Administration (TSA), 52
Travel Assistance International, 45
travel insurance, 44, 45
U.S. National Park Service, 36
Washington State Ferries, 173
Washington State Parks, 207–208
Western Union (wire service), 122
Wilderness Information Center, 235
wildlife
  dolphins, 172, 186
  refuge, 22, 273, 274
  safety issues, 235–236
  sea lions, 172, 180
  watching, 246–247
  whale-watching, 186, 208, 210, 276
winter, 15, 18, 30, 64
Wooden Boat Festival, 21–22, 266–267
Woodland Park Zoo, 173

• *Y* •

Yahoo! Travel (online reservations),
    65–66

• *Z* •

zoo, 173

Accomodations Index

Ace Hotel, 90
Alexis Hotel, 90–91
Chambered Nautilus Bed & Breakfast
    Inn, 91
College Inn, 104
Courtyard by Marriott, 91
Four Seasons Olympic Hotel, 94
Grand Hyatt Seattle, 94
Hampton Inn and Suites, 94–95

Homewood Suites by Hilton, 95
Hostelling International-Seattle, 95
Hotel Edgewater, 64, 95–96
Hotel Monaco Seattle, 96
Hotel Vintage Park, 96–97
Inn at Harbor Steps, 97
Inn at the Market, 97
Inn at Queen Anne, 104
MarQueen Hotel, 97–98
Marriott Residence Inn, 98
Mayflower Park Hotel, 98
Mediterranean Inn, 99
Paramount Hotel, 99
Pensione Nichols, 104
Pioneer Square Hotel, 104
Renaissance Madison Hotel, 99
The Roosevelt, 100
Salisbury House, 100
Salish Lodge & Spa, 100
Seattle Marriott Waterfront, 101
Sheraton Seattle Hotel and Towers, 101
Sixth Avenue Inn, 105
Sorrento Hotel, 101–102
University Inn, 105
University Tower Hotel, 102
W Seattle, 102–103
The Wall Street Inn, 102
The Westin Seattle, 103
Willows Lodge, 103
Woodmark Hotel, 104

Restaurant Index

Andaluca, 132
Anthony's Pier 66, Bell Street Diner,
    and Fish Bar, 132
Bell Street Diner, 132
Brasa, 133
The Brooklyn Seafood, Steak &
    Oyster House, 133
Buca di Beppo, 127, 133–134

Cafe Juanita, 134
Campagne, 134
Canlis, 134–135
Carmelita, 135
Cascadia, 135, 282
Cassis, 138
Chandler's Crabhouse, 138
Chinook's at Salmon Bay, 138
The Crab Pot Restaurant and Bar, 139
Dahlia Lounge, 124, 139, 282
Daniel's Broiler, 139
Dick's Drive-Ins, 140
Earth & Ocean, 140
El Gaucho, 123, 140
Etta's Seafood, 141
Fandango, 141
Fish Bar, 132
Fleming's Prime Steakhouse &
    Wine Bar, 141
Flying Fish, 141–142
The Georgian Room, 127, 142
The Herbfarm, 142
iCon Grill, 142–143
Ivar's Salmon House, 143
Julia's on Broadway, 143
Kaspar's, 143–144
Le Pichet, 144
Metropolitan Grill, 144
Nishino, 144
Oceanaire Seafood Room, 145
Palace Kitchen, 145, 220
Palisade, 145
Ray's Boathouse and Cafe, 146
Rover's, 73, 146
Salty's on Alki Beach, 146–147
Sazerac, 147
Shiro's, 147
Tia Lou's, 147–148
Tulio Ristorante, 148
Waterfront, 148
Wild Ginger, 148–149

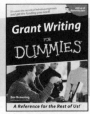

FOR DUMMIES®

A world of resources to help you grow

TRAVEL

Italy FOR DUMMIES

0-7645-5453-0

Hawaii FOR DUMMIES

0-7645-5438-7

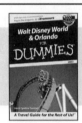

Walt Disney World & Orlando FOR DUMMIES

0-7645-5444-1

Also available:

America's National Parks
For Dummies
(0-7645-6204-5)

Caribbean For Dummies
(0-7645-5445-X)

Cruise Vacations For
Dummies 2003
(0-7645-5459-X)

Europe For Dummies
(0-7645-5456-5)

Ireland For Dummies
(0-7645-6199-5)

France For Dummies
(0-7645-6292-4)

Las Vegas For Dummies
(0-7645-5448-4)

London For Dummies
(0-7645-5416-6)

Mexico's Beach Resorts
For Dummies
(0-7645-6262-2)

Paris For Dummies
(0-7645-5494-8)

RV Vacations For
Dummies
(0-7645-5443-3)

EDUCATION & TEST PREPARATION

Spanish FOR DUMMIES

0-7645-5194-9

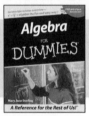

Algebra FOR DUMMIES

0-7645-5325-9

U.S. History FOR DUMMIES

0-7645-5249-X

Also available:

The ACT For Dummies
(0-7645-5210-4)

Chemistry For Dummies
(0-7645-5430-1)

English Grammar For
Dummies
(0-7645-5322-4)

French For Dummies
(0-7645-5193-0)

GMAT For Dummies
(0-7645-5251-1)

Inglés Para Dummies
(0-7645-5427-1)

Italian For Dummies
(0-7645-5196-5)

Research Papers For
Dummies
(0-7645-5426-3)

SAT I For Dummies
(0-7645-5472-7)

U.S. History For Dummie
(0-7645-5249-X)

World History For
Dummies
(0-7645-5242-2)

HEALTH, SELF-HELP & SPIRITUALITY

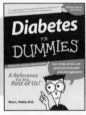

Diabetes FOR DUMMIES

0-7645-5154-X

Sex FOR DUMMIES

0-7645-5302-X

Parenting FOR DUMMIES

0-7645-5418-2

Also available:

The Bible For Dummies
(0-7645-5296-1)

Controlling Cholesterol
For Dummies
(0-7645-5440-9)

Dating For Dummies
(0-7645-5072-1)

Dieting For Dummies
(0-7645-5126-4)

High Blood Pressure For
Dummies
(0-7645-5424-7)

Judaism For Dummies
(0-7645-5299-6)

Menopause For Dummie
(0-7645-5458-1)

Nutrition For Dummies
(0-7645-5180-9)

Potty Training For
Dummies
(0-7645-5417-4)

Pregnancy For Dummies
(0-7645-5074-8)

Rekindling Romance For
Dummies
(0-7645-5303-8)

Religion For Dummies
(0-7645-5264-3)

FOR DUMMIES®

A world of resources to help you grow

HOME & BUSINESS COMPUTER BASICS

0-7645-0838-5

0-7645-1663-9

0-7645-1548-9

Also available:

Excel 2002 All-in-One
Desk Reference For
Dummies
(0-7645-1794-5)

Office XP 9-in-1 Desk
Reference For Dummies
(0-7645-0819-9)

PCs All-in-One Desk
Reference For Dummies
(0-7645-0791-5)

Troubleshooting Your PC
For Dummies
(0-7645-1669-8)

Upgrading & Fixing PCs
For Dummies
(0-7645-1665-5)

Windows XP For
Dummies
(0-7645-0893-8)

Windows XP For
Dummies Quick
Reference
(0-7645-0897-0)

Word 2002 For Dummies
(0-7645-0839-3)

INTERNET & DIGITAL MEDIA

0-7645-0894-6

0-7645-1642-6

0-7645-1664-7

Also available:

CD and DVD Recording
For Dummies
(0-7645-1627-2)

Digital Photography
All-in-One Desk
Reference For Dummies
(0-7645-1800-3)

eBay For Dummies
(0-7645-1642-6)

Genealogy Online For
Dummies
(0-7645-0807-5)

Internet All-in-One Desk
Reference For Dummies
(0-7645-1659-0)

Internet For Dummies
Quick Reference
(0-7645-1645-0)

Internet Privacy For
Dummies
(0-7645-0846-6)

Paint Shop Pro For
Dummies
(0-7645-2440-2)

Photo Retouching &
Restoration For Dummies
(0-7645-1662-0)

Photoshop Elements For
Dummies
(0-7645-1675-2)

Scanners For Dummies
(0-7645-0783-4)

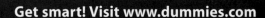

Get smart! Visit www.dummies.com

- **Find listings of even more Dummies titles**

- **Browse online articles, excerpts, and how-to's**

- **Sign up for daily or weekly e-mail tips**

- **Check out Dummies fitness videos and other products**

- **Order from our online bookstore**

™

Available wherever books are sold. Go to www.dummies.com or call 1-877-762-2974 to order direct